Event Processing in Action

Event Processing in Action

OPHER ETZION
PETER NIBLETT

MANNING
Greenwich
(74° w. long.)

For online information and ordering of this and other Manning books, please visit
www.manning.com. The publisher offers discounts on this book when ordered in quantity.
For more information, please contact:

Special Sales Department
Manning Publications Co.
180 Broad Street
Suite 1323
Stamford, CT 06901
Email: orders@manning.com

Manning Publications Co.   Development editor: Sebastian Stirling
180 Broad Street   Copyeditor: Betsey Henkels
Suite 1323   Proofreader: Katie Tennant
Stamford, CT 06901   Typesetter: Marija Tudor
                                          Cover designer: Marija Tudor

ISBN: 9781935182214
Printed in the United States of America
1 2 3 4 5 6 7 8 9 10 – MAL – 16 15 14 13 12 11 10

brief contents

contents

vii

PART 3   PRAGMATICS 253

foreword

Modern event processing is fast becoming a foundation of today's information society. This is a technology that emerged in the late 1990s, but event processing is nothing new. For sixty years it has been, and still is, a technological basis for discrete event simulation, weather simulation and forecasting, networks and the internet, and all manner of information gathering and communications—just to name a few areas. In the 1990s, there were one or two university research projects dedicated to developing new principles of event processing, called complex event processing (CEP). After 2000, CEP began to appear in commercial IT applications, and more recently, starting around 2006, the number of event processing applications and products in the marketplace has grown rapidly.

The Power of Events, a book that I published in 2002, was about this new area of event processing theory and applications and it offered a vision for an embryonic industry. Much has happened since then. Companies have been developing and marketing event processing products ever more rapidly. Indeed, complex event processing has become an established market area for commercial applications. University courses have sprung up around the world. It is now a developing area of computer science. It is time for more books on event processing!

This new book, *Event Processing in Action,* by Opher Etzion and Peter Niblett, is a very welcome contribution to the field. Both authors are prominent contributors to event processing and the first author is the founder of the internationally active Event Processing Technical Society (EPTS).

This is a book on the technology underlying event processing, and can be used by software professionals who wish to learn the event processing perspectives as well as serve as a basis for a university course on the subject. It deals with foundational matters such as what an event is, types of events, and different types of event processing agents. The book emphasizes distributed event processing, event-driven architectures, communicating networks of event processing agents, and how to build them. There are detailed examples throughout. It covers all the topics needed to bring the reader to a point where he or she can start building useful event processing software. The book takes a modern object-oriented approach to software throughout, so the reader should indeed be a software specialist.

The principles and technology in this book form one of the cornerstones needed to build the next generation of information technology and mobile applications based on event processing. Of course, commercial applications are often developed without the underlying technical principles being explicitly stated or studied. The principles come later! I believe this book will set the record straight. If you are at all interested in a systematic approach to both present and future distributed information processing and mobile applications, this is a book you should read.

DAVID LUCKHAM

AUTHOR OF *THE POWER OF EVENTS*

preface

Event processing is an emerging area. The term *event processing* refers to an approach to software systems that is based on the idea of events, and that includes specific logic to filter, transform, or detect patterns in events as they occur. Recent years have seen the appearance of various commercial products and open source offerings that serve as generic event processing software platforms. According to some studies, this is the fastest growing segment of enterprise middleware software. Although interest in this subject is growing, gaining a deep understanding of event processing is still a challenge. As it is a relatively new area, it is not surprising that several different approaches to event processing have been evolving in parallel. This means that when trying to understand what event processing is, it can be difficult to see the forest for the trees. Our intention in writing this book was is to dive deeply into the meaning of event processing (the forest) and to give you an opportunity to experience event processing by using some of its languages and tools (the trees).

ABOUT THIS BOOK

This is a book intended for those interested in understanding what's behind event processing technologies and how they should be employed to design and implement applications. This book is the first comprehensive view of event processing for the technical reader. It treats event processing as a generic technology, in a way that fits all the different implementation approaches, and thus familiarizes you with the entire forest, and not just one particular tree. The book provides a deep dive into all the concepts that need to be understood in order to design event processing applications, and guides you through these concepts by showing the construction of a single example application that uses event processing—the Fast Flower Delivery application.

If you are interested, you also have the unique opportunity of learning how to implement this example using representatives of today's programming styles: SQL extensions, rule-based languages, and imperative languages. These languages may have either textual or graphical user interfaces, or a mix of the two. The website that accompanies the book provides examples based on the Fast Flower Delivery application, with instructions on how to download trial versions of various commercial and open source event processing products. This allows the reader to see the concepts applied in action, to play with the code, and to devise further examples. The book also discusses implementation issues and the authors' opinion about event processing of the future.

THE INTENDED READERSHIP

The book is intended for those who want to gain understanding about event processing concepts in depth; its primary audience is technical, consisting of architects, designers, developers, and students. The book will benefit designers and architects who wish to know how to design applications that use event processing, and developers who would like to understand the relationship of these concepts to current event processing languages and products. It can also serve as a textbook for an academic or professional course on event processing, and for this reason each chapter includes an additional reading list along with a few exercises.

THE BOOK'S METHODOLOGY

In this book we have taken a top-down approach by describing the concepts (the forest), and then providing the reader an opportunity to view the trees (representatives of the different approaches) and experiment with them through the associated website. This is different from the bottom-up approach of describing a single language or product. We have used this method because there are several different ways to implement event processing applications, and it's not easy to transfer thinking from one to another. We use a general model that consists of seven building blocks, which we believe is an effective way to explain the concepts and facilities of event processing. We feel that there are advantages in using this level of abstraction when designing and developing applications.

To illustrate these concepts we use a single example which we follow throughout the course of the book. This example, based on flower delivery, can be understood with no prior domain knowledge, but nevertheless contains many of the concepts that we discuss in the book.

Terminology varies among different event processing products, so in this book we have tried to define all the terms and concepts that we use, and we provide a summary of these definitions in appendix A. Our definitions are written in an explanatory style rather than in a formal style, to make them accessible to a broad audience. Where possible we use definitions that are consistent with the terminology established by the Event Processing Technical Society (EPTS); however our scope of terms is broader.

ROADMAP

The book has three parts. The first consists of chapter 1 and chapter 2 and is an introduction to the subject and to the terms and concepts that we use. If you are already familiar with event processing, you can browse through part 1, noting the definitions we use.

- Chapter 1 is the entry point, with some examples and basic terms. It introduces the Fast Flower Delivery example.
- Chapter 2 explains basic architectural and programming principles.

Part 2 delves into the concepts in detail, showing how the seven building blocks can be used to describe an event processing application, illustrating them in the context of the Fast Flower Delivery example:

- Chapter 3 deals with events: event types, event schema descriptions, and relationships among event types.
- Chapter 4 deals with event producers: the types of event producers and the ways events are obtained from a producer.
- Chapter 5 covers event consumers: the types of event consumers, and some current examples.
- Chapter 6 deals with the event processing network, a key concept in event processing, and its associated building blocks, such as event processing agents, channels, and global state elements.
- Chapter 7 discusses the notion of context and its major role in event processing.
- Chapter 8 looks in greater detail at event processing agents that filter and transform events.
- Chapter 9 examines event pattern matching, the jewel in the crown of event processing.

Part 3 deals with additional issues that relate to the implementation of event processing applications:

- Chapter 10 surveys implementation issues, both engineering aspects, such as scalability, and software engineering aspects, such as programming style and development tools.
- Chapter 11 surveys some of the semantic challenges that developers and users of event processing systems should be aware of, in order to avoid anomalies when building event processing applications.
- Chapter 12 discusses emerging trends and technology directions in the area of event processing.

FURTHER READING

Some topics mentioned in the book are not thoroughly discussed, because they fall outside the scope of the book and they are the subject of books in their own right.

Business topics, such as a review of the types of event processing applications being used and analysis of current event processing products, are beyond the scope of the book. Chapter 1 contains an additional reading list for those of you who want to explore business topics further. We provide event processing application examples in chapter 1, but these are intended to motivate the use of event processing rather than to give a detailed survey of applications.

Many technologies and architectural concepts are related to event processing, starting from service-oriented architecture (SOA), and including Enterprise Integration Patterns (EIP), and other disciplines such as business process management (BPM), business intelligence (BI), and Business Activity Monitoring (BAM). In chapter 1 we briefly survey the relationship of event processing to each of these areas and provide an additional reading list.

CODE CONVENTIONS AND DOWNLOADS

All source code in listings or in text is in a `fixed-width font like this` to separate it from ordinary text. Code annotations accompany many of the listings, highlighting important concepts. In some cases, numbered bullets link to explanations that follow the listing.

Source code for all working examples in this book is available for download from the publisher's website at http://www.manning.com/EventProcessinginAction.

THE *EVENT PROCESSING IN ACTION* WEBSITE

This book's website is hosted by the Event Processing Technical Society and can be found at http://www.ep-ts.com/EventProcessingInAction.

The website contains implementations of the Fast Flower Delivery example that accompanies this book in several different event processing languages representing different programming styles. Some code samples from these solutions are embedded inside the book, but if you wish to learn a specific language you should download the documentation from the appropriate link on the website. There is also a link to an editor that will let you create a model of the Fast Flower Delivery application using the building block language described in this book.

AUTHOR ONLINE

The purchase of *Event Processing in Action* includes free access to a private forum run by Manning Publications where you can make comments about the book, ask technical questions, and receive help from the authors and other users. To access and subscribe to the forum, point your browser to http://www.manning.com/EventProcessingin Action. This page provides information on how to get on the forum once you are registered, what kind of help is available, and the rules of conduct in the forum.

Manning's commitment to our readers is to provide a venue where a meaningful dialogue between individual readers and between readers and the authors can take place. It's not a commitment to any specific amount of participation on the part of the authors, whose contribution to the book's forum remains voluntary (and unpaid). We suggest you try asking the authors some challenging questions, lest their interest stray!

The Author Online forum and the archives of previous discussions will be accessible from the publisher's website as long as the book is in print.

acknowledgments

Many people have contributed to this book, either by creating the body of knowledge that it contains, or by making helpful comments during its writing.

The building block approach and the event processing network architecture presented in this book originated in the work of the IBM Software Group Architecture Board Workgroup on Event Processing. Besides the two authors, this workgroup included the following IBM colleagues: Allen Chan, Amir Bar-or, Andrew Coleman, Avshalom Houri, Beth Hutchison, Billy Newport, Brent Miller, Bruce Wallman, Eric Erpenbach, Eric Wayne, Greg Porpora, Henry Chang, Idan Ben-Harrush, Jeffrey Garratt, Joachim Frank, Kristian Stewart, Kun-Lung Wu, Mamdouh Ibrahim, Mark Hubbard, Michael Spicer, Oskar Zinger, Prasad Vishnubhotla, Rob Phippen, Steven De Gennaro, Thomas Freund, and Vish Narayan.

The section discussing the various language styles is based on the DEBS 2009 tutorial of the Event Processing Technical Society workgroup on language analysis cochaired by Jon Riecke and Opher Etzion, with the following members: Adrian Paschke, Alex Kozlenkov, Arno Jacobsen, Bala Maniymaran, Bob Hagmann, David Tucker, Dermot McPeake, Francois Bry, Guy Sharon, Louis Lovas, Michael Eckert, Pedro Bizarro, Richard Tibbetts, Robert McKeown, Susan Urban, Simon Courtenage, and Serge Mankovskii. Nir Zolotorevsky helped us with the geospatial terminology and contributed to the discussion of spatial data types, contexts, and patterns.

Many people have provided invaluable comments on the manuscript, either through the anonymous review process, or directly to the authors via Manning's Author Online forum. We acknowledge in particular the contributions of Hans Gilde and Rainer von Ammon, who provided many detailed comments throughout the process, as well as Christian Hunt, Roland Stühmer, Roy Schulte, Ady Kemp, Richard Veryard, Asaf Meir, Tim Henley, Christian Siegers, Mark Palm, Ben Hall, Andrew Rhine, Andy Dingley, Joshua White, Dimitar Dimitrov, Amin Mohammed-Coleman, Dru Sellers, Gregor Hohpe, Amos Bannister, Paul Benedict, Awais Bajwa, Christophe Avare, Tony Niemann, John Griffin, Chris Bleuel, David Dossot, Brian Connell, and the reviewer known to us only as *coffee fan*.

The draft version of this book was used to teach an event processing course in the Technion-Israel Institute of Technology, and the students in this course helped in constructing the book's website and in validating the various implementations on the website. The team of students who coordinated this work and created the website included Asaf Meir, Greg Arutiunian, and Veronika Bogina, the building block editor was developed by Ronen Vaisenberg.

We would also like to thank the various organizations who worked with us to provide the example implementations that you can find on our website, and in particular our contacts: Alexandre Vasseur (ESPER), Bob Hagmann (Aleri/CCL), Darko Anicic (ETALIS), Eddie Galvez (StreamBase), Roland Olsson (ruleCore), and Stanphenie Yao (Progress/Apama).

Many thanks to our IBM colleague Ella Rabinovich, who served as the teaching assistant for the first course based on this book, and contributed many insights and suggestions that helped us improve the book. And we would like to express our appreciation to David Luckham, author of *The Power of Events* and Professor Emeritus at Stanford University, for agreeing to read the manuscript early on and for contributing the foreword to this book.

Last but not least we would like to thank our editors at Manning, Tara McGoldrick Walsh and Sebastian Stirling, our technical proofreader Samujjwal Bhandari, and the production team, Mary Piergies, Betsey Henkels, Katie Tennant, Janet Vail, and Marija Tudor, who helped us make the transition from casual writing to a professional book.

about the cover illustration

On the cover of *Event Processing in Action* is "A habitant of Risi," a hamlet in the interior of the peninsula of Istria in the Adriatic Sea, off Croatia (see map). The illustration is from a recent reproduction of a book of Croatian dress customs, *Characterization and Description of Southwestern Wende, Illyrians and Slavs,* by Balthasar Hacquet, originally published around 1800. The illustrations were obtained from a helpful librarian at the Ethnographic Museum in Split, Croatia, itself situated in the Roman core of the medieval center of the town: the ruins of Emperor Diocletian's retirement palace from around AD 304. The book includes finely colored illustrations of figures from different regions of Croatia, accompanied by descriptions of the costumes and of everyday life. About Risi we learn that

> In this part of Istria, men wear black felt hats, jackets made of brown meslanka,[1] trousers with garters below the knee, as well as white socks and shoes with clasps. Short vests with small buttons are worn over dark red shirts. The men carry a bag with small personal items and weapons such as an axe, rifle, or sword. An Istrian is generally of medium height with black hair. His ancestry is a mix of Italian and Slav, and he is considered both impulsive and bold.

---

[1] This Croatian word comes from the Italian "mezzo lana," which means a mixture of wool.

Istrian dances recall Greek dances and the accompanying music is played on vidalice,[2] harps, bagpipes, or fiddles. Highland populations produce a variety of objects made of wood, such as paddles, drums, boxes, and so on. Because roads are rare, they use donkeys to transport these goods, and the rest of what they need is brought to the towns by sea. The main occupation of the population is mountain cattle and sheep breeding, not only for the wool, but mainly for the sake of trade and the good prices of meat.

Our particular Istrian is carrying a bag with his personal items and he has a number of daggers and pistols in his belt, but no rifle or axe. Instead he is holding an impressively long pipe.

Dress codes and lifestyles have changed over the last 200 years, and the diversity by region, so rich at the time, has faded away. It is now hard to tell apart the inhabitants of different continents, let alone of different hamlets or towns separated by only a few miles. Perhaps we have traded cultural diversity for a more varied personal life—certainly for a more varied and fast-paced technological life.

Manning celebrates the inventiveness and initiative of the computer business with book covers based on the rich diversity of regional life of two centuries ago, brought back to life by illustrations from old books and collections like this one.

---

[2] Double flute made of a single block of wood. They have a single mouthpiece, but two channels that direct the air flow into two separate pipes.

Part 1

The basics

In this book we discuss events. Many people associate the word *event* with a meaningful happening in their lives such as a graduation party or wedding. If you wanted to plan a wedding event, you would need to understand the basics, such as terminology for discussing plans with service providers, the family constraints that affect the nature of the event, and the different types of ceremonies available.

We start this book by explaining the basics of event processing. If you are already familiar with the basics you can browse through part 1, taking note of the terminology that we use in this book. If you're not sure that you know what event processing is all about, this part of the book should fill in the blanks for you.

Part 1 consists of chapters 1 and 2. Chapter 1 provides a bird's-eye view of event processing. It explains what we mean by *events* and *event-driven behavior*. It includes some examples and relates them to different types of event processing. It also positions event processing within the enterprise computing universe and introduces the Fast Flower Delivery example application that will accompany us throughout the book. Chapter 2 discusses the architectural concepts and building blocks required to construct event processing systems.

Entering the world
of event processing

I am more and more convinced that our happiness or unhappiness depends far more on the way we meet the events of life, than on the nature of those events themselves.

—Wilhelm von Humboldt

Some people say that event processing will be the next big development in computing; others say that event processing is old hat with nothing new. There is some truth in both viewpoints but before exploring them let's clear up the confusion about what *event processing* actually is. This confusion stems from misconceptions and mixed messages from vendors and analysts, and also from lack of standards, lack of agreement on terms, and lack of understanding of the basic issues. This book aims to clear up this confusion.

We use the phrase *event processing* in this book, much as the terms *database management* and *artificial intelligence* are used, to refer to an entire subject area. Our definition of event processing is therefore fairly broad, namely, any form of computing that performs operations on events. We elaborate on what this means as the chapter progresses.

This chapter includes the following:

- An explanation of what we mean by events, using examples from daily life
- Examples of computerized event processing in use, and the reasons for its use
- An introduction to the main concepts of event processing
- The idea of a dedicated event processing platform and its business value

- The relationship of event processing to other computing concepts
- An introduction to the Fast Flower Delivery application that accompanies us throughout this book
- A description of the *Event Processing in Action* website, http://www.ep-ts.com/EventProcessingInAction

Before clearing up the confusion surrounding event processing, we need to look at its background and examples of event processing in daily life.

1.1 *Event-driven behavior and event-driven computing*

We intend this book to disperse the fog around event processing by supplying a clear, comprehensive, and consistent view of what event processing is. We start by explaining the concept of event-driven behavior in daily life, and then look at how this carries across to the world of event-driven computing. As we go through the book we define the terms we use. You can find an alphabetically sorted list of these definitions in appendix A.

1.1.1 *What we mean by events*

Before going further we should clarify what we mean by an *event*.

> **EVENT** An *event* is an occurrence within a particular system or domain; it is something that has happened, or is contemplated as having happened in that domain. The word *event* is also used to mean a programming entity that represents such an occurrence in a computing system.

We give two meanings to the word *event*. The first meaning refers to an actual occurrence (the *something that has happened*) in the real world or in some other system. The second meaning takes us into the realm of computerized event processing, where the word *event* is used to mean a programming entity that represents this occurrence. It's easy to get caught up in a rather pedantic discussion about the difference between these two, but in practice we can safely use the word *event* to have either meaning as it's usually easy to tell the meaning from the context. You should note that a single event occurrence can be represented by many event entities, and also be aware that a given event entity might capture only some of the facets of a particular event occurrence.

As this is such an important term, it's worth commenting on three of the phrases used in the definition. The first of these is "system or domain." In event processing we are chiefly concerned with real-world events–that is, events that occur in real life, such as an order being placed or a plane landing. But the techniques of event processing can also be applied to things that happen in artificial domains such as training simulators, virtual worlds, and similar virtual environments.

Next, the definition includes things that are "contemplated as having happened." It is possible to have events that don't correspond to actual occurrences. To explain what we mean, imagine a fraud detection system being used in a financial institution. Such a system monitors financial transactions and generates events when it suspects that a fraud is being conducted. These systems can generate false positives, so further investigation is usually required before you can be sure whether a fraud has actually taken place or not.

Finally, the definition contains the phrase "programming entity." Elsewhere in this book we use the phrase *event object*, as this sounds more natural than *event programming entity*, but we need to make it clear that we aren't necessarily talking about an object as defined in object-oriented programming. In some contexts you might encounter events represented as OO objects, but you can also find events that appear in other forms, such as records in a relational database, structures in a language like C or COBOL, or messages transmitted between systems. We have therefore chosen to use the more general expression *programming entity* in our definition.

The word *event* is sometimes used in event processing literature to refer to a type or class of events rather than to a specific event instance. In this book we either use the term *event type* in such cases, or we use the name of the type as an adjective, for example, `Account Overdrawn` event, unless it is obvious from the context that we mean the type rather than a specific instance.

1.1.2 *Event-driven behavior in daily life*

The event concept is simple yet powerful. Suppose you are working on your laptop in a coffee shop, and since you entered this coffee shop several things have happened: people have come in and out and the waitress has brought you coffee. These are all events, but none of them is particularly exciting. Imagine now what would happen if a robber entered the coffee shop and demanded people's money. This would disrupt the peaceful atmosphere and compel people to react. Suppose that someone surrenders his wallet to the robber, triggering further events. After recovering from the shock, the victim might call credit card companies to cancel his stolen credit cards, which in turn would trigger further activities.

Let's leave scary scenarios and look at how coffee shops work.[1] Some work in a synchronous fashion: a customer walks up to the counter and asks for coffee and pastry; the person behind the counter puts the pastry into the microwave, prepares the coffee, takes the pastry out of the microwave, takes the payment, gives the tray to the customer, and then turns to serve the next customer. Another way to organize things is to have the person behind the counter take the order and payment and then move on to serve the next customer, while other people in the background deal with the pastry and coffee. When both are ready they'll call the customer, or bring the items directly to the table, allowing the customer to sit down, take out a laptop, and write books while waiting. Figure 1.1 illustrates these two approaches.

---

[1] The synchronous/asynchronous natures of coffee shops were discussed by Gregor Hohpe in his article, "Gregor Hohpe: Your Coffee Shop Doesn't Use Two-Phase Commit." IEEE Software 22(2): 64-66 (2005) http://www.computer.org/portal/web/csdl/abs/mags/so/2005/02/s2064abs.htm.

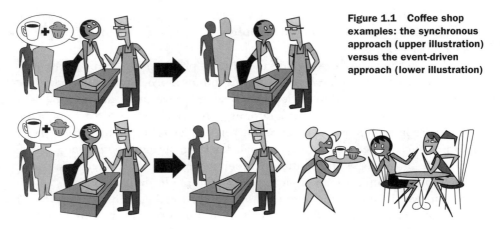

Figure 1.1 Coffee shop examples: the synchronous approach (upper illustration) versus the event-driven approach (lower illustration)

The first approach resembles traditional information systems—you issue a request and wait for the response, typically doing nothing in between. The second approach is asynchronous, and everything is based around events. In particular there is an `order is completed` event which is a combination of two other independent events: `coffee is ready` and `pastry is heated`. The `order is completed` event is a routine event for the coffee shop and customers, whereas the robbery is an unexpected event. Both result in reactions from those involved.

We encounter events all the time in our daily lives. Some events are quite basic—the phone rings, an email arrives, somebody knocks at the door, or a book falls on the floor. Some events are unexpected—the robbery event, coffee being spilled on the laptop creating a short circuit, a late flight causing you to miss a connection. It's also an event when you then find out that your luggage didn't arrive. Not all unexpected events are negative. They can include winning the lottery, getting a large order from an unexpected customer, or finding a significant amount of natural gas under the sea.

Some events can be observed very easily, for example, things that we see and hear during our daily activities; some require us to do something first, for example, subscribing to news groups, or reading a newspaper. In other cases we need to do some work in order to detect the event that actually happened, as all we can observe are its symptoms. As an example, suppose your laptop couldn't connect to your wireless home router. This might be a symptom of an event which had occurred earlier, and identifying the event could require 90 minutes of investigation by a skilled technician. As another example, suppose you recently noticed that your family's consumption of milk had increased, and you needed to add an additional carton of milk to your weekly grocery list. You might reach this conclusion when you ran out of milk in three consecutive weeks, convincing you that this was a consistent phenomenon. In this example `running out of milk` is an observable event, whereas the `milk consumption has increased` event is a higher level event that can be deduced from observing lower level events.

The main reason for learning that events have occurred is that it gives us the opportunity to react to them. In the previous example you might react to the `milk` consumption has increased event by increasing your weekly purchase of milk. Many of the events around us are outside the scope of our interest. Some events are background noise and do not require any reaction, but some do require reaction, and those we call *situations*.

SITUATION   A *situation*[2] is an event occurrence that might require a reaction.

One of the main themes in event processing is the detection and reporting of situations so that they can be reacted to. The reaction might be as simple as picking up the phone or changing the weekly shopping list, or it might be more complicated. If we miss a flight connection there may be several alternative reactions depending on the time of the day, the airport where we are stranded, the airline policies, and the number of other passengers in the same situation.

In these examples, event processing has been performed by human beings. Let's now move from the world of people to the world of information systems.

1.1.3   *Examples of computerized event processing*

Using events in information systems is not new. In the early days of computing, events appeared in the form of exceptions whose role was to interrupt the regular flow of execution and cause alternative processing to happen. For example, if a program tried to divide by zero an exception event would be raised that enabled the programmer to end the program with an error message, or to perform corrective action and then continue with the computation process. More recently, events were featured in graphical user interface systems (such as Smalltalk or Java AWT) where user interface components (for example, buttons or menus) are designed to react to UI events such as mouse clicks or key presses.

In this book we are mainly concerned with computing events that correspond to events that occur in the real world. These examples show different ways in which automated event processing is used today:

Example 1: A patient is hooked up to multiple monitors that perform various measurements. The measurements take the form of events, which are then analyzed by an event processing system. A physician can configure this system, on a patient-by-patient basis, so that a nurse is alerted if certain combinations of measurements are detected within a certain time period, and so that the physician is alerted if other combinations occur. This example demonstrates the use of event processing to allow timely response to emergency situations, or as part of a personalized diagnosis program.

Example 2: In an airline luggage handling system a radio-frequency identification (RFID) tag is attached to every piece of luggage. RFID readers are located along the luggage route (the sorting device, the cart going to the aircraft, the aircraft's unloading dock, and more). Events from the RFID readers are analyzed to provide exception alerts,

---

[2]   The term *situation* has been used in this way by several people including Asaf Adi and Opher Etzion: "Amit - the situation manager." VLDB J. (VLDB) 13(2):177-203 (2004). http://www.springerlink.com/content/nb1qa1d02vvdre00/.

such as luggage is on the wrong cart; luggage did not arrive at the aircraft; luggage did not even arrive at the sorting device; as well as a routine alert when luggage is approaching the carousel. This example demonstrates the use of event processing for detecting and eliminating errors within an automated processing system. The fact that an event did not occur is one of the most common event processing patterns, called the *absence pattern*, discussed in chapter 9. Some people refer to it as a "non-event."

Example 3: A manufacturing plant with restricted access zones uses RFID tags to monitor compliance with safety regulations. Each person working or visiting the plant carries an RFID tag, and an RFID reader in each zone generates an event when it detects the presence of that person. These events can then be analyzed to detect safety violations—simple ones such as a person entering an unauthorized zone, or more complex ones such as an authorized person working unaccompanied in a zone which requires the presence of two or more authorized people. This example demonstrates the use of geospatial event processing to detect policy violations.

Example 4: A personal banking system allows bank customers to set up alerts when certain events occur, such as when the sum withdrawn from a given customer's accounts within a single day is greater than $10,000; or when a particular investment portfolio has gone up by more than 5 percent since the start of the trading day. This example demonstrates the use of event processing for personalized information dissemination.

Example 5: A financial institution wishes to detect frauds or a financial regulator wishes to catch illegal trading patterns. They collect events from banking or trading systems and analyze them. Certain patterns of activity might suggest that a person is possibly (but not necessarily) in the process of committing a fraud or other illegal activity. This example demonstrates the use of event processing to detect evolving phenomena.

Example 6: An emergency control system informs and directs first responders and people at risk in case of an incident (for example, a fire or the leakage of hazardous materials). In this case the event is a report on an incident, and the main focus of the system is the dissemination of information: who should be informed about what and at what time, given the nature of the incident.

Example 7: An online trading system matches buy requests and sell requests in an auction. It needs to maintain fairness practices (for example, first person to make the bid has first chance). In this case the complexity lies in the matching itself. The events are the buy and sell requests and the matching process is required to match using patterns that apply fairness criteria such as priority based on order, matching conditions, and prior information about the level of risk of the buyer and seller based on trade history. This example demonstrates the use of event processing to dynamically manage business processes.

Example 8: A manufacturing plant management system diagnoses mechanical failures based on observable symptoms. In this case the events are symptoms, describing things that do not work properly, and the main purpose of the event processing is to find the root cause of these symptoms. This example demonstrates the use of event processing for problem determination and resolution.

Example 9: A road tolling system detects the entry and exit points of a vehicle using a toll road and bills the owner. Vehicles are detected based on analysis of a video stream that captures their license plates. Here the main difficulty is extracting and interpreting the vehicles' license plates from the video stream in order to generate the events themselves. This example demonstrates the use of event processing to trigger business processes, where the events need to be obtained as a result of analysis.

Example 10: A social networking site starts a multiparty chat when five people from a group are online. In this case an event occurs when a person goes online or offline. Event processing is used to analyze these events to decide when to start a chat session. This example demonstrates the use of event processing for real-time collaboration.

This list of examples isn't intended to be a comprehensive review of event processing applications. At the end of this chapter we give references, which detail the types of applications in which event processing is employed, and the business value of using these applications. In the next section we provide a classification of event processing systems according to their business use.

1.1.4 *Categories of event processing applications*

The examples given in the previous section and many others can be classified as shown in figure 1.2:

- *Observation*—Event processing is used to monitor a system or process by looking for exceptional behavior and generating alerts when such behavior occurs. In such cases the reaction, if any, is left to the consumers of the alerts; the job of the event processing application is to produce the alerts only. The patient

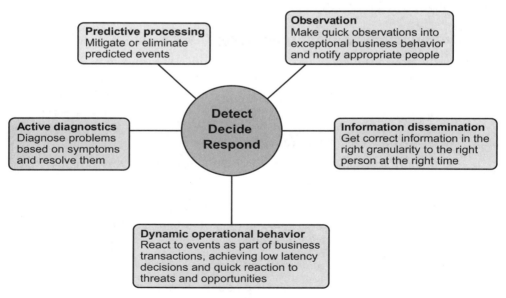

Figure 1.2 Five categories of an event processing application

monitoring system (example 1) comes under this heading, as does the luggage monitoring system (example 2) and the safety regulation compliance system (example 3).

- *Information dissemination*—Another reason for using event processing is to deliver the right information to the right consumer at the right granularity at the right time, in other words, personalized information delivery. Examples of this type are the personalized banking system (example 4) and the emergency system that sends alerts to first responders (example 6).
- *Dynamic operational behavior*—Event processing is often used to drive the actions performed by a system dynamically so as to react to incoming events. The online trading system (example 7) falls into this category, as do examples 9 and 10. In all these examples the output of the application is directly affected by the input events.
- *Active diagnostics*—Here the goal of the event processing application is to diagnose a problem, based on observed symptoms. The mechanical failure case (example 8) is such an example; a help-desk system is another example.
- *Predictive processing*—Here the goal is to identify events before they have happened, so that they can be eliminated or their effects mitigated. The fraud detection system (example 5) is of this kind.

These different classes of use are not exclusive of each other; a specific application may fall into several of the categories that we have listed.

You may notice that we have started using the term *event processing* without explaining what we mean by it. We now introduce the term briefly, though of course it is the subject of the rest of this book.

1.2   Introduction to event processing

In the previous section we introduced the idea of events in real life and their representation in computing systems, and we looked at some of the uses of event processing. We now look at what we mean by *event processing* and describe some of the components of an event processing application and an event processing platform.

1.2.1   What we mean by event processing

In the introduction to this chapter we explained that we are using a fairly broad definition of event processing:

> **EVENT PROCESSING**   *Event processing* is computing that performs operations on events. Common event processing operations include reading, creating, transforming, and deleting events.

There are two major themes within this area:

- The design, coding and operation of applications that use events, either directly or indirectly. We saw some examples of applications like this in section

1.1.3. We refer to this as *event-based programming*, although it is sometimes also called *event-driven architecture.*[3]

- The processing operations that you can perform on events as part of such an application. These include filtering out certain events, changing an event instance from one form to another, and examining a collection of events to find a particular pattern. These operations can often result in new event instances being generated. Many of the examples in section 1.1.3 used event processing operations to analyze low-level events and derive further events from them.

It's possible, of course, to write event-based programs without using explicit event processing operations, and people have been doing event-based programming for many years. The three things that distinguish event processing from simple event-based programming, and which open up such a rich range of possibilities are as follows:

- *Abstraction*—Operations that form the event processing logic can be separated from the application logic, allowing them to be modified without having to change the producing and consuming applications.
- *Decoupling*—The events detected and produced by one particular application can be consumed and acted on by completely different applications. There's no need for producing and consuming applications to be aware of each others' existence, and they may be distributed anywhere in the world. An event emitted by a single producing application can be acted on by many consuming applications. Conversely you can arrange for an application to consume events produced by many different producing applications.
- *Real-world focus*—Event processing frequently deals with events that occur, or could occur, in the real world.

Let's pick up on the *real-world focus* idea and explore it in a bit more detail.

1.2.2 *Event processing and its relationship to the real world*

All the examples that we listed in section 1.1.3 use event processing to detect or report on situations, events that occur in the real world that may require a reaction, human or automated. In this section we use a couple of further examples to explore the relationship between events in the real world and their representation in an event processing system. These examples illustrate two kinds of relationships:

- *Deterministic*—There is an exact mapping between a situation in the real world and its representation in the event processing system.
- *Approximate*—The event processing system provides an approximation to real world events.

Our first example is a system that detects violations of payment on a toll bridge. In this case the situation occurs when a vehicle goes through a highway toll booth (figure 1.3) without paying.

---

[3] See the book by Chandy and Schulte that we reference at the end of this chapter.

Figure 1.3   A highway toll booth. In this example there is an exact mapping between the real-world events at the toll bridge and their representation in the event processing system.

This can happen in two ways:

1   A vehicle uses an automatic payment system lane without having the device that identifies the car.

2   A vehicle uses a manual lane and manages to sneak through without paying.

In both cases the system detects the situation and sends a picture with the vehicle license plate to the officer on duty on the other side of the bridge. From the event processing perspective we can devise a simple event processing application that detects the fact that a vehicle did not pay and sends this observation along with the picture to a consumer (the officer). This is a deterministic example; the derived event that flows to the consumer implies that the situation has occurred. Conversely when the officer does not receive an event, he or she can assume that no violation has occurred.

In our second example, events in the event processing system only approximate the real world. The setting is a service provider's help desk (figure 1.4). The situation involves a customer who gets so frustrated with the service that he threatens to cancel his account. The service provider wants to detect this situation so that it can assign a skilled customer relations officer to call the customer.

Figure 1.4   A service provider help desk. In this example the mapping between real-world events and their representation in the event processing system is not as clear cut as in the toll booth example.

In this example things are not so straightforward. A human agent can detect frustrated customers by the tone of their voices or electronic messages, but this might not catch all frustrated customers. So in addition we might use an event processing system to look at patterns of user activity, for example, one that detects when a customer contacts the help desk three or more times within a single day. Although we can construct an event processing application that detects this pattern and sends a notification to the appropriate customer relations officer, the detection of this pattern is neither a necessary nor sufficient indication that the situation has occurred. In this case the derived event generated by the system is an approximation to the situation, as there may be false positives and false negatives. Ways of dealing with uncertainty in event processing are discussed briefly in part 3 of this book.

1.2.3　*Reasons for using event processing*

One question you might ask is why you might want to use an event processing approach in the first place. Here are some reasons:

- Your application might be naturally centered on events, as are many of the examples in section 1.1.3. They involve sensors that detect and report events, and the purpose of the application is to analyze and react to these events.
- Your application might need to identify and react to certain situations (either good or bad) as they occur. An event-driven approach, where changes in state are monitored as they happen, lets an application respond in a much more timely fashion than a batch approach where the detection process runs only intermittently.
- Event processing can give you a way of extending an existing application in a flexible, non-invasive manner. Rather than changing the original application to add the extra function, it's sometimes possible to instrument the original application by adding event producers to it (for example, by processing the log files that it produces). The additional functionality can then be implemented by processing the events generated by these event producers.
- Intermediary event processing logic can be separated out from the rest of the application. This can allow the application to be adapted quickly to meet new business requirements, sometimes by the application business users themselves.
- The application might involve analysis of a large amount of data in order to provide an output to be delivered to a human user or another application. This data can be organized into streams of events which are then distributed to multiple computing nodes allowing separate parts of the analysis to be performed in parallel.
- There are potential scalability and fault tolerance benefits to be gained by using an event-driven approach. An event-driven approach allows processing to be performed asynchronously, and so is well suited to applications where events happen in an irregular manner. If event activity suddenly spikes, it may be possible to defer some processing to a subsequent, quieter time.

We are not claiming that event processing is a universal solution, and that existing batch, online transaction processing, or database-centric applications should be rewritten using event processing technology. However, event processing plays an important part in complementing these approaches. With some applications an event-driven approach will give you a more timely response, better throughput, or greater flexibility through the separating out of event processing logic from the mainstream application code. It doesn't have to be a case of either/or; many applications incorporate a mixture of event-driven and other approaches.

Next we discuss the idea of an event processing platform and its business value.

1.3   *The business value of an event processing platform*

The examples in section 1.1.3 differ one from another, but all follow the same pattern: events are reported, sometimes by multiple event producers, and some processing of the events is performed. This processing can be made up of several phases, and at the end it creates additional events that are consumed either by humans or by automated processes.

The producers of the events may be different from their consumers. For example, in the luggage management system (example 2), events are produced by the check-in process (which emits an event when luggage is initially deposited) and by the various radio-frequency identification (RFID) readers, which emit events about the movement of the luggage in the system. The events generated by the event processing system are consumed by the luggage control system itself, by airport staff, or even by the passengers themselves.

Many event processing applications keep the logic that processes the events separate from the event producers and consumers, as shown in figure 1.5.

One consequence of adopting this pattern is that you can run the event processing logic on a dedicated event processing platform. Several commercial or open source event processing platforms are available (you can find some references on our website). An event processing platform provides some or all of the following:

- A language for expressing event processing logic
- Tools to design and test event processing logic

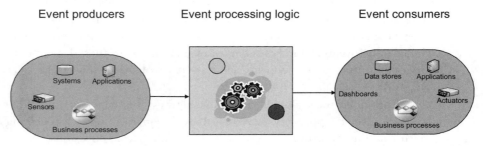

Figure 1.5   **The structure of an event processing application, showing the separation of event processing logic from the event producers and event consumers**

- A runtime to execute event processing logic
- An event distribution mechanism
- Operational management tools

People frequently ask this question: Is there business value in employing dedicated event processing software, such as an event processing platform, to construct such applications, or is it sufficient to understand the concepts of event processing and apply them using regular programming languages and existing software tools? From observing the current market and reading analyst reports one can draw two conclusions about the current usage of event processing software:

- The use of dedicated event processing software is growing rapidly; analysts claim that this is the fastest growing segment of enterprise application middleware.
- Dedicated event processing software is used in only a small fraction of its potential market.

In this section we briefly explain some of the criteria you can use to decide whether event processing software might have business value in a particular case.

1.3.1 Effectiveness issues

The use of event processing software can substantially reduce the total cost of ownership of an event processing application. The cost reduction comes from the level of abstraction, and is similar to the benefit you get from using a database management system to hold data rather than using a file system. Event processing software typically provides abstractions for handling events that are at a higher level than those provided by conventional programming languages. This can decrease the cost of development and maintenance, and thus the total cost of ownership. In some cases these higher level abstractions can also enable semi-technical persons to author event processing rules. We return to this point in chapter 12, when discussing the event processing of tomorrow.

Another effectiveness issue is business agility. You might need to change your event processing functionality relatively quickly, and it's much easier to make quick changes to functions that are expressed using higher level programming abstractions and that are detached from mainstream application logic. Furthermore, if the event processing logic is separated out in this way, nontechnical users might be able to author and maintain it. This would increase the speed of initial implementation and subsequent changes, allowing the event processing logic to be specified and implemented directly by the application's business users.

1.3.2 Efficiency issues

In some cases the sheer volume of events to be processed, or the complexity of the processing required, necessitate implementations that can scale up and meet high performance requirements. We discuss this issue further in chapter 10, when talking about implementation issues. In these cases, the use of software optimized for this purpose might be crucial to achieve this goal, as it may not be easily achievable using regular programming.

Applications may also be concerned with other non-functional properties such as reliability, availability, and security. Event processing platforms can provide specific support for these properties, along with operational tools to manage event processing applications when they are put into production.

1.3.3   *When to use dedicated event processing software*

Generic software platforms are now being used in many areas. To take just two examples, organizations typically use database management systems to manage their data and process queries, and they use message-oriented middleware to connect enterprise applications. In a similar fashion, we think that for many applications it has become more cost effective to use an event processing software platform rather than to implement one's own.

As in any build-versus-buy decision, there are cases when it might not be cost effective to use a dedicated event processing platform. In some cases the event processing functionality required is quite simple, with no special performance requirements, and the usage of event processing within the enterprise is limited. In these cases it might not be worth investing the time or money required to purchase, learn, and assimilate event processing software. It might also be more reasonable to use a self-built solution when the required functionality is unique and is not expressible naturally within any of the languages provided by event processing platforms.

If you decide to build your own event processing application from the ground up, you can still follow the principles described in this book. You can structure your application as shown in figure 1.5 and develop a set of software components, each of them written to perform a specific function, corresponding to the event processing agents that we discuss in this book. These software components can communicate by sending event instances over a messaging system, such as Java Message Service (JMS). You might want to use an enterprise service bus to perform some of the simpler event processing functions, such as transformation, filtering, and routing.

We provide a set of additional references at the end of this chapter for readers interested in reading more about the business aspects of event processing.

1.4   *Event processing and its connection to related concepts*

Now that we've given a brief introduction to event processing, it's time to see how it relates to some other concepts that exist in the IT environment. We discuss the following areas: business process management (BPM), Business Activity Monitoring (BAM), business intelligence (BI), business rule management systems (BRMSs), Network and Systems Management (NSM), message-oriented middleware (MOM) and stream computing. This section covers a lot of ground at quite a high level, so at the end of the chapter we provide some references for the reader who is interested in finding out more about some of these areas.

1.4.1   *Event-driven business process management*

Business process management deals with computerized support of modeling, managing, orchestrating, and executing some or all of an enterprise's business processes. BPM software has evolved from workflow systems, and is now frequently included in service-oriented architecture platforms. We discuss the relationship of event processing to service-oriented architecture in the next chapter.

There are two major standards related to BPM software: BPMN (business process modeling notation),[4] an Object Management Group (OMG) standard that deals with the modeling side, and WS-BPEL (Business Process Execution Language),[5] an OASIS standard that deals with the execution side. The synergies between BPM and event processing are listed here:

- The BPM system can serve as an event producer, generating events that report on state changes within the BPM system, which are then analyzed by the event processing system, with the resulting derived events either being returned to the BPM system, or disseminated to other applications.
- The BPM system can act as an event consumer, reacting to situations detected by the event processing system after it has analyzed events from outside the BPM system. An event sent from an event processing system could interact with the BPM system in several ways: the event could trigger a new instance of business process, it could affect a decision point within the flow of a business process that is already running, or it could cause an existing process instance to stop running. We'll give an example from human resources management. In this example a fictional enterprise uses a managed business process to make management appointments. This process consists of a number of activities: advertising the position, identifying candidates, evaluating them, and reaching a decision. Several events could trigger this process to start, such as retirement or promotion of an existing manager. After the process has started it could be affected by a number of external situations. Let's look at two examples of external situations that affect the process. First, event processing could be used to detect that fewer candidates have applied than expected, and this could cause the process to launch an activity to encourage more applications, such as additional publicity or the use of a recruitment agency. Second, during this process there might be an organizational change that eliminates the position (in which case the process should be canceled) or an organizational change made to alter the set of skills required for the job (which might remove some candidates from consideration).

At the time of writing, there are some BPM products that embed their own ad hoc event processing capabilities. In the future we might see more integration between

---

[4] http://www.omg.org/spec/BPMN/
[5] http://www.oasis-open.org/committees/tc_home.php?wg_abbrev=wsbpel

BPM and event processing products, given the increasing importance of event processing to the BPM space. We provide some references at the end of the chapter for readers interested in pursuing this topic further.

1.4.2 Business Activity Monitoring (BAM)

Business Activity Monitoring (BAM) is a term coined by Gartner.[6] BAM software typically tracks key performance indicators (KPIs). For example, a book publisher uses the number of copies sold per month of an important book as a KPI. The BAM concept, in principle, is wider than KPI tracking and may include monitoring of any kind of business related event.

BAM software systems typically contain some event processing functionality. Systems that are centered on KPI tracking perform filtering, transformation, and most importantly aggregation of events. This can be done in batch mode, calculating KPIs at the end of each day, week, or month as appropriate, or in online mode so that the current value of the KPI can be continually tracked, typically on a dashboard. We cover the dashboard concept in chapter 5, while discussing event consumers.

Two trends in the evolution of BAM software will require more event processing functionality: the drive to provide richer types of observation, which necessitates more event processing functions such as event pattern detection; and the need to provide more online observations when data comes from multiple event sources. We anticipate that these trends will lead to more use of event processing software in tightly or loosely coupled integration with BAM software.

1.4.3 Business intelligence (BI)

Business intelligence (BI) is a collection of analytics techniques and software used to help organizations make decisions based on data that they have collected.

Today's BI systems differ from event processing systems in that they are request driven. A typical BI system takes as its input a set of data that has previously been collected in a data warehouse. It analyzes the data retrospectively, and does not respond to events as they happen. This approach is so different from event processing that it makes sense to think of business intelligence and event processing as separate disciplines, dealing with different problems.

We are beginning to see the appearance of software that provides online analytics for decision making. This is a kind of event-driven BI, because it involves versions of the BI analytics that can run online, triggered by events. The term *operational intelligence*[7] is sometimes used to describe this area. Whereas mainstream BI functionality will remain request oriented for the foreseeable future, event-driven BI is useful to some segments of the BI marketplace, and so we expect to see this functionality being included in BI software.

---

[6] http://www.gartner.com/resources/105500/105562/105562.pdf

[7] The Wikipedia entry for operational intelligence provides some explanation: http://en.wikipedia.org/wiki/Operational_intelligence.

1.4.4   *Business rule management systems (BRMSs)*

Business rule management systems (BRMSs) are software systems that execute rules, typically in the form of *condition-action* or *if-then,* which are kept separate from mainline application logic. This means that the rules can be modified without requiring change to the application code. The rules are expressed in declarative languages and are managed by dedicated software platforms.

There is often confusion between the concepts of BRMS and event processing, mainly due to the fact that some event processing software is based on rule-oriented languages, and the term *rule* is sometimes used to mean the basic processing primitive of event processing (in this book we use the term *event processing agent* instead). However BRMS and event processing systems have fundamental differences:

- Event processing is invoked by the occurrence of events; business rules are invoked by requests made from application logic.
- Business rules operate on states; event processing operates on events but can consult state.
- A business rule system makes inferences from a knowledge base of business rules; the main functionality of event processing is event filtering, transformation, and pattern detection.

These differences result in different functionality, different execution mechanisms, and different types of optimization. Attempts have been made to implement business rules functionality using event processing software and to implement event processing functionality using BRMS software, for example, adding temporal extensions to BRMS to express the equivalent of the event processing temporal patterns that we will examine in chapter 9. It is, however, difficult to optimize both types of functionality in a single implementation.

There are also synergies between event processing and business rules:

- Business rules can be used in the routing and filtering decisions made by event processing software.
- Event processing functionality can be expressed in a rules-based programming style.
- Business rules and event processing rules could be authored by the same person, particularly when the products involved aim their level of abstraction at the business user.
- The occurrence of an event, or the detection of a situation by event processing software, can be used to trigger a BRMS business rule. In this case the BRMS is a consumer of events produced by the event processing system.

These synergies, coupled with the growing quantity of applications that require both event processing and business rules functionality, may serve as a motivation for tighter integration between BRMS and event processing, including common programming models and common product packaging.

1.4.5   Network and System Management

Network and Systems Management (NSM) applications are event driven. One of NSM's major goals is to monitor error events (sometimes called *symptoms*) and analyze them to find their root causes. An underlying problem may give rise to many symptoms, for example, a malfunctioning network router could cause a number of services to fail. Network and Systems Management software uses a technique called *event correlation*[8] to examine symptoms and identify groups of symptoms that have a common root cause. These systems also look for particular patterns among the events that they monitor.

NSM products predate more general-purpose event processing software, and have continued to evolve in parallel with it. They have been focused on management applications, whereas event processing has concentrated more on business applications.[9] They also have different types of users (NSM users are typically system administrators) and different non-functional assumptions.

Some applications (such as Business Activity Monitoring) may require a combination of systems management and event processing applications, and this might be a motivation for developing more synergy between the two areas, but we expect that they will continue to move along separate tracks, at least for the near future.

1.4.6   Message-oriented middleware (MOM)

Message-oriented middleware (MOM) complements event processing, but also partially overlaps it. MOM provides a transport layer that event processing may employ as an infrastructure to implement event channels. The filtering functionality of event processing is similar to the filtering functionality in MOM, as is some of the transformation functionality. There are also differences:

- Whereas an event instance may be represented as a message, a message does not necessarily represent an event. For example, if you send a picture as a message using a MOM system, the picture does not necessarily represent an event.
- Whereas messages in message-oriented middleware can have temporal semantics, such as timestamps, expiry, and ordering, these are not hard requirements. In contrast, temporal properties are fundamental to event processing.
- MOM typically handles each message separately, whereas event processing usually includes functions that operate on collections of events, for example, aggregation and pattern detection.

Event processing may be implemented using a combination of MOM and dedicated event processing components, using the MOM to route event messages between event processing components and to perform filtering. You can find a good description of the

---

[8] A Computerworld article described event correlation in network and system management at http://www. computerworld.com/s/article/83396/Event_Correlation?taxonomyId=16&pageNumber=1.

[9] For an interview with Tom Bishop, CTO of BMC Software, on this topic see http://complexevents.com/ wp-content/uploads/2008/11/an-answer-to-a-question3.pdf.

MOM pattern and related concepts in Hohpe and Woolf's *Enterprise Integration Patterns.*[10] This book includes several of the concepts that we cover; it provides a message-oriented view, whereas we describe the concepts from an event processing viewpoint.

1.4.7 Stream computing

The term *event stream processing* is sometimes used as an alias for event processing but sometimes just refers to a subset of it. Stream computing is a much wider subject, encompassing streams that contain data that we would not normally view as events, for example, video streams and audio streams. Stream computing uses an infrastructure based on a dataflow model, which may be used to run various types of applications.

Event processing intersects and synergizes with stream computing as follows:

- You can use a stream processing platform to implement the event processing functionality described in this book.
- Functions implemented on top of a stream computing framework can serve as event producers. For example, in a security application you might use a stream processing platform to extract events out of video streams, which are then forwarded to an event processing platform for further analysis.

Additional reading on stream computing is detailed at the end of this chapter.

We now introduce the Fast Flower Delivery application that accompanies this book and is demonstrated on the book's website.

1.5 The Fast Flower Delivery application

Before presenting numerous concepts and details, we introduce our example event processing application. This example is used throughout the book to explain and demonstrate the concepts and facilities of event processing. We have chosen a supply chain management example centered on flower delivery that illustrates many of the features found in event processing applications, but which can be understood without application-specific knowledge.

This example is demonstrated using the book's website:

http://www.ep-ts.com/EventProcessingInAction

The website provides you an opportunity to see this example implemented using a number of event processing platforms and tools, and lets you experiment with a number of these platforms so you can see how the concepts described in this book are applied in practice.

In this section we provide a specification of our example—the Fast Flower Delivery application—in a detailed, yet informal, type of specification. As we proceed through the book we examine each aspect of this application in some detail. Appendix B contains a more formal specification of the application, using elements of our modeling language. We start with figure 1.6 which summarizes the main event flows in the application:

---

[10] http://www.eaipatterns.com/

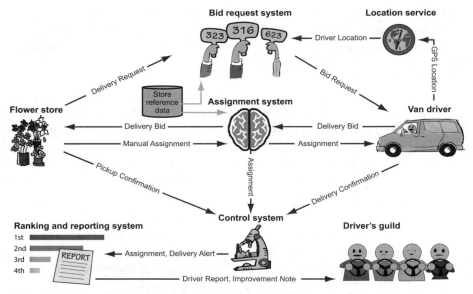

Figure 1.6   Parts of the Fast Flower Delivery application. The arrows represent the flow of events, and the pictures represent the various entities involved in the network.

1.5.1   *General description*

A consortium of flower stores in a large city has established an agreement with local independent van drivers to deliver flowers from the stores to their destinations. When a store gets a flower delivery order, it creates a request which is broadcast to relevant drivers within a certain distance from the store, with the time for pickup (typically *now*) and the required delivery time. A driver is then assigned and the customer is notified that a delivery has been scheduled. The driver makes the pickup and delivery, and the person receiving the flowers confirms the delivery time by signing for it on the driver's mobile device. The system maintains a ranking of each individual driver based on his or her ability to deliver flowers on time. Each store has a profile that can include a constraint on the ranking of its drivers; for example, a store can require its drivers to have a ranking greater than 10. The profile also indicates whether the store wants the system to assign drivers automatically, or whether it wants to receive several applications and then make its own choice.

1.5.2   *Skeleton specification*

Let's go through the various phases of the skeleton specification:

PHASE 1: BID PHASE

The communication between the store and the person who makes the order is outside the scope of the system, so as far as we're concerned a delivery's lifecycle starts when a store places a `Delivery Request` event into the system. The system *enriches* the `Delivery Request` event by adding to it the minimum ranking that the store is prepared to accept (each store has a different level of tolerance for service quality). Each van is equipped with a GPS modem which periodically transmits a GPS Location event. The system *translates* these events, which contain raw latitude and longitude values, into events that indicate which region of the city the driver is currently in. When it receives a Delivery Request event, the system matches it to its list of drivers. It selects only those authorized drivers who satisfy the ranking requirements and who are currently in nearby regions. A Bid Request event is then broadcast to all these drivers.

PHASE 2: ASSIGNMENT PHASE

A driver responds to the Bid Request by sending a Delivery Bid event designating his or her current location and committing to a pickup time. Note that here the term *request* means a message that asks drivers to bid; it should not be confused with a service request issued in a request-response protocol. Two minutes after the Bid Request broadcast, the system starts the assignment process. This is either an automatic or a manual process, depending on the store's preference. If the process is manual the system collects the Delivery Bid events that match the original Bid Request and sends the five highest-ranked to the store. The store chooses one of these five drivers and creates the Assignment event itself. If the process is automatic, the first bidder among the selected drivers wins the bid, and the Assignment event is created by the event processing application. The pickup time and delivery time are set and the Assignment is sent to the driver.

There are also alerts associated with this process: if there are no bidders, an alert is sent both to the store and to the system manager; if the store has not performed its manual assignment within 1 minute of receiving its Delivery Bid events, both the store and system manager receive an alert.

PHASE 3: DELIVERY PROCESS

When the driver arrives to pick up the flowers from the store, the store sends a Pickup Confirmation event; when the driver delivers the flowers, the person receiving them confirms by signing the driver's mobile device, and this generates a Delivery Confirmation event. Both Pickup Confirmation and Delivery Confirmation events have associated timestamps, and this allows the system to generate alert events.

- A Pickup Alert is generated if a Pickup Confirmation wasn't reported within 5 minutes of the committed pickup time.
- A Delivery Alert is generated if a Delivery Confirmation wasn't reported within 10 minutes of the required delivery time.

PHASE 4: RANKING EVALUATION

The system evaluates each driver's ranking every time that driver completes 20 deliveries. If the driver did not have any Delivery Alerts during that period, the system generates a Ranking Increase event indicating that the driver's ranking has increased by one point. Conversely, if the driver has had more than five delivery alerts during that time, the system generates a Ranking Decrease to reduce the ranking by one point. If the system generates a Ranking Increase for a driver whose previous evaluation had been a Ranking Decrease, it generates an Improvement Note event.

PHASE 5: ACTIVITY MONITORING

The system aggregates assignment and other events and counts the number of assignments per day for each driver for each day in which the driver has been active. Once a month the system creates reports on drivers' performance, assessing the drivers according to the following criteria:

- A *permanently weak driver* is a driver with fewer than five assignments on all the days on which the driver has been active.
- An *idle driver* is a driver with at least one day of activity that had no assignments.
- A *consistently weak driver* is a driver whose assignments, when active, are at least two standard deviations lower than the average assignments per driver on that day.
- A *consistently strong driver* is a driver whose daily assignments are at least two standard deviations higher than the average number of assignments per driver on each day in question.
- An *improving driver* is a driver whose assignments increase or stay the same day by day.

As we have said, this application accompanies us throughout the book, and provides us with a good view into the various functions performed by an event processing system. You will find implementation material for this application on the book's website, which we describe next.

1.6   *Using this book's website*

The *Event Processing in Action* website is a valuable resource for you, because it bridges the concepts explained in this book with products and open source offerings in the event processing domain. The website's URL is

http://www.ep-ts.com/EventProcessing InAction

On the website you can find the following:

- A specification of the Fast Flower Delivery example application, containing material from section 1.5 of this chapter. As well as demonstrating the concepts of this book, this example helps you understand the various languages that can be accessed from the website.
- Links to the participating languages. Each of the participating languages has a link to a site from which you can download the language, documentation, and an implementation of the Fast Flower Delivery application.
- An open source editor allowing you to create definition elements using the modeling language that is introduced in this book.
- Excerpts from each of the chapters in this book.

We briefly discuss the part of the website which deals with the participating languages in the sections that follow.

THE LANGUAGE-BASED PART OF THE WEBSITE

In order to experience event processing programming you need to choose the language that you would like to use. The website contains examples in several different languages. You can pick one of these languages and go into it in depth or look at several to get a better feel for the various ways to do event processing.

We include here a few examples illustrating some of the different language styles that you can find on the website. These examples show how to implement the automatic driver assignment step that occurs in phase 2 of the Fast Flower Delivery application.

APAMA EVENT PROCESSING LANGUAGE

The imperative language style is illustrated by the MonitorScript Event Programming Language (EPL) from Apama, a division of Progress Software. The syntax of Monitor-Script is similar to Java or C++ as shown in listing 1.1.

Listing 1.1 Example of the MonitorScript event programming language from Apama

```
if isAuto then {
  DeliveryBid db;
  on DeliveryBid(store=dr.store):db within(ASSIGNMENT_TIME){        ❶ Detect
    assignmentTimer.quit();                                            pattern
    route Assignment(dr.requestId,
                     dr.store,                              ❷ Send
                     db.driver,                                event
                     dr.addresseeLocationPointX,
                     dr.addresseeLocationPointY,
                     db.committedPickUpTime,
                     dr.requiredDeliveryTime);
    watchForPickUp(dr, db.driver, db.committedPickUpTime);
    watchForDelivery(dr, db.driver);
  }
}
```

In this code snippet, `DeliveryBid` and `Assignment` are event types. The listener ❶ reacts when it detects the first incoming `DeliveryBid` and then executes the block of code contained in curly braces { } that follow it. This includes statement ❷, which creates and emits an `Assignment` event. This uses attributes from the original delivery request, as well as from the `DeliveryBid`.

ESPER

Esper is an open source event processing implementation, and like several other event processing platforms it uses a stream-oriented language that is an extension of SQL. It can be embedded into Java applications.

```
on pattern[every b=BidRequest(storeManual=true)->timer:interval(2 min)]   ❶
insert into AssignmentManual                              ❷ Send
select d.* from DeliveryBid d where requestId=b.requestId    event   Detect
order by ranking desc limit 5;                                       pattern
```

As you can see, the syntax of this language is similar to SQL but it has been extended with the on `pattern` statement ❶ which performs a similar role to the on statement in the MonitorScript EPL. A SQL `insert` statement ❷ is used to send the `Assignment` event.

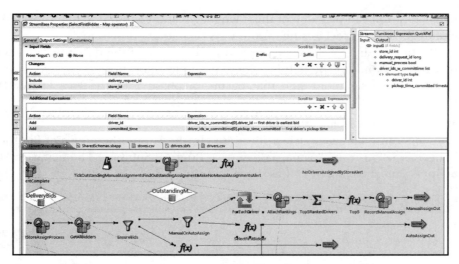

Figure 1.7   The graphical interface for StreamBase StreamSQL EventFlow

STREAMBASE STREAMSQL EVENTFLOW

The StreamBase product also uses an extension of SQL, but programmers are encouraged to use the graphical user interface provided by the StreamBase Studio shown in figure 1.7, known as StreamSQL EventFlow, instead of entering the StreamSQL as text.

At the bottom of this illustration you can see the control flow of the application. The driver assignment is performed by the `SelectFirstBidder` operator, represented by one of the icons in the flow. You configure details of this operator using the tabbed property sheets that appear at the top.

These examples show some of the different language styles that are available; more languages and language styles are displayed on the website. We conclude this chapter with table 1.1, which gives a list of languages currently available.

Table 1.1   Event processing languages classified by language style

Language style	Language or product name	Vendor or open source
Stream-oriented	Aleri	Aleri
	CCL	Aleri/Coral8
	Esper	Open source
	CQL	Open ESB IEP (open source)
	Oracle CEP	Oracle
	RTM Analyzer	RTM Realtime Monitoring
	SPADE	IBM
	StreamInsight	Microsoft
	StreamSQL EventFlow	StreamBase

Table 1.1 Event processing languages classified by language style *(continued)*

Language style	Language or product name	Vendor or open source
Rule–oriented:		
ECA Rules	Amit	IBM (Research Asset)
	AutoPilot M6	Nastel
	Reakt	RuleCore
	RulePoint	Informatica/Agent Logic
	SENACTIVE InTime	UC4 / SENACTIVE
	StarRules	Starview Technology
	Vantify	WestGlobal
	WebSphere Business Events	IBM
Inference rules	DROOLS Fusion	JBoss (open source)
	TIBCO BusinessEvents	TIBCO
Logic Programming	Etalis	Open source
	Prova	Open source
Imperative	MonitorScript	Progress Software
	Netcool Impact Policy Language	IBM

After you have chosen a language style, you can use links on the website to get more information about languages that implement it.

1.7   *Summary*

Although we process events all the time in our daily lives, traditional software paradigms have not been oriented towards event-driven functionality, but instead have focused on more synchronous request-driven interactions. Many kinds of applications benefit from an event-driven approach. Imagine that you have an employee who sits idle and only works when explicitly told exactly what to do—that isn't an effective way to handle a business. Likewise there are cases in which software is more effective if, rather than waiting to be told what to do, it can detect when an event has happened and can decide whether and how to react.

There can also be benefits in separating the logic that processes events from mainstream application logic, so that an event processing application is made up of event producers, event consumers, and intermediary event processing. Although you can implement event processing logic by hand in a conventional programming language, there are advantages in using a dedicated event processing platform. Such platforms usually have their own languages and tools, and as we have seen, several different language styles are currently in use.

You should now be familiar at a high level with the basic concepts covered in this book. Reading the rest of the book will give you a more detailed understanding of these concepts and their proper use in constructing event processing applications, starting with the discussion of the technical principles behind event processing in chapter 2.

1.7.1   Additional reading

Chandy, K. M., and W. R. Schulte. 2009. *Event Processing: Designing IT Systems for Agile Companies, 1st ed.* McGraw-Hill Osborne Media. http://www.amazon.com/Event-Processing-Designing-Systems-Companies/dp/0071633502/ref=sr_1_1?ie=UTF8&s=books&qid=1258816511&sr=8-1. This book is an excellent reference on the business motivation for event processing, as well as the positioning of event processing against Service-Oriented Architecture (SOA) and other related concepts. It includes a discussion of terminology, for example, the various interpretations of the term *event*.

Luckham, David. 2002. *The Power of Events: An Introduction to Complex Event Processing in Distributed Enterprise Systems.* Addison-Wesley Professional. http://www.amazon.com/Power-Events-Introduction-Processing-Distributed/dp/0201727897/ref=sr_1_2?ie=UTF8&s=books&qid=1258816511&sr=8-2. This is the first book published about event processing. It introduced early versions of many of the concepts discussed in this book such as event processing networks and event processing agents.

Arasu, Arvind, et al.2003. STREAM: The Stanford Stream Data Manager. "SIGMOD Conference": 666. http://dblp.uni-trier.de/rec/bibtex/conf/sigmod/AbadiCCCCEGHMRSSTXYZ03. This article describes the STREAM project from Stanford University, which introduced the Continuous Query Language (CQL).

Zimmer, Detlef, and Rainer Unland. 1999. "On the Semantics of Complex Events in Active Database Management Systems." ICDE: 392-399. http://www.informatik.uni-trier.de/~ley/db/conf/icde/ZimmerU99.html. This article is a good survey of related concepts in active databases; several of the concepts we discuss later had their origin in work done in the context of active databases.

von Ammon, Rainer. 2009. "Event-Driven Business Process Management." Encyclopedia of Database Systems: 1068-1071. http://www.springerlink.com/content/p267j78082568086/. This is an encyclopedia entry explaining event-driven business process management.

1.7.2   Exercises

1.1   Provide your own examples of real-life activities which involve events and reactions to them.

1.2   Classify the ten examples given in section 1.1.3 into the categories given in section 1.1.4. Remember that an example can fit into more than one category.

1.3 Provide three of your own examples of the use of automated event processing, and analyze the benefits of automation.

1.4 List all event types used in the Fast Flower Delivery application.

1.5 List all the event processing agents in that application.

1.6 List the event types consumed and emitted by each event processing agent in the Fast Flower Delivery application.

1.7 Describe three additional functions that could be added to the Fast Flower Delivery application.

Principles of event processing 2

An apprentice carpenter may want only a hammer and saw, but a master craftsman employs many precision tools. Computer programming likewise requires sophisticated tools to cope with the complexity of real applications, and only practice with these tools will build skill in their use.

—Robert L. Kruse

In the previous chapter we briefly introduced event processing. In this chapter we explore the technical concepts behind event processing in more detail. The chapter is divided into three main sections:

- In section 2.1 we look at the event-based programming part of event processing. This covers the *event* aspect of event processing. The remainder of the chapter then discusses the *processing* part of event processing.
- In section 2.2 we introduce the main concepts of event processing, and define the terminology we use to describe them.
- In section 2.3 we introduce the modeling language that we use in this book to describe the concepts from section 2.2.

This chapter focuses on the general principles underlying these topics. In part 2 of this book we show them being used in the Fast Flower Delivery example that we introduced in the previous chapter.

2.1 Events and event-based programming

In the first part of this chapter we look more closely at events in computerized event processing, their interactions with application components, and the ways they are distributed between these components. As a lead into this, however we start by looking at how applications components typically interact when they *aren't* using events.

2.1.1 The background: request-response interactions

Everyone who has used a web browser (figure 2.1) will have had first-hand experience of the request-response interaction pattern. When you use a browser, you formulate a request, usually by clicking on a link or filling in a form, which is sent across the internet

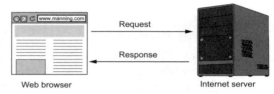

Figure 2.1   Request-response on the World Wide Web

to a web server. You then wait while the server constructs a response. This response is returned across the internet and then displayed by the browser.

In a request-response interaction the request can be a request for information (sometimes called a *query*) or it can be a request for something to happen (sometimes called an *update*). An *update* can be anything that causes a change of state at the server side, for example, placing an online shopping order. In the query case the response returns the information asked for; in the update case it usually carries a confirmation that the requested action has been carried out successfully. The response to an update request can contain extra information; for example, if the request was to place an order, the response might give an indication of the time when that order will be fulfilled.

Request-response[1] interactions are used frequently in distributed computing and form the basis of most service-oriented architectures. In the general interaction pattern, one application or application component, termed a *service requestor* (or sometimes a *client*) sends a request to another, known as a *service provider* or *server,* and sometime afterwards the requestor receives a response. The great majority of request-response interactions are synchronous in nature.

> **Synchronous interactions**
>
> In a synchronous interaction the provider is expected to send a response back fairly promptly. This usually means a few tenths of a second at the longest, though response times of several seconds are sometimes encountered in web applications. The requestor's thread of execution blocks waiting for the response to arrive without doing anything else in the interim. In practice there is often a timeout mechanism so that

---

[1]   Request-response as well as some of the other terms are discussed in depth in the book *Enterprise Integration Patterns: Designing, Building, and Deploying Messaging Solutions* by Gregor Hohpe and Bobby Woolf. Addison-Wesley, 2003; http://www.amazon.com/Enterprise-Integration-Patterns-Designing-Deploying/dp/0321200683/ref=sr_1_1?ie=UTF8&s=books&qid=1258829949&sr=1-1.

(continued)

the requestor thread waits only for a finite period before deciding that there must have been some kind of failure and that the response is never going to arrive.

Figure 2.2 shows a Unified Modeling Language (UML) sequence diagram of a request-response interaction.

Sequence diagrams

In a sequence diagram time travels down the page, and each entity that interacts is represented with a vertical lifeline. The interactions, or messages, between these entities are shown using horizontal arrows.

In this diagram you can see the requestor, an order processing application, sending a stock query request to an inventory system to determine whether a particular item is in stock or not. The order processing application blocks waiting for the response to this query.

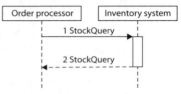

Figure 2.2   Request-response in distributed computing

The request-response interaction pattern is a convenient programming technique. It is used when interacting with all representational state transfer (REST)-style web services[2] and most SOAP-style[3] services, and it forms the basis for the remote procedure call (RPC) invocation pattern used in most distributed object systems. The request-response interaction pattern has the advantage of being familiar to programmers who have made a procedure or function call in a procedural programming language or who have invoked a method in an object-oriented language and often fits naturally into the design of an application. When writing a program you reach a point where the program needs a piece of additional information, or where it needs to make sure that something takes place that is external to it, and the natural thing to do at such a point is to invoke an external component or service to return the information or to perform the operation. As we noted earlier, the arrival of the response indicates that the request has been received by the service provider and has been acted upon. (This is only part of the story, because an application might still have to cope with the situation where a failure means that no response is received. In such circumstances the requestor cannot immediately tell whether the request was acted upon or not.)

---

[2] Roy T. Fielding, Richard N. Taylor. 2002. Principled design of the modern Web architecture. *ACM Transactions on Internet Technology.* 2(2): 115-150. http://portal.acm.org/citation.cfm?doid=514183.514185.

[3] http://www.w3.org/TR/soap/

2.1.2   *Events and the principle of decoupling*

Events differ from requests in the following important way:

> **EVENT** An *event* is an indication of something that has already happened, whereas a request, as its name implies, expresses the requestor's wish that something specific should happen in the future.
>
> As a result we use slightly different terminology for the participants in an interaction involving events. Instead of talking about a service requestor and a service provider, we refer to an *event producer* and an *event consumer*.

To take two obvious examples, if you consult an airline booking service to find out what flights are available on a given date, you are sending that service a request, but when your chosen flight actually takes off, there is an event.

In fairness we should point out that not everything is as clear cut, and it's sometimes possible to view something either as an update request or as an event. Suppose you want to place an order to sell stock on an online trading system. Your interaction with the system can be seen either as a request, because you're hoping that stock will be sold for you, or as the event that you have placed an order. By viewing it as an event, we allow for the possibility that there might be several consumers (either within the trading system proper or outside it) for the event. You will see later that we have events like this in the Fast Flower Delivery application.

In some cases, it's possible for an event to represent the underlying occurrence completely. Consider, for example, a temperature sensor that sends an event every minute. These events could contain all there is to know: the location of the sensor, the time of day, and the temperature value. However, in other cases there may be many features of an occurrence that could be observed (and even some that aren't directly observable) and an event object can still represent the occurrence without necessarily containing all this information. As an example, a medical monitoring device might be able to perform multiple measurements of a patient's condition, but when it's used it reports only those kinds of measurement that are relevant to the individual patient's treatment.

Furthermore it's possible that a single occurrence could be represented by more than one event instance. This could be the case if there are multiple applications all interested in different aspects of the occurrence. Consider, for example, a new employee hired occurrence. A payroll application would be interested in things like the employee's name, serial number, job level, and starting salary, whereas a physical security application would require the employee's office location and information on his or her job responsibilities.

Events are sometimes used to represent changes of state, and this approach is used in many monitoring-style applications. The system being monitored is represented as a set of *resources* (these could be physical things like sensors or logical things like business processes) each of which is associated with state information. There's usually a way to query each resource directly in order to read its state (for example, the current temperature in the case of the temperature sensor) but the resources also act as event producers and send events whenever one or more of their internal state values change. This allows monitoring applications to be notified immediately when something happens, without their having to continually poll all the resources.

An event has meaning that is independent of its producer and of its consumers, and as a result event producers and event consumers can be completely decoupled from each other. The idea of using the event itself to decouple the event producer and event consumer is a significant difference between event-based programming and application design based on request-response interactions.

There is of course a degree of decoupling in a request-response interaction. When you implement a service provider, you generally code it to provide that particular service without regard to the nature or purpose of the service requestor, so the provider is *decoupled* from the requestor. However the service requestor depends on the service provider performing an agreed function. In contrast, in event processing we can get mutual decoupling of producer and consumer; a producer can be decoupled from a consumer and the consumer decoupled from the producer. We can summarize this as the *principle of decoupling*.

> **Principle of decoupling**
>
> In a decoupled event processing system an event producer does not depend on a particular processing or course of action being taken by an event consumer. Moreover, an event consumer does not depend on processing performed by the producer other than the production of the event itself.

In a decoupled system there can be more than one consumer of an event, and the action taken, if indeed any action is taken at all, can vary significantly between consumers. It can also vary during the lifetime of the application. As an event producer does not know what an event consumer is going to do with an event, or even how many consumers there are, it usually does not make sense for the event producer to expect a response to its events.

At this point we should point out that even though a producer itself does not expect a response, in some situations a producer forms part of a larger application component that does expect to receive incoming events. Let's consider the Fast Flower Delivery application that was introduced in chapter 1. In that application a flower store has an event producer that produces a `Delivery Request` event which is submitted to the delivery scheduling system. Shortly after this, if it has chosen to do manual assignment, the store will receive a number of `Delivery Bid` events. These `Delivery Bid` events are caused indirectly by the `Delivery Request` but we view them as events in their own right rather than as direct responses to the request event. As such they are handled by an event consumer portion of the store's application rather than by the event producer responsible for the original `Delivery Request`. This distinction may look unnecessarily subtle at first, but by keeping a clear separation of producers and consumers and viewing the `Delivery Bids` as separate events we can build more flexible and adaptable applications.

A corollary of the principle of decoupling is that an event can, and usually does, have meaning outside the context of a particular interaction between its producer and consumers. In contrast, a request in a request-response interaction generally has meaning only within that interaction.

2.1.3 *Push-style event interactions*

Interactions that use events differ from request-response interactions in a number of ways, the two biggest differences being these:

- An event producer does not, in general, expect consumers to take any specific action when they receive events that it has sent them.
- Events are often sent as *one-way* messages. In other words, after a producer has sent an event message, it can get on with other things without having to wait for responses.

Figure 2.3 shows a UML sequence diagram that depicts one-way event interactions.

You can see that, in this style of distri-bution, communication is initiated by the producer when it has an event to distrib-ute. It *pushes* the event to each consumer as a one-way message. In this particular example, the producer sends a copy of its first event to two separate consumers, but then sends two more events, this time just to consumer 1.

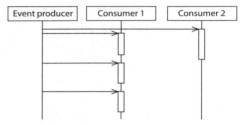

Figure 2.3   Typical push-style event distribution

In none of these four interactions does the event producer wait for a response from the consumer. One reason for this is that a response would relate to the action taken by the consumer, and as we have said the producer is not aware of what this is going to be. Another reason is that the number of such consumers is often not known when the event producer is being designed and coded (and in some cases the number of consumers can vary dynamically while the application is running).

Figure 2.3 illustrates three commonly found characteristics of event distribution:

- The consumer does not send a response to the producer, other than possibly an indication that it has received the event. This means that the consumer can pro-cess the event *asynchronously* to the producer.
- A given event instance may be delivered to more than one consumer, and each consumer can process that event in a different way.
- A given producer may produce a sequence of events over time.

Using push-style distribution can result in reduced processing latency because the producer can send an event as soon as it has one to distribute (this is in contrast to the *pull* style, which we look at later).

Events and messages

There's one area of possible confusion that it is worth clearing up at this stage, and that is the distinction between an event and a message. As we mentioned in the previous section, message passing systems are often used to distribute events between event producers and event consumers, and it's tempting to equate events with the messages used to transmit them. Indeed we ourselves sometimes use the phrase *send the event.*

The difference here is that the event is the entity that records information about the event occurrence, whereas the message is the mechanism used to exchange that information. There are messages that don't contain events, and conversely there are events that aren't in the form of messages (for example, event records held in an event log).

A message used to convey an event entity is sometimes called a *notification*; it contains a serialized form of the event entity. So the phrase *send an event* is convenient shorthand for *send a notification message containing the event.* We should mention two more aspects of notification messages:

- We have already seen that in some event processing applications events are stored in log files or databases. In these applications you may encounter a notification message that doesn't contain the actual event data, but instead contains a reference to the log entry for the event (in other words, the message tells you that something has happened, but doesn't provide all the information about it). When a consumer receives one of these messages it can use the reference to retrieve the event data from the log or database.
- It's also possible for a single message to carry several events—this can be convenient when there are many events to be transferred, for example, when retrieving events from an event log.

Push distribution directly from producers to consumers is used in some event processing applications, but a common variation of this pattern is to use an intermediary event channel, and we'll see this next.

2.1.4 *Channel-based event distribution*

In the simple push interactions shown in figure 2.3, each event is sent directly from the producer to its consumer, and in some cases this means that the producer has to send multiple copies of the same event. The implication of this is that the producer has to be aware, at least at runtime, of the number of consumers and their identities (for example, in figure 2.3 you can see that the event producer is aware of consumer 1 and consumer 2). This can be done in three ways:

- Knowledge of the consumers can be configured statically into the event producer.

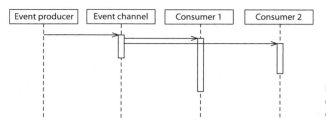

Figure 2.4 Push-style event distribution with an intermediary event channel

- The event producer can find their identities by consulting an external information source, such as a directory service.
- The event producer can require the consumers to register themselves dynamically before they can receive events.

All these approaches impose extra work on the event producer, which can be avoided if the event producer delegates the distribution of events to another entity, as shown in figure 2.4.

In figure 2.4 you can see that the event producer sends a single copy of the event to an intermediary which we call an *event channel*. This channel then takes care of forwarding the event to the event consumers.

The sequence diagram shown in figure 2.4 might give you the impression that an event channel is just another piece of application code. In practice, though, an event channel can be implemented in a number of different ways:

- It could be an intermediary service or other piece of software (sometimes called a *broker*).
- It could be implemented using a multicast protocol, such as IP Multicast.
- It could be implemented using message-oriented middleware (MOM), such as a Java Message Service (JMS) provider.

How does the channel know which consumers it should forward the event to? This depends partly on how it is implemented. In the IP Multicast case, the event is automatically forwarded to a consumer that is listening on the particular multicast group address that the producer has used. In broker or MOM implementations, the channel could be statically configured with the list of consumers, or the consumers could register themselves (or even be registered by someone else) with the channel. If dynamic consumer registration is involved, the pattern is known as *publish/subscribe* and the consumer registrations are referred to as *subscriptions*.

Push-style interactions, either intermediated via an event channel or direct from producer to consumer, are the most commonly found kinds of interaction in event processing, but there are occasions when request-response interactions are used to distribute events, and we look at those in the next section.

2.1.5 *Using request-response interactions to distribute events*

We now take a look at situations where the request-response interaction pattern is used to distribute events. In these interactions an event is passed as a parameter on

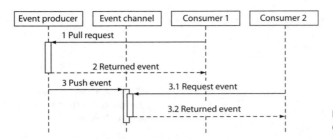

Figure 2.5   Pull-style event distribution

either the request or the response. The most important are *pull-style* interactions where events are passed in the response, as shown in figure 2.5.

In pull-style distribution, the consumer uses the standard request-response pattern to request an event from a producer, or from an intermediary channel. It receives that event in the response part of the interaction. In the examples in figure 2.5, we see event consumer 1 sending a pull request directly to the event producer (message 1), which responds by returning an event in message 2. To avoid having to hold on to events and to avoid having to service requests from multiple consumers, an event producer may choose to delegate this job to an intermediary event channel, similar to the way it can use a channel to help with push-style distribution. Figure 2.5 also shows this: the producer uses a regular push (message 3) to send the event to the channel, and consumer 2 requests it (message 3.1) from the channel. Our examples show only a single event being returned, but this approach can be extended to send multiple events in the response messages. This is useful as there could be more than one undelivered event pending at the producer or channel when a consumer makes a pull request.

Although push-style distribution is more widely used in event processing, there are situations where pull is used instead. These include situations where there is the following:

- A consumer that is only available occasionally, or is only intermittently connected to the distribution system (for example, a handheld mobile device)
- A consumer that wants to regulate its processing of events and have control over exactly when it receives them
- A consumer that is physically unable to receive unsolicited incoming events, for example, a computer system behind a firewall
- A producer that is unable to distribute events

A common example of a producer that is unable to distribute events is writing events to an event store or log. This is a file or database system that is used for medium- or long-term event storage. It doesn't distribute event objects when it is updated, but it can provide a pull-style producer interface, allowing other entities to read events from the log using request-response style queries.

An event store might also provide an interface that allows events to be written to it using a request-response pattern. This is an example of a request-response interaction where an event is supplied as part of the request message.

Now we have covered the basics of event-based programming, we can conclude this section of the chapter by examining the relationship of event processing to service-oriented architecture.

2.1.6 *Event processing and service-oriented architecture*

In recent years there has been much use of the terms *event-driven architecture* (EDA) and *service-oriented architecture* (SOA). Because they both end with the word *architecture*, you might imagine that they are alternatives and that you have to choose whether to adopt one of these styles or the other. It is our contention that this is not the case, and that it is perfectly possible to use event processing within an overall SOA. In fact the term *event-driven SOA* is now used by some analysts and vendors to denote the combination of EDA and SOA.[4]

To explain this, we need to look at what we mean by EDA and by SOA. In this book we have avoided using the term *EDA*, preferring the term *event-based programming*, largely because of the confusion the term EDA often causes.

> **EVENT-BASED PROGRAMMING** *Event-based programming*, also called *event-driven architecture* (EDA) is an architectural style in which one or more components in a software system execute in response to receiving one or more event notifications.

If you adopt a narrow definition of SOA, which states that every application has to be built from request-response oriented services, and *only* from request-response oriented services, then it is true that you would be limited to request-response interactions and wouldn't be able to benefit from all of the advantages of event processing. However, we claim that there is nothing fundamental to SOA that dictates the exclusive use of request-response.

The main idea in SOA is to move away from a monolithic way of designing applications to one where applications are composed of reusable, shareable components. For this to be possible the components need to have well-defined interfaces that are independent of their implementations, and it must be possible to incorporate a given component into more than one application. The emphasis is on the flexibility that comes from this reuse, so that IT systems can be adapted quickly and easily to respond to new business conditions. Much of the focus of SOA is on the design principles and lifecycle and governance issues involved in such an approach—for example, identifying what services are available and who is responsible for developing and maintaining them.

There is nothing in the previous paragraph that implies that the SOA components (services) have to be exclusively request-response oriented. SOA's reusability requirement calls for a degree of decoupling among components but, as we saw in section 2.1.2, event producers and event consumers are even more decoupled than request-response components, so they can easily be used within SOA.

---

[4] See the Wikipedia entry: http://en.wikipedia.org/wiki/Event-driven_SOA for more discussion and some references.

An event-based programming approach can be mixed with request-response components in a SOA in two ways:

- It is possible for a component to implement both approaches. In other words, it can provide or consume a request-response interface and also be an event producer or event consumer. As an example, consider a service that fulfils orders via a request-response interface and produces an event when it detects low stock levels.
- The SOA infrastructure that hosts the SOA components can provide instrumentation that produces events on behalf of request-response style services. For example, you could instrument the order fulfillment service just mentioned so that an event is produced each time an order is fulfilled. These events are then processed by event processing components.

You can view event processing components as extending the repertoire of components used inside a SOA, and an event processing network (EPN) as being a kind of SOA composite service. (We introduce event processing networks in section 2.2.2.) The lifecycle and governance aspects of SOA apply equally well to these components, although of course their interfaces are defined slightly differently—an event producer is defined in terms of the events it produces rather than the request-response interfaces that it relies on, and an event consumer is defined in terms of the events it consumes rather than the request-response interfaces that it implements.

Now that we have covered the basic principles of events and event-based programming, we turn our attention to the remaining aspects of event processing.

2.2   *Main concepts of event processing*

In this section we outline the main concepts that we explore in the remainder of the book and introduce some of the terminology that we use. In section 2.3 we introduce our modeling language which can be used to record the details of an event processing application. We start with an overview of the architecture of event processing to provide a framework for the key concepts.

2.2.1   *Event processing architecture*

Don't be put off by the rather grandiose title of this section. What we're going to look at is the general way that event-driven computing applications are constructed, and the building blocks used to construct them. We go into the details of these building blocks later in this book.

Not all event processing applications are the same, of course, but by and large most of them have a structure something like that shown in figure 2.6.

An application contains one or more components that generate the events. We refer to these as *event producers*, following the terminology we used in section 2.1, and they are shown on the left side of figure 2.6. Event producers can come in a wide range of shapes and sizes: for example, they might be hardware sensors that produce events when they detect certain physical occurrences; they might be bits of software

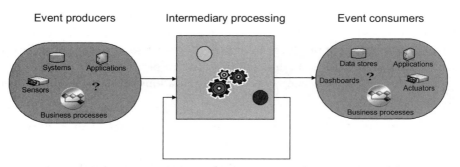

Figure 2.6 The major architectural components of event processing, showing the logical separation of event processing logic from the event producers and event consumers

instrumentation that produce events when certain error conditions are detected; or they might be explicit bits of application programming logic. We discuss event producers further in chapter 4.

The counterparts of the event producers are called *event consumers*. These are the components that ultimately receive the events and typically act on them. Again, their functions vary—they might, for example, store events for later use, display them in a user interface, or take action as a result of receiving them. Event consumers are discussed further in chapter 5.

Event producers and event consumers are linked by event distribution mechanisms, illustrated by the arrows in figure 2.6, and some intermediary event processing often takes place between the event producers and the event consumers. Event distribution is frequently performed using asynchronous message passing technology, which is why we often talk about the producers *sending* events, and the consumers *receiving* them. However other mechanisms can be used, for example, an event producer might simply write its events to an event log file, which is subsequently read by the event consumers. The event distribution mechanism is usually one-to-many so that an event, after being sent, can be received by multiple event consumers.

We discuss the intermediary event processing more fully as this book progresses. In simple cases this processing may just involve routing and/or filtering of the events sent by the event producers; however, much of the richness in event-driven architectures comes from the fact that the intermediate event processing can generate additional events. These events can then be distributed to the event consumers, but they can also be subjected to further event processing, as suggested by the feedback arrow in figure 2.6.

This diagram shows the intermediary event processing as a monolithic component. In practice, event processing systems often allow this intermediary processing to be specified as a sequence of subcomponents which we refer to as *event processing agents*.

It is important to note the decoupling of the event consumers and the event producers, which we mentioned in section 2.1.2. Here the event takes center stage. The event producer has a relationship with each event that it produces, rather than a direct relationship with the event consumers. It is unaware of how many event consumers there are, and has no idea what action (if anything) the consumer is going to take when it receives the event. Likewise the event consumer reacts to the event itself rather than the specific event producer (although in some cases the identity of the event producer forms part of the data that makes up the event).

We summarize this section with formal definitions of the new terms that we have been using.

> **EVENT PRODUCER**   An *event producer* is an entity at the edge of an event processing system that introduces events into the system.

This definition might look strange at first—you might imagine that it would also have to detect the occurrence that gave rise to the event, create the object that is going to represent it, and populate that object with data. We have deliberately made the definition as general as possible because although an event producer may do all those things, it doesn't necessarily do so (it might be a proxy that relays events in from somewhere else). More importantly, the rest of the system (the distribution mechanism, intermediary processing, and event consumers) can't actually tell how an event producer generates its events; what's important to the rest of the system is that it emits them.

Having seen the definition of event producer, the definition of event consumer should hold no surprises.

> **EVENT CONSUMER**   An *event consumer* is an entity at the edge of an event processing system that receives events from the system.

As we mentioned earlier, the intermediary event processing shown in figure 2.6 can be made up of a number of event processing agents.

> **EVENT PROCESSING AGENT**   An *event processing agent* is a software module that processes events.

An event processing agent ingests events and can forward events or emit new ones, so at one level they can be said to consume and produce events. However we don't regard event processing agents as either event producers or event consumers, as we reserve those terms for entities that are outside the event processing system. We also distinguish between two types of event: raw events and derived events.

> **RAW EVENT**   A *raw event* is an event that is introduced into an event processing system by an event producer.

The definition of a raw event relates only to its source and not to its structure; a raw event may or may not be composed of other events.

> **DERIVED EVENT**   A *derived event* is an event that is generated as a result of event processing that takes place inside an event processing system.

Note that this definition is relative to the system being considered. An event object can be generated in one event processing system (and thus be a derived event in that system) and then be passed to a second event processing system where it would be viewed as a raw event.

In the sections that follow we look more closely at intermediary event processing. In section 2.2.2 we discuss how event processing agents can be assembled to form event processing networks, and in section 2.2.3 we describe operations that event processing agents can perform.

2.2.2 *Event processing networks*

We have already remarked that the intermediary event processing shown in figure 2.6 is typically not monolithic, but instead is composed of a number of event processing agents. Such agents are specified using an event processing language, and there are a number of styles of event processing languages currently in use. These include the following:

- Rule-oriented languages that use production rules
- Rule-oriented languages that use active rules
- Rule-oriented languages that use logic rules
- Imperative programming languages
- Stream-oriented languages that are extensions of SQL
- Other stream-oriented languages

We look at these in more detail in chapter 10, but for now we are concerned with how the various agents can be assembled together, regardless of the language used to code them. We introduce a new term to describe this.

> **EVENT PROCESSING NETWORK** An *event processing network* (EPN) is a collection of event processing agents, producers, consumers, and global state elements (explained in section 2.3.3) connected by a collection of channels.

An event processing network is depicted in figure 2.7.

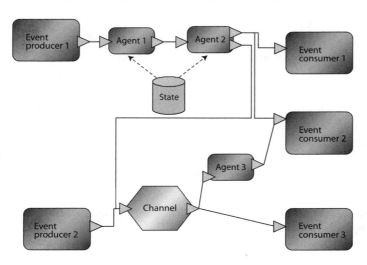

Figure 2.7 **This is an example of a particular event processing network showing the event processing components. The event producers appear at the extreme left of the diagram, and the event consumers at the far right.**

Figure 2.7 shows an EPN with all of its components. At the edges you can see the event producers and event consumers, with the event processing agents in between them. The wiring lines show the flow of events among the various agents, and are referred to as *implicit channels* (you'll recall from section 2.1.4 that channels can be implemented in a variety of ways). There is also an explicitly modeled channel. (Chapter 6 discusses channels further.) Each agent accepts a stream of one or more input events delivered to it through a channel, and it in turn emits further events, which are carried through one or more channels to further agents or to event consumers.

An event processing network can be used to describe a single application (such as those described in section 1.1.3), but a single EPN can also be used to deliver multiple related applications. Suppose that the event processing network shown in figure 2.7 has been established in order to implement a particular application. This application contains a pair of agents (agent 1 and agent 2) that take events from event producer 1 and process them to produce a stream of new derived events. Now suppose that we wish to develop a second event processing application that requires the same set of derived events. Instead of duplicating agent 1 and agent 2 in the second application, we can extend the network so that the output from agent 2 is fed to further agents that perform the processing needed for the second application.

2.2.3 *Types of intermediary event processing*

As we saw earlier, one of the powerful ideas in event processing is the abstraction (separating out) of event processing logic so that it sits between event producers and event consumers rather than being hardcoded into them; we introduced the idea of an event processing network containing event processing agents as a way to achieve this abstraction.

In this section we briefly introduce the types of intermediary processing that are most commonly performed by such agents. Intermediary event processing is the central topic of this book, and is covered in depth in chapters 6 through 9; this section is intended to be a brief summary to whet your appetite.

STATELESS EVENT PROCESSING

The simplest form of event processing takes events from the event producers and distributes them to the event consumers. This often involves filtering of the events, because not every event will be of interest to every event consumer (and in some cases there may be sensitive events that a particular consumer is not authorized to receive). Filtering and routing of this sort is sometimes performed by the same infrastructure that is providing the event distribution, particularly if that infrastructure has publish/subscribe capabilities. Alongside simple basic filtering and routing, intermediary processing might include logging events for audit purposes in an event store. Filtering, routing and logging are all examples of *stateless event processing*.

> **STATELESS EVENT PROCESSING** An event processing agent is said to be *stateless* if the way it processes one event does not influence the way it processes any subsequent events.

Moving up in sophistication, the intermediary processing might involve *translating* the events—either to change their representation or to add information to them (*enrichment*) or remove information from them (*projection*). The techniques used here are similar to those used in enterprise application integration and can be implemented using similar approaches and tools.[5]

STREAMS AND STATEFUL EVENT PROCESSING

The operations we have just discussed take a *one-event in/one-event out* form, but it is also possible to have event processing agents that take collections of events as their input or create one or more new events as their output:

- An incoming event may be *split* into multiple events, each containing a subset of the information from the original event.
- A stream of multiple incoming events may be *aggregated* to produce a stream of derived events. The derived events are typically computed from more than one event from the input stream (for example, an output event might contain a running total of a value contained in the input events).
- Two streams of incoming events may be *composed* to produce a stream of derived events.

You'll see that we have introduced a new concept here—*event stream*—so let's define this now.

> **EVENT STREAM** An *event stream* (or *stream*) is a set of associated events. It is often a temporally totally ordered set (that is to say, there is a well-defined timestamp-based order to the events in the stream). A stream in which all the events must be of the same type is called a *homogeneous* event stream; a stream in which the events may be of different types is referred to as a *heterogeneous* event stream.

Streams can be a convenient way to think of and model an event processing application. Some event processing systems make the stream their major abstraction. It can be more natural to think of an event processing agent as operating on an entire stream of events, rather than as operating on each event one by one. The stream concept can be particularly useful in applications that involve time series events, such as the periodic reading of a sensor or periodic quotes of a stock price.

Agents that aggregate or compose event streams exhibit stateful event processing.

> **STATEFUL EVENT PROCESSING** An event processing agent is said to be *stateful* if the way it processes events is influenced by more than one input event.

Let's look at a simple example to illustrate the idea of a stateful agent. Suppose we have an application that receives an event every time a quantity of a given product is

---

[5] See *Enterprise Integration Patterns: Designing, Building, and Deploying Messaging Solutions* by Gregor Hohpe and Bobby Woolf. Addison-Wesley. 2003. http://www.amazon.com/Enterprise-Integration-Patterns-Designing-Deploying/dp/0321200683/ref=sr_1_1?ie=UTF8&s=books&qid=1258829949&sr=1-1.

sold, and we are interested in knowing the total quantity that has been sold. We can use an event processing agent to compute a running total. Each time it receives a sale event, the agent emits a new event containing the updated total. This meets our definition of a stateful agent, because each of the events emitted by the agent depends on all the events that it has previously received.

Note that a stateful agent does not necessarily emit a derived event every time it receives an input event. Suppose, in our example, that the volume of incoming sale events is high. We might decide that we don't want an updated total event to be emitted every time a new sale event comes in, so we arrange for the agent to emit derived events less frequently, for example, every tenth time it sees an input event, or perhaps only at the end of every day.

In this running total example, the total starts at zero when we start up the agent and carries on increasing during the lifetime of its associated input stream, so each total event that is emitted is influenced by all the sale events that have been received up to that point. This might be what is wanted in this particular example, but it's easy to come up with cases where we want the agent to consider only a subset of the input events. Suppose that, instead of computing a running total, our agent computes an average sale size. We might then be interested in seeing a rolling average of the last ten or last hundred sale events so as to be able to spot emerging trends.

To allow for requirements like this, stateful agents can be defined so that they operate only on subsets of the input events that they receive. In stream processing terminology, such a subset is often referred to as a *window* into the stream. We return to the idea of windows and their generalization, *event context*, in chapter 7.

We conclude this section with a comment on the way stateful processing is handled in implementation languages. We have already noted that there are a variety of different event processing languages, and they have different ways of handling state. Two approaches are commonly used:

- Some languages take an event-driven approach where the function performed by the agent is defined as an operation on a single event (just as in the stateless case) but this operation can also read or write items of state data that are associated with the agent. This state data is then carried forward from an operation performed on one event to the operation performed on the next event that is received by the agent. Our running total example could be implemented in this manner. To do so the agent would retain a piece of state data representing the current value of the total. This would be updated each time a new event is received, and used when the output event is generated.

- Some languages, particularly those that emphasize the stream abstraction, have an explicit window concept. In these languages incoming events are gathered into a window, and the language defines an operation to be performed on all the events in that window. This is a convenient approach to use for our rolling average example. To implement this you could set up a *sliding window*. Each time a new event arrives the oldest event is evicted from the window, and the new event is added. The average can then be recomputed using all the events that are in the window at that time.

As the running total and rolling average examples show, the event-driven approach is more natural in some cases, and the window-driven approach in others, and so some languages offer a mixture of both approaches.

These are the basic concepts that accompany us throughout this book. We now look at the modeling language that we use to describe them.

2.3　*Modeling event processing networks*

Many computing books explain concepts by providing examples in a particular programming language or by using a particular product implementation. We could have chosen to use such an *implementation-up* approach, but as there are many different languages and products available, picking one would have restricted our thinking to the constructs that implementation chose to use as primitives.

Instead we follow a more *top-down* or *model-driven* approach. We provide a language that lets you describe an EPN as a collection of platform-independent *definition elements*. These definition elements are abstractions that can be used by application designers and are distinct from the system-level artifacts that implement them. Each definition element is an instance of one of seven basic *building blocks*. You'll recall that in section 2.2 we introduced event processing agents, event producers, event consumers, and event channels; these are all building blocks in our modeling language.

The building block abstraction allows us to talk about the important features of a concept without getting caught up with the details of a particular implementation. It also acknowledges the fact that there may be more than one way to implement a particular concept.

If you want to acquire hands-on experience with event processing tools, the *Event Processing in Action* website provides an opportunity to download and experiment with various implementations of these concepts. The website includes a link to a graphical editor that lets you to experiment using the building blocks. The website can be found at

　　http://www.ep-ts.com/content/view/74/108/.

The direct link to the building block editor is

　　http://code.google.com/p/epdleditor/.

2.3.1　*What is a building block?*

An event processing building block represents an event processing concept and is used to create platform-independent definition elements, which are implementation-neutral instances of this building block. For example, we can use the *event type* building block to create implementation-neutral representations of the event types needed by an application such as the `Delivery Request` event type used in the Fast Flower Delivery application. Each application is made up of a collection of these definition elements, customized to perform a particular role and connected together to form an event processing network.

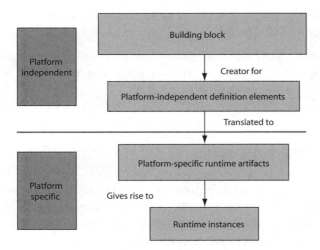

Figure 2.8   Building blocks, definition elements, and runtime instances and how they relate to each other

When the application is implemented, these platform-independent definition elements have to be translated into one or more platform-specific *runtime artifacts*, using platform-specific tools. In this book we are not particularly concerned about the nature of these artifacts, which will depend on the tool that is being used to develop the application (they could, for example, be statements or classes in a programming language, or they might be configuration files or entries in a database table). After it has been developed, the application will be run and this will result in the creation of one or more runtime instances of these platform-specific artifacts.

Figure 2.8 shows the relationship between building blocks, element definitions, and runtime instances.

To illustrate the relationships in figure 2.8, let's look at the concrete example shown in figure 2.9, where we are using the event type building block to define the event types needed for our application. In particular we have created a `Delivery`

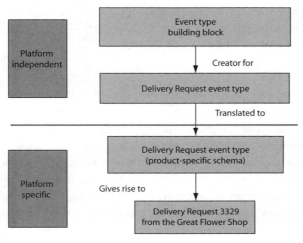

Figure 2.9   Event type building block and corresponding artifacts

Request event type definition element which corresponds to the platform-specific artifact representing that event type. There are likely to be many event instances of this particular event type that occur when the application runs. In figure 2.9 we see one of these: Delivery Request 3329 is a specific instance of the Delivery Request event type created by the Great Flower Shop. It contains specific attributes that match the schema of the event type defined by the Delivery Request definition element.

2.3.2 *Information in a definition element*

The different types of building blocks have a similar structure. We illustrate this by looking at a specific example, the event channel building block shown in figure 2.10.

Chapter 6 explains the full details of this particular building block; this figure is intended to demonstrate the various parts of a building block:

- Each building block has a name, and this name determines the type of platform-independent definition elements that it describes. In this example the name is *event channel*. It also has an icon, which can be used to depict these definition elements in graphical representations.

- In order to create a definition element from a building block, you need to provide certain pieces of information. The building block describes what this information is. In this example you have to provide a channel identifier (a name for the event channel) define input terminals and output terminals, and specify a routing scheme and quality of service assertions.

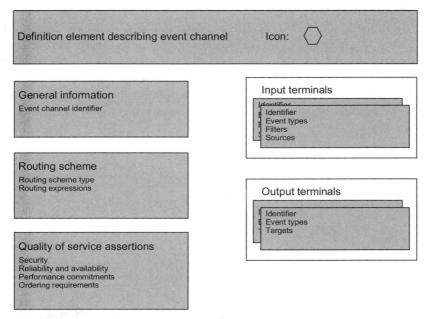

Figure 2.10   Information contained in the event channel building block

In part 2 we explain all the concepts used to build an event-driven computing application in terms of these building blocks, and we demonstrate this by using building blocks to specify the Fast Flower Delivery application.

2.3.3 *The seven fundamental building blocks*

In section 2.3.1 we introduced the idea of an event processing building block. These building blocks give us the primitive components, which are put together to form event-driven applications. To use a metaphor from chemistry, the building blocks are like chemical elements, definition elements are like atoms, and the applications built from them correspond to molecules. In this section we review the different types of building blocks (the periodic table in our metaphor), and in the next section we look at the event processing network—the mechanism used to build applications from these atoms.

There are seven fundamental building blocks and these are shown in figure 2.11. Some building blocks contain references to others, and some of these relationships are shown by arrows in the figure.

We give detailed descriptions of each of these building blocks in part 2, where you'll also be able to see how they are used in the Fast Flower Delivery application, but we give a brief summary of each of them here.

Any event-driven application will involve one or more different types of events and, as its name suggests, the event type building block allows us to describe these types. This building block defines the structure of an event (this is sometimes called an *event schema*) along with some of its semantics.

The *event producer* and *event consumer* building blocks are used to represent the concepts of the same name. The event producer represents an application entity that emits events into the EPN, and the event consumer an application entity that receives them. These building blocks model only those bits of the behavior of the event producer or consumer that are visible to other components of an event processing network. So the event producer building block does not specify how an event producer

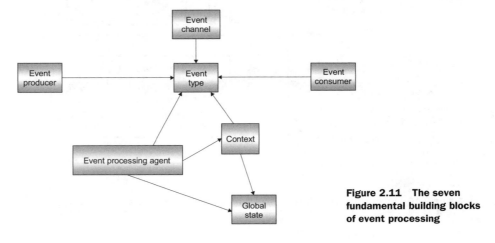

Figure 2.11 The seven fundamental building blocks of event processing

instance actually comes to emit an event, and the event consumer building block does not specify what an event consumer instance does when it consumes an event.

The event producer or event consumer definition element can represent either a single producer or consumer instance, or a whole class of such instances. In some applications there might be just one instance of the producer (for example, if the producer is a firewall router raising alert events); in other cases there might be many instances (for example, smoke detectors in a building). Where there are many instances it would be tedious to require every one to be represented by a separate definition element.

The *event processing agent* building block represents a piece of intermediary event processing logic inserted between event producers and event consumers. In contrast to the event producer and event consumer, the event processing agent building block models the behavior of the agents built from it. In a minute we'll look at the various different kinds of event processing agents.

An *event channel's* principal job is to route events between event producers and event consumers (recall the example of a channel being used in figure 2.4). We look at channels a bit more when we examine EPNs in the next section.

The five building blocks we have mentioned so far should be familiar to you because they represent concepts that we have already introduced. We have two further building blocks to explain: the context building block and the global state element building block.

A *context* element collects a set of conditions from various dimensions (temporal, spatial, segmentation-oriented, and state-oriented), giving us a way to categorize event instances so that they can be routed to appropriate agent instances. For example, you can use a segmentation-oriented context to make sure that events relating to different customers are handled by different event processing agent instances. Chapter 7 discusses contexts further.

A *global state* element refers to data that is available for use both by event processing agents and by contexts. This data may be system-wide global variables, reference data used to enrich events, and event stores that hold past events. Chapter 6 discusses global state elements further.

2.3.4 Event processing agents

There are several different kinds of event processing agents, and so there are several variants of the event processing agent building block, as shown in figure 2.12.

This figure shows the inheritance hierarchy of the various EPA building block types. Filter, Transformation, and Pattern detect are all specializations of *event processing agent,* but Transformation can itself be further subdivided.

We cover these agents in detail in later chapters so we confine ourselves to a few brief comments here:

- *Filter agents*—These are used to eliminate uninteresting events. A Filter agent takes an incoming event object and applies a test to decide whether to discard it

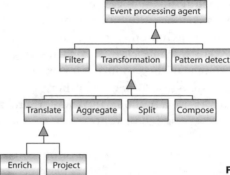

Figure 2.12   Different kinds of event processing agents

or whether to pass it on for processing by subsequent agents. The Filter agent test is usually stateless, in other words, a test based solely on the content of the event instance. An example would be a test that discards a `transaction reported` event if its value is less than $100.

- *Pattern detect agents*—These take collections of incoming event objects and examine them to see if they can spot the occurrence of particular patterns. For example, you can use a Pattern detect agent to discard the first two failed `logon attempt` events, but pass through subsequent ones. Pattern detect agents can emit derived events that describe the pattern that they have detected instead of, or in addition to, passing through the incoming event objects.
- *Transformation agents*—These modify the content of the event objects that they receive.

Transformation agents can be further classified based on the cardinality of their inputs and outputs.

- *Translate agent*—This takes each incoming event object and operates on it independently of preceding or subsequent event objects. It performs a *single event in, single event out* kind of operation.
- *Split agent*—This takes a single incoming event and emits a stream of multiple event objects—it performs a *single event in, multiple events out* operation.
- *Aggregate agent*—This takes a stream of incoming event objects and produces an output event that is a function of the incoming events. It performs a *multiple events in, one event out* operation.
- *Compose agent*—This takes two streams of incoming event objects and operates on them to produce a stream of output events. This is similar to the join operator in relational algebra, except that it joins streams of events rather than tables of data.

Two special kinds of translation appear sufficiently frequently for it to be worth assigning them their own building blocks. They are the *Enrich* agent, which augments an event object with additional information (for example, a customer address derived from a customer identifier in the incoming event), and the *Project* agent, which deletes information from the incoming event.

You may notice that these descriptions have referred to "incoming events" and have talked about passing events on to subsequent agents for further processing. This leads us naturally to the question of how event processing agents are connected to form applications—and that's what we're going to look at in the next section.

2.3.5 *Event processing networks*

In this section we go a bit deeper into the concept of an event processing network and we introduce a graphical notation to describe them. This section serves as an introduction; we fill in more of the details in part 2.

We have already met the main ingredients of an EPN—they are none other than the *producer, consumer, event processing agent* and *channel* definition elements. Before we move on to networks,

Figure 2.13   External appearance of an event processing agent

we need to take a look at the externals of these definition elements. We start with the *event processing agent*, illustrated in figure 2.13, which also serves as an introduction to our graphical notation.

We represent each agent definition element as a rounded square box containing one or more named *input terminals* which can receive events from other entities, and one or more *output terminals*, through which it emits events. The number of terminals varies depending on the kind of agent it is.

The input and output terminals can be labeled with a set of event types to show what they are prepared to receive (input terminals) and what they are able to emit (output terminals). In addition, input terminals can be assigned filter conditions, which restrict the set of event instances that will be accepted by the agent. A purist might argue that the ability to specify a filter is not strictly needed, because one could achieve the same effect by inserting an explicit filter agent upstream from the agent in question. The reason for including a filter in the specification of the agent is that the logic of the agent proper might be dependent on the filter, and it therefore makes sense for the processing logic and the filter to be specified in a single entity.

The definition elements for *event producers* and *event consumers* have similar graphical representations and are shown in figure 2.14. They also have terminals—although producers have only output terminals, and consumers have only input terminals.

Now we are ready to assemble a collection of event producers, event consumers, and event processing agents to form an event-driven application. We do this by specifying an event processing network. An EPN allows us to define the set of event producers

Figure 2.14   Event producer and consumer definition elements

and event consumers that participate in the application, to specify the possible routes by which events from the producers can find their way to the consumers, and to specify the intermediate event processing (if any) to be applied to these events *en route* between producers and consumers. In addition, an EPN is a vehicle for specifying nonfunctional characteristics (including ordering constraints, reliability, security, and performance requirements).

An event processing network can be completely static, containing a fixed set of producers, consumers, and event processing agents, or it can be more dynamic:

- Producer or consumer instances may come and go dynamically.
- The set of event processing agents and the interconnections between them may vary dynamically.

It is important to note that an EPN is an abstraction. An underlying implementation does not have to slavishly reproduce the artifacts in the event processing network. What is important is that an implementation should reproduce the behavior specified by the EPN. An implementation also has to worry about a physical provisioning of artifacts to computing nodes (something that looks like a single agent in an EPN may in fact be realized by multiple processes running on multiple computers).

An event processing network is made by taking a collection of producers, consumers, and agents, and connecting their input and output terminals. Figure 2.15 shows the components of a simple EPN. We have left some details out of this picture, such as labels attached to the terminals, to make it easier to see the main features of the representation.

The picture in figure 2.15 looks straightforward, but it's worth taking a few minutes to walk through it. The presence of the event producer box indicates that the application consists of just one class of event producer. We use the word *class* here deliberately. You'll recall that we wrote earlier that a single event producer definition element can represent many instances of a physical event producer (for example, all the smoke detectors in a building). This makes it easier for a diagram to represent a dynamic network. So in the smoke detector example there is no need to modify the diagram each time a new detector is added. Similarly, the event consumer box implies the presence of a class of consumers, and this allows for dynamic consumer registration to be modeled. (You'll recall that in section 2.1.4 we noted that dynamic consumer registration is a feature of publish/subscribe systems.)

The link between the event producer and the Project agent indicates that every event instance emitted by the event producer is distributed to the Project agent. As we noted earlier, there might be a filter associated with the input terminal to the Project agent, in which case a particular event instance might not actually be processed by the

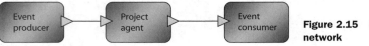

Figure 2.15 Simple event processing network

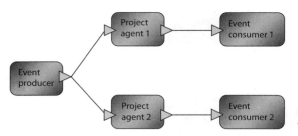

Figure 2.16 A producer with an output terminal connected to two agents

agent. Also the word *distributed* should not be taken too literally—the event processing network diagram is a logical representation, and an implementation could choose to optimize the event flow so as to filter out events further upstream. The direction of flow of events is implied by the terminals involved. In this case events flow from the output terminal of the event producer to the input terminal of the Project agent. The presence of a link does not necessarily imply that events are distributed in a push fashion, as an input terminal can instead pull events from an output terminal. Moreover, a link does not prescribe a particular mechanism for transporting events, though there might be quality of service requirements associated with it which influence this.

An event processing network graph can include a more complex distribution pattern such as that shown in figure 2.16. In this example two links emerge from a single output terminal on the event producer. This means that when the producer emits an event through this terminal, two copies of the event instance are distributed, one to Project agent 1 and the other to Project agent 2 (subject to filters on the input terminals of these two agents). The network does not impose constraints on the order in which this happens—in one implementation the two events could be distributed concurrently, whereas in another the distribution could be serialized, so that distribution to one of the two producers does not start until after the event has been distributed to the other one.

It is also possible to have two different output terminals linked to a single input terminal, as shown in figure 2.17. In this somewhat contrived example we have events from a single producer being processed in two different ways by two different agents after which they are delivered to a single consumer. The fact that two links converge on a single input terminal implies that events from the two agents are interleaved in some order. It says nothing about the particular order of interleaving—if the order is important, the application should use an agent to perform the interleaving explicitly.

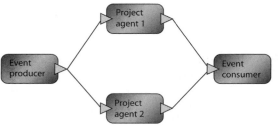

Figure 2.17 Two agents connected to a single consumer input terminal

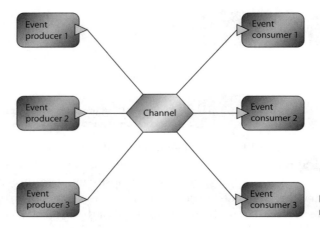

Figure 2.18   Use of an explicitly modeled channel to route events

The links that we have been talking about, shown as lines in the graphical notation, are special cases of event channels. Simple channels like these do not need to be explicitly modeled using definition elements because each one connects only a single input terminal to a single output terminal and their behavior is fully specified by the constraints and requirements attached to those terminals. (A simple one-to-one channel with no filtering might be implemented by nothing more complicated than a function call between producer and consumer.) However, more sophisticated routing is sometimes required, and for these we can use a fully modeled event channel definition element (using the event channel building block) as illustrated in figure 2.18.

We saw one use of a channel in figure 2.5—to convert between push and pull distribution and thus allow an input terminal that supports only pull to be connected to an output terminal that supports only push. Modeled channels have further advantages:

- They have identifiers, which means that producers, consumers, and agents can be linked to a channel rather than to each other. This reduces the complexity of the event processing diagram (compare figure 2.18 with figure 2.19, which shows a similar topology that does not include a channel). It also means that you can add or remove producers, consumers, or agents without having to know the names of other producers, consumers, or agents in the network.
- They have their own configuration parameters. This means that you can specify particular routing behavior or associate particular quality of service requirements with a modeled channel and have that apply to all events that pass through the channel.

Note that, as is the case with event processing agents, there are several ways in which a channel can be realized at runtime in an event processing implementation, and its representation in figure 2.18 as a box does not imply that it is a separate piece of executable code. For example, one way to implement a channel might be as a topic in a publish/subscribe system.

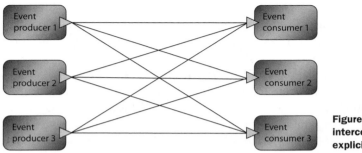

Figure 2.19 Additional interconnects required if an explicit channel is not used

As figure 2.19 shows, to connect n producers to m consumers, you need $n \times m$ interconnecting links if you don't use an explicit channel, whereas with an explicit channel you can reduce this to $n+m$ links. If n or m is large, this can be significant.

2.4 Summary

In this chapter we started with the basic principles of event-based programming (sometimes called event-driven architecture) and examined its relationship with service-oriented architecture (SOA). In particular we saw how event producers and event consumers can be decoupled from one another in event-based programming, and we examined the interaction patterns used to distribute events between them.

In the second half of the chapter we discussed the main concepts of event processing and introduced the modeling language that we use to describe it. This includes the various types of event processing building blocks, and the graphical notation we use to depict an event processing network.

We have now introduced all the concepts that we use in the book, and in part 2 we move to an in-depth discussion of each of them.

2.4.1 Additional reading

Hohpe, Gregor, and Bobby Woolf. 2003. *Enterprise Integration Patterns: Designing, Building, and Deploying Messaging Solutions.* Addison-Wesley. http://www.amazon.com/Enterprise-Integration-Patterns-Designing-Deploying/dp/0321200683/ref=sr_1_1?ie=UTF8&s=books&qid=1258829949&sr=1-1. This book explains in depth many of the concepts discussed here, such as request-response. It is also the major book that describes message-oriented functionality.

Smith, Bud. 1997. *Push Technology for Dummies.* IDG Books Worldwide. http://www.amazon.com/Push-Technology-Dummies-Bud-Smith/dp/076450293X/ref=sr_1_2?ie=UTF8&s=books&qid=1258830719&sr=1-2. This book describes the fundamentals of push technology.

Taylor, Hugh, et al. 2009. *Event-Driven Architecture, How SOA Enables the Real-Time Enterprise.* Addison-Wesley Professional. http://www.amazon.com/Event-Driven-Architecture-Enables-Real-Time-Enterprise/dp/0321322118/ref=sr_1_1?ie=UTF8&s=books&qid=1258889333&sr=1-1. This book uses examples to explain what EDA is and how it is related to SOA.

Hurwitz, Judith, et al. 2006. *Service Oriented Architecture For Dummies*. Wiley Publishing. http://www.amazon.com/Service-Oriented-Architecture-Dummies-Computer/dp/ 0470054352/ref=sr_1_2?ie=UTF8&s=books&qid=1259174835&sr=8-2. This is one of many books that explain SOA.

Wu, Kun-Lung, et al. 2007. "Challenges and experience in prototyping a multi-modal stream analytic and monitoring application on System S." VLDB 2007: 1185-1196. http://www. vldb.org/conf/2007/papers/industrial/p1185-wu.pdf. This article provides an example of a general stream computing platform.

Frankel, David S. 2003. *Model Driven Architecture: Applying MDA to Enterprise Computing*. Wiley Publishing. http://www.amazon.com/Model-Driven-Architecture-Enterprise-Computing/ dp/0471319201/ref=sr_1_1?ie=UTF8&s=books&qid=1258889376&sr=1-1- spell. This book explains the principles of model-driven architecture.

2.4.2   Exercises

2.1   Give examples of two applications where you would use pull distribution to retrieve events from an event producer, one example using periodic pull, and one using ad hoc pull.

2.2   Provide an example of an application in which an event producer also serves as an event consumer.

2.3   Can events be distributed using a request-response (remote procedure call) message exchange pattern? Give an example or alternatively explain why this is not possible.

2.4   Draw the event processing network for an application that can produce or consume Twitter events and that uses at least five different types of event processing agents.

2.5   Give an example of an application in which a channel needs to be programmed explicitly.

2.6   Give an example of an application that contains a component that is both an event consumer and an event producer. Is the fact that both producer and consumer are combined in a single component significant to the event processing system? If so, to what purpose can this information be used?

2.7   Give your own examples of classification schemes that use a four-level classification similar to that shown in figures 2.8 and 2.9.

2.8   Try to define a platform-independent definition element of one of the event channels that exist in the Fast Flower Delivery application.

2.9   An event processing network diagram looks similar to a workflow diagram, such as Business Process Modeling Notation (BPMN) or a diagram used to represent Web Services Business Process Execution Language (WS-BPEL) as both of them use directed graphs. Can you explain the differences in the semantics of nodes and edges between these two kinds of diagram?

2.10 Do you think that it is possible, or makes sense, to create a unified graph that contains both workflows and event processing networks?

Part 2

The building blocks

When planning an event such as a wedding, one realizes that it is made up of several standard building blocks: the ceremony itself, the food, the music, and the photography.

Part 2 discusses in depth the seven building blocks that are required to construct event processing applications. Each of its chapters describes one or more building blocks and their attributes using examples. The chapters also show examples of the building blocks being used to describe the Fast Flower Delivery application, with code samples from various event processing languages to show how the building blocks are implemented in practice.

Chapter 3 deals with the event type building block which represents the event metadata. Chapter 4 discusses event producers that introduce events into event processing systems. Chapter 5 discusses event consumers that consume the output events. Chapter 6 covers the notion of an event processing network and its associated building blocks: event processing agent, event channel, and global state element. Chapter 7 discusses the context building block. Chapters 8 and 9 go into specific types of event processing agents in depth. Chapter 8 discusses the transformation and filtering types of event processing agents, and chapter 9 discusses pattern detection event processing agents.

Defining the events

3

When I can't handle events, I let them handle themselves.

—Henry Ford

Before delving into how events are processed, we spend a chapter discussing what events are and how they are defined. This is a good place to start our in-depth exploration of event processing, as it's natural to begin the detailed design of an application by defining the event types that it uses. It's good practice to base the design of an event processing application on a clearly thought-out set of event types. It also gives your first opportunity to see definition elements in use.

In this chapter we discuss the following topics:

- The logical structure of an event, and what we mean by an event type
- What you specify in an *event type* definition element
- Event header attributes, in particular the timestamp attributes
- Event payload attributes, including attributes referring to application entities
- Relationships between event types, such as generalization and specialization

We illustrate these topics by showing some of the event types used in the Fast Flower Delivery application, and we conclude the chapter with a discussion of how real-life event processing systems represent events and event types.

3.1   *Event types*

You will recall that in chapter 1 we discussed two meanings for the word *event*. One of these refers to something that has happened (the *event occurrence*) and the other refers to the programming entity that is used to represent it (the *event object*). In this chapter we talk about the design of event objects, so it's the second of these meanings that we're mainly concerned with. However, when designing an event object you need to think about the event occurrence and decide which aspects of it should be included in its representation.

In an event processing application you usually encounter many event objects that have a similar structure and a similar meaning: consider, for example, the stream of events coming from a temperature sensor. All the events contain the same kind of information, though of course each event will have a different timestamp and will report a different temperature reading. So instead of defining the structure of each event individually, you specify the structure of this entire class of events. This is similar to defining a reusable type in a programming language, and we refer to this specification as an *event type*.

> **EVENT TYPE**   An *event type* is a specification for a set of event objects that have the same semantic intent and same structure; every event object is considered to be an instance of an event type.

Each event type has a unique event type identifier. In this book we use simple descriptive text strings for these identifiers, and we write them in `this typeface`. We also use the event type identifier as an adjective to describe an event instance; the phrase "`Delivery Request` event" reads more easily than the clumsy alternative "event of type `Delivery Request`." If you revisit the section in chapter 1 where we introduced our Fast Flower Delivery application, you will see that we have already mentioned several event types in this way. While we are talking about terminology, we should explain that we are using the term *event instance* as a synonym for *event object*.

Some event processing systems use untyped events. These systems do not enforce any particular structure on their event objects, for example, they might simply represent each event object as a single character string. However, the applications running in such systems usually impose their own typing systems on these events. In this book, therefore, we assume that all events have types associated with them, and that any event objects that start life as untyped events either get associated with a type or are translated to typed events before being processed by the event processing application proper. This restriction is not as onerous as might at first appear, because we allow event instances to contain *open content*, that is to say, free-format data in addition to the attributes defined by the event type.

3.1.1   *Logical structure of an event*

An event type specifies the information that is contained in its event instances. It does this by defining a set of event attributes.

ATTRIBUTE An event *attribute* is a component of the structure of an event. Each attribute has a name and a data type.

The values of these event attributes should help answer questions such as this: What happened? When did it happen? Where did it happen? What other information is associated with its happening? The answers to these questions can be recorded at various levels of precision. Whereas all these questions might be relevant for some applications, for other applications only some are. Although lack of information is a problem, surplus information is a burden, so when designing an event type you need to consider the amount of information that will be required by the applications that use it.

> **Capitalization convention**
>
> Every attribute has a name, and when we refer to an attribute in the text part of this book we use a lowercase name with spaces in it, for example, *occurrence time*, since this looks more natural in written English. In examples we use medial capitals—for example, *occurrenceTime*—because this form is easier to use in programming languages and with machine readable formats such as XML.

We distinguish between three kinds of information carried in an event object, and these are shown in figure 3.1.

The *header* consists of meta-information about the event, for example, its occurrence time. (The word *header* is used because when an event object is serialized into a message, this data is usually put at the start of the message.) This information is carried using well-known attributes, and so can be recognized by a processor that might not understand the remainder of the event instance. The second part—the *payload*—contains specific information about the occurrence itself. An event can also contain free-format open content information. The event type dictates the set of attributes that can appear in the payload, but does not constrain the open content portion of the event. Every event instance has a header portion, but need not have a payload or open content.

Some event processing platforms or event type standards provide a set of predefined header attributes to be used in all event instances. In keeping with the implementation-neutral approach that we are following in this book, we define some platform-independent header attributes with fixed names and data types, which can

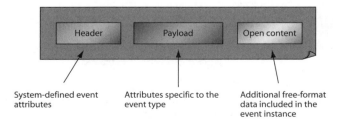

System-defined event attributes | Attributes specific to the event type | Additional free-format data included in the event instance

Figure 3.1 Logical structure of an event instance, showing its three constituent parts

be mapped to the platform-specific attributes used in an actual implementation. The header attributes that we are going to define fall into two categories:

- Attributes that describe the event type. These include an attribute that provides the event type identifier, an attribute that indicates whether this is a composite event or not, and one that gives the precision of any timestamp header attribute values.
- Attributes that provide generic information about the event. These carry information specific to this instance of the event, such as its instance identifier or its occurrence time. Some of these attribute values may be inserted into the event instance by the event processing platform rather than by the event processing application.

As we mentioned earlier, you might not want every event object to carry the full complement of header attributes, so we use the event type definition to specify which header attributes are required, which are permitted, and which are forbidden in an instance of that type.

The event payload consists of a collection of attributes, defined by the event type. Each attribute has a data type, which can be a simple data type, such as a string or numeric value, or (in some systems) a complex data structure. The event type definition can also indicate how many times a given attribute is required or permitted to appear in the payload. Note that in some languages, each event instance is required to have exactly one instance of each payload attribute.

3.1.2 *Event type building block*

In this section we give a quick summary of the event type building block by looking at its definition element. In the sections that follow we work through all the header and payload parts of an event, describing the attributes that they contain and the corresponding entries that appear in the definition element.

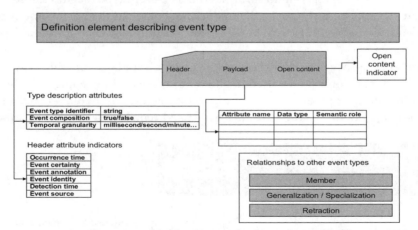

Figure 3.2   The event type definition element consists of attributes that describe the contents of the event header and payload, and a list of relationships between this event type and other event types.

Figure 3.2 shows the structure of the definition element. As we saw in chapter 2, every definition element contains information specific to that kind of definition element (in this case, it's an event type definition element). It can also contain references to other definition elements (in this case, references to related event type definitions).

As you can see from figure 3.2, an event type definition element contains the following information:

- Type description attribute values
- Header attribute indicators
- Payload attribute definitions
- Open content indicator
- Relationships with other event types

We now describe each of these in turn, and at the same time discuss the header and payload attributes that appear in the event instances themselves.

3.2 *Header attributes*

You will recall that some header attributes (the type description attributes) have values that are fixed as part of the event type definition. These values appear in the event type definition element, and can also appear in the event instances. We describe these in section 3.2.1, and then in section 3.2.2 we move on to the remaining header attributes. The definition element does not fix a value for these remaining attributes, because their values can vary instance by instance. It does, however, contain indicators that show whether an event instance has to carry each attribute or not.

3.2.1 *Event type description attributes*

The event type building block has three type description attributes, shown at the upper left of figure 3.2. The values of these attributes are contained in an event type definition element, and they may also appear in the headers of corresponding event instances. We describe each in turn.

> **EVENT TYPE IDENTIFIER** The *event type identifier* attribute uniquely identifies the type described by the definition element.

As we said earlier, we are concerned only with event processing systems that support typed events, so we can assume that every event object is an instance of a particular event type. The event type identifier attribute is generally carried in the event instance so that an event consumer or event processing agent that receives the event instance can discover its type. Note that in some systems the type can be inferred from the context, or *compiled in* to the producer, consumer, or agent code, and so does not physically need to be included in the event instance. However this can be viewed as an implementation-provided optimization.

> **EVENT COMPOSITION** The *event composition* attribute is a Boolean attribute that denotes whether the specific event type is the composition of other events or not.

Many systems support composite events (a *composite event* is one whose payload is made up of several different event instances, possibly themselves of different types). A composite event has a special kind of event type that constrains the content of the event by defining the types of the events that it is allowed to contain. The event composition attribute forms part of the event type definition element but can be included as a header attribute in an event instance as a convenience to any processor of that instance. The default value of this attribute is false, so an event type is considered as noncomposite if this attribute is not explicitly specified in the definition element.

Our final type description attribute, the temporal granularity or chronon attribute, refers to the precision of the event header's timestamps.

> **TIMESTAMP AND TEMPORAL GRANULARITY**   A *timestamp* is a data type that denotes a certain point in time; its precision is given by the temporal granularity that applies to the event type.
>
> The *temporal granularity* (or *chronon*) attribute denotes the *atom of time* from a particular application's point of view, for example: second, minute, hour, or day.

Different applications have different requirements when it comes to the precision at which time measurements are taken, and this is normally specified by the application as opposed to being part of an event type definition. However, an application might want the timestamps for a particular event type to be recorded at higher or lower precision than other events. In the Fast Flower Delivery application we define the default temporal granularity for timestamps to be one minute, but we override it for the `Delivery Bid` event type which has a granularity of a second.

The value of this attribute applies to an event's *occurrence time* and *detection time* attributes (which we define in the next section), and affects the temporal-related processing of events of this type. It also lets an event producer know how accurate these timestamps have to be when it is constructing an event instance. It can appear in the event type definition element and also, as a convenience, in an event object. The value to be used is that specified in the event object or definition element. If these are absent, the value to be used is that specified as an application default, and if none is provided there either, an implementation default can be used.

In table 3.1 we show the event type description attributes for the `Delivery Bid` event type from our Fast Flower Delivery application. Later in this chapter we show concrete examples of event definitions in various languages.

Table 3.1   The type description attributes for the `Delivery Bid` event type

Attribute name	Attribute value
eventTypeIdentifier	Delivery Bid
eventComposition	false
temporalGranularity	second

In this example the *event type identifier* tells us the event type, and we can see that it is not a composite type (this is actually the default and does not need to be specified). The temporal granularity is *second*, which overrides the application's default of *minute*. The rationale here is that for most events in this application a minute's granularity is sufficient. However we need to have a finer granularity for bids because we may want to place bid event instances in order using the time at which they were sent.

Next we discuss the information covered in the header of each event instance.

3.2.2   *Header attribute indicators*

An event instance header can include further attributes containing meta-information that is useful when processing the event. The name and meaning of these header attributes is not specific to a particular event type.

An event type definition element can indicate which of these header attributes must, may, or must not appear in an event instance. If an attribute is required to appear in every event instance, it is shown as *required*. If it is permitted but not required, it is shown as *optional*, and if its presence is forbidden we show it as *not applicable*. If a definition element does not specify whether an attribute should appear or not, the requirement for that particular attribute is specified by the application itself as an *application default*.

These attributes fall into two groups:

- Attributes whose values are generally set by the application: occurrence time, event certainty, and event annotation
- Attributes whose values can be system generated: event identity, detection time, and event source

We now discuss the meaning of each attribute.

OCCURRENCE TIME   The *occurrence time* attribute is a timestamp with a precision given by the event type's temporal granularity (chronon). (The actual representation may be presented in a finer granularity, but for all processing purposes, it should be rounded to the chronon granularity.) It records the time at which the event occurred in the external system.

The occurrence time value is provided by the event producer or event processing agent that detects or derives the event. For example, an in-car GPS system can insert an occurrence time timestamp derived from the GPS satellites. Although we define occurrence time as a timestamp, the occurrence time is sometimes better represented by a time interval and not a single time point. We discuss interval-based occurrence time in chapter 11.

In some cases, the event producer might not be able to determine the time when the event actually occurred and so cannot provide a true occurrence time, for example, if the producer works by examining the state of some external entity only at periodic intervals. In such cases you must have either the event producer set an approximate occurrence time, or you must ignore occurrence time altogether, and use the system-generated detection time (described later in this section) instead. There may also be problems of inaccuracy if each event producer has its own time-of-day clock, especially when using a short time granularity. We discuss this and other temporal issues section in chapter 11.

There are two more application settable attributes, *event certainty* and *event annotation*.

EVENT CERTAINTY The *event certainty* attribute denotes an estimate of the certainty of this particular event.

The event certainty attribute has a value of 1.0 if it is certain that this event occurred in reality in the way described by the event payload, down to a value of 0 if it is certain that the event did not occur as described. Event uncertainty handling is an advanced topic that we discuss briefly in chapter 11. It isn't handled in a systematic way in today's event processing platforms, and we do not include this attribute in any of the events used in the Fast Flower Delivery application.[1]

EVENT ANNOTATION The *event annotation* attribute provides a free-text explanation of what happened in this particular event.

The event annotation attribute provides a mechanism that an event producer or event processing agent can use to annotate an event instance with a human-readable explanation. This annotation may be used for documentation purposes. The text can also be processed by an event processing agent, or set by an agent when it creates a derived event. Again, this attribute may be required, optional, or not applicable for a certain event type, or for an entire application.

System-generated attributes are attributes which, if they appear in the event instance at all, are generated automatically by the event processing system rather than being inserted by an event producer or an event processing agent. We discuss three such attributes: event identity, detection time, and event source.

EVENT IDENTITY The *event identity* attribute is a system-generated unique ID for each individual event instance.

The designer of the event type can determine whether the event identity value appears in event instances or not, because some applications care about tracing individual events and some do not. Note that if the system is implemented in an object-oriented language, each event object will usually have an object identity, and it might be possible to use this as the event identity.

DETECTION TIME The *detection time* attribute is a timestamp (in the event type's temporal granularity) that records the time at which the event became known to the event processing system.

---

[1] If you are interested in reading about uncertain events, refer to this article: Segev Wasserkrug, Avigdor Gal, Opher Etzion, Yulia Turchin, "Complex event processing over uncertain data." DEBS 2008: 253-264. http://portal.acm.org/citation.cfm?doid=1385989.1386022.

Note that in practice different systems generate this timestamp in different ways. Some record the time when the event producer calls a system API to submit the event; some record the time when the event is placed into a buffer for processing; others use the time when the event is retrieved from the buffer and the actual processing starts. The user can sometimes tune the way that an implementation sets the detection time, and some systems make it a required attribute of all event instances.

The significance of the detection time is that many event processing platforms use it in order to establish the relative order of events, or to determine whether an event occurred in a particular time interval or not (in later chapters we look at event processing agents for which the order of events is significant and applications where the fact that an event happened within a certain time interval is important).

Some implementations allow the use of buffering as a way of collecting and re-ordering events so that they can be processed in order of occurrence time regardless of the order in which they were actually detected. The application or the event processing agent specifies whether occurrence time ordering or detection time ordering is used, and this choice does not form part of the event type definition.

EVENT SOURCE   The *event source* attribute is the name of the entity that originated this event. This can be either an event producer or an event processing agent.

This is another attribute that can be generated by the system and included in the event instance if permitted by the event type definition element. It is sometimes useful for an event processor to know where an event instance came from; in the Fast Flower Delivery application an `Assignment` event can be emitted either by a `Store` event producer or by an `Automatic assignment` event processing agent.

Table 3.2 shows an example of the header attribute indicators we have just discussed. Once again we're using the `Delivery Bid` event type from the Fast Flower Delivery application as our example.

Table 3.2   The header attribute indicators for the `Delivery Bid` event type

Attribute type	Occurrence
occurrenceTime	required
eventAnnotation	optional
eventCertainty	not applicable
eventIdentity	required
detectionTime	required
eventSource	required

Occurrence time is defined as a required attribute for each event of this type, *event annotation* as optional, and *event certainty* is shown as not applicable. All the system-generated attributes are required.

In summary, the major questions answered by the header are as follows:

- What kind of occurrence is this? This is denoted by the *event type identifier*.
- When did this event occur? This is denoted by the *occurrence time* and *detection time*.
- What emitted this event? This is denoted by the *event source*.

Having looked at the header we now move on to the event's payload.

3.3   *Payload attributes*

An event's header attributes carry meta-information about the event, such as what type of event it is, and when and where it occurred. This is generic metadata in that its syntax and interpretation are independent of the actual event type. In contrast, the attributes that make up the event payload are used to carry the data that describes the actual occurrence. You can liken this to a file in a computer file system; the payload corresponds to the contents of a file, whereas the header corresponds to file metadata such as its name, time of last access, and so on.

We start by discussing data types, and then talk about a couple of specific semantic roles that attributes can play.

3.3.1   *Data types*

Every payload attribute has a data type. (Each header attribute also has a data type, but their types are predefined, whereas payload attribute data types need to be declared explicitly.) In our model we have a few basic data types that are well known from programming languages, and a couple that are more advanced. In addition, attributes can have complex data types; these are structures composed of other data types. The simple data types are as follows:

- String
- Integer
- Float (floating point number)
- Decimal (fixed precision number)
- Binary encoded data
- Boolean
- Date
- Time
- DateTime
- Location
- Reference to another event

Most of these are straightforward and map to the data types used in an implementation language, though some implementation languages subdivide them further. For example, Java has several integer data types of different sizes. In addition there are differences in the ways that dates and times are handled in different languages. The location data type is somewhat more complicated and we need to discuss that a bit more.

> **LOCATION** A *location* data type[2] is used to designate a real-world location associated with the event; it can refer to the location using domain-specific geospatial terms, for example, lines and areas that are defined in a particular geospatial domain.

A location attribute can take two forms:

- An explicit representation using a coordinate system, for example, a point might be represented as a latitude/longitude pair
- An identifier of a spatial entity, for example, the name of a building or city

In addition, the data type can represent either a point, a line (or polyline), or an area:

- *Point*—The event is considered as occurring in a specific geometric point in the space, using some coordinate system (2D or 3D). Example: the GPS coordinates of a specific vehicle.
- *Line*—The event is considered as occurring on a line or polyline. Example: the road (represented by a polyline) that a vehicle is currently driving along.
- *Area*—The event is considered as occurring within a certain geographical area or volume (2D or 3D). Example: the local authority jurisdiction that a vehicle is currently located in.

Figure 3.3 shows these different representations being used by applications that monitor traffic on a certain highway.

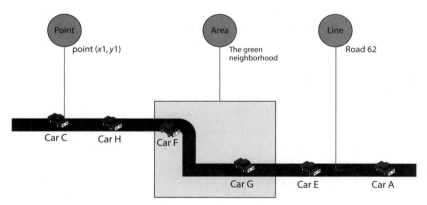

Figure 3.3   A traffic monitoring example showing three different location data types (point, line, and area) used by different intelligent transport applications

[2] For a complete discussion of location data types refer to Martin Erwig, Ralf Hartmut Güting, Markus Schneider, Michalis Vazirgiannis, "Spatio-Temporal Data Types: An Approach to Modeling and Querying Moving Objects in Databases." GeoInformatica 3(3): 269-296 (1999).

In this example there are three applications that each require different information:

- The first application is interested in the exact location of each car; the event that designates the location of car C is a point location determined by the car's GPS device.
- The second application is interested in knowing which neighborhood (area) each car is in; the events that designate the locations of cars F and G show that they're in the same neighborhood, and its name is returned as the value of their location.
- The third application is interested in cars being on a certain road; all the cars in this picture are located on Road 62; so the location attribute returned is a line (a polyline in this case).

The meaning of a payload attribute can be entirely local to the event type in which it appears, or it can have a meaning that extends beyond that type definition. We now look at two such semantic roles that a payload attribute can play.

3.3.2 *Attributes with semantic roles*

Attributes may also have semantic roles, and we discuss two such roles: entity references and common attributes. We start with entity references.

> **ENTITY REFERENCE**   An event *entity reference* is an event attribute whose value is a reference to a particular entity external to the event.

In the context of this definition, an *entity* is something modeled by the application and given a unique identifier by that application. It frequently models something that exists in the application's business domain, for example, a customer or an order. In the Fast Flower Delivery application we model the participating flower stores and drivers as entities; as you will see in section 3.5 many of the event types used in that application have attributes that refer to stores and drivers.

An event processing agent or consumer can use the reference to look up information about the entity, for example, the `driver` attribute in a `Delivery Bid` can be used to find the current ranking of the driver making the bid. The reference data type includes a scheme that tells the processor how to do this lookup, for example, the attribute value might be a key used to retrieve the data from a particular database table. As well as providing a way of finding out additional information, an entity reference attribute can be used to partition the context that is used to process the event. In our example the space of all `Pickup Confirmation` and `Delivery Confirmation` events and their associated alerts and derived events can be partitioned using the value of the `driver` attribute.

In some cases we have attributes in two or more event types that, although they don't reference an external entity, nevertheless have the same meaning. We refer to these as *common attributes*. Sometimes it's possible for an event processing application to infer a connection between two distinct event instances that have a matching common attribute value. You can use common attributes, as you can entity references, as part of a context that partitions the space of events into sets of related event instances. See chapter 7 for a longer discussion of contexts.

> **COMMON ATTRIBUTE** A *common attribute* is an event attribute whose semantics are defined by the attribute name. All common attributes with the same name in a given application domain are considered to be semantically equivalent.

In the Fast Flower Delivery application the common attribute called `request id` is used in a number of event types. It is used to relate event instances back to the original customer delivery request event.

3.3.3 *Open content indicator*

An event payload can also contain free-format open content information. The event type definition element does not constrain the open content portion of the event, but it contains an open content indicator, which specifies whether open content must, may, or must not appear in an event instance.

If open content is required to appear in every event instance, the indicator takes the value *required*. If open content is permitted but not required, the indicator shows it as *optional*, and if its presence is forbidden the indicator says *not applicable*. The default is not applicable.

3.3.4 *Payload example*

Table 3.3 shows the domain-specific payload attributes for the `Delivery Bid` event type.

Table 3.3   Payload attributes for the `Delivery Bid` event type

Attribute name	Data type	Occurrence	Semantic role
requestId	Integer	required	Common attribute
driver	String	required	Reference to driver entity
store	String	required	Reference to store entity
committedPickupTime	DateTime	required	
ranking	Integer	optional	

This event type has five attributes in its payload, four of which are required to be present. Each attribute has a type: Integer, String, or DateTime, and three have semantic roles. The `driver` and `store` attributes are references to entities that are stored in the application's global state elements (`Driver status` and `Store reference`); `request id` is a common attribute which appears in other event types used in the application.

Next we discuss relationships between event types.

3.4   *Relationships between event types*

An event type definition may contain references to other event types when there is semantic relationship between them. The event type definition element lists the referenced event types and gives the nature of each relationship. We discuss four types of relationships: membership, generalization, specialization, and retraction.

In section 3.2.1 we noted that a composite event type defines the event types that it is allowed to contain. We use the membership relationship to do this.

> **MEMBER AND MEMBERSHIP**   An event type is said to be a *member* of a composite event type if its instances can be included in instances of the composite event type. The *membership* relationship applies only to composite event types. It indicates that the related event type is a member of the composite event type.

The membership relationship is part of the definition of the composite event type, not the member event type. Our next two relationships, specialization and generalization, come as a pair and are converse relationships. In some cases it is more convenient to define the generalization relationship, and in other cases it is more convenient to define the specialization.

> **GENERALIZATION AND SPECIALIZATION**   The event *generalization* and *specialization* relationships indicate that an event type is a generalization or specialization of another event type, possibly conditioned by a predicate.

The notion of specialization (and its converse, generalization) originated in semantic data models[3] and has become popular through object-oriented programming. The essence is that an event type E2 is said to be a specialization of event type E1 if event type E2 inherits the definition of event type E1 with possible additions and modifications, such that each instance of event type E2 can also be considered as an instance of event type E1. This means that a consumer or event processing agent that is able to handle an event of type E1 can also handle an event of type E2. The additions and modifications in E2 must not substantially alter the meaning of the event. In the Fast Flower Delivery example the Manual Assignment event type is a specialization of the Assignment event type.

There are cases in which you might want to restrict the conditions under which events of type E2 can also be considered as instances of events of type E1, by making the specialization relationship contingent on a predicate. This is best explained by taking an example (not from the Fast Flower Delivery example). Let's say that we have a help-desk system that handles problems with office equipment; there are event types related to problems with printers, screens, phones, fax machines, and scanners. These problem events are all specializations of a single Hardware Problem event type, because the help desk has a single service covering all these types of equipment.

---

[3]   These terms were first introduced in John Miles Smith and Diane C. P. Smith, "Database Abstractions: Aggregation and Generalization," ACM Trans. Database Syst. 2(2): 105-133(1977).

However, suppose that some people have laser printers in their offices, and that service for these printers is provided by local technicians rather that by the help desk service. In this case you might want only a `Printer Problem` event to be considered a specialization of the `Hardware Problem` event type in cases when the printer in question is not a laser printer.

The final relationship we discuss is used to indicate that a given event can be reversed, or retracted, by another event type.

> **RETRACTION**   A *retraction* event relationship is a property of an event type referencing a second event type. It indicates that the second type is a logical reversal of the event type that references it.

We discuss the idea of retraction briefly in chapter 11. In our example `Delivery Request Cancellation` is a retraction of the `Delivery Request` event type, because a `Delivery Request Cancellation` terminates any processing related to the delivery.

Now that we have described the event type definition element, we can take a look at the event type definitions in the Fast Flower Delivery application.

3.5   *Event types in the Fast Flower Delivery example*

In this section we include the complete definitions of all the raw event types used in the Fast Flower Delivery example. This application also uses derived event types, but we leave those until our discussion of event processing agents in later chapters.

3.5.1   *Header attributes*

Most of the event types in this application have the same set of header attributes, so to avoid repetition, we list the header attribute indicators here. You can see them, along with the default temporal granularity, in table 3.4.

Table 3.4   Application defaults for the Fast Flower Delivery application

Attribute type	Default setting
temporalGranularity	minute
eventAnnotation	optional
eventCertainty	not applicable
eventIdentity	required
occurrenceTime	required
detectionTime	required
eventSource	required

The values shown in this table apply to all event types used in the application, so in the discussion that follows we don't repeat any of these entries unless their values differ from those in the table.

3.5.2   *Event type definition elements*

The Fast Flower Delivery application has seven different raw event types. In this section we look at each of these, giving details of their event payloads, relations with other event types, and any other attributes that differ from the defaults shown in table 3.4.

DELIVERY REQUEST

We start with the `Delivery Request` type, shown in table 3.5. An event of this type is created when a customer's request is fed into the system, and it starts the whole delivery cycle going.

Table 3.5   Payload attributes in the `Delivery Request` event type

Attribute name	Data type	Occurrence	Semantic role
requestId	Integer	required	Common attribute
store	String	required	Reference to store entity
addresseeLocation	Location	required	Common attribute
requiredPickupTime	DateTime	required	Common attribute
requiredDeliveryTime	DateTime	required	Common attribute
minimumRanking	Integer	optional	
neighborhood	Location	optional	Reference to neighborhood entity

The first five attributes in this list are required in all instances of this event type. They are attributes that are supplied by the flower store event producer when it creates the event. The `minimumRanking` attribute shows the minimum driver ranking that the flower store is prepared to accept. This value is not filled in by the flower store, but instead it is added by the Fast Flower Delivery application, when it enriches the event. The application takes the value of `store`, looks up that store's minimum ranking requirement and neighborhood from the `Store reference` table, and adds them to the event instance.

   Several of the attributes are shown as *common attributes* because, as we'll see shortly, they appear in other event types in the application. In particular the value of the `request id` attribute can be used to match up instances of these different event types that refer to the same delivery.

   This event type has one relationship: the `Delivery Request Cancellation` event type is a retraction of this type.

GPS LOCATION

Events of the `GPS Location` type are sent periodically to the system by the vehicle's GPS sensor. As you can see from table 3.6 they have a simple payload.

Table 3.6   Payload attributes in the `GPS Location` event type

Attribute name	Data type	Occurrence	Semantic role
driver	String	required	Reference to driver entity
driverLocation	Location	required	

The semantic role for the driver attribute indicates that it is a key that can be used to look up details of the driver in the Driver status table.

DELIVERY BID

A Delivery Bid event is sent by those drivers who decide that they are interested in making a particular delivery. We used this event type as our example earlier, and you'll recall from table 3.1 that Delivery Bid has a temporal granularity of one second. In table 3.3 you can see its payload attributes. These include the committed pickup time and the request id, which the driver's producer sets to show which delivery request is being bid for. The producer does not supply a value for the ranking attribute; this is filled in later by an event enrichment agent.

MANUAL ASSIGNMENT

Manual Assignment events are produced by a store, in cases where it has elected to assign a delivery to a driver, rather than have the event processing application do this for it. Table 3.7 shows the payload of this event.

Table 3.7 Payload attributes in the Manual Assignment event type

Attribute name	Data type	Occurrence	Semantic role
requestId	Integer	required	Common attribute
store	String	required	Reference to store entity
driver	String	required	Reference to driver entity
addresseeLocation	Location	required	Common attribute
requiredPickupTime	DateTime	required	Common attribute
requiredDeliveryTime	DateTime	required	Common attribute

This event type has two relationships. It is a specialization of the Assignment event type, and has the Delivery Request Cancellation as a retraction type.

PICKUP CONFIRMATION

A flower store issues a Pickup Confirmation event when a driver has collected an order of flowers and has set off to deliver them. Table 3.8 shows its payload.

Table 3.8 Payload attributes in the Pickup Confirmation event type

Attribute name	Data type	Occurrence	Semantic role
requestId	Integer	required	Common attribute
store	String	required	Reference to store entity
driver	String	required	Reference to driver entity

You will see that this type doesn't contain a specific collection time timestamp. That's because the event type also contains an *occurrence time* header attribute, as this was included in the application defaults shown in table 3.4.

DELIVERY CONFIRMATION

A `Delivery Confirmation` event is produced by the driver's handheld device when the person receiving the flowers signs for them on the device. Table 3.9 shows its payload.

Table 3.9   Payload attributes in the `Delivery Confirmation` event type

Attribute name	Data type	Occurrence	Semantic role
requestId	Integer	required	Common attribute
driver	String	required	Reference to driver entity

Our final event type is the `Delivery Request Cancellation` type, which as we have already seen is a retraction event for two other event types.

DELIVERY REQUEST CANCELLATION

A `Delivery Request Cancellation` event, as its name suggests, is issued when a store cancels the delivery of a particular order. Table 3.10 shows its simple payload.

Table 3.10   Payload attributes of the `Delivery Request Cancellation` event type

Attribute name	Data type	Occurrence	Semantic role
requestId	Integer	required	Common attribute

You can see in table 3.10 the use of a common attribute (`request id`) to indicate the order that has been cancelled.

3.5.3   *Event instance example*

We conclude this section with table 3.11, which shows the information that might be carried in an instance of one of these types. We have chosen to show a `Delivery Request` event.

Table 3.11   A particular instance of the `Delivery Request` event type

Attribute name	Attribute value
eventTypeIdentifier	Delivery Request
eventIdentity	455244535
occurrenceTime	20 March 2009,15:15
detectionTime	20 March 2009,15:16
eventSource	Flower Power store
requestId	R429531
store	Flower Power

Table 3.11   A particular instance of the `Delivery Request` **event type** *(continued)*

Attribute name	Attribute value
addresseeLocation	5 Main Street
requiredPickupTime	20 March 2009,15:30
requiredDeliveryTime	20 March 2009,16:30

This listing shows an example `Delivery Request` event instance. The first five entries are header attributes, and show that this is a `Delivery Request` event produced by the Flower Power store at the indicated date and time. The event identity 455244535 is a unique value generated by the event processing system to distinguish this event object from other event instance objects.

The remaining attributes form the payload of the event. You can see the application-generated `request id` attribute. This is the common attribute used to correlate this event with other events that relate to this same order.

We have been using a simple tabular format to present the examples in this chapter. We conclude with a brief discussion of the various ways in which event types and instances are represented in practice.

3.6   Event representation in practice

There is, at present, no single standard for the way that event instances or event types are represented. Each event processing language has its own definition of what an event instance contains, and there are structural differences among these languages that affect the information that can be carried in an event. The event type model that we have presented in this chapter can be mapped onto these languages; however, some things (for example, optional attributes) in the model aren't directly supported in all event processing languages.

In this section we discuss these structural differences and their consequences for implementations of our Fast Flower Delivery application. We then have a brief discussion of tools and languages used to define event types, and conclude this chapter with a quick look at the interchange of event types and event instances between event processing systems.

3.6.1   Event structure

Every event processing platform has an implementation-specific way to represent an event instance when it is being processed by the platform. The API used to access event attributes obviously varies by language, but more significantly there are differences between the nature and structure of the attributes themselves. There are several areas of difference:

- The complexity of the payload. Some languages support payloads containing structures, repeating and optional attributes, and allow open content.

- The set of data types that can be used for event attributes.
- The set of predefined header attributes supported by the platform.

We take a closer look at each of these areas.

PAYLOAD COMPLEXITY

Many platforms, including most of those with stream-oriented languages, process only events that have flat structures. Each attribute defined by an event type appears exactly once in every instance of that type; these attributes are permitted to have only simple data type, so an event instance looks like a relational tuple, and a stream of identically typed events looks like a relation.

Flat event types have the advantage that it is easy to access an event's attributes from the event processing language. In stream-oriented or rules-oriented languages, like Continuous Computation Language (CCL) or Etalis, attribute names can be used directly in the statements that make up the language. In object-oriented imperative programming languages, like Apama's, the attributes can be exposed as methods or properties of the event object.

On the other hand, flat event types can't naturally handle events that have a complicated or variable structure, such as purchase order events that contain the order details, or composite events. We have avoided using event types like this in the Fast Flower Delivery application, but some event processing applications require them, particularly applications that have to process events that arrive from event producers in the form of Extensible Markup Language (XML) documents. Three approaches can be used to handle events that have complicated structures like this:

- You could preprocess the event instance to turn it into one that has a flat event type. For example, if the event arrives as an XML document, you can transform it using Extensible Stylesheet Language Transformations (XSLT) (we talk more about XSLT in chapter 8). Many event processing platforms provide adaptors for well-known event formats that let you do this; alternatively you can use an enterprise service bus (ESB) to do it outside the event processing platform proper.
- If the event processing platform supports open content you could preprocess the event to extract a flat set of payload attributes, as in the previous approach, but then append the original structured event data as open content. This means you can do filtering, routing, pattern detection, and other event processing operations on the flat set of attributes, but still have the original structured event data if it is required by an event consumer.
- You could use an event processing platform that natively supports structured event objects. We discuss one of these, ruleCore, when we look at event type tools in section 3.6.2.

We expect that the number of platforms providing native support for complex payload structures will grow over time, and so we allow for such event types in our building block modeling language.

Before we leave the subject of payload complexity, note that the `Delivery Request` event type from the Fast Flower Delivery application contains an optional attribute called `minimum ranking`. This attribute is not set by the flower store event producer, but is added later by the Fast Flower Delivery application, when it enriches the event. If your event processing platform does not support optional attributes, you could work around this by defining two different event types, one that includes `minimum ranking` and one that does not. However, this approach would get out of hand if you have an event type with several optional attributes. An alternative approach, for languages that don't support optional attributes, is to have the event producer supply a special *sentinel value* for the attribute, indicating that it is not really there. In the particular case of the Fast Flower Delivery application, there's no need for a special sentinel value, because the application can ignore any value already in the event when it enriches it.

ATTRIBUTE DATA TYPES

Different event processing languages have different specifications for the simple data types that can be used for their event attributes. The set of data types usually depends on the language style. Languages based on SQL generally use SQL data types, and this makes an event instance look like a row in a SQL table. Other languages use data types based on Java primitive types, or on XML Schema's simple data types.

In section 3.3.1 we gave a list of the simple data types used in our modeling language. These should be sufficient to model the data types used in most common event processing languages.

HEADER ATTRIBUTES

In section 3.2 we listed the header attributes that we include in our building block modeling language, and in 3.5 we stated that the Fast Flower Delivery application requires four of them (occurrence time, detection time, event identity, and event source) to be present in every event instance.

Event processing platforms vary widely in their support for header attributes. Most support an event type identifier, though the strongly typed nature of some languages means that you might never have to interrogate an event instance to ask it for its type. Most platforms have an equivalent of detection time, and they use this to establish event ordering, but again they don't always surface this to the application (chapter 11 contains a fuller discussion of occurrence time and detection time).

You can consider two things if your event processing logic needs one of these header attributes but your language doesn't support it. If you're using a Java Message Service (JMS) implementation (or other message-oriented middleware) to transport events, you might be able to use the JMS message header fields (for example, JMSMessageID could be used as the event identity). Alternatively you can add the attribute you need into the payload of the event type.

3.6.2 Defining event types in current event processing platforms

Some event processing platforms provide graphical tools to let you enter and manage event type definitions as part of their IDEs. In figure 3.4 we show an example of the event type editor part of the WebSphere Business Events Design Data tool.

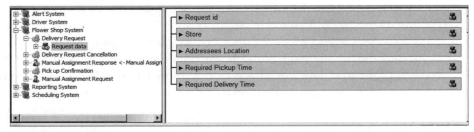

Figure 3.4   The `Delivery Request` **event type, shown in the WebSphere Business Events Design Data tool. You can see the payload attributes at the right of the picture.**

In some platforms you define event types programmatically or by using a file format. In particular, several platforms let you export or import event types in an XML file format. You can use XML in two ways to represent an event type. In listing 3.1 we show the approach used by the ruleCore language.

Listing 3.1   `DeliveryRequest` event type defined using ruleCore

```
<EventDef eventType="DeliveryRequest">
  <Description>Event: DeliveryRequest</Description>
  <Properties>
    …
    <Property name="requestId">
      <base:XPath>string(base:EventBody/user:requestId)</base:XPath>
    </Property>
    <Property name="store">
      <base:XPath>string(base:EventBody/user:store)</base:XPath>
    </Property>
    <Property name="addresseeLocation">
      <base:XPath>string(base:EventBody/user:AddresseeLocation)
      </base:XPath>
    </Property>
    <Property name="requiredPickupTime">
      <base:XPath>string(base:EventBody/user:requiredPickupTime)
      </base:XPath>
    </Property>
    <Property name="requiredDeliveryTime">
      <base:XPath>string(base:EventBody/user:requiredDeliveryTime)
      </base:XPath>
    <Property name="minimumRanking">
      <base:XPath>string(base:EventBody/user:minimumRanking)
      </base:XPath>
    </Property>
  </Properties>
</EventDef>
```

In ruleCore an event instance is modeled as an XML document, and has a fixed set of header attributes common to all event types. The payload part of the event type is defined using a sequence of XML elements (the Property elements). Each Property element gives the name of the attribute, and an XPath expression that shows where the attribute can be found in the event document. This means that the event instance can have a complex structure, but the attributes can be given simple names.

An alternative approach, shown in listing 3.2, is to use XML Schema directly and define an event payload as an XML Schema element.

Listing 3.2   The `DeliveryRequest` event type defined using XML Schema

```
<element name="DeliveryRequest" type="tns:deliveryRequestType" />    ◁──┐   Payload
                                                                       ❶  element
<complexType name="deliveryRequestType">          ◁──┐   Payload
    <sequence>                                       ❷  type
            <element ref="tns:requestId" />
            <element ref="tns:store" />
            <element ref="tns:addresseeLocation" />          ❸  Common
            <element ref="tns:requiredPickupTime" />            attributes
            <element ref="tns:requiredDeliveryTime" />
            <element name="minimumRanking" type="positiveInteger" />   ◁──
    </sequence>                                                     Local
</complexType>                                                      attribute ❹

<element name="requestId" type="anyURI" />
<element name="store" type="anyURI" />
<element name="addresseeLocation" type="epia:locationType" />   ❺  Common
<element name="requiredPickupTime" type="dateTime" />               attribute
<element name="requiredDeliveryTime" type="dateTime" />             declarations
```

In this example, the `DeliveryRequest` payload is represented by element ❶ and the payload attributes are listed in its XML Schema type definition ❷. XML Schema provides a useful way to represent common attributes. This event type uses five common attributes, and they are declared as XML Schema global elements ❺. After being declared, a global element can be included by reference in a complex type, and we use this mechanism ❸ to include the common attributes in our event type. They can be included in other event types in a similar fashion. In contrast, `minimumRanking` is not a common attribute so we declare it as a local element ❹ inside `delivery-RequestType`. This means that it can be only used as part of this event type. Another event type might also have an attribute called `minimumRanking`, but if this were so it would have to have a separate local declaration within that type. As these two `minimumRanking` attributes would then have separate declarations, we cannot infer any connection between the two, other than a coincidence of their names. Note that when we declared the `addresseeLocation` common attribute we had to extend the XML Schema type system to include a location data type.

The approach used in listing 3.2 has the advantage of using standard XML Schema, and so it can be handled by regular XML Schema tools. It can cope with complex XML Schema structure types, although this results in complex XPath expressions showing through to the event processing logic.

3.6.3   *Standards for interchanging event types and event instances*

As we noted earlier, there is no single standard for describing event types, and no single format for interchanging event instances between systems. However, several organizations have defined standards in this area. These organizations have, in the main, been concerned with the development of standardized sets of event types to be used in particular industries, for example, healthcare, insurance and financial trading, and certain cross-industry domains such as security and network and systems management. In order to define event types they have had to find languages to describe them, and formats to allow their event instances to be exchanged.

Although these organizations have focused mainly on defining event payloads, many of their specifications have recognized that some attributes are common to all their event types, and so they have a header and payload structure similar to the one we have described in this chapter. An example of this is the Web Services Distributed Management standard from OASIS. This standard contains a flexible and extensible event format (the WSDM Event Format) intended primarily for network and systems management applications. This format has a rich header structure, including categorization attributes that allow events to be filtered and routed by processors that don't necessarily understand the entire event type.

The event types described in these specifications frequently have complex structures like those described in section 3.6.1, but they can be used with the event processing platforms and languages that we mention in this book. This is normally done by using an adaptor to convert between the standard's type and format and the native type and representation used by the platform, as described in that section.

Earlier specifications (for example, the healthcare industry's HL7[4] v2 standards) use a concise character encoding for event instances, but more recent specifications (such as HL7 v3) use XML. With XML it is straightforward to pass the encoded event instance in a web service message. Existing or emerging standards in this area include the following:

- WS-Topics is an OASIS standard that allows event types to be classified into topics. It assumes that an event payload is described using an XML Schema global element definition (as shown in listing 3.2).
- WS-EventDescriptions is a specification developed by the W3C, to provide a standard way of describing event types used in web services. It also uses the approach shown in listing 3.2.

These two specifications focus on the payload portion of events; their assumption is that the attributes that we describe as headers are either included in these payloads or are transported alongside the payload elsewhere in the web service message. We discuss the wider question of standardization and event processing in chapter 11.

3.7   *Summary*

In this chapter, the first of our deep dives, we discussed what is meant by an event type, and described our platform-independent definition of an event type. There is,

---

[4] You can find out more about the HL7 standards at the Health Level Seven International website, http://hl7.org.

at present, no single agreed-upon standard for how events or event types are to be represented, so in this chapter we focused on the information that needs to be carried by events. This is made up of the payload that carries the event's own information, and a header that provides additional meta-information about the event. We also listed the raw event types used in the Fast Flower Delivery application.

In chapter 4 and the chapters that immediately follow it, we move on to look at event producers and the other entities that make up an event processing network.

3.7.1 Additional Reading

Galton, Antony, and Juan Carlos Augusto, *Two Approaches to Event Definition*, DEXA 2002: 547-556. http://www.springerlink.com/content/46mbb6ajt6t20qvd/. This article discusses various approaches for event definition.

Jensen, Christian S., et al. "The Consensus Glossary of Temporal Database Concepts—February 1998 Version." In Opher Etzion, Sushil Jajodia, and Suryanarayana Sripada, *Temporal Databases Research and Practice*, Springer, 1998: 367-405. http://www.springerlink.com/content/03981447077588rj/. Temporal concepts such as chronon and other temporal concepts are taken from this temporal databases concepts' glossary. Note that the entire book contains various articles on temporal databases.

Vambenepe, William, Steve Graham, and Peter Niblett, *Web Services Topics 1.3*, OASIS Standard, 1 October 2006. http://docs.oasis-open.org/wsn/wsn-ws_topics-1.3-spec-os.pdf. This standard uses XML Schema to describe event types for use with web services.

Kreger, Heather, Vaughn Bullard, and William Vambenepe, *Web Services Distributed Management: Management Using Web Services* (MUWS 1.1) Part 2, OASIS Standard, 01 August 2006. http://docs.oasis-open.org/wsdm/wsdm-muws2-1.1-spec-os-01.pdf. This standard includes a definition of the WSDM Event Format.

3.7.2 Exercises

3.1 Add three more event types to the Fast Flower Delivery application and list their definition elements.

3.2 In which cases is the use of occurrence time important? Provide an example.

3.3 In which cases is the use of spatial properties important? Provide an example.

3.4 Provide scenarios (not from the Fast Flower Delivery example) that use event generalization and retraction events.

3.5 Create two event instance examples, in the manner of table 3.11, for each of the raw event types described in section 3.5.

3.6 Find documentation of two different event processing commercial products, study the way event types are defined, and translate the event types defined in section 3.5 to these representations. Use the products to create the instance examples you defined in exercise 3.5.

Producing the events 4

We've heard that a million monkeys at a million keyboards could produce the complete works of Shakespeare; now, thanks to the Internet, we know that is not true.

—Robert Wilensky

In chapter 2 we discussed the architecture of event processing applications and introduced the model that we are using to describe event processing systems. In this model, and in the majority of event processing systems, there is a distinction between entities that introduce event objects into the event processing system (event producers), the software artifacts that process the events (event processing agents, or EPAs), and the entities that receive the events after processing by the event processing system (event consumers).

We now continue our detailed examination of event processing applications by looking at event producers; we discuss event consumers in chapter 5 and event processing agents in chapter 6. In this chapter we examine the following:

- The notion of an event producer, its role, and the definition element describing it
- The different kinds of event producers
- The different ways of interacting with an event producer

We also include a specification of the event producers used in the Fast Flower Delivery application. We start by defining the event producer.

4.1   Event producer: concept and definition element

In chapter 2 we defined an event producer as something that introduces event objects into the event processing network from the world outside. This definition is deliberately broad and doesn't impose restrictions on why, how, or when the event producer introduces these events. Whether you view something as an event producer or not depends on the EPN you're discussing. Imagine you have two EPNs linked together, so that the first network sends events to the second. The second EPN then would view the first EPN as an event producer, and the first EPN would see the second as an event consumer.

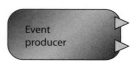

We represent an event producer in our model as a node that has only output terminals, as shown in figure 4.1. The absence of input terminals is one of the differences between an event producer and an event processing agent. Another difference is that an event processing agent's logic is explicitly specified as part of the event processing network definition, whereas the logic of an event producer is

Figure 4.1   Event producer with two output terminals

not. We make this second distinction in order to set clear borders between the event processing that is specified by the EPN and the preprocessing or post-processing that lie outside its scope.

When talking about an event producer, it is important to recognize that we can use the concept to refer to three slightly different things:

- An abstract type of event producer, for example, a GPS sensor.
- A collection of event producer instances, all of the same type, which feature in a given application. We refer to such a collection as a *class*, for example, we have the class of all GPS sensors deployed in our Fast Flower Delivery application.
- A single instance of an event producer, for example, the GPS sensor inside driver John Galt's vehicle.

It is often helpful to be able to model a class of instances rather than to have to refer to each producer instance individually as some applications can involve hundreds or even thousands of producers. Moreover, in many applications the number of producers is not fixed but varies over time; for example, the number of drivers involved in our Fast Flower Delivery application can vary day by day.

An event producer node in an event processing network diagram, and its corresponding definition element, can represent either a single event producer instance, or a class made up of multiple event producer instances. In the latter case the definition element represents the things that the producer instances all have in common including the event types that they emit through their output terminals.

4.1.1   Event producer definition element

In the previous section we observed that there are three aspects to the event producer concept, and we use the event producer definition element to model all three. We use

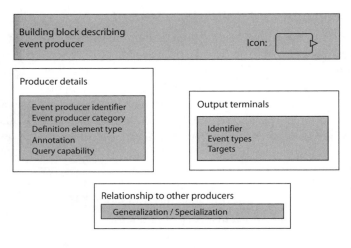

Figure 4.2   The event producer definition element contains details about the definition element itself, a list of output terminals, and a list of relationships to other event producer definitions

it to define abstract event producer types, event producer classes, and event producer instances. Recall also that the event producer definition element is concerned only with the interaction between the producers that it represents and the rest of the EPN and does not describe the internal logic of the event producers.

The definition element consists of three parts: producer details, output terminals, and relationships to other producer types. A producer definition element that represents a class or instance will have one or more of its output terminals connected to other entities in the EPN (we talk more about this in chapter 6). A definition element that represents an abstract type of event producer can't be included directly in an event processing network, and so its output terminals are left disconnected.

We now describe the three parts of the definition elements shown in figure 4.2: producer details, output terminals, and relationships to other producers.

4.1.2   *Event producer details*

The *producer details* part of the definition element contains attributes that describe the producer or producers represented by the definition element, along with an attribute that indicates whether the definition element represents an instance, class, or abstract type.

- *Event producer identifier* gives the name of the producer abstract type, producer class, or producer instance described by the definition element. It can be used when referring to this definition element from elsewhere.
- *Event producer category* indicates the kind of event producer that is being described by the definition element (for example, it could be a software trace point, or an RFID reader). This attribute is used for descriptive purposes and has no effect on the way that events are handled by the event processing network itself. We give some suggestions for categories in section 4.2.

- *Definition element type* is an attribute which indicates whether the definition element represents an abstract type, a class of producer instances, or a single instance. Its possible values are abstract type, producer class, or producer instance. When the definition element is being used as a node in an EPN, it represents either a producer class or producer instance.
- *Annotation* is an optional attribute that provides more information about the event producer instance, class, or abstract type.
- *Query capability* is a Boolean attribute which indicates whether the producer can be queried or not. See section 4.3.2 for more details.

Next we describe the output terminals.

4.1.3 *Output terminal details*

The second part of the definition element describes the event producer's output terminals. An event producer emits events through these output terminals. Each output terminal has one or more event types associated with it, and it also has a number of *targets*—references to entities that receive events that are emitted through the terminal. There are no targets on the output terminals in an abstract type definition element; one or more targets can be added when a definition element is used as a node in an event processing network, as then it is being used to describe a class or instance.

An event producer can have one or more output terminals and each output terminal has the following attributes:

- *Identifier*—Used to distinguish this terminal in cases where the event producer has more than one output terminal.
- *Event types*—A collection of event type identifiers showing the types of events that can be emitted through this output terminal. An output terminal can have one or more event types associated with it. This association is not exclusive (an event producer can have the same event type associated with multiple output terminals).
- *Targets*—A list of the *identifiers* of the input terminals of entities which are to receive events from this output terminal. Each output terminal can have zero or more targets. If the definition element represents an abstract producer type, none of its output terminals have targets assigned to them.

In figure 4.3 we show an example of an output terminal connected to an explicitly modeled channel. In this case the event producer is connected to an explicit channel, but an output terminal can also be connected to an input terminal of an event processing agent, or even an event consumer. In such cases we say that it is connected through an implicit channel.

Figure 4.3   Event producer connected to an explicitly modeled channel

4.1.4   Producer relationships

An event producer definition element can specify that it is a specialization of another event producer definition element, and this can be used as a way of indicating that a particular definition element has a particular abstract event producer type. This is useful if the application involves several classes of producer that all have the same abstract type.

In order to qualify as a specialization, the definition element must have output terminals that correspond to the output terminals of the definition element that it specializes. The event types on these output terminals must be the same as the types on the terminals of the element being specialized, or specializations of those types. The definition element may contain additional output terminals.

An element representing an event producer class or instance can be a specialization of one that represents an abstract type, and an abstract type can itself be a specialization of another abstract type. For example, the Fast Flower Delivery application's GPS sensor producer type might be a specialization of a more general Sensor producer type.

The converse of specialization is the generalization relationship. In all cases the definition element that is the generalization must be an abstract type.

We now take a look at the different kinds of event producers.

4.2   The various kinds of event producers

As we have already said, the event producer definition elements that appear in an event processing network model attempt to capture only the EPN-facing interfaces of the event producers that they represent. The nature of an event producer, and its inner workings, are opaque, and all you see in the EPN model are, in effect, proxies that represent the real producers. However, the real producers do make up an important part of the event processing application, and so it is worth discussing them.

We do this by classifying them into categories and giving examples of each. Figure 4.4 shows three categories: hardware, software, and human interaction.

Any classification of this sort is subjective—in reality a producer may well involve a mixture of hardware, software, and human elements. Also there's sometimes a choice about where to set the boundary of an event producer. When talking in the abstract it can be difficult to be precise about where the event producer stops, and the rest of the

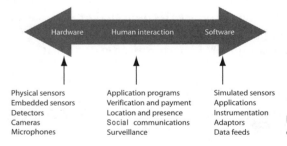

Figure 4.4   **Different kinds of event producers encountered in event processing applications**

event processing network begins, though this rarely causes a problem when describing or designing an application in practice.

4.2.1 Hardware event producers

Hardware producers are used extensively in a number of application areas:

- Medical equipment and personal body sensors (for example, heart-rate monitors)
- Device management (computer systems or industrial equipment)
- Defense and military applications
- Security applications
- Traffic management systems
- Logistics and supply chain management
- Weather reporting and forecasting

The archetypal hardware event producer is a sensor that generates events that report on one or more aspects of the physical environment in which it is situated, for example, a smoke detector.

A sensor can be packaged as a discrete piece of hardware, such as the smoke detector example; or it can be embedded into another piece of equipment, for example, a sensor that detects the fan speed on a computer motherboard. The simplest kind of sensor reports on just one aspect of its environment, for example:

- Motion of the sensor itself including vibration
- Tilt or angle of orientation of the sensor
- Rotation of a rod attached to the sensor
- Temperature
- Humidity
- Light (intensity or color)
- Infrared or radio waves
- Sound (intensity of frequency)
- Air (or other gas) pressure
- Physical pressure applied to the sensor itself
- Magnetic field
- Level or pressure of a liquid
- Airflow
- Electric current or potential
- Electrical conductivity
- Chemical environment (for example, pH level, or presence of a particular chemical)
- Mechanical strain
- Ionizing radiation

More sophisticated detectors use one or more of the physical detection mechanisms previously listed to make specific observations or look for particular kinds of occurrence. Here is a small list of examples:

- A sensor that detects motion external to itself, such as a passive infrared (PIR) sensor. This can be used to detect the presence of people in the vicinity of the sensor, for example, when reporting on room occupancy or when looking for intruders.
- A sensor that detects whether the door on the casing of equipment is open or closed.
- An RFID reader used to detect the presence of an RFID tag. This can be used in supply chain or many other application areas.
- A seismometer used to detect and report on earthquakes or nuclear tests.
- A traffic speed detector. Apart from their obvious use in penalizing speeding drivers, speed detectors can also be used in intelligent traffic management systems.
- GPS location devices. These are used in a wide variety of tracking and location-aware services.

Cameras (both still and video), microphones, telephones, and radio receivers can also be viewed as event producers because the data that they produce can be processed by event processing applications. For example, you could have a security application that processes frames coming from a video camera looking for the presence of unauthorized personnel in a secure area.

4.2.2   *Software event producers*

Although software is often associated with a hardware producer, some event producers are made up of software only.

The first category consists of *simulated sensors*. These are software simulations of the kinds of hardware producers discussed in section 4.2.1. Simulated sensors are used when the entire external system is itself a simulation, for example, a flight training simulator or virtual reality game, and they can also be used to stand in for a real piece of hardware when testing an event processing application.

An event producer could be a first-class part of a software *application*. By this we mean that it is a piece of application logic that explicitly generates an event object and submits it to the event processing network. This may happen as a result of a human interaction (see the next section) but sometimes events can be generated less directly. For example, a financial trading system might include a settlement application that automatically generates payment events. This application uses a programming interface to submit the event, as discussed in section 4.3.

Events can be produced indirectly by a technique known as *instrumentation*. Here the events are not generated by application code itself, but instead are produced by software that is monitoring the application, looking for noteworthy activity. This kind of producer is sometimes called a *monitor* or *probe*. A wide range of events could be viewed as noteworthy, from tracing program start-up and shutdown or tracing function calls within the application, through detecting updates that the application makes to its data, reporting computer performance statistics, or spotting and reporting on hardware or software errors if they occur. Instrumentation can be provided by the operating system or the container that runs the application, or by database or messaging middleware that the application uses. Examples include workflow engines which can generate events when a particular workflow goes through a state transition, security subsystems which can generate alerting events when they detect attempted security violations, and message queuing systems which can generate events when the number of messages waiting in a queue exceeds a certain threshold.

We use the term *adaptor* to refer to a producer that doesn't directly detect events itself, but instead collects information available from elsewhere and uses that to generate events. Adaptors can be used to provide the instrumentation we mentioned in the previous paragraph, for example, adaptors that run against application or database log files, but they are also used to connect hardware sensors to an event processing network. A single adaptor can be used to connect multiple sensors to a network, and so act as a concentrating gateway, as well as translating from the protocol used by the sensor into the protocol used by the EPN. It is sometimes convenient to view the adaptor as the event producer, rather than having each sensor appear as a separate producer.

Our final category of software producer is a news or data *feed*. This is a mechanism that brings data in from outside the organization that owns the EPN. For many years financial trading applications have used stock feeds provided by news agencies or individual exchanges. These feeds contain price information about recent trades of stocks or other financial instruments, as well as a variety of other pieces of financial information. More recently web-based feeds that use Atom Syndication Format or Really Simple Syndication (RSS) have emerged. Literally tens of thousands of them are available on the internet.

4.2.3 *Human interaction*

Some events are generated directly by human interaction, albeit with a bit of software and hardware assistance. Two of the producers in our Fast Flower Delivery example are of this kind: the `Store` producer, which lets a store employee enter or cancel requests, pick drivers, and confirm pickups, and the `Driver` producer that represents the drivers who bid for work and confirm delivery.

Human interaction can be facilitated by an *application program* with a user interface that in effect allows the user to enter the event. In our example we could imagine that each store has a web application, and store personnel use a form-style interface to place a delivery order request.

Events can also be generated using a *verification* or *payment* device, for example, the delivery confirmation produced by the driver's handheld device in our application, or a purchase event being generated by a till in a retail store.

Some producers detect our *presence*, for example, the swiping of an identity card (or having a personal RFID tag scanned) when entering a secure area, the use of an NFC (near field communications) tag to go through a ticket barrier on public transport or pass through immigration control. Instant messaging applications (and increasingly telephony applications) can produce presence events that indicate when a user has turned a computer or handheld device on or off, and these presence events sometimes include information about the user's location or actions.

This brings us to our next area, *social communications*. As well as providing its regular web browser interface, the popular Twitter internet service offers RSS feeds that can be used to communicate presence (and other) events. Events can also be produced from other social networking applications (recall the final example in section 1.1.2).

The final category is *surveillance*. We are all familiar with CCTV cameras, but a more controversial area is web activity monitoring, where a user's website interactions are captured and tracked.

4.3   *Interfacing with an event producer*

Having looked at the wide range of possible producers, we now turn to how they interface with the rest of the event processing network. We start by looking at the interaction patterns that they use and then at the mechanics of how they connect.

4.3.1   *Interaction patterns*

A quick examination of the producers reviewed in section 4.2 shows that interaction patterns fall into two categories:

- *Sensor style*—These are producers that sense environment or state, for example, temperature sensors.
- *Detector style*—These are producers that detect specific occurrences and report on them through events. These occurrences can be rare (for example, an intruder alarm) or frequent (a human heartbeat, or a customer walking through a turnstile) but they are nevertheless identifiable as separate occurrences.

It's clear that the event objects generated by a detector style producer describe the occurrences that the producer detects, but what about the sensor style producers? What kind of event objects do they produce and, more importantly, when should they produce them? You could claim that they just report status rather than real event occurrences, and that therefore they should not be counted as event producers at all. That would, however, be to deny the fact that they are used in event processing applications, and that the event objects that they emit can be treated in the same way as the event objects produced by the detector style of producer.

The event objects generated by a sensor-type producer usually record the current value of whatever it is that the sensor is measuring. A sensor-type producer can adopt three strategies as to when it emits the event. First is to emit an event only when it detects an appreciable change in the value of what it is measuring; for example, a temperature sensor might generate an event if the temperature has moved by more than 0.5° C from the value that it last reported. This approach is closest to that of an event detector, because it is in effect reporting the *temperature has changed* occurrence. The second strategy is simply to report the current value, whatever it is, on a periodic basis, and the third approach is to never emit an event spontaneously, but instead record the current value and return it to anyone who requests it. This third approach is sometimes referred to as *polling*, and is similar to the pull-style event distribution that we discussed in chapter 2.

The same choices are available to the detector-style of event producer. It can implement a push-style interface, which means that it emits an event object each time it detects the corresponding occurrence. It can hold onto the event and on a periodic basis emit an object corresponding to the last event detected (this approach is rarely used in practice). Or it can wait until polled before returning an event object describing the last occurrence(s) that it detected.

The designer of the producer usually chooses the approach, a choice influenced by considerations such as the nature of the events themselves, as well as the capabilities of the producer implementation. For example, it would be difficult to implement the polling approach if the producer has no mechanism for receiving incoming requests. In general, a push approach is used if low latency is important, or if every event is important. A polling approach can be used if only the most up-to-date value is important—if the latest event generated by the producer makes earlier events obsolete. We discussed other reasons for using a pull approach in chapter 2.

4.3.2 Queriable event producers

Many of the event producers we discussed in section 4.2 simply forget about an event occurrence after they have emitted the corresponding event object. They might, of course, have to hold on to an event object for a while before emitting it, particularly if they support a pull interface, but in this section we are concerned with more open-ended, longer term retention of events. Some producers do retain a longer-term history of events that have occurred. This could be for purposes of nonrepudiation or other legal or regulatory reasons or to assist with subsequent problem determination. Some software producers (for example, log or database adaptors or feed producers) continue to have access to the raw data that they use to produce events.

Producers that retain historical event data in this way can provide an interface to allow this data to be queried by an event processing application, and we use the definition element's *query capability* to indicate if this is the case or not. In the area of *active diagnostics* that we mentioned in chapter 1, the ability to query past events is useful, because events which seem insignificant at the time when they occur can prove important when diagnosing a problem that is detected later. If the producer of such events can be queried, an active diagnostics application does not have to maintain its own store of historical events.

4.3.3 Interfacing mechanisms

An event producer interacts with the event processing network using an event distribution mechanism (we introduced event distribution in chapter 2). An EPN can support one or more event distribution mechanisms, and these mechanisms can either be protocol based or API based.

In a protocol-based mechanism the event producer uses a transport protocol supported by the event processing platform. This could be a proprietary protocol or a standardized one, and describes both how event objects are serialized as well as the transport protocol used to transmit them. The protocol can support either push-style or pull-style distribution or both. The protocol might also include a way for the event distribution network to provide a filter to exclude certain events. To see why this might be useful, consider an event processing application that is monitoring a piece of equipment and needs to know when its temperature exceeds 40° C. The application could take every temperature change event from the sensor and filter out all events that don't go above this temperature, but it can reduce the number of events being produced, distributed, and processed by delegating the task of filtering to the producer itself. You could do this by programming the temperature threshold value (40° C) into the design of the sensor, but the dynamic approach where the value is supplied by the EPN itself allows it to be changed easily if required.

In the API approach, the event processing platform provides a programming interface for the event producer to use, and this approach is frequently used by software event producers. The programming interface shields the event producer from the underlying protocol that is used by the middleware. There are two main styles of API. One is the kind of programming interface provided by message-oriented middleware, such as the Java Message Service API, where the producer explicitly constructs an event object and uses the API to transmit it. In the other style of API (sometimes found in management applications) the API provides access to one or more resources (objects recording aspects of the current state of the producer). Rather than having to construct an event object explicitly, the producer makes updates to the state held in these resources, and these updates in turn cause resource state change event objects to be created and distributed.

Now that we have discussed the theory, let's look at how these ideas are put into practice in our Fast Flower Delivery application.

4.4   *Producers in the Fast Flower Delivery application*

This section contains a short discussion of the different event producer definition elements that can be found in our model of the Fast Flower Delivery application.

4.4.1   *The four event producers*

In the Fast Flower Delivery example there are four event producers: `Store`, `Driver`, `GPS sensor`, and `Vehicle`. We look briefly at each in turn.

THE STORE EVENT PRODUCER

We start with the definition element for the `Store` producer. Its definition element type is *producer class* because the application treats all the participating flower stores in a similar manner, so we can have a single event producer definition that represents them all.

Its event producer category is *human interaction*, as personnel in the flower store enter its events, and it has four output terminals, as shown in table 4.1.

Table 4.1　Output terminals for the Store event producer

Identifier	Event types	Targets
Request	Delivery Request	Request enrichment EPA
Assignment	Manual Assignment	Assignment channel
Confirm Pickup	Pickup Confirmation	Pickup alert EPA
Cancellation	Delivery Request Cancellation	Delivery cancellation channel

The Assignment and Cancellation terminals have explicit channels as their targets. The other two terminals are connected through implicit channels, and so they are shown as directly targeting event processing agents.

We have chosen to model the event store with four output terminals, one for each event type. This is because there is no direct logical connection between them (for example, it doesn't make sense to think of a stream made up of Request and Assignment events). It is also convenient to use separate terminals in this application, because we want the different types of events to go to different targets. This would still have been possible with a single output terminal, but we would have had to include filter specifications to make sure that the right events go to the right targets.

THE DRIVER EVENT PRODUCER

The Driver event producer definition element represents all the drivers using the application, so it too has *producer class* as its definition element type. Although the driver uses a handheld device to submit events, we still give the definition element an event producer category of *human interaction*, because it is the driver that we are modeling, not the device (we are assuming that there's a one-one association of drivers to devices). The event producer's output terminals are shown in table 4.2.

Table 4.2　Output terminals for the Driver event producer

Identifier	Event types	Targets
Bid	Delivery Bid	Driver enrichment EPA, Daily assignments calculator EPA
Confirm	Delivery Confirmation	Delivery alert EPA

Again, we have chosen to use separate output terminals for the two types of event emitted by this event producer.

THE GPS SENSOR EVENT PRODUCER

We have included the GPS sensor event producer to illustrate producer specialization. This event producer is abstract, so naturally its definition element type is *abstract type*, and, as you might expect, its event producer category is *sensor*. The type has just one output terminal, as shown in table 4.3.

Table 4.3   Output terminal for the `GPS sensor` abstract event producer

Identifier	Event type	Targets
Report	GPS location	-

As this is an abstract type, its terminals are not connected to any targets.

THE VEHICLE EVENT PRODUCER

Our final definition element is the `Vehicle` event producer. Its definition element type is *producer class* as it represents all the vehicles that are being used for flower delivery. It is a specialization of the `GPS sensor` type, reflecting the fact that there is a physical GPS sensor in each vehicle, and the events are actually produced by that sensor. Its event producer category is therefore *sensor*, just like the `GPS sensor` type and, as you can see from table 4.4, it has the same output terminal.

Table 4.4   Output terminal for the `Vehicle` event producer

Output terminal	Event type	Targets
Report Location	GPS Location	Location service EPA

As this definition element is not an abstract type, we can supply a target for its output terminal.

4.5   *Summary*

In this chapter we have introduced the first part of the event processing flow, the event producer. We discussed the event producer definition element, and noted that it can be used to represent an abstract producer type, a concrete event producer, or a class of multiple concrete event producers. We also remarked that the event producer's internal logic is outside the scope of the event processing network and that an event producer node in an EPN is a proxy that represents the connection from one or more real event producers to the rest of the EPN. We discussed a number of different kinds of producers and looked at interactions between producers and the rest of the network.

This is the first node from the EPN that we have examined, and we now jump to the other end of the network and discuss event consumers.

4.5.1   *Additional reading*

The Workflow Management Coalition Specification, Workflow Management Coalition, White Paper—Events. http://lists.ebxml.org/archives/ebxml-bp/200005/pdf00001.pdf. This white paper describes the use of workflow as a producer and consumer of events.

IBM Redbooks, "Implementing Event Processing with CICS." http://www.amazon.com/ Implementing-Event-Processing-Cics-Redbooks/dp/0738433365/ref=sr_1_1?ie= UTF8&s=books&qid=1258899442&sr=1-1. This book describes an example of software instrumentation acting as an event producer.

Cordeiro, Carlos De Morais, Dharma P. Agrawal: *Ad Hoc & Sensor Networks: Theory and Applications*, World Scientific Publishing company, 2006. http://www.amazon.com/Ad-Hoc-Sensor-Networks-Applications/dp/9812566821/ref=sr_1_3?ie=UTF8&s=books&qid= 1258899679&sr=1-3. This book provides an introduction to sensor networks.

4.5.2 Exercises

4.1 Explain, with examples, why it is useful to have the concept of a class of event producers.

4.2 Provide an example of an event producer class that contains multiple instances.

4.3 We have stated that all the members of an event producer class must have the same type. Explain why we impose this requirement.

4.4 Provide an example of an application using multiple event producer classes in which it is helpful to have an abstract producer type.

4.5 Provide three examples of useful instrumentation of programs, explain what events will be created in each case, and what purpose they might serve.

Consuming the events 5

What information consumes is rather obvious: it consumes the attention of its recipients. Hence, a wealth of information creates a poverty of attention and a need to allocate that attention efficiently among the overabundance of information sources that might consume it.

—Herbert Simon

We now move on to the event consumer. This is the mirror image of the event producer that we discussed in chapter 4, so we recommend that you read that chapter before reading this one. In this chapter we look at

- The notion of an event consumer, its role, and the definition element that describes it
- The different types of event consumers
- The different types of interaction with an event consumer
- The distinction between an event consumer and a subscriber

We also include a specification of the event consumers used in the Fast Flower Delivery application. We start by defining the event consumer, the core concept of this chapter.

5.1   *Event consumer: concept and definition element*

The event consumer is the logical complement of the event producer. An event consumer accepts event objects from entities in an event processing network and processes them. How it actually processes the event objects lies outside the scope of the EPN model.

We represent an event consumer as an event processing network node that has only input terminals, as you can see in figure 5.1.

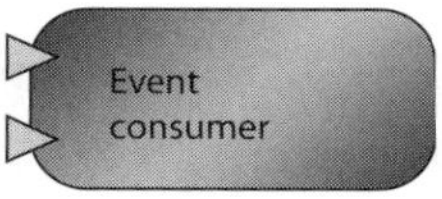

An event consumer node, like that shown in figure 5.1, is similar to an event producer in that it can represent either a single event consumer instance or a class of several similar event consumer instances.

Figure 5.1   An event consumer with two input terminals

5.1.1   *Event consumer definition element*

The event consumer definition element can be used in one of three ways:

- To define an abstract event consumer type
- To represent a class of concrete event consumer instances
- To represent a single concrete event consumer instance

Recall that the event consumer definition element is concerned only with the interaction between the consumer or consumers that it represents and the rest of the event processing network; it does not describe the internal logic of the event consumers.

The definition element consists of three parts: consumer details, input terminal specifications, and relationships to other consumers. An event consumer definition element that represents a class or instance has one or more of its input terminals connected to other entities in the EPN; a definition element that represents an abstract type cannot have its input terminals connected to anything.

Figure 5.2 illustrates the event consumer definition element.

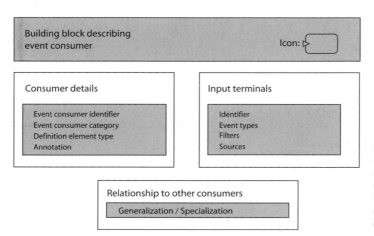

Figure 5.2   The event consumer definition element contains details about the definition element itself, a list of input terminals, and a list of relationships to other event consumer definitions.

We now describe the three parts of the definition element shown in figure 5.2: consumer details, input terminals, and relationships to other consumers.

5.1.2   *Event consumer details*

The *event consumer details* part of the definition element contains some attributes that describe the consumer or consumers represented by the definition element, along with an attribute that indicates whether the definition element represents an instance, class, or abstract type. These attributes are similar to those found in the event producer definition element.

- *Event consumer identifier* gives the name of the consumer abstract type, consumer class, or consumer instance described by the definition element. It can be used to refer to this definition element from elsewhere.
- *Event consumer category* indicates the kind of event consumer that is being described by the definition element, for example, it could be a dashboard or a hardware actuator. This attribute is used for descriptive purposes and has no effect on the way that events are handled by the event processing network itself. We give suggestions for categories in section 5.2.
- *Definition element type* is an attribute which indicates whether the definition element represents an abstract type, class of consumer instances, or a single instance; its possible values are *abstract type, consumer class,* or *consumer instance.* When the definition element is being used as a node in an EPN, it represents either a consumer class or a consumer instance.
- *Annotation* is an optional annotation that provides more information about the event consumer instance, class, or abstract type.

Next we discuss the input terminals.

5.1.3   *Input terminal details*

The second part of the definition element describes the event consumer's input terminals. An event consumer can receive events through any of its input terminals. Each input terminal has one or more event types associated with it, and it can also have one or more *sources*—references to entities from which the terminal is to receive events. There are no sources on the input terminals in an abstract type definition element; one or more sources can be added when a definition element is used as a node in an event processing network, as then it describes a class or instance.

An event consumer can have one or more input terminals and each input terminal has the following attributes:

- *Identifier*—This is used to distinguish this terminal in cases where the event consumer has more than one input terminal.

- *Event types*—This is a list of event type identifiers showing the types of events that can be accepted by this input terminal. An input terminal can have one or more event types associated with it.
- *Filters*—The list of event types on an input terminal is a form of filter expression, as the input terminal admits only events whose type is on the list. However an input terminal can have additional filter expressions that further limit the set of event objects that can be received by the terminal. These filter expressions could, for example, include expressions that filter events based on the values of particular event attributes. Chapter 8 examines filters further.
- *Sources*—This is a list of identifiers of output terminals of entities that can send events to this input terminal. These entities can be modeled channels (as shown in figure 5.3), event producers, or event processing agents. Each input terminal can have zero or more sources. If the event consumer definition element represents an abstract consumer type, none of its input terminals can have sources assigned to them.

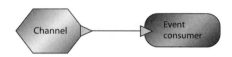

Figure 5.3   An event consumer with an explicitly modeled channel as the source for its input terminal

An event consumer can be associated with a source of events without having a source explicitly specified on its input terminal. This is because the input terminal can itself be specified as a target on an output terminal of the source entity.

5.1.4   Consumer relationships

A definition element that represents a class, instance or type can be a specialization of another definition element that represents a type, and conversely a type definition element can be a generalization of another type, class, or instance.

In order to qualify as a specialization the definition element must include all the input terminals of the definition element that it specializes, although the event types on such a terminal may be specializations of the types on the terminal being specialized. The definition element may contain additional input terminals. As with event producers, the specialization relationship can be used as a way of indicating the abstract type definition element that corresponds to a particular instance or class.

Next we discuss the different kinds of consumers.

5.2   The various kinds of event consumers

In the previous section we described the *event consumer category* attribute. This is a free-format text attribute that indicates what kind of event consumer is being described. In this section we give examples which could be used as categories.

In figure 5.4 we show three broad families of event consumers: hardware, software, and human interaction.

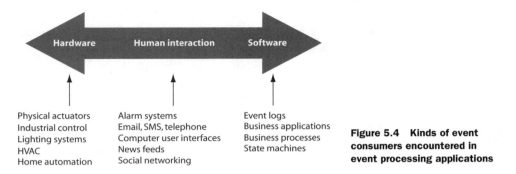

Figure 5.4   Kinds of event consumers encountered in event processing applications

As is the case with event producers, there aren't clear dividing lines among these classifications; you may well encounter consumers that involve a mixture of hardware, software, and human interaction elements.

5.2.1 *Hardware event consumers*

A piece of hardware that consumes events is often referred to as an *actuator*, and is the counterpart of the hardware *sensor* that produces events. An actuator takes an incoming event and reacts to it by performing a physical action, often in order to control something in the physical world. This might involve physical motion (if the actuator includes some kind of motor), changing a magnetic field, or producing an electrical or radio signal.

Here are some examples of actions that could be performed by an actuator:

- Locking or unlocking a door
- Raising or lowering a barrier
- Applying the brakes on a vehicle
- Opening or closing a valve
- Controlling a railroad switch
- Turning a piece of equipment on or off

An actuator could be physically packaged alongside a sensor in the same piece of hardware, but when this happens we still model the sensor and actuator as a separate producer and consumer.

Figure 5.4 suggests specific areas where actuators can be used. In industrial control applications actuators are used to power equipment on and off, to control the operation of machinery, and to control the flow of liquids. In intelligent building applications, actuators can be used to control lighting, heating, and air conditioning systems. With the emergence of home automation, actuators can be used to perform tasks such as opening or closing garage doors or window blinds, as well as for controlling lighting and heating.

5.2.2　*Human interaction*

The actuators described in the previous section react to events by directly controlling something in the physical world. There is another style of event consumer whose job is to interface with human beings. This might be to alert someone about a serious occurrence that needs immediate attention, to report something less urgent that, nevertheless, might be of interest, or to update the information shown by a visual display of some sort.

People can be alerted to important and urgent events by alarm systems (for example, bells or flashing lights) or by system-generated telephone calls. For less urgent alerts, you could use a consumer that generates an email or a Short Message Service (SMS) text message.

Consumers frequently convey information about events through the medium of a computer user interface. This interface is implemented either by a specially written client application or, increasingly frequently, via a web application that allows the event data to be viewed on a web browser without requiring the installation of specialist software.

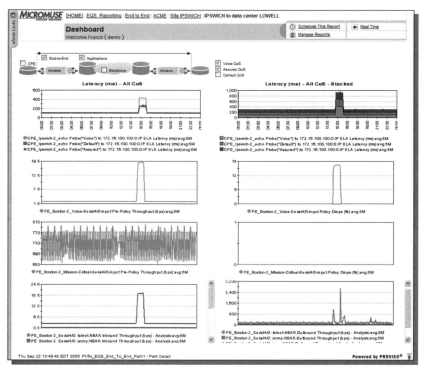

Figure 5.5　Performance monitoring dashboard. This event consumer takes a variety of performance measurement events and displays them as graphs.

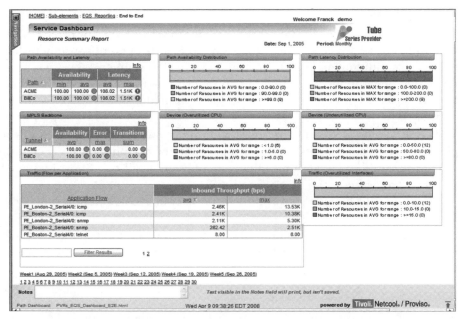

Figure 5.6   A dashboard screen showing the use of color-coding to indicate out-of-line situations. The window at the top right indicates that all the resources being monitored exceeded the maximum acceptable value for path latency.

The name *dashboard* is given to a particular kind of user interface that gathers information on past and present events, often from multiple sources. Dashboards are used by applications that provide monitoring capability, for example, performance monitoring or business activity monitoring tools. Figure 5.5 shows an example from a network performance tool. This tool uses a portal-like dashboard to show routine performance-related information.

As well as gathering raw data, monitoring systems also calculate metrics or key performance indicators. These are values computed from the raw data that have meaning to the business concerned. Dashboards can use graphical techniques to let people know when these metrics or indicators show that something is not behaving as expected. Figure 5.6 shows a number of network performance metrics displayed in a dashboard panel.

In this example raw performance events from a variety of network resources have been analyzed, and a number of metrics have been computed and averaged over the previous month (for example, CPU utilization, traffic, and path latency). The averaged metrics have then been compared against predefined value ranges, and are displayed as red, orange, or green bars (in the print version of this book, the red bars are darker and the green bars are lighter).

A busy executive can get a quick summary of the dashboard using a device such as the Ambient Orb from the Ambient Devices company, shown in figure 5.7. This can be programmed to change color in response to data from the event processing application, and so can be used to show the status of a particular metric or collection of metrics.

Event processing applications can use consumers specifically designed to display event data in a way that is appropriate to the type of event in question (this is sometimes referred to as *event visualization*). In figure 5.8 we can see a consumer that provides the visual display part of a vehicle-tracking application.

This application uses a map with overlays to indicate the locations (past and present) of the item being tracked. Such map-like interfaces are often used for displaying events relating to specific locations.

Figure 5.7   The Ambient Orb. The orb can be programmed to change color to reflect the general health of an organization, or to show the status of a specific key indicator.

Other styles of user interface include travel departure and arrival boards and sports scoreboards. These can be simulated by computer applications or implemented as physical displays. The difference between these two is blurring as more and more display boards are being implemented in software; the physical departure board is rapidly becoming a thing of the past.

Event processing applications can also make people aware of events by distributing them via web feeds (using Atom or RSS protocols). Users can view such events through

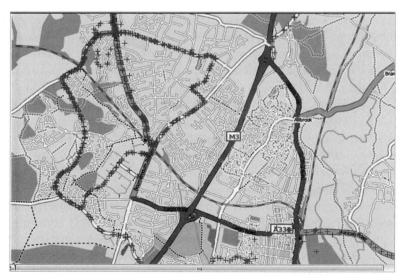

Figure 5.8   A visual display from a location tracking application. The individual markers show the positions that a particular vehicle (in this case a bus) has visited in the previous 24 hours.

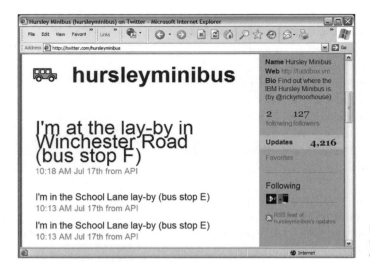

Figure 5.9   Twitter can be used to report the position of a vehicle.

readily available feed reader software. In a similar vein, event notifications can be posted to a wide community using Twitter or social networking sites. Figure 5.9 shows Twitter[1] being used. The panel shown in figure 5.9 is part of the same vehicle-tracking application that we saw in figure 5.8.

5.2.3   *Software event consumers*

The third family consists of event consumers that comprise only software and that do not themselves offer a user interface.

Software consumers can keep a record of the events they receive, either in a flat file or a database. We refer to such consumers as *event logs*. An event log can be useful in active diagnostic applications; when analyzing a problem it is frequently useful to be able to go back in time and look at events that took place in the run-up to the occurrence of the problem itself, but which appeared unremarkable at the time. Another use of an event log is to provide an audit trail. When designing an event log, you need to consider what bits of event data need to be recorded, and what kinds of searches are going to be performed against that data. If the log is going to be read only occasionally, you should consider implementing the log in a way which optimizes writing of the data rather than reading it.

Software consumers also include what might be called *line of business* applications—application logic not modeled in the event processing network itself. The event consumer is in effect the gateway between the EPN and this application code. This category covers a wide range of core business applications, for example, asset and inventory management, enterprise resource planning, and personnel systems.

---

[1]   http://twitter.com/hursleyminibus

The consumer can integrate with the line of business application in various ways. If the application has been constructed using a service-oriented architecture approach, or if it has been adapted to provide SOA interfaces, the consumer can use these interfaces. If this is not the case, the consumer might have to be implemented in the form of an adapter to the application.

Another approach is for the consumer not to interface directly to a single line of business application, but rather to interface to a business process management (BPM) system; the BPM system then orchestrates the interaction with one or more applications. There are two commonly used BPM programming models. In a workflow model, which is embodied by the Business Process Modeling Notation (BPMN) and WS-BPEL standards, a business process is defined as a graph of activities. Figure 5.10 (which comes from the BPMN 1.2 specification) shows a simple business process.

The receipt of an event by the consumer can be used to trigger the start of a new instance of the process (in this example, the arrival of an order would be such an event), or to terminate a process that is already running. The receipt of an event could be used to cause an already-running process to transition from one activity to the next. BPM systems also make use of *state machine* programming models, and in a similar fashion the arrival of an event at the consumer can be used to instantiate a new process, or cause a state change within an existing state machine.

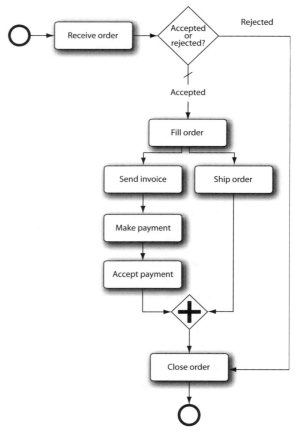

Figure 5.10   A simple business process modeled using BPMN. A process instance is created when a new order is received and proceeds through a sequence of activities.

5.3   *Interfacing with event consumers*

In this section we look at how event consumers attach to the rest of an event processing network. We start by looking, in an abstract way, at the interaction patterns that they use, and then we look at the mechanics of how they connect in practice.

5.3.1   *Interaction patterns*

In chapter 4 we saw that the designer of an event producer has to choose a strategy for when it produces an event. We don't have to worry about such complexities when it comes to event consumers. An event consumer interacts in pretty much the same way as any other node within an EPN. Its input terminals identify, by means of filters, the set of event types and instances that the consumer is prepared to accept.

The complications that occur with event consumers arise from the fact that an event consumer definition element can (and often does) represent a class of multiple concrete consumer instances (we refer to them as *members* of the class). The first complication is that the members of the class may change over time (in other words, the class could be dynamic). This is particularly likely to happen if the consumer provides a visualization interface, as there could be a new concrete consumer each time a new user opens the visualization application. In such cases the system has to provide a dynamic registration interface, allowing concrete consumer instances to be registered or deregistered. We refer to the act of registering a consumer instance as *subscribing*, and the act of deregistering as *unsubscribing*. The entity that submits the subscribe request is called a *subscriber*. In many cases it is the would-be consumer instance that submits the subscribe request (the subscriber and consumer are one and the same), but there are cases where one entity can request a subscription on behalf of another.

The second complication occurs because an event consumer's input terminal applies to all members of the class, and so you would expect that an event that arrives at an input terminal (and meets the requirements of any filters on that terminal) would be delivered to every member of the class. In some cases, however, the event processing application might want to control which members actually get to see the event. A case in point occurs in our Fast Flower Delivery application, where we want Bid Request events to be delivered only to drivers who happen to be in an appropriate geographical location and who meet the flower store's reputation and reliability criteria.

> **NOTE** An individual member of the class is free to ignore the event, and because the behavior of consumer instances is not modeled by the definition element, there's nothing to stop some members from processing it and some from ignoring it.

In some cases it's best to use smaller classes of consumers, or even to avoid using class type consumers, and model each consumer instance as its own separate definition element, but this leads to unnecessarily complex event processing network models as the number of concrete consumer instances grows. Having to revise the model each time a consumer joins or leaves is also a problem.

We can continue to benefit from the advantages of class type consumer definition elements if the events sent to the consumer class contain attributes that identify, directly or indirectly, the members of the class which are to receive the event. When an event object is received by a class type event consumer, it is tested against any filters present on the input terminal (these filters are defined at the class level and so apply across the board to all consumer instances represented by the class). If the event passes them, a copy of it is distributed to the relevant member consumer instances. We see an example of this in section 5.4 when looking at the `Driver` event consumer from the Fast Flower Delivery application.

5.3.2   *Interfacing mechanisms*

The mechanisms that can be used to interface an instance-type event consumer with the rest of the EPN are similar to those used with event producers. An event processing network can support one or more event distribution mechanisms, and these mechanisms can either be protocol based or API based.

In a protocol based mechanism the consumer uses a transport protocol supported by the EPN implementation. This could be a proprietary protocol or a standardized one; it describes how event objects are serialized as well as the protocol used to transfer them between the EPN and consumer implementations. The protocol can support either push-style or pull-style distribution or both (push and pull were discussed in chapter 2). The protocol might also include a way for the consumer to provide a filter expression to exclude certain events; this allows for more efficient implementations than if the filtering is left to the consumers themselves, because it might be possible for a channel implementation in the EPN to combine filters from multiple consumers and thus do filtering earlier on in the distribution process.

In the API approach, the event processing network provides a programming interface for the consumer to use. As is the case with producers, there are two main styles of API. One is the kind of programming interface provided by message-oriented middleware, such as the Java Message Service API, where the consumer receives an explicit event object across the API. With the other style the API provides access to one or more resources and the event processing network communicates with the consumer by making updates to the state held in these resources.

In section 5.3.1 we saw that there can be two complications if the definition element represents a class of consumers:

- There could be a need to be able to register new concrete consumers dynamically.
- There could be a need for logic that inspects the incoming event, identifies the members (consumer instances) that are to receive copies, and then forwards the event to only the relevant members.

Both these capabilities can be implemented by the event processing platform if it provides a mechanism (either protocol based, or API based, or both) by which the concrete consumer instances can be registered as members of the consumer class. As part of this registration process the consumer instance is associated with a filter expression that determines which events it is to receive. For example, if Java Message Service (JMS) is being used, each concrete consumer instance can subscribe itself and register a message selector that picks out only events that are intended for its consumption. In practice things aren't quite as neat as this with JMS, because JMS message selectors cannot operate directly against the message payload, so the attributes needed for the selector have to be set into JMS message properties.

Now let's turn our attention to the Fast Flower Delivery application.

5.4   Consumers in the Fast Flower Delivery example

This section contains a short discussion of the different event consumer definition elements that can be found in our model of the Fast Flower Delivery application.

When modeling a consumer that can process more than one type of event, you can choose how to assign these event types to input terminals. At one extreme you can have a separate input terminal for each event type—at the other extreme you can have a single input terminal for all event types. We have assigned each event type to a separate input terminal, except when there is a connection between the event types in question.

5.4.1   The three event consumers

Our Fast Flower Delivery application contains three event consumer definition elements: Driver, Store, and Drivers' Guild. We show the consumer details and input terminals for each of these in turn.

THE DRIVER EVENT CONSUMER

The Driver definition element represents the class of all drivers and has a definition element type of *consumer class*.

Its event consumer category is *human interaction*, and it has two input terminals as shown in table 5.1.

Table 5.1   The input terminals for the Driver class

Input terminal	Event types	Source
Bids	Bid Request	Bid Request channel
Assignments	Assignment	Assignment channel

Drivers have to handle two different types of events: Bid Request events, issued during the bid phase, and Assignment events, if they are selected during the assignment phase. We have chosen to model this event consumer with two separate input terminals, though we could also have combined both event types on a single input terminal.

Bid Request and Assignment events do not go out to all the drivers represented by the class. Both these event types contain driver attributes which indicate which drivers are to receive the event in question. When a new driver joins the Drivers' Guild, part of the joining process involves registering a new concrete event consumer instance with the system. This instance is registered only to receive event instances that contain the driver's name.

THE STORE EVENT CONSUMER

The Store definition element represents all the florist stores that participate in the program, and so it too has *consumer class* as its definition element type.

Its event consumer category is *human interaction*, and it has two input terminals, as shown in table 5.2.

Table 5.2 The input terminals for the `Store` class

Input terminal	Event types	Source
Bids	Delivery Bid	Assignment request channel
Alerts	No Bidders Alert Manual Assignment Timeout Alert Pickup Alert Delivery Alert	Alerts channel

A store that has elected to do manual assignment will receive `Delivery Bid` requests from drivers bidding for work on its `Bids` input terminal. Stores also receive alert events if something goes wrong in the process, and we have chosen to have all alerts handled by a single input terminal.

THE DRIVERS' GUILD EVENT CONSUMER

The `Drivers' Guild` event consumer feeds evaluation reports to the guild. Its definition element type is *consumer instance*, as there is only one guild.

Its event consumer category is *human interaction*, and it has a single input terminal, as shown in table 5.3.

Table 5.3 The input terminals for the `Drivers' Guild`

Input terminal	Event types	Source
Evaluation	Improvement Note Driver Report	Improving note EPA Consistent strong driver EPA Consistent weak driver EPA Permanent weak driver EPA Idle driver EPA Improving driver EPA

This consumer receives all its input events through this single input terminal.

5.5   Summary

In this chapter we have moved to the other end of the event processing network and looked at the event consumer. We discussed the event consumer definition element, and noted that it can be used to represent an abstract consumer type, a concrete event consumer, or a class of multiple concrete event consumers. Similar to an event producer, the event consumer's internal logic is outside the scope of the EPN and an event consumer node represents the connection to one or more real event consumers from the rest of the EPN. When the consumer definition element does represent more than one real consumer, we may need to use an attribute or attributes in the event object to target an event at a subset of these real consumers. We also discussed a number of different kinds of consumers and looked at interactions between consumers and the rest of the network.

Now that we have looked at producers and consumers, it is time to turn to the EPN itself, and the way that it is used to connect event processing entities to one another.

5.5.1   *Additional reading*

Rasmussen, Nils H., Manish Bansal, and Claire Y. Chen. 2009. *Business Dashboards: A Visual Catalog for Design and Deployment.* Wiley. http://www.amazon.com/Business-Dashboards-Visual-Catalog-Deployment/dp/0470413476/ref=sr_1_2?ie=UTF8&s=books&qid=1258900014&sr=1-2. This book discusses the concept of business dashboards and their implementation.

5.5.2   *Exercises*

5.1   Give an example of when it is useful to have an event consumer definition element representing an abstract type.

5.2   Explain, with examples, how generalization and specialization relationships apply to event consumer definition elements.

5.3   List two ways to avoid using event attributes to route events in the Fast Flowers Delivery application. What are the advantages or disadvantages of these approaches?

5.4   Give an example of an application of the Ambient Orb, and describe the coloring scheme.

5.5   Give an example in which the consumer is a workflow, and events are used to start a new process, stop an existing process, and modify the state of an existing process.

5.6   Give two examples of applications that use dynamic consumer subscriptions, and one where all the consumer instances are statically defined.

5.7   Give an example which involves third-party subscribers, in which a consumer instance is registered by a separate entity.

5.8   Describe the possible security implications of third-party subscriptions. Suggest ways in which they can be mitigated.

The event
processing network
6

If you have built castles in the air, your work need not be lost; that is where they should be. Now put the foundations under them.

—Henry David Thoreau

The event processing network is the central concept in this book, and we start this chapter with a summary of the concept and the notation that we introduced in chapter 2 and then take a more detailed look. The EPN links two fundamental building blocks, the event producers of chapter 4 and the event consumers of chapter 5. It provides a way of modeling the processing that takes place between these producers and consumers. This intermediate processing is represented by three additional building blocks: event processing agents (EPAs), global state elements, and channels.

In this chapter we look at the EPN and these three building blocks. In particular we discuss the following:

- The event processing network itself. We start with a summary of the concept and the notation that we introduced in chapter 2 and then look at further details.
- The concept and anatomy of EPAs, and a discussion of the different types of EPAs. We explore these types in more depth in chapters 8 and 9.
- The concept and functions of an event channel.
- The way that we represent global state in an event processing network.

To help illustrate the main concepts of the chapter and show how they can be put together to model the Fast Flower Delivery application, we list the EPAs, channels, and global state elements used in the application.

6.1   *Event processing networks*

When we introduced EPNs in chapter 2, we showed how an event processing network can be viewed as a collection of *event processing agents, event producers,* and *event consumers* linked by *channels.*

We start with a brief recap of this idea, showing the graphical notation that was introduced in that chapter, and extending it to add elements that represent global state. We then look at how you can nest EPN models inside one another, to simplify complex networks and to allow EPN models to be reused. We conclude this section with a look at how an EPN model relates to the implementation artifacts that you find in an event processing system, and give a summary of the benefits of having an EPN model in the first place.

6.1.1   *Event processing network and its notation*

Figure 6.1 shows our graphical notation and illustrates a number of features of an EPN. We represent a network as a kind of graph and the various processing elements that make up the network (producer, agent, consumer, and channel) are shown as shapes that make up the nodes of this graph. These nodes have input or output terminals, shown as triangles (a triangle pointing into a shape is an input terminal; a triangle pointing outwards is an output terminal).

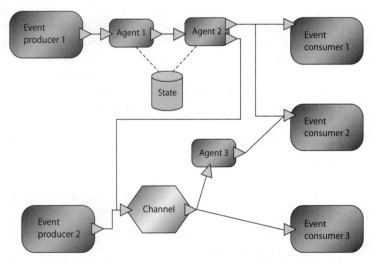

Figure 6.1   An example event processing network, showing the graphical notation we are using, and illustrating some of the features of an EPN

An output terminal can be connected to an input terminal by a solid line. We refer to these lines as *links* or *edges,* and you can see there are several of them in the figure. These links show the flow of event instances through the network.

> **NOTE** The presence of a link indicates that any event object emitted by the output terminal is to be distributed to the corresponding input terminal. If you prefer to think about event distribution in terms of streams, you can picture a stream of events emerging from the output terminal and flowing along the link.

In figure 6.1 two links emerge from one of the output terminals of agent 2. This means that when agent 2 emits an event through this terminal, two copies of the same event instance are distributed. In this case one copy goes to consumer 1 and the other to consumer 2. The notation does not dictate the order in which these two copies are distributed. In some implementations the two copies are distributed concurrently, in others one after the other. In stream terms, the stream that emerges from the output terminal splits into two equal copies, one copy of the stream flowing along each link.

It's also possible to have two links connected to the same input terminal, as shown with the input terminal for consumer 2 in figure 6.1. This means that the input terminal can receive events from either link, and the streams of events coming in along these links are interleaved. The manner in which this interleaving occurs is implementation dependent. To impose a specific order on the interleaved stream you use a Pattern detect event processing agent, or an explicit Compose agent with two separate input terminals. We say more about these agents in chapters 8 and 9.

As you can see from the example in figure 6.2, it's also possible to create event processing networks that contain feedback loops.

In this example agent 2 emits a stream of events which are then fed back into agent 1. What happens in networks like this depends very much on how the agents process their events. You might have a network where agent 1 sends an event to agent 2 but agent 2 sends it back to agent 1 for further processing (clearly you need to be careful to avoid infinite recursion in cases like this). The event sent from agent 2 to agent 1 could be a completely different kind of event. For example, agent 2 might be a Pattern detect agent monitoring the events that are flowing out of agent 1. When it

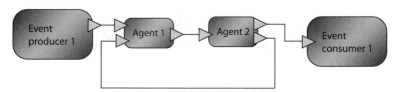

Figure 6.2   An example of feedback in an event processing network. Some of the events emitted by agent 2 are fed back into agent 1.

detects an anomaly in these events it sends a derived event to agent 1 to stop agent 1 from processing any further events.

> **NOTE** A link can be specified between an output terminal and an input terminal either by setting the target attribute of the output terminal equal to the identifier of the input terminal, or by setting the source attribute of the input terminal equal to the identifier of the output terminal.

While it is often convenient to connect producers, consumers, and event processing agents using links, you can also connect them using an explicit channel node. You can see an example of a channel being used at the bottom of figure 6.1. The advantage of representing a channel with a processing element (and thus having it appear as a node in the diagram) is that it lets you specify how you would like the channel to behave, and you can have this specification included as part of the overall EPN model.

An event processing network diagram can contain one further type of node called a *global state element*. These elements, which we discuss further in section 6.4, represent stateful data that can be read by event processing agents when they do their work. Our EPN notation includes additional edges to record the relationship between global state elements and the EPAs that use them. These edges differ from the edges we have discussed so far, in that they represent the transfer of data from a global state element, rather than the transfer of events between elements, so we show them using dashed rather than solid lines. You can see examples at the top of figure 6.1 where agent 1 and agent 2 both use the global state element called State.

6.1.2 *Nested event processing networks*

The graphical representation of a large EPN can be somewhat unwieldy, but this can be simplified by nesting one EPN inside another. This also means you can use a hierarchical approach[1] to designing and maintaining an EPN.

The nesting process works like this: an event processing agent node in the diagram can represent a nested event processing network instead of representing a single agent. The input and output terminals of the event processing agent correspond to producers and consumers of the EPN that it contains. Figure 6.3 shows an example of this. This process could continue again, and some of the EPAs in the nested network could themselves contain further sub-nested networks.

The diagram at the top of figure 6.3 shows part of the unexpanded network consisting of four nodes: A1 through A4 and the links between them. At the bottom of the figure we see the expanded network diagram; agent A2 is expanded to an EPN that contains three event processing agents—A21, A22, and A23. Similarly A3 is expanded to an event processing network that contains agents A31, A32, and A33. You will see that the input terminals of A2 correspond to producers P21 and P22 in the leftmost nested EPN, and the output terminals of A2 correspond to consumers C21, C22, and C23.

---

[1] A hierarchical approach to the design of software is quite common. See HIPO (Hierarchical Input Process Output methodology); William S. Davis and David C. Yen, *The Information System Consultant's Handbook*, CRC Press, 1998. http://www.hit.ac.il/staff/leonidM/information-systems/ch64.html.

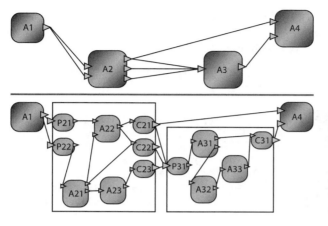

Figure 6.3   An example showing nested event processing networks. The upper part of the figure shows an EPN with four nodes. Two of these (A2 and A3) are agents that contain nested EPNs. The lower half of the figure shows the full network with these nodes expanded to reveal the agents inside them.

6.1.3   Implementation perspective

Our event processing modeling language gives us a way to represent the behavior of an event processing application (or an event processing system comprising several such applications). A model in this language, represented by an EPN diagram, is made up of a number of platform-independent definition elements, each of which describes a piece of event processing functionality in an abstract manner. If you look at the implementations of the Fast Flower Delivery application on the *Event Processing in Action* website, you'll see they realize these definition elements as concrete software or hardware runtime artifacts in different ways. We use the term *runtime artifact* to mean a software module which can be an event processing engine, an instance of such an engine that deals with a specific function, or a special piece of code that implements a specific function.

The event processing network model is therefore an abstraction that describes the functional behavior of the event processing system, without necessarily representing the physical realization of this functionality. This means that the EPN diagram can be set out in a way that expresses this behavior as clearly as possible.

When implementing or managing an event processing application you have to deal with the implementation or runtime artifacts that are supported by your event processing platform and language. Although there is a relationship between these artifacts and the platform-independent definition elements in the EPN model, it is usually not a one-one correspondence. There are many different ways in which you can realize the elements from the model as runtime artifacts, and we show some of these approaches in figure 6.4.

At the top left of figure 6.4 we can see an EPN, made up of a number of event processing agents performing different functions. As we saw in chapter 2, some of these EPAs could be stateful, for example, one might be an Aggregate agent that is computing a running total of the money spent. If we want to keep separate totals for the money spent by each customer, we need to have separate *instances* of that agent, one for each customer, running in our system. It is inconvenient to have to represent every

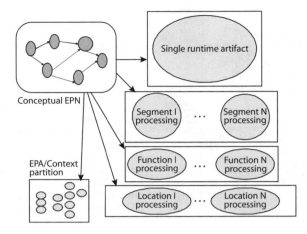

Figure 6.4   How an event processing network model (shown at top left) can be mapped to the runtime artifacts that implement it in an event processing platform

event processing agent instance in the event processing model (in the same way that it can be impractical to represent every event consumer instance).

NOTE   There can be many event processing agent instances corresponding to a single event processing agent definition element in the model. Moreover, it's quite common for these instances to be created and destroyed during the lifetime of an event processing application, and for there to be more than one of these instances active at any given time.

Figure 6.4 shows ways in which these instances can be implemented in a runtime system:

- The entire event processing network could be rendered into a single centralized runtime artifact; this single runtime artifact contains the functionality of all the event processing agent instances and routes all events between them. Many of the existing event processing products started in this manner, and some still only offer a centralized implementation like this.
- The other extreme is one where a separate runtime artifact for each event processing agent instance and a messaging system is used to distribute events between them. This is shown at the bottom left of figure 6.4. It provides maximum modularity as each artifact can be placed on a different server, allowing much of the event processing agent work to be performed in parallel.

Between these two extremes there are several other ways in which you could assign event processing agent instances to runtime artifacts, and they are shown at the bottom right of figure 6.4:

- You could assign agent instances to artifacts using a segmentation context (see chapter 7). For example, all processing of platinum customers is performed by one runtime artifact, and all processing of gold customers is done by another runtime artifact, and so on.
- You could assign instances based on function. For example, in the Fast Flower Delivery application you could have all the processing related to `Bid Request`

and `Assignment` events performed by one runtime artifact, all timeout handling by another runtime artifact, and all rankings done by a third runtime artifact.

- You could assign instances by geographical location, for example, having a dedicated runtime artifact for each store in the Fast Flower Delivery application.

By now you should have a good idea of what an event processing network model is; we conclude this section with a short discussion of why one is useful.

6.1.4 Benefits of an event processing network model

Some event processing systems do not present their users with an EPN concept. An application designer using one of these systems defines various functions, and the relationships between them are inferred by the system and are not made visible. However, our experience shows that there are benefits from making EPNs explicit and visible to the designers, developers, and even end users. The following benefits can be gained by using a model like the one we have described:

- People tend to place more trust in systems in which the flow is explicit. Even if the flow does not have to be defined explicitly, it should be visible, and updatable. This view is based on experience and user feedback.

- If you have an explicit representation of an EPN, you can validate the network using static and dynamic analysis techniques to detect possible problems such as termination, inaccessible nodes, nondeterministic behavior, and contradictions. You can also make other observations about the behavior of the application. We return to the subject of validation in chapter 10.

- An explicit representation of an EPN can be used to perform performance optimization. For example, you can select a good mapping of event processing agent instances to runtime artifacts, or find a good distribution of those artifacts among threads and servers.

Now we move from a general discussion of the event processing network to various components of the network, starting with EPAs.

6.2 Event processing agents

The event processing agent is one of the seven event processing building blocks. It plays a major part in the EPN model and, as we explained in the previous section, event processing agent instances can be mapped in different ways to runtime artifacts. We enumerate below several types of EPAs, but first we look at the logical structure of an agent and the kinds of functions that an agent can include.

6.2.1 Functions of an event processing agent

Figure 6.5 shows the stylized anatomy of an event processing agent with its three logical functions:

- *Filtering*—Selecting which of the input events participate in the processing. Filtering can be performed in several logical places inside an event processing agent and is discussed further in chapter 8.

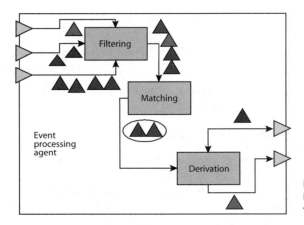

Figure 6.5 An example showing the internals of an event processing agent that contains all three logical functions

- *Matching*—Finding patterns among events and creating sets of events that satisfy the same pattern, as discussed in chapter 9.
- *Derivation*—Using the output from the matching step to derive new events and setting their content, as discussed in chapter 8.

Figure 6.5 illustrates the logic and internal flow of one particular agent. In this example there are three input terminals, which are the entry points to the agent. Event instances flow into the agent through these terminals. As we saw in chapter 2, each terminal can have a filter condition associated with it that selects event instances based on their type and/or based on the values of the various attributes of the event. An event processing agent can also be associated with a context and, if this is the case, filtering associated with this context is also performed at this stage (we discuss contexts further in chapter 7). The filtering step takes each incoming event as an input, and applies the filter conditions. In general it eliminates any event instance that does not meet these conditions. In the next section we see that sometimes we are also interested in processing events that are filtered out.

The matching step takes all events that have been left by the filtering step, and looks for matches between them, using an event processing pattern or some other kind of matching criterion. It creates matching sets, each of which contains a collection of event instances that satisfy the criterion. In the example in figure 6.5 the single matching set contains two events of different types.

The derivation step takes the matching set as an input and derives new events, applying derivation formulae to the events in the matching sets. Many EPA types omit one or more of these steps, for example, a *Transformation* EPA contains only filtering and derivation. Events inside a Transformation agent flow directly from the filtering step to the derivation step without matching in between.

We now turn from the internal structure of event processing agents to look at their behavior as seen from the outside. We examine specific types of event processing agents, including the Transformation agent that we just mentioned.

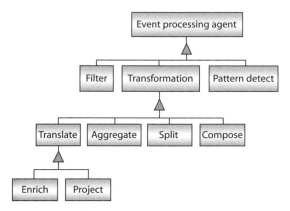

**Figure 6.6   Event processing agent types.
This diagram shows an inheritance
hierarchy, for example, Enrich and Project
are special cases of Translate, which in
turn is a special case of Transformation.**

6.2.2   Types of event processing agents

Of the many different types of EPAs, we give in this section a set of types which are sufficient to express the functionality most commonly found in today's event processing
applications. This isn't a minimal set, as there is some overlap between them (you may
notice that we have an explicit Filter agent, but we said earlier that all agents can perform filtering). Our objective is to provide a useful set that lets you describe the
behavior of an application in a clear and natural fashion. In some applications you
might need to extend this set with some additional EPA types, for example, agents that
use advanced analytic techniques to filter events, or that use machine learning techniques to classify events; however, in this book we discuss only the EPA types illustrated
in figure 6.6 (which you may have seen earlier as figure 2.12).

Figure 6.6 shows the event processing agent types grouped in an inheritance hierarchy. Two of them, the Transformation type and the root Event processing agent
type, are abstract, that is to say they don't appear directly in our models. We include
them in this figure to show that the types that appear under them have something in
common. In the sections that follow we include some formal definitions of these event
processing agent types, to supplement the informal descriptions from chapter 2.

6.2.3   Filter event processing agent

Event processing applications sometimes involve event producers which generate a
large volume of events, not all of which are of interest to the application. A *Filter* EPA
can be used to reduce this volume by excluding unwanted event instances. Although
any EPA can perform filtering, because each input terminal can have an associated filter expression, it's helpful to have an EPA that focuses solely on filtering.

> **FILTER**   A *Filter* agent is an EPA that performs filtering only and has no match-
> ing or derivation steps, so it does not transform the input event.

A Filter agent, shown in figure 6.7, has one Input terminal and three output terminals, which we discuss shortly. It also has a filter expression which determines which

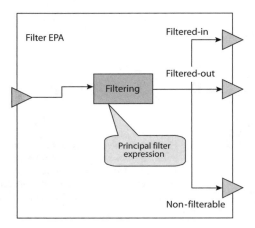

Figure 6.7   The Filter EPA showing the Input terminal and three output terminals

event instances are to be *filtered in* (selected) by the agent and which are to be *filtered out*. A Filter agent may be intended to handle multiple different event types, in which case the filter expression should be well-defined for each of these event types. For example, an expression that filters events depending solely on the value of an attribute called `Driver` will work as intended against any event type that contains a `Driver` attribute. We go into more details on filter expressions in chapter 8.

There are three possible output terminals, although of course when constructing an event processing network you do not need to have edges connected to all three. These output terminals are

- *Filtered-in*—Any input event that satisfies the filtering expression flows out through this terminal.
- *Filtered-out*—Any input event for which the expression can be evaluated, but which does not satisfy the filtering expression flows out through this terminal.
- *Non-filterable*—Any input event for which the expression cannot be evaluated flows out through this terminal. Note that the definition of a nonfilterable event depends on the language used for the filter expression. Some languages, for example, XPath, are reasonably tolerant and will generally attempt to filter events either in or out.

The Filtered-out terminal is a special feature of this agent. You can connect the Filtered-in and Filtered-out terminals to different targets to arrange for an event instance that doesn't satisfy the filter expression to be processed differently from one that does.

As you can see from its definition, a *Filter* agent transfers an event from its Input terminal to one of the output terminals and does not make any transformation of its content. We now look at EPAs that specifically focus on transforming events into new derived events.

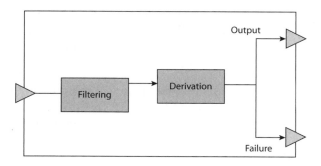

Figure 6.8   The Transformation EPA

6.2.4 *Transformation event processing agents*

Transformation EPAs take input events and create output events that are functions of these input events, as shown in figure 6.8.

> **TRANSFORMATION** A *Transformation* EPA is an EPA that includes a derivation step, and optionally also a filtering step.

Transformation EPAs can be stateless, processing each event instance individually, or stateful, in which case the way a particular event instance is processed can depend on other instances that have been processed by the agent. Figure 6.9 shows the several different types of Transformation EPAs.

Transformation EPAs differ in the kind of transformation they perform, for example, some are stateful and others stateless. They also differ depending on whether they take a single input stream or multiple input streams, and whether they emit a single output stream or multiple output streams. We discuss each type in turn starting with the simplest, the *Translate* EPA.

> **TRANSLATE** A *Translate* EPA is a stateless Transformation EPA that takes a single event as its input, and generates a single derived event which is a function of the input event, using a derivation formula.

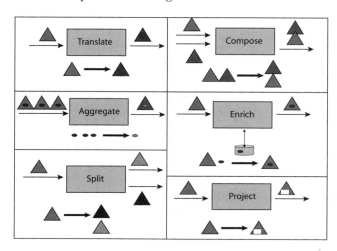

Figure 6.9   Six subtypes of the Transformation EPAs, showing the inputs, outputs, and transformation type

The Translate EPA can be used to convert events from one type to another, or to add, remove, or modify the values of an event's attributes. For example, a Translate agent might use an XSLT program to convert an event instance from one XML format to another. *Enrich* and *Project* are special cases of the Translate EPA type.

ENRICH   An *Enrich* EPA is a Translate EPA that takes a single input event, uses it to query data from a global state element, and creates a derived event which includes the attributes from the original event, possibly with modified values, and can include additional attributes. The new and changed values are calculated using the results from the global state query.

Enrich agents can be used to add information to an event (for example, an event containing a customer number can be enriched with the customer's name and address) or to correct information in an event (data cleansing).

PROJECT   A *Project* EPA is a Translate EPA that takes an input event, and creates a single derived event containing a subset of the attributes of the input event.

A Project EPA is similar to the project operator in relational algebra; it selects a subset of the attributes of a single event.

Now we look at our first stateful transformation agent, the *Aggregate* EPA.

AGGREGATE   An *Aggregate* EPA is a Transformation EPA that takes as input a collection of events and creates a single derived event by applying a function over the input events.

The input of the Aggregate EPA is a collection of events and the output is a single derived event. The illustration in figure 6.9 shows an aggregation over a single attribute, but the aggregate operation may involve multiple attributes. Note that the input events may be processed together as a set after they have all arrived, or processed one by one so that the aggregation is computed incrementally. Examples of aggregation functions are sum, average, maximum, and minimum; there are, of course, many more aggregation functions.

Next we define the *Split* EPA.

SPLIT   A *Split* EPA is a Transformation EPA that takes as an input a single event and creates a collection of events. Each of them can be a clone of the original event, or a projection of that event containing a subset of its attributes.

The Split EPA creates multiple derived events as a result of processing a single input event instance. A Split agent can be used to send different portions of the input event to different targets.

COMPOSE   A *Compose* EPA is a Transformation EPA that takes groups of events from two input terminals, looks for matches using a matching criterion, and creates derived events based on these matched events.

The Compose EPA creates a set of derived events; each of them is a function of a collection of events taken from both input terminals. This is similar to the join operator in relational algebra.

It's possible to concatenate a number of these Transformation EPAs to produce a more complex transformation. These Transformation EPAs could be combined to form a composite agent using the nesting approach described in section 6.1.2. Here are some examples:

- An event e1 is input to an Enrich agent which derives the event e2. This is, in turn input to a Split agent that creates the events e3, e4, and e5.
- The events e1, e2, e3 are aggregated by an Aggregate agent which produces the derived event e4. This is enriched by an Enrich agent to create the derived event e5.

The last of our event processing agents is the Pattern detect agent. We are going to devote the whole of chapter 9 to this agent, so we introduce it briefly here.

6.2.5 *Pattern detect event processing agent*

A Pattern detect agent uses all the different steps described in section 6.2.1. It examines a stream of incoming event instances looking for occurrences of a specific pattern in that stream.

> **PATTERN DETECT** A *Pattern detect* EPA is an EPA that performs a pattern matching function on one or more input streams. It emits one or more derived events if it detects an occurrence of the specified pattern in the input events.

The notion of pattern is defined and discussed in length in chapter 9. A Pattern detect EPA can have one or more input terminals and examines collections of multiple events received from these terminals. These events can be of more than one event type. As with all EPAs, each input terminal may specify a filter condition. The result of a pattern matching is a matching set that contains all the events that meet the pattern. This matching set can serve as an input to a derivation step that transforms the events in the matching set into one or more output events. If no derivation is specified, the events that are in the matching set flow out unchanged through the Output terminal. The Fast Flower Delivery application uses a simple Pattern detect agent to raise an alert event if a driver has not met the committed pickup time.

We conclude this section by describing the definition elements that we use to represent EPAs.

6.2.6 *Event processing agent definition element*

Now that we've discussed a number of different types of EPAs, it's time to see how to represent them in our event processing network model. The *event processing agent* is one of the seven fundamental building blocks, and each event processing agent in an EPN is represented by an EPA definition element (though, as we see in chapter 7, there can

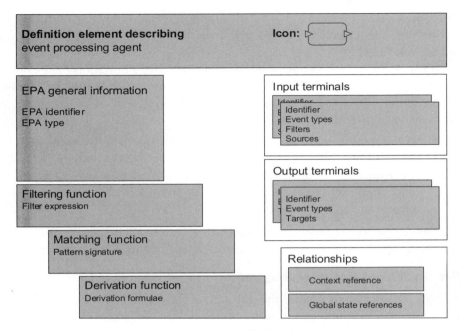

Figure 6.10   Generic event processing agent definition element

be many event processing agent instances corresponding to each definition element). The information contained in these definition elements varies a little depending on the agent's type, but they all have a shape similar to that shown in figure 6.10.

Regardless of what type it is, every event processing agent definition element contains a *general information* section. This section contains the following:

- *Event processing agent identifier*—The name of the agent described by the definition element. It can be used to uniquely identify this EPA definition.
- *Event processing agent type*—The type attribute describes the function performed by the agent, and determines the shape of the rest of the definition element (for example, some types have a fixed number of input and output terminals). The value of this attribute can be one of the nonabstract types from figure 6.6, such as Split or Translate, or it can be the special value *Event Processing Network* indicating that the event processing agent is in fact a nested EPN as described in 6.1.2.

The definition element contains details of the agent's *input terminals* and *output terminals*. These are specified in the same way as they are for event producers (see section 4.1.3) and event consumers (section 5.1.3).

Some event processing agents, in particular Enrich agents, read data from global state elements. The definition element for such an agent contains references to the global state elements that it uses (shown at the bottom left of figure 6.10). You may recall that we show these references as dashed lines in EPN diagrams. The definition element can also have a reference to a context element. We discuss event processing contexts in chapter 7.

The definition element also contains parameters that control the function performed by the agent. The set of parameters varies depending on the particular agent type, but they fall into three categories, filtering, matching, and derivation, these being the three main internal functions of an event processing agent. We go into detail on filter expressions and derivation formulae in chapter 8, and we define pattern signatures in chapter 9.

6.2.7 *Event processing agents in the Fast Flower Delivery application*

We now illustrate some of these types of EPAs by looking at the Fast Flower Delivery application. We won't go into all their details here, as we do this in chapters 8 and 9. You'll recall from figure 1.6 that the application is made up of a number of individual systems, and we describe the agents system by system, starting with table 6.1, which lists the agents in the bid request system.

Table 6.1   Event processing agents in the bid request system

Identifier	EPA type	Input event type	Output event type	References
Request enrichment	Enrich	Delivery Request	Delivery Request	Store reference
Bid Request creator	Enrich	Delivery Request	Bid Request	Driver status

These two EPAs are connected to each other, as shown in figure 6.11.

The `Request enrichment` agent takes a `Delivery Request` event, submitted by a flower store's `Store` producer, and queries the store's preferences (held in the `Store reference` global state element) to find the minimum ranking that the store is prepared to accept. This is added to the event instance, which is forwarded to the `Bid Request creator` agent. This is another Enrich agent. It queries the `Drivers` global state element, finds out which drivers are in the neighborhood and meet the minimum ranking requirement (this is the attribute supplied by the `Request enrichment` agent) and creates a `Bid Request` event. This contains details from the original `Delivery Request` along with the IDs of the chosen drivers. It sends this event, through the `Bid Request` channel, to the `Driver` consumer which distributes it to the drivers registered with those IDs.

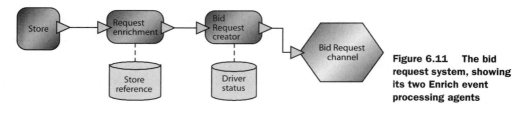

Figure 6.11   The bid request system, showing its two Enrich event processing agents

In order to know which drivers are in the right neighborhood, the application needs to know where the drivers are at any point in time. The drivers are tracked by the location service, which includes a single event processing agent, shown in table 6.2.

Table 6.2   Event processing agents in the location service

EPA identifier	EPA type	Input event type	Output event type	References
Location service	Translate	GPS Location	Driver Location	Neighborhoods

This is a Translate EPA whose job is to compare the raw latitude/longitude readings that come from a vehicle's GPS device against a map of the city to determine what part of the city the driver is currently in. It is shown in figure 6.12.

Figure 6.12   Location service event processing agent

This agent inserts the name of the neighborhood into the output event, which is used to update the `Driver status` global state element.

The core of the application is the assignment system, which takes each `Bid Request` from the bid request system and matches it against the `Delivery Bid` events that come back from the drivers. The system either selects a driver itself, or gets the flower store to select one. Table 6.3 lists the assignment system's event processing agents.

Table 6.3   Event processing agents in the assignment system

EPA identifier	EPA type	Input event types	Output event types	References
Driver enrichment	Enrich	Delivery Bid	Delivery Bid	Driver status
Assignment manager	Compose	Delivery Bid, Bid Request	Delivery Bid, No Bidders Alert	
Bid enrichment	Enrich	Delivery Bid	Delivery Bid	Store reference
Bid routing	Filter	Delivery Bid	Delivery Bid	
Manual assignment preparation	Pattern detect	Delivery Bid, Bid Request	Delivery Bid	
Automatic assignment	Pattern detect	Delivery Bid	Assignment	

Figure 6.13 shows how these agents are connected.

The `Assignment manager` is a Compose agent. It takes `Bid Request` events from the bid request system, and also receives `Delivery Bid` events from the drivers (after these have been enriched with driver rankings by the `Driver enrichment` agent). It

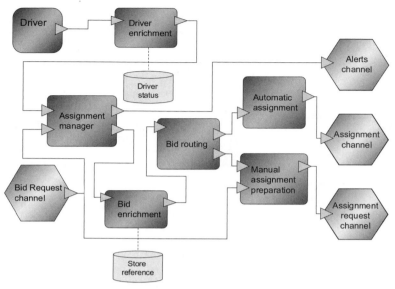

Figure 6.13 Event processing agents that make up the assignment system

checks that the committed pickup times in these bids match the pickup times from the corresponding Bid Requests. If it doesn't find any acceptable bids in the 2-minute period, it generates a No Bidders Alert. If it does find bids, it forwards the Delivery Bid events to the Bid enrichment agent. This takes each event and looks up the flower store's preference, adding an attribute to the event to indicate whether the store wishes to assign the driver itself or not, before passing it to the Bid routing agent. This is a Filter agent that routes the event either to the Manual assignment preparation agent or to the Automatic assignment agent, depending on the value of this attribute. The Manual assignment preparation agent accumulates the Delivery Bid events from the top five ranked drivers and forwards them to the Store consumer, through the Assignment request channel. The Automatic assignment agent picks the first Bid Request that it encounters and converts it into an Assignment event. It is then forwarded, through the Assignment channel, to the driver and other interested parties.

The control system is responsible for checking that drivers and stores are using the application correctly. It has three Pattern detect agents, listed in table 6.4

Table 6.4 Event processing agents in the control system

EPA identifier	EPA type	Input event types	Output event types
Assignment not done	Pattern detect	Delivery Bid, Manual Assignment	Manual Assignment Timeout Alert
Pickup alert	Pattern detect	Pickup Confirmation, Assignment	Pickup Alert
Delivery alert	Pattern detect	Delivery Confirmation, Assignment	Delivery Alert

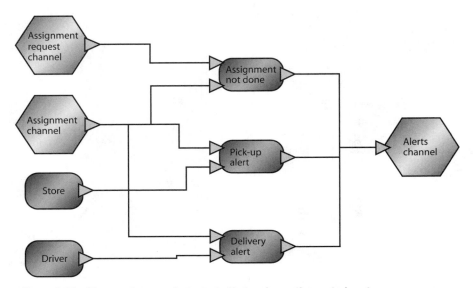

Figure 6.14   The event processing agents that make up the control system

These agents take `Assignment` events from the `Assignment` channel, `Pickup Confirmation` events from the stores, and `Delivery Confirmation` events from the drivers, as shown in figure 6.14.

The `Assignment not done` agent monitors stores to make sure that they are performing manual assignments on time when they are sent `Delivery Bids`. The `Pickup alert` and `Delivery alert` agents monitor the delivery after it has been assigned. They raise alert events if the driver does not pick up the flowers or deliver them by the times stated in the `Assignment` event.

The ranking and reporting system contains a number of event processing agents, shown in table 6.5, that assess driver performance.

Table 6.5   Event processing agents in the ranking and reporting system

EPA identifier	EPA type	Input event types	Output event types
Ranking increase	Pattern detect	Delivery Alert	Ranking Increase
Ranking decrease	Pattern detect	Delivery Alert	Ranking Decrease
Improving note	Pattern detect	Ranking Increase, Ranking Decrease	Improvement Note
Daily assignments calculator	Aggregate	Assignment, Delivery Bid	Daily Assignments
Daily statistics creator	Aggregate	Daily Assignments	Daily Statistics
Performance evaluation	Compose	Daily Assignments, Daily Statistics	Relative Performance

Table 6.5 Event processing agents in the ranking and reporting system *(continued)*

EPA identifier	EPA type	Input event types	Output event types
Permanent weak driver	Pattern detect	Daily Assignments	Driver Report
Idle driver	Pattern detect	Daily Assignments	Driver Report
Consistent strong driver	Pattern detect	Relative Performance	Driver Report
Consistent weak driver	Pattern detect	Relative Performance	Driver Report
Improving driver	Pattern detect	Daily Assignments	Driver Report

We discuss these agents in more detail in chapters 8 and 9, but figure 6.15 shows how they fit together.

The agents at the top of this diagram perform the Fast Flower Delivery phase 4 ranking evaluations, which are conducted every 20 deliveries; the others do the phase 5 activity monitoring, which generates reports once per month.

Event processing agents play a critical role in an event processing network, as they perform the intermediary processing that takes place in the application. However we can't finish our discussion of EPNs without mentioning the two other building blocks that they can contain. These are *event channels*, which route events between EPAs, and *global state elements*, which support the EPAs by providing shared state data for them to use.

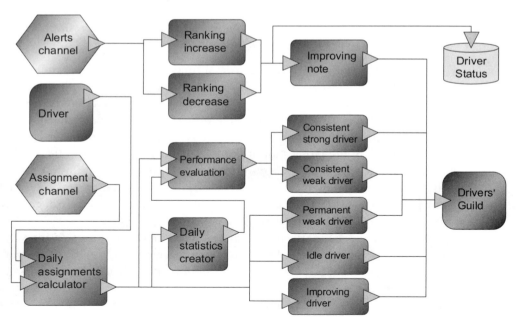

Figure 6.15 The event processing agents in the ranking and reporting system

6.3   Event channels

In chapter 2 we explained the rationale for using event channels as intermediaries between EPAs. We noted that there are advantages in representing channels as explicit nodes in the EPN, both because this adds clarity in cases where there are many processing elements to be connected, and also because a channel provides a way to specify routing behavior explicitly.

> **NOTE**   Some implementations employ a single channel to perform all the routing between event processing agents; such a channel is called an *event bus*.

We start this section by defining the concept of the event channel and then discuss routing schemes.

6.3.1   Event channel notion

An event channel routes event instances from one processing element to another in the EPN. (We refer to agents, producers, and consumers as *processing elements*.) As with the other building blocks, a channel can be implemented as a runtime artifact in various ways. For example, it could be implemented as a queue, a function call, or a publish-subscribe topic. The best choice for an implementation depends on the function required of the channel, the environment in which it runs, and the nature of the processing elements to which it is connected.

> **EVENT CHANNEL**   An *event channel* is a processing element that receives events from one or more source processing elements, makes routing decisions, and sends the input events unchanged to one or more target processing elements in accordance with these routing decisions.

The simplest channels accept events from a single source and route them all to a single target. We don't require simple channels like this to have an explicit definition element or to appear as explicit nodes in the conceptual EPN diagram. If all you want to do is to route events from a source element to a target element, you can just link the two by setting the target attribute of the source's output terminal or by setting the source attribute of the target's input terminal. This defines a link in the model, and is shown as an edge in the EPN diagram (there is still, of course, a runtime channel artifact; it's just that it doesn't appear as an explicit node in the diagram). This makes the event processing network presentation simpler and less crowded. You can see these implicit channels in use in figures 6.11 to 6.15.

More complex channels, such as channels that make routing decisions, appear as nodes in the EPN diagram, and so we have a building block in our EPN modeling language that is used to define event channel definition elements. An event channel definition element has one or more input terminals, and these receive events through a link (an edge in the EPN diagram) just like the input terminals on an event processing agent or an event consumer. A link to a channel is usually created by setting the target attribute of the source's output terminal to point at the channel's input terminal.

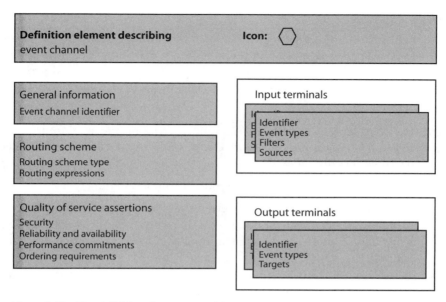

Figure 6.16   The definition element describing an event channel

An explicit event channel can have multiple output terminals. The channel takes the events it receives on its input terminals and forwards them through its output terminals. The choice of which output terminal or terminals to use depends on the channel's *routing scheme*. With some routing schemes, it is possible for an event instance received on an input terminal to be forwarded through multiple output terminals. If this happens, each event instance that is forwarded is a logical copy of the original event; in other words, each event object is independent of all the others. The event processing network model makes no assertions about the order in which these events are emitted by a runtime channel implementation.

In figure 6.16 we show the contents of an event channel definition element. The different parts of this definition element are as follows:

- *Event channel identifier*—The name of the channel described by the definition element. It can be used to refer to this definition element from elsewhere.
- *Terminals*—Input and output terminals are defined in the same way as they are in event processing agents, event producers, and event consumers.
- *Routing scheme*—This specifies the type of information used when making routing decisions. This is further discussed in section 6.3.2.
- *Quality of service assertions*—These specify non-functional characteristics that the channel is required to exhibit. They can come from several domains, for example, security requirements, performance objectives, reliability and availability requirements, and constraints on event ordering.

We discuss non-functional characteristics further in part 3 of this book.

6.3.2   *Routing schemes*

As we mentioned earlier, one of the reasons for having an explicitly modeled event channel is that it gives us a place in the model to specify how events are to be distributed. One aspect of this is the routing scheme that determines which processing element or set of processing elements is to receive any particular event instance handled by the channel.

> **ROUTING SCHEME**   A *routing scheme* denotes the type of information used by a channel to make a routing decision. The possible routing schemes are fixed, type-based, and content-based.

Here is a short description of each of these routing schemes:

- *Fixed*—The channel routes every event that it receives on any input terminal to every output terminal. In cases where there are multiple output terminals this means that separate copies of each input event are transmitted on each output terminal.
- *Type-based*—The channel makes routing decisions based on the event type of the event that is being routed.
- *Content-based*—The routing decision is based on the event's content. This can be phrased as decision trees or decision tables, and is based on the input event content, and possibly also on context information.

A routing scheme may be composed from multiple routing schemes, which means that an event is only routed to an output terminal if it would have been routed to it by all of these routing schemes. An example is a routing scheme that is composed from a type-based scheme and a content-based scheme.

6.3.3   *Channels in the Fast Flower Delivery application*

Table 6.6 shows the simple channels used in the Fast Flower Delivery application. These appear as edges in the event processing network diagram.

Table 6.6   Implicit channels in the Fast Flower Delivery application

Input terminal sources	Output terminal targets	Event types
Store	Request enrichment EPA	Delivery Request
Request enrichment EPA	Bid Request creator EPA	Delivery Request
Vehicle	Location service EPA	GPS Location
Location service EPA	Driver status global state element	Driver Location
Driver	Driver enrichment EPA	Delivery Bid
Driver enrichment EPA	Assignment manager EPA	Delivery Bid
Assignment manager EPA	Bid enrichment EPA	Delivery Bid
Bid enrichment EPA	Bid routing EPA	Delivery Bid

Table 6.6   Implicit channels in the Fast Flower Delivery application *(continued)*

Input terminal sources	Output terminal targets	Event types
Bid routing EPA	Automatic assignment EPA	Delivery Bid
Bid routing EPA	Manual assignment preparation EPA	Delivery Bid
Store	Pickup alert EPA	Pickup Confirmation
Driver	Delivery alert EPA	Delivery Confirmation
Driver	Daily assignments calculator EPA	Delivery Bid
Ranking increase EPA	Improving note EPA, Driver status global state element	Ranking Increase
Ranking decrease EPA	Improving note EPA, Driver status global state element	Ranking Decrease
Improving note EPA	Drivers' Guild	Improvement Note
Consistent strong driver EPA, Consistent weak driver EPA, Permanent weak driver EPA, Idle driver EPA, Improving driver EPA	Drivers' Guild	Driver Report
Daily assignments calculator EPA	Daily statistics creator EPA, Permanent weak driver EPA, Idle driver EPA, Improving driver EPA	Daily Assignment
Daily statistics creator EPA	Performance evaluation EPA	Daily Statistics
Performance evaluation EPA	Consistent strong driver EPA, Consistent weak driver EPA	Relative Performance

This table shows the types of events that flow across each channel, and the names of the processing elements attached to the channel.

Table 6.7 shows the explicit channels that are used in the application. We have chosen to use explicit channels to link the various systems illustrated in figures 6.11 to 6.15.

Table 6.7   Explicit channels in the Fast Flower Delivery application

Channel identifier	Routing scheme	Event type	Input terminal sources	Output terminal targets
Bid Request channel	Fixed	Bid Request	Bid Request creator EPA	Driver, Assignment manager EPA, Manual assignment preparation EPA
Alerts channel	Fixed	All Alert types	Assignment manager EPA, Assignment not done EPA, Pickup alert EPA, Delivery alert EPA	Ranking increase EPA, Ranking decrease EPA

Table 6.7   Explicit channels in the Fast Flower Delivery application *(continued)*

Channel identifier	Routing scheme	Event type	Input terminal sources	Output terminal targets
Assignment channel	Fixed	Assignment	Store, Automatic assignment EPA	Driver, Assignment not done EPA, Pickup alert EPA, Delivery alert EPA, Daily Assignments calculator EPA
Assignment request channel	Fixed	Delivery Bid	Manual assignment preparation EPA	Store, Assignment not done EPA
Delivery cancellation channel	Fixed	Delivery Request Cancellation	Store	Cancellation EPA *(not described in this book)*

We conclude this chapter with a discussion of the sixth of the seven building blocks: the global state element. This is the last of the building blocks that can appear as a node in the event processing network diagram.

6.4   *Global state elements*

We have already encountered several cases where event processing logic needs access to more information than that which it can obtain from a single event. Some event processing agents maintain their own local state allowing them to carry information over from one event to the next. However, there are cases where an agent needs access to data that is external to the event processing application, or where two EPAs need to have access to the same stateful data. We refer to this shared stateful data as the *global state* of the EPN. This global state can take a number of forms:

- Historical events retained in an event store so that they can be processed at a later phase.
- Reference data that event processing agents can access, for example, to enrich or cleanse event data. Reference data is not maintained by the event processing system, but can affect the output of the event processing.
- State of external entities that, like reference data, is not maintained by the event processing system but which can be used as part of processing events. Examples include the following: current state of a business process, an airport alert level, and weather-related states (sun, clouds, rain, and snow). This state could change as a result of a (raw or derived) event being processed by an event consumer.
- Event processing state (whether persisted to disk or held in shared memory) that is accessible across event processing agents, and can be updated by an event processing application. This is typically maintained by the event processing platform.

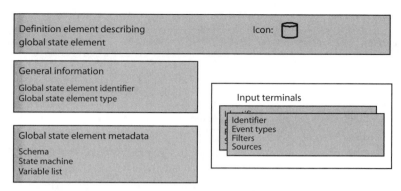

Figure 6.17   The definition element describing a global state element

Global state is one of the seven building blocks, and as such is defined using definition elements. Figure 6.17 shows what the definition element for a global state element looks like.

The *general information* section contains the following:

- *Global state element identifier*—The name of the state entity described by the definition element. It can be used to refer to this definition element from elsewhere.
- *Global state element type*—This indicates the type of the item. It can take one of the following values: event store, reference data, external state or event processing state, as explained previously.

Two of the global state types (event store and event processing state) can accept updates directly from an event processing application. These global state elements can have input terminals, defined like the input terminals for an event consumer. An event store global state element takes an incoming event and adds it to the store; an event processing state element uses the values of the incoming event's attributes to update its state.

The *metadata* section describes how the state data is organized. If the state is held as a relational table, the metadata includes the database schema. If it is an external state machine, the metadata contains an enumeration of its possible states. If the state is held as a hash table, the metadata describes the constraints there may be on the hash keys and values.

Table 6.8 shows the global states that are used in the Fast Flower Delivery example.

Table 6.8   Global state elements in the Fast Flower Delivery application

Element identifier	Element type	Metadata	Input event type
Neighborhoods	Reference data	Geospatial database schema	
Driver status	Event processing state	Driver ID, Driver ranking, Current neighborhood	Ranking Increase Ranking Decrease Driver Location

Table 6.8   Global state elements in the Fast Flower Delivery application *(continued)*

Element identifier	Element type	Metadata	Input event type
Store reference	Reference data	Store name, Minimum ranking, Store location, Store region, Automatic assignment flag	

The application has three global state elements. Neighborhoods is a geospatial reference database that divides the city into regions. It is used by the location service when converting GPS latitude and longitude coordinates into a neighborhood identifier. Driver status is a shared table that keeps each driver's current ranking and last-known neighborhood. It can be updated by sending appropriate events to its Input terminal (see figures 6.12 and 6.15). Store reference contains reference data relating to a store. This reference data comprises five attributes: the store's name, its location in address form, the region of the city in which it is located (this is represented as a neighborhood identifier), the minimum driver ranking it is prepared to accept, and a flag to indicate whether the store wishes the application to assign drivers automatically or not.

6.5   *Event processing networks in practice*

In this section we show some examples of the concepts described in this chapter implemented in various languages. For a thorough look at various implementations we invite the reader to use the *Event Processing in Action* website.

Figure 6.18 shows a graphical representation of part of an EPN. It is taken from the StreamBase implementation of the Fast Flower Delivery application. This might not look like a code listing to programmers who are used to an imperative coding language, but developers use this user interface to build StreamBase StreamSQL applications.

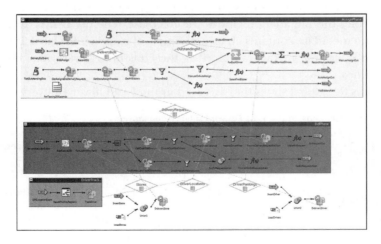

Figure 6.18   An example of using a graphical user interface to define an event processing network. This example uses StreamBase StreamSQL Event Flow.

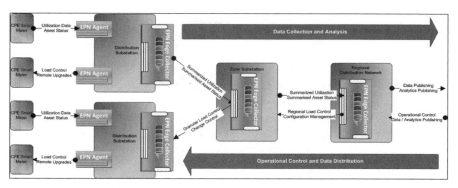

Figure 6.19   An explicit event processing network representation from Event Zero. Note that the EPN semantics in this illustration differ slightly from those we use in this book, but the principle is similar.

This kind of graphical interface lets you develop an EPN in a top-down and explicit fashion. Figure 6.19 shows another example of the top-down approach taken from Event Zero, which also has an explicit EPN model. Event Zero is not one of the participants on the *Event Processing in Action* website, so additional information about their language can be obtained directly from the company.

Some event processing languages do not make the EPN explicit. In these languages you construct applications in more of a bottom-up approach. EPAs are constructed independently, and the EPN is built automatically by matching up their input and output event types.

Event processing languages sometimes combine routing capability with the event processing agent functionality, rather than providing it as a separate channel entity. Some platforms are able to delegate channel routing function to message-oriented middleware software.

6.6   Summary

In this chapter we covered the event processing network, the central concept in this book, and the tool we use to model the functional definition of an event processing application. We gave a brief summary of the EPN itself, and then looked at three of the processing elements it can contain. These were event processing agents, which perform intermediary processing, the channels that link them together, and the global state elements that represent the state that is accessed by the EPAs.

We look at EPAs in greater depth in chapters 8 and 9, but in chapter 7 we encounter *context*, the seventh and final event processing building block.

6.6.1   Additional reading

Kahn, Gilles, *The Semantics of Simple Language for Parallel Programming*, IFIP Congress 1974: 471-475. This is a classic article which introduced data flow networks. The event processing network described in this book is a descendant of a data flow network.

Sharon, Guy, and Opher Etzion. 2008. *Event processing network: Model and Implementation*, IBM System Journal, 47(2):321–334. This paper defines the event processing network and many related concepts, such as the event channel. It can be considered as an ancestor of this chapter (our thinking has evolved since this paper was written).

Hohpe, Gregor, and Bobby Woolf. 2003. *Enterprise Integration Patterns: Designing, Building, and Deploying Messaging Solutions*, Addison-Wesley. http://www.amazon.com/Enterprise-Integration-Patterns-Designing-Deploying/dp/0321200683/ref=sr_1_1?ie=UTF8&s=books&qid=1258829949&sr=1-1. This book has patterns related to channels and routing schemes.

6.6.2   *Exercises*

6.1   We have described several ways in which an event processing agent can be mapped to executable runtime artifacts. Can you think of another variation we did not mention? What do you think are the benefits of each of these mappings?

6.2   Can you suggest a validation feature that can be enabled using an explicit event processing network representation?

6.3   Can you think of examples in which the use of events that are filtered out and non-filterable events are useful?

6.4   Devise an example which has at least one event processing agent of each of the Transformation agent types.

6.5   Devise extensions of the Fast Flower Delivery application that have channels with content-based and typed-based routing.

6.6   What role can event processing have in implementing state machines? Give an example.

6.7   What role can state machines have in implementing event processing? Give an example.

Putting events in context

7

The skill of writing is to create a context in which other people can think.

—Edwin Schlossberg

The way we view things in our daily life is affected by their context. This context can relate to the time of day; for example, at night you can open your car with the remote control from quite a long distance, but you may have to come quite close on a sunny day. Context can also relate to location: you might feel safe enough to carry money in your wallet in your own city, whereas in countries which have a reputation for muggings, you hide your money. Context may relate to other external conditions such as the state of the traffic. The route you choose to drive to the airport might depend on your knowledge of likely traffic conditions, or on congestion reports that you have picked up from the radio. In this chapter we introduce context as an explicit building block in our event processing model and dive deeply into the idea of context applied to event processing by covering the following topics:

- Discussion of the notion of context and its role in event processing
- Detailed discussion of the various context dimensions: temporal, spatial, state-oriented, and segmentation-oriented
- Context composition
- Context in the Fast Flower Delivery application
- Context definitions in practice

7.1   *The notion of context and its definition element*

Context plays the same role in event processing that it plays in real life. A particular event can be processed differently depending on the context in which it occurs, and it may be ignored entirely in some contexts. Context is used by some of the Fast Flower Delivery agents that we introduced in chapter 6, for example, the `Assignment manager` agent deals with a driver's `Delivery Bid` event differently depending on that event's timing relative to an earlier `Bid Request` event.

Event processing applications use context in three main ways:

- A stream, as we have defined it, can comprise an open-ended set of event objects. If you want to perform an operation on the stream you can't wait until all these event objects have been received. Instead you have to divide the stream into a sequence of context partitions, or *windows*, each of which contains a set of consecutive events. You can then define the operation in terms of its effect on the events in a window. The rule that determines which event instances are admitted into which window is something we call a *temporal context*.

- A stream could contain events that aren't particularly connected to one another, even though they might occur close together in a temporal sense. They might, for example, refer to occurrences in different locations, or to occurrences involving different entities in the real world. Suppose you were to process the stream with a stateful agent, such as a simple Aggregate agent that counts the number of events. By default this would count all the events in the stream, but what if you want to see separate totals for each location where the events occurred? To do this you need to have a separate agent, or at least a separate *instance* of the agent, processing the events for each location. *Spatial* contexts and *segmentation-oriented* contexts let you assign related events to separate context partitions. You can then have each partition processed by a distinct instance of the event processing agent, so that events in one context partition are processed in isolation from the events in other partitions.

- Context also allows event processing agents to be context sensitive, so that an agent that is active in some contexts may be inactive in others. We refer to this as *state-oriented* context.

You could try to achieve these effects using the event processing constructs that you met in chapter 6, using a separate agent for each context and using filtering and routing to direct event instances through different routes in the event processing network depending on the context associated with them. However, this could lead to large and unwieldy networks. Context-dependent event processing occurs sufficiently frequently that it is worth separating context out and treating it as an explicit construct in the EPN model. We now look at what that means.

The notion of context in computer science has been explored in the discipline known as *context aware computing*. A number of definitions of context have been proposed, all of which have the same net result: they take a cloud of event instances and classify them into one or more sets (we call these *context partitions*). An event process-ing operation that is associated with a context operates on each of these context parti-tions independently.

> **NOTE** In our EPN model operations are performed by event processing agents, and if an agent is associated with a context, every partition of that context is handled by a separate instance of that agent. If the agent is stateful, each instance has its own local state. Events in different context partitions are thus kept separate from one another when they are processed by the agent.

You can see that context is particularly useful in connection with stateful event pro-cessing agents and, as we see in the next chapter, they can act as filters when used with stateless agents.

A context partition can be semantic, for example, in the Fast Flower Delivery appli-cation we have a partition for all events that relate to a particular `Delivery Request`. A context partition can be based on spatial properties, for example, all events within 1 km from a given location, or it can be based on time. As well as affecting how events are processed, context has an important role in optimizing implementations. If you have partitioned the event space appropriately, you can process the different parti-tions concurrently.

Contexts are realized in different ways in event processing languages. Some lan-guages have the notion of context as a primitive language construct, whereas others have one construct for temporal grouping (this is usually called a *window*), and a sepa-rate mechanism for content grouping (like the SQL *group by* clause). In our model we view both temporal grouping and content grouping as kinds of context because they have a similar role.

> **CONTEXT** *A context* is a named specification of conditions that groups event instances so that they can be processed in a related way. It assigns each event instance to one or more *context partitions*. A context may have one or more *context dimensions* and can give rise to one or more context partitions.

The context dimension tells us what aspect of the event is used to do the grouping. At the start of this section we introduced four context dimensions, namely temporal con-text, spatial context, state-oriented context, and segment-oriented context. We discuss these dimensions, and the various types of context associated with them, in the follow-ing sections of this chapter.

We refer to the set of conditions that make up a context as the *context specification*, and the groups of event instances as context partitions, though where it is clear which one we mean we use the single word *context*. Despite their name, context par-titions do not always partition the space of events in the mathematical sense because you can have context specifications which have overlapping context partitions. In these kinds of contexts a single event instance can belong to more than one of the context's partitions.

The nature of a context partition depends on the context specification:

- Some context specifications give rise to just one context partition. We see an example later when we look at state-oriented context.
- Some context specifications give rise to a fixed number of context partitions, for example, distance location contexts.
- Some context specifications, for example, some temporal contexts, don't have a fixed number of partitions. Instead new context partitions are created dynamically over time.

Context is one of the seven fundamental building blocks, and we use definition elements to represent context specifications in our event processing modeling language. Figure 7.1 shows the shape of the context definition element.

Each context definition element contains details:

- *Context identifier*—The name of the context specification described by the definition element. It can be used to refer to this definition element from elsewhere.
- *Context dimension*—This tells us whether the definition is for a *temporal, spatial, state-oriented,* or *segmentation-oriented* context, or whether it is a *composite* context, that is to say one made up of other context specifications. We explain these in subsequent sections of this chapter.
- *Context type*—This determines the approach used to assign event instances to context partitions. The possible values of context type depend on the dimension.

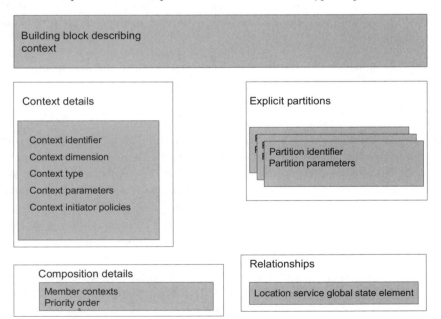

Figure 7.1   The context definition element

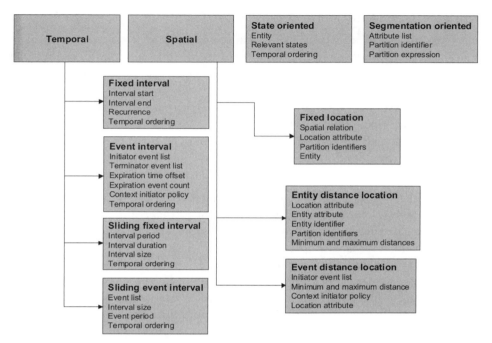

Figure 7.2 The different types of context showing their context parameters and partition parameters. This diagram also shows the principal dimension associated with a type, for example, the *fixed location* type is concerned with the spatial context dimension.

Each context has a collection of *context parameters* which provide its detailed specification. These parameters are specific to the context type and are discussed in the following sections. Some context types give rise to a finite number of partitions, and their specification includes an enumeration of all the partitions in the definition element. These *explicit partitions* can be given identifiers. Some context types can have a *context initiator policy*, a concept that is discussed later in this chapter.

If the context dimension is *composite*, the definition element also includes a list of its *member contexts*, and indicates the *priority order* used in their composition. Figure 7.2 shows a number of different context types, organized by dimension, and lists the parameters associated with each type.

We now discuss each of these four dimensions and look at the types of context associated with them.

7.2 *Temporal context*

We start this section with a general definition of temporal context, and then look at each of the four types of temporal context.

TEMPORAL CONTEXT A *temporal context* consists of one or more time intervals, possibly overlapping. Each time interval corresponds to a context partition, which contains events that happen during that interval.

We illustrate this with a couple of examples:

- An event processing agent that raises an alert if someone attempts to make more than three withdrawals from an ATM machine within a single day. In this example each day (starting at midnight) is a separate context partition containing the withdrawal events that occur during that day.
- An event processing agent that raises an alert if someone attempts to make more than three withdrawals within a 24 hour period. We can use the same agent that we used in the previous example, but this time with a context partition that starts whenever a given customer withdraws money from an ATM machine and ends 24 hours later.

When an event processing agent is associated with a temporal context, it processes only events that are associated with a partition of that context. If the context has more than one partition, each partition is handled by a different instance of the agent; no local agent state is carried across between these instances. If the event processing agent has only one input terminal, the context partitions break the incoming stream into one or more sets of events, which are often referred to as *windows*. These windows can overlap, and if this happens a single event instance can belong to more than one window. If the event processing agent has more than one input terminal, the context takes all incoming events into consideration, regardless of the input terminal that receives them. The context partitions, or windows, can thus contain events from more than one input stream.

Each partition is defined by a time interval with a starting time and an ending time. There are several different ways to specify these boundaries, and we identify four different types of temporal context which we show, with examples, in figure 7.3.

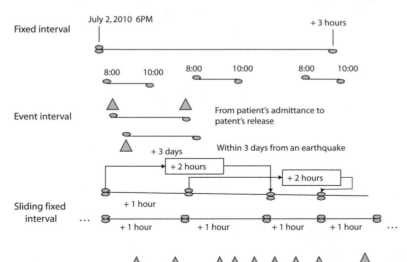

Figure 7.3   Different types of temporal context with their context partitions

Looking at figure 7.3 you can see cases with one partition and cases with potentially unbounded sequences of partitions. If there are multiple partitions, they can overlap, abut one another, or have gaps between them.

After a time interval has been established, the partition consists of all the events from the relevant stream or streams that lie inside that interval, but what does *lie inside* mean here? That depends on how the interval's boundaries are defined:

- If the boundary is defined as a point in time, we take a timestamp associated with the event, and compare it with the boundary timestamp. This tells us which side of the boundary the event lies on. Several event timestamps may be available to us: the event's occurrence time, its detection time (in effect the time when the event processing agent receives the event), or another timestamp in the event.

- If the boundary is determined by an event, we are interested in the events that are before or after that event. This means there needs to be an order relationship (ordering) between the events we are interested in. There may be several different ways to infer an ordering. If all the events have an occurrence time, we can use that to determine the order (up to the temporal granularity at which it is recorded). If there is a sequence number in all the events, we can use that. Otherwise we can use the order in which the events are detected by the event processing agent (the detection time).

Each of our four temporal context types contains a temporal ordering parameter, which indicates which of these techniques is to be used. Temporal ordering is a challenging area which we return to in chapter 11.

We now describe each of the context types shown in figure 7.3, but before we do that, a quick word on terminology. In the sections that follow we refer to temporal context partitions as windows and use the phrases *opening a window* or *closing a window* to mean the same as *starting a context partition* or *ending a context partition*.

7.2.1 *Fixed interval*

The *fixed interval* context is used to represent either a single fixed-length time period, or a fixed-length time period that repeats in a regular fashion, for example, the trading hours of a financial market. These time periods do not overlap.

> **FIXED INTERVAL CONTEXT** In a *fixed interval* context each window is an interval that has a fixed time length; there may be just one window or a periodically repeating sequence of non-overlapping windows.

With fixed interval contexts, events are only assigned to windows if they contain a timestamp that is compatible with the context's temporal ordering. Each time interval is considered to be a half-open interval. So if you have an interval *[Ts, Te)* starting at *Ts* and ending at *Te*, an event with timestamp τ is included in the window if $Ts \leq \tau < Te$.

The *context parameters* for this type are as follows:

- *Interval start*—This gives the start time for the first (or only) interval. It can either be a DateTime or a Date. If a Date value is given by default, the interval starts at midnight local time on the specified day, however, an application can set its own start of day time to apply to all fixed interval contexts.

- *Interval end*—This gives the end time for the first (or only) interval. It can be a Date or DateTime or it can be a duration giving the length of the interval. If it is specified as a Date, by default the interval ends at midnight that day; however, the application can specify an alternative time for end of day.
- *Recurrence*—This specifies how frequently the interval is to repeat, if at all.
- *Temporal ordering*—This parameter indicates whether the assignment of events to windows is based on their detection time or on their occurrence time timestamp. The event instance is only assigned to a window if it has the appropriate timestamp.

Here are two non-repeating interval examples:

- Super Bowl XLIV (start = 7 February 2010 6pm EDT, end = 3 hours duration)
- The months of July and August 2009 (start = 1 July 2009, end = 1 September 2009)

Here are two examples with periodically repeating intervals:

- Every working day between 8 - 10 A.M. (start = 1 July 2009 08:00, end = 1 July 2009 10:00, recurrence = daily, working days only). This is the second example in figure 7.3.
- Every year during the month of December (start = 1 December 2000, end = 1 January 2001, recurrence = yearly).

These examples use fixed interval contexts:

- Calculating the total value of purchases from a web store for each individual hour of the day
- Monitoring a patient for a fixed time after an operation
- Calculating daily stock market indicators

The windows in a fixed interval context are time triggered. We now look at a different kind of temporal context in which the windows are triggered by specific events.

7.2.2 Event interval

In an *event interval* context, a window is opened or closed when an event processing agent receives a particular event as its input. You can see an example in figure 7.3 where there is a window that is opened by a `patient admittance` event and closed by a `patient release` event.

> **EVENT INTERVAL CONTEXT** In an *event interval* context each window is an interval that starts when the associated event processing agent receives an event that satisfies a specified predicate. It ends when the EPA receives an event that satisfies a second predicate, or when a given period has elapsed.

A window is opened when the event processing agent receives a prespecified event (called the *initiator*). It closes when the event processing agent receives a prespecified event (the *terminator*). The initiator and terminator can be specified as specific event instances, or they can be specified more broadly, for example, the context could specify that any instance of a particular event type acts as an initiator. The window may also close even if a terminator event has not been detected, either when a given period of time has elapsed or when the window has reached a given size.

The parameters for an event interval context are as follows:

- *Initiator event list*—A new window is opened when the event processing agent receives any of the events specified in the list. An event may be specified by its event type, in which case any instance of that event type will open the window, or it may be specified by the combination of an event type and a predicate expression. If the predicate is present, the window will be opened only if the event instance also satisfies the predicate (that is to say if the predicate expression returns TRUE when evaluated on the event instance).

- *Terminator event list*—The window is closed when the event processing agent receives any of the events specified in the terminator list. The terminator list is similar to the initiator list; each entry in the list consists of an event type and optionally a predicate expression. If the predicate expression is present, the window will only be closed if the event instance satisfies the predicate.

- *Expiration time offset*—The window is closed after this time period has elapsed, even if no terminator event has been received. By default this is an offset from the time the window was opened, but it can also be specified as an offset from any attribute of the initiator event whose data type is DateTime.

- *Expiration event count*—The window is closed after it has reached this size, even if no terminator event has been received.

- *Context initiator policy*—This parameter specifies what is to happen if a second initiator event is encountered. Context initiator policies are discussed in section 7.6.

- *Temporal ordering*—This parameter indicates whether inclusion of events in the window depends on the order in which they are detected, on their *occurrence time* timestamp, or on another specified attribute in the event that has a value that increases over time (a timestamp or an application-specified sequence number).

The context specification must include an initiator event list, and at least one of the following: terminator event list, expiration time offset, or expiration event count. If an expiration time offset is specified, the temporal ordering parameter must indicate ordering by timestamp.

NOTE The initiator event is included in the window that it initiates. The terminator event is not included in the window that it terminates. If an event is both an initiator and a terminator, it closes an existing window before opening a new one. An event that causes the expiration event count limit to be reached is included in the window (unless it happens also to be the terminator event).

The following are event interval context examples:

- From patient admittance to patient release (initiator event = `patient admittance`, terminator event = `patient release`).
- From entrance to the parking lot until exit from the parking lot, but no more than 8 hours (initiator event = `parking lot entrance`, terminator event = `parking lot exit`, expiration time offset = + 8 hours).
- Within three days of an earthquake (initiator event = earthquake, expiration time offset = + 3 days).
- From an `Assignment` event to a `Delivery Confirmation` event, with expiration time offset of `Assignment.requiredDeliveryTime` + 5 minutes. This example comes from the Fast Flower Delivery application; see table 7.9.
- A book review process, starting with the call for reviews and ending when four reviews have been received (initiator event = `Review process start`, expiration event count = 5).

We now look at a type of temporal context in which each the start of each window is determined as a time offset from the start of its predecessor.

7.2.3 *Sliding fixed interval*

In a *sliding fixed interval* context, new windows are opened at regular intervals. Unlike the non-sliding fixed interval context, these windows are not tied to particular times. Instead each window is opened at a specified time after its predecessor. Each window has a fixed size, specified either as a time interval or a count of event instances. In figure 7.3 you can see an example where a new window is opened every hour, and each window lasts for exactly an hour.

> **SLIDING FIXED INTERVAL CONTEXT** In a *sliding fixed interval* context, each window is an interval with a fixed temporal size or a fixed number of events. New windows are opened at regular time intervals relative to one another.

Events are only assigned to windows if they contain a timestamp that is compatible with the context's temporal ordering. Each time interval is considered to be a half-open interval. So if you have an interval starting at Ts and ending at Te, an event with timestamp τ is included in the window if $Ts \le \tau < Te$.

The parameters for a *sliding fixed interval* context are as follows:

- *Interval period*—The time period that elapses between the start of each window.
- *Interval duration*—The time period for which each window stays open.
- *Interval size*—The maximum number of event instances to be included in each window.
- *Temporal ordering*—This parameter indicates whether the assignment of events to windows is based on their detection time or on their occurrence time timestamp.

The specification must include an interval period parameter and either an interval duration or interval size (or both). Sliding intervals may be overlapping or non-overlapping.

They are overlapping if and only if the interval period < interval duration. Here are a couple of examples:

- Start a sliding interval of 1 hour every 10 minutes (interval period = 10 minutes, interval duration = 1 hour). In this case there will be six partially overlapping windows at any point in time.
- Start a sliding window of 1 hour every hour (interval period = 1 hour, interval duration = 1 hour). In this case there is only one window open at any point in time.

Sliding fixed interval contexts are typically used with Aggregate agents.

7.2.4 *Sliding event interval*

The *sliding event interval* context is similar to the sliding fixed interval context. The difference is that the criterion for opening a new window is specified as a count of events, rather than as a time period. In figure 7.3 you can see an example where each group of three successive blood pressure measurements is assigned into a new window, irrespective of the times at which the measurements were taken.

> **SLIDING EVENT INTERVAL CONTEXT** In a *sliding event interval* context the opening of each new window, and its duration, is determined by counting the number of events received by the event processing agent.

When it is associated with a sliding event interval context, an event processing agent monitors its input, counting the number of times it receives certain kinds of event. This count determines when windows are opened and closed. This is a continuous process, and it's possible to have back-to-back windows one after the other, or to have overlapping windows.

The parameters for a *sliding event interval* context are as follows:

- *Event list*—This specifies which events count towards the *interval size* and *event period*. The event processing agent may receive events not specified in this list; such events are included in the window but do not count towards the window size. Each entry in the list contains an event type. This type can be accompanied by a predicate expression, in which case an instance of the event type is only counted if it satisfies the predicate, that is to say, if the predicate returns TRUE when evaluated against the event instance.
- *Interval size*—This determines the size of each window. It is specified as the number of events (of a kind specified by the event list parameter) that are to be included in the window.
- *Event period*—The number of events (as specified by the event list parameter) received by the event processing agent before a new window is to be opened. If this parameter is not specified, it defaults to the interval size, which means that a new window is opened each time the previous window closes.
- *Temporal ordering*—This parameter indicates whether inclusion of events in the window depends on the order in which they are detected, on their *occurrence time*

timestamp, or on some other attribute in the event that has a value that increases over time (a timestamp or an application-specified sequence number).

If the event list encompasses all the events that can be received by the event processing agent, an event interval context divides this set of input events into a sequence of equal size partitions. Aggregate agents frequently use this kind of sliding event context, as in the following examples:

- A physician looking at trends in a patient's blood pressure wishes to see an average of every three successive blood pressure readings (as shown at the bottom of figure 7.3). In this example there is only one event type, and the sliding event interval parameters are event list = blood pressure reading; event period = 3; interval size = 3. This means that each blood pressure reading is included in only one window and so only participates in one aggregation operation.
- Now suppose that the physician wishes to see three-point moving average values. To do this we can use the same event processing agent, but this time the sliding event interval parameters are event list = blood pressure reading; event period = 1; interval size = 3. This means that each reading is included in three successive windows and is aggregated three times with three other readings.

Temporal context is widely used in event processing as many languages support some kind of time window, but we are aware of a growing number of applications that make use of event location. This idea of location awareness is part of the wider concept we call spatial context, which we discuss next.

7.3   *Spatial context*

A spatial context groups event instances according to their geospatial characteristics. This type of context assumes that the event contains an attribute that assigns a location to the event. The precise meaning of this attribute depends on the event type: it could mean that the event actually occurred at that location, or it could mean that the event involved arrival at that location or departure from it. An event instance is only classified into a partition of a spatial context if it contains such an attribute.

The event's location attribute can specify the location using any of the location data types mentioned in chapter 3 (points in space, areas, and so on) although there are some data types that can't be used with some spatial context definitions and we mention these restrictions as we look at how spatial context is specified. The location attribute can take two forms:

- An explicit representation using a coordinate system, for example, a point might be represented as a latitude/longitude pair
- An identifier of a spatial entity, for example, the name of a building or city

If the attribute is expressed as an identifier we need a way of interpreting it in order to apply the context. This is done by having a service or database table that can convert between an identifier and a coordinate representation (the conversion from identifier

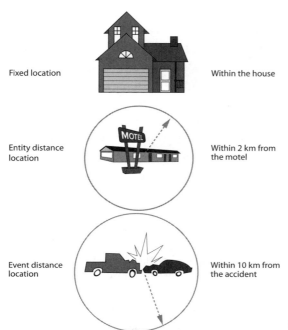

Fixed location — Within the house

Entity distance location — Within 2 km from the motel

Event distance location — Within 10 km from the accident

Figure 7.4   Examples of spatial context

to geographic coordinates is known as *geocoding*). In this case, the spatial context definition element contains a *location service* reference. This is a reference to the global state element that provides this conversion capability. The location identifier is converted by the location service into coordinate form and it is then handled as if it had been supplied as coordinates.

As you can see in figure 7.4, there are several types of spatial context: *fixed location, entity distance location*, and *event distance location*.

We now discuss these three types of spatial context.

7.3.1   Fixed location

A *fixed location* context has one or more context partitions, each of which is associated with a spatial entity, sometimes referred to as a *geofence*. An event instance is classified into a context partition if its location attribute correlates with the spatial entity in some way.

> **FIXED LOCATION CONTEXT**   A *fixed location* context has predefined context partitions based on specific spatial entities. An event is included in a partition if its location attribute indicates that it is correlated with the partition's spatial entity.

The parameters for the fixed location context are the following:

- *Spatial relation*—The type of comparison used to determine if the event is correlated with the entity
- *Location attribute*—The identifier of the event's location attribute

The context definition element may also contain a reference to a global state element that provides the *location service* for this context. The definition element may additionally specify one or more explicit partitions. If present, these partition specifications include the following:

- *Partition identifier*—An identifier assigned to this partition. It can be used to refer to this partition from elsewhere.
- *Entity*—Identifier of the spatial entity associated with this partition. This identifier can be used to retrieve the coordinate representation of the entity from the *location service* global state element.

If the context definition has explicit partitions, an event instance is included in all partitions that it matches. This means that a copy of the event is processed by each corresponding event processing agent instance. If the event doesn't match any partition, it is not handled by any instance of the event processing agent.

If the context definition doesn't have explicit partitions, it has an implicitly defined partition corresponding to every spatial object known to the location service. Each event is matched against all the spatial objects held by the location service global state element.

Here are some examples of fixed location contexts:

- The Drivers' Guild decides to extend the Fast Flower Delivery application to discover how much time its drivers are spending in a particular area of the city. To do this it uses a fixed location context defined by the boundaries of this area to monitor drivers' GPS Location events. To determine which events occurred within the area the context uses the Neighborhoods global state element.
- In a physical security application the event types building entered and building exited have a point location attribute that corresponds to the door through which the entry or exit occurred. The context has an explicit partition for each building that is being monitored. The comparison now involves taking the point location from the event and testing it to see which building is involved, so that the appropriate event processing agent instance can be used.

We still need to explain the *spatial relation* parameter. Recall that a location may be represented as one of three types: point; line or polyline; or area or volume. When evaluating a fixed location context we have two such locations, the event location and the entity location. The *spatial relation* parameter tells us how to compare these two locations in order to decide whether to include the event instance in the context partition or not. There are six possible values for spatial relation: *contained in, contains, overlaps, disjoint, equals* and *touches*. In figure 7.5 we show examples of these relations using various combinations of entity and event location types (for simplicity we show only 2D area examples).

The relations illustrated in figure 7.5 are straightforward:

- The *contained in* relation is satisfied if the entity location is completely enclosed within the event location.

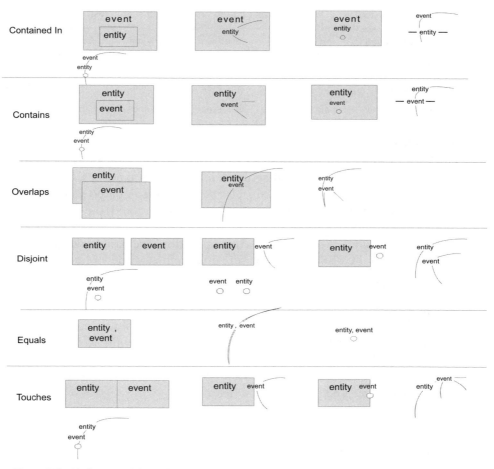

Figure 7.5 Various spatial relation types. Each row illustrates a different relation type, showing examples for which the relation is satisfied.

- The *contains* relation is satisfied if the event location is completely enclosed within the entity location.
- The *overlaps* relation is satisfied if there is an overlap between the entity location and event location, but neither of them is contained within the other.
- The *disjoint* relation is satisfied if there is no overlap between the entity location and event location.
- The *equals* relation is satisfied if the entity location and event location are identical.
- The *touches* relation is satisfied if the event location borders the entity location.

Not every combination of entity location type and event location type is valid. Table 7.1 shows which combinations can be used for each spatial relation type.

Table 7.1   Combinations of location types that are valid for each spatial relation type

Entity	Contained in	Contains	Overlaps	Disjoint	Equals	Touches
point	line, area			point, line, area	point	line, area
line	line, area	point, line	line, area	point, line, area	line	point, line, area
area	area	point, line, area	line, area	point, line, area	area	point, line, area

The rows of this table correspond to the entity location's data type, and the table entries show the event location data types that are valid for a given relation. Among other things, this table shows that any combination of types can be compared using the *disjoint* relation, but only identical types can be compared using the *equals* relation. If the combination of entity and event types is not valid, the event is not included in the corresponding partition.

In the next kind of spatial context, the partitions are based not on separate spatial entities, but on the distance between the event and an entity of interest.

7.3.2   *Entity distance location*

An *entity distance location* context gives gives rise to one or more context partitions, based on the distance between the event's location attribute and some other entity. This entity may be either stationary or moving. If the entity is moving, the distance relates to the location of the entity at the time that the event occurred (its occurrence time). The entity may be either one that is specified by another attribute of the event, or one that is specified in the context definition.

> **ENTITY DISTANCE LOCATION CONTEXT**   An *entity distance location* context assigns events to context partitions based on their distance from a given entity. This entity is either specified by an event attribute or is given as part of the context specification.

The locations of the event and the entity can be specified using point, line, or area location types. We define the distance between the two locations to be the shortest distance between any pair of points taken from the two locations. This means that if you want to base the context on the distance from the center of a spatial area (such as a city), you should define that entity location as a point type.

The parameters for the *entity distance location* context are as follows:

- *Location attribute*—The identifier of the attribute in the event that gives the event's location
- *Entity attribute*—The identifier of the attribute in the event that gives the identifier of the entity
- *Entity identifier*—The identifier of the entity

The definition element must contain either an entity attribute or an entity identifier, but not both. As with the fixed location context, it may contain a reference to a global state element that provides the *location service* for this context. It must also contain one or more explicit partition specifications. A partition specification includes the following:

- *Partition identifier*—An identifier assigned to this partition. It can be used to refer to this partition from elsewhere.
- *Minimum and maximum distance*—An event is included in the partition if the shortest distance between the event and the entity is less than the maximum distance and not less than the minimum.

Here are some examples of entity distance location:

- The example shown in figure 7.4 where the entity is a motel and the context is used to track fire alarms within 2 km of the motel, in order to alert the motel manager of possible danger. This context has a single partition, and both the event location and the entity location are given as points.
- Vehicle breakdown events partitioned according to their distance from a particular service center. They are grouped by distance as follows: less than 10 km, between 10 km and 30 km, between 30 km and 60 km, and more than 60 km. In this case the service center is a fixed entity specified in the context definition, and the partition specifications are maximum distance 10 km; minimum distance 10 km, maximum distance 30 km; minimum distance 30 km, maximum distance 60 km; minimum distance 60 km. This example is not illustrated in figure 7.4.
- An alerting service at a big conference, which attendees can use to receive alerts when they are in the proximity of another person. Attendees send periodic events giving their own location, and these events include the name of the person they are interested in meeting. This example shows the use of an entity distance location context where the entity is itself moving. The context specification has an entity attribute which tells the context which attribute from the event gives the name of the person being tracked and an explicit partition with a maximum distance of 100 m. This means that the alert generation event processing agent is invoked only if the two people are less that 100 m apart.

Our final spatial context type does not have predefined partitions. In this type of context, the creation of partitions is triggered by the occurrence of certain events.

7.3.3 *Event distance location*

In this type of context, as with an event interval context, a new partition is created when an event processing agent receives a particular event as its input. Subsequent events, of whatever type, are then included in this partition if they occurred within a specific distance of the initiating event. Distance is defined as in the entity distance location context. A given event may be included in more than one partition.

> **EVENT DISTANCE LOCATION CONTEXT** An *event distance location* context assigns events to context partitions if they occurred within a specific distance from the location of the event that triggered the creation of the partition.

The parameters for the *event distance location* context are as follows:

- *Initiator event list*—A new partition is created when the event processing agent receives any of the events specified in the list. An event may be specified by its event type, in which case any instance of that event type will create the partition, or it may be specified by the combination of an event type and a predicate expression. If the predicate is present, the partition will be created only if the event instance also satisfies the predicate (that is to say, the predicate expression must return TRUE when evaluated on the event instance).

- *Location attribute*—The identifier of the attribute in the event that gives the event's location.

- *Minimum and maximum distance*—An event is included in the partition if the shortest distance from the location of the initiator event is less than the maximum distance and not less than the minimum.

- *Context initiator policy*—See section 7.6.

As is the case with the other spatial contexts, the definition element may contain a reference to a global state element that provides the *location service* for this context.

The following are examples of event distance location contexts:

- Detecting the presence of a vehicle within a 10 km radius of an accident (initiator event list is `accident`, maximum distance is 10 km), as illustrated in figure 7.4.

- Detecting a case of scarlet fever within a distance of 100 km from a previous outbreak of this disease (event type is `disease report`, predicate is `disease= "scarlet fever"`, maximum distance is 100 km).

Temporal and spatial contexts group events based on data from the events themselves. We now look at another kind of context, state-oriented context. This type of context is based entirely on the state of an external entity and takes no notice of the type or content of the event instance itself.

7.4 *State-oriented context*

State-oriented context is the third of the four context dimensions. It differs from the other dimensions in that the context is determined by the state of some entity that is external to the event processing system. This is best illustrated with examples:

- An airport security system could have a `threat level` status taking values `green`, `blue`, `yellow`, `orange`, or `red`. Some events may need to be monitored only when the `threat level` is `orange` or above, whereas other events may be processed differently in different threat levels (entity = `threat level`, relevant states = `orange`, `red`).

- Traffic in a certain highway has several status values: `traffic flowing`, `traffic slow`, and `traffic stationary`. Some events are monitored only during traffic jams in order to reroute vehicles or alert people to expect late arrivals (entity = `Traffic on highway A3`, relevant states = `traffic stationary`).

There is only one state-oriented context type and it is defined as follows:

> **STATE-ORIENTED CONTEXT** A *state-oriented* context has a single partition. It is controlled by an external entity, and the decision of whether to include an event in the partition is based on the state of the external entity at the time when the event occurs or is detected.

The parameters for state-oriented context are as follows:

- *Entity*—The identifier of the external entity whose state controls this context
- *Relevant states*—A list of the external entity states which cause an event to be included in the partition
- *Temporal ordering*—Indicates whether the decision to include or exclude is made using the value of the state at the event instance's occurrence time or at its detection time

An event processing agent associated with a state-oriented context will process incoming events only if the entity is in one of the states specified by the relevant states parameter.

The last dimension to discuss is segmentation-oriented context.

7.5   *Segmentation-oriented context*

A *segmentation-oriented* context is used to group event instances into context partitions based on the value of an attribute or collection of attributes in the instances themselves. As a simple example, consider an event processing agent that takes a single stream of input events, in which each event contains a `customer identifier` attribute. The value of this attribute can be used to group events so that there's a separate context partition for each customer. Each context partition contains only events related to that customer, so that the behavior of each customer can be tracked independently of the other customers.

In this kind of segmentation-oriented context, the context specifies just the attribute (or attributes) to be used, and this implicitly defines a context partition for every possible value of that attribute. Alternatively, a segmentation-oriented context definition can list its context partitions explicitly. Each partition specification includes one or more predicate expressions involving one or more of the event attributes; an event is assigned to a context partition if one of its predicates evaluates to TRUE.

> **SEGMENTATION-ORIENTED CONTEXT** A *segmentation-oriented* context assigns events to context partitions based on the values of one or more event attributes, either using the value of these attribute(s) to pick a partition directly, or using predicate expressions to define context partition membership.

There is only one type of segmentation-oriented context. It is the segmentation context and it has a single parameter:

- *Attribute list*—List of one or more attributes used to determine the context partition

If the attribute list is present, the context partitions are determined by the value of a single attribute (if the list only has one attribute), or by the combination of values of the listed attributes. Here are examples: if the attribute list contains just the `driver` attribute, events are grouped into partitions according to the value of this attribute, so each driver has its own partition; if the attribute list contains both `driver` and `store`, there is a separate partition for each combination of the values of `driver` and `store`. An event must contain all of the attributes in the attribute list; otherwise it is not assigned to a partition.

Instead of having an attribute list, the context specification may contain one or more explicit partitions. If present these partition specifications include the following:

- *Partition identifier*—An identifier assigned to this partition. It can be used to refer to this partition from elsewhere.
- *Partition expressions*—One or more predicate expressions referring to attributes in the event instance. In order to be included in the partition, an event instance must satisfy at least one of these expressions.

If the context definition has explicit partitions, an event instance is included in all partitions that it matches. This means that a copy of the event is processed by each corresponding event processing agent instance. If the event does not match any partition, it isn't handled by any instance of the event processing agent.

As an example of explicit partitions, consider an application where events contain a person's age. The application can use a segmentation context to group together events from different age ranges. To do this it has an explicit partition for each range, for example:

- age < 21
- age ≥ 21 and age < 30
- age ≥ 30 and age < 50
- age ≥ 50 and age < 67
- age ≥ 67

We have now completed our review of the four context dimensions and the context types associated with them. In this discussion we have mentioned a context initiator policy, and we turn to look at that next.

7.6   *Context initiator policies*

We need to tune up the semantics for a couple of the context types that we have mentioned. These are types in which events determine the boundaries of the context partitions. If this kind of context is used, there is the possibility that several context initiator events may occur over the time that a context partition is active.

Recall the event interval subtype where a new window is opened when a particular event occurs and consider the example given in section 7.2.2:

Within three days of an earthquake
(initiator event = `earthquake`, *expiration time offset* = *+ 3 days).*

Assume that there is an earthquake at 10:00 on May 5, 2007. This would establish a window corresponding to the interval [May 5, 2007 10:00, May 8, 2007 10:00). However, suppose that another earthquake event happens at 06:00 on May 7. This lies in the middle of this interval. We need to specify how this case should be handled, and to do this we introduce the idea of the *context initiator policy*.

CONTEXT INITIATOR POLICY   A *context initiator policy* is a semantic abstraction that defines the behavior required when a window has been opened and a subsequent initiator event is detected. The possible policies are open another window, ignore the new initiator event, refresh the window, or extend the window.

In the event interval case, the effects of the various context initiator policies are

- *Add*—A new window is opened, alongside the existing one. In the earthquake example, another window will be added with the interval [May 7, 06:00, May 10, 06:00), while the original window is still open. Relevant events that occur within the intersection of the two intervals will be classified to both context partitions, so if we are monitoring the number of heart attacks within the period of three days from an earthquake in a certain area, we include every heart attack event in both context partitions.
- *Ignore*—The original window is preserved. The new earthquake event does not cause a new window to be opened.
- *Refresh*—The original window is closed, and a new window is opened.
- *Extend*—The timeout processing (expiration event count or expiration time offset) is reset to start with the new initiator event. In the earthquake example an expiration time offset is being used, so the window is extended to May 10, 06:00.

Figure 7.6 illustrates these policies:

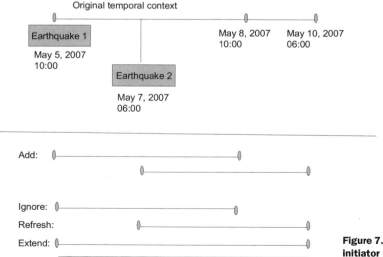

Figure 7.6   The various context initiator policy options

This policy also applies to the event distance location context subtype. Recall the example in section 7.3.3:

> Detecting the presence of a vehicle within a 10 km radius of an accident (initiator event list is `accident`, maximum distance is 10 km).

Suppose that a context partition has been established for this context and then a second `accident` event occurs, which should, in principle, open the same context partition again. The possibilities are

- *Add*—Another partition related to the new accident will be added to the spatial context.
- *Ignore*—The second accident is ignored; the focus is on the original accident only.
- *Refresh*—The original context is closed, so the location in this context always relates to only the most recent accident.
- *Extend*—The context partition is extended to be the union of 10 km distance from both locations.

Each context type that we have discussed so far belongs to just one of the four context dimensions. However, in practice many applications use contexts that involve multiple dimensions. We refer to these as composite contexts.

7.7   *Composite contexts*

Event processing applications often use combinations of two or more of the simple context types that we have discussed so far. In particular a temporal context type is frequently used in combination with a segmentation-oriented context, and we show an example of this in figure 7.7.

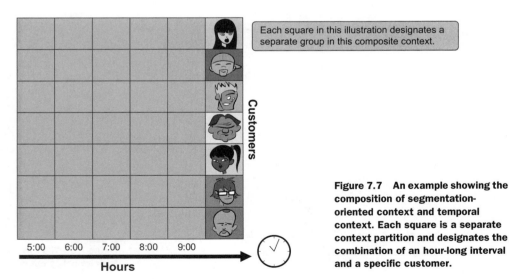

Each square in this illustration designates a separate group in this composite context.

Customers

5:00   6:00   7:00   8:00   9:00

Hours

Figure 7.7   An example showing the composition of segmentation-oriented context and temporal context. Each square is a separate context partition and designates the combination of an hour-long interval and a specific customer.

We look first at the basic definition of composite context, and then explain why we may need to assign an order of priority to the components that make up a composite context.

7.7.1 *The notion of composite context*

We start by looking at the definition of composite context.

COMPOSITE CONTEXTS A *composite context* is a context that is composed from two or more contexts, known as its *members*. The set of context partitions for the composite context is the Cartesian product of the partition sets of the member contexts.

With two member contexts, the composition process works like this: Event instances are first classified into context partitions using one of the two contexts (the order of classification is determined by the *priority order*, discussed in section 7.7.2). Each of these context partitions is then further subdivided using the other context. This process is then repeated if more than two contexts are involved. The contexts that are composed together may be of any dimension and any type, and in practice they are often of different types, as the following examples show:

- *Composition of segmentation-oriented context and temporal context*—This is illustrated in figure 7.7 where the segmentation-oriented context groups event instances by customer, and the temporal context is a sliding fixed interval context with a duration and frequency of 1 hour. In the resulting composite context each context partition groups together the events that relate to a single customer for a single hour.
- *Composition of spatial context and state context*—In this example, imagine that we have a fixed location spatial context relating to the city of Trento in Italy and a state context relating to the state of the weather (clear, cloudy, rain, snow). The composite context has four partitions, one for each state of the weather applied to events that occur within the city of Trento.
- *Composition of segmentation-oriented context and spatial context*—In this example suppose that the segmentation context relates to car type, and the spatial context is the distance from Malpensa Airport (near Milan, Italy). If the segmentation context has 20 different car types, and the spatial context has three context partitions (for example, for distances 0-5 km, 5-10 km, 10-30 km), the composite context will have sixty partitions, one for every combination of car type and distance range.

These three examples of composite contexts are all multidimensional. The first example combines segmentation-oriented (by customers) with sliding fixed interval temporal context (by hour); every combination of hour and customer creates another context partition. The second composite context combines state-oriented (weather) and fixed location (neighborhood). The third composite event combines segmentation-oriented context and spatial context.

Note that in some cases a member context may have a separate existence outside the composite context, and in some cases one or more of the member contexts have meaning only within the composite context. If you look at the Pickup interval context from the Fast Flower Delivery application (see table 7.12), you can see that it is made up of a segmentation-oriented context called Request context, which partitions events according to the delivery request that they relate to, and a temporal context that starts when the assignment is made and ends either when pickup is done or 5 minutes after the committed pickup time. The segmentation-oriented context is independent of the composite context and is used both as a stand-alone context and as a member of other composite contexts. The temporal context in this example is specific to this composite context and is not used elsewhere. It can therefore be defined as part of the composite context specification.

Next we explain priority ordering.

7.7.2 *Priority ordering in context composition*

In the examples of the previous section, it doesn't matter what order we apply the two contexts. In the example in figure 7.7, we get the same collection of events in each context partition, whether we classify the events according to time first and according to customers second, or vice versa. However, this is not true for every composite context, because some context types have relative rather than absolute semantics, so the order of classification may yield different results. We demonstrate this with the following example.

Let's assume that we are monitoring the length of calls in a call center dealing with customer problems to find the average duration of a phone call per service agent, over each group of three calls. To do this we use a composite context, made up of a temporal context and a segmentation-oriented context. The temporal context is a sliding event interval with event period = 3 and interval size = 3, so that it creates windows containing three events each. The segmentation context partitions the space of events by service agent. The composite context is associated with an aggregate event processing agent that calculates the average call duration. Note that this is a simplified example, and that in reality we would probably calculate the average in units that are much bigger than three calls, but we wanted to show an example that did not involve hundreds of event instances.

Each call is represented by an event, and in table 7.2 we show a 3-hour history of these events.

Table 7.2   Events recording calls handled between 08:00 and 11:00

Event identity	Detection time	Employee	Duration (seconds)
E1	08:01	John	40
E2	08:12	Mike	60
E3	09:00	John	100

Table 7.2   Events recording calls handled between 08:00 and 11:00 *(continued)*

Event identity	Detection time	Employee	Duration (seconds)
E4	09:21	Gayle	40
E5	09:23	Gayle	180
E6	09:24	John	60
E7	09:44	Gayle	120
E8	10:00	Mike	600
E9	10:21	Gayle	120
E10	10:30	Gayle	30
E11	10:33	Mike	100
E12	10:49	Gayle	90
E13	10:50	John	150
E14	10:55	John	60
E15	10:57	John	120

If we take the temporal context first, we get five partitions, each containing three successive events, regardless of the employee involved: let's call them `first`, `second`, `third`, `fourth`, and `fifth`, where first consists of the events {`E1, E2, E3`}, second consists of the next three events, and so on. After classifying the event according to this dimension, we further classify them using the segmentation context. Table 7.3 illustrates the results.

Table 7.3   Assignment of events to context partitions when the temporal context is applied first and the segmentation-oriented context second

Context partition identity	Temporal partition	Segmentation partition	Event instances included	Average result
CI1	First	John	E1,E3	70
CI2	First	Mike	E2	60
CI3	Second	Gayle	E4, E5	110
CI4	Second	John	E6	60
CI5	Third	Gayle	E7, E9	120
CI6	Third	Mike	E8	600
CI7	Fourth	Gayle	E10, E12	75
CI8	Fourth	Mike	E11	100
CI9	Fifth	John	E13, E14, E15	110

Table 7.3 shows that as the `first` temporal partition included events for only John and Mike, it yielded only two composite partitions. Furthermore, only partition `CI9` actually contained three events. This is not really what we intended, as we wanted to partition the contexts (and calculate the average) for each successive three calls for a single service agent. To do this we have to classify the events applying the segmentation-oriented context first and the temporal context second. Table 7.4 shows that we now take all six of John's calls and classify them into two temporal partitions, each containing three events. This means that when we average them, we get the results we wanted.

Table 7.4   Assignment of events to context partitions when the segmentation-oriented context is applied first and the temporal context second

Context partition Identity	Segmentation partition	Temporal partition	Event instances included	Average result
CI1	John	First	E1, E3, E6	66.6
CI2	John	Second	E13, E14, E15	110
CI3	Mike	First	E2, E8, E11	253.33
CI4	Gayle	First	E4, E5, E7	113.33
CI5	Gayle	Second	E9, E10, E12	80

The order makes a difference to the result in this case because the boundaries of the sliding event interval are relative to the stream of events rather than absolute points in time. So when defining a composite context, you may specify the order in which the member contexts are applied. We call this the *priority order.*

Priority order can also be needed when composing three or more contexts. Our examples so far have included two contexts, but we now look at the context definitions used in the Fast Flower Delivery application, and you'll see that one of these is composed of three contexts.

7.8   *Contexts in the Fast Flower Delivery application*

The Fast Flower Delivery application uses several segmentation-oriented, temporal, and composite contexts, which we describe in this section. The first of these is the straightforward segmentation-oriented context shown in table 7.5.

Table 7.5   `Driver` context

Context identifier	Context dimension	Context type	Attribute list
Driver	segmentation-oriented	segmentation	driver

This groups events that relate to a given driver. The only event processing agent that is directly associated with this context is the `Improving  note` agent that traces the driver's ranking modifications to check whether the driver has improved; in addition this context participates in several composite contexts.

The application also uses a segmentation context, shown in table 7.6, which groups events that are related to a particular delivery request.

Table 7.6 `Request` context

Context identifier	Context dimension	Context type	Attribute list
Request	segmentation-oriented	segmentation	requestId

This context makes use of the fact that many of the events in the application contain the `request id` common attribute. The one agent directly associated with this context is the `Automatic assignment` agent from the assignment system (see figure 6.13). This context is also used as part of composite contexts.

We now look at the temporal contexts used by the application. The first of these is shown in table 7.7. This context assigns events into contiguous month-long windows. This context does not have any event processing agents directly associated with it, but is used as part of composite contexts.

Table 7.7 `Monthly` context

Context identifier	Context dimension	Context type	Interval start	Interval end	Recurrence
Monthly	temporal	fixed interval	2000-01-01	2000-02-01	Monthly

The `Daily` context, shown in table 7.8, assigns events into contiguous day-long windows. The `Daily statistics creator` and `Performance evaluation` agents are directly associated with this context; these agents calculate aggregates for all drivers on a daily basis.

Table 7.8 `Daily` context

Context identifier	Context dimension	Context type	Interval start	Interval end	Recurrence
Daily	temporal	fixed interval	2000-01-01	2000-01-02	Daily

The remaining contexts are all composite contexts that combine temporal contexts with one of the segmentation contexts that we have already defined. The first of these is the `Delivery interval` context, shown in tables 7.9a and 7.9b. The context denotes the time interval within which delivery is expected. It expires when the delivery is confirmed, or when the timeout occurs. The `Delivery alert` agent is directly associated with this context; this agent creates an alert if no confirmation is received in the interval.

Table 7.9a shows the composite context; the `Request` context member (which we met earlier in table 7.6) ensures that a new window is opened for each separate bid request, whereas the temporal member (table 7.9b) opens a window each time that an `Assignment` is made.

Table 7.9a `Delivery interval` **context**

Priority order	Member contexts
1	Request
2	Temporal delivery interval

Table 7.9b shows the temporal member context, which lasts for up to 10 minutes from the `required delivery time`.

Table 7.9b `Temporal delivery interval` **member context**

Identifier	Context type	Initiator	Terminator	Expiration time offset	Initiator policy
Temporal delivery interval	event interval	Assignment	Delivery Confirmation	requiredDeliveryTime +10 minutes	Ignore

The next composite context, shown in table 7.10a, is the `Bid interval` composite context; the `Request` context member (which we met earlier in table 7.6) ensures that a new window is opened for each separate bid request, whereas the temporal member (table 7.10b) opens a window each time that a bid request is encountered; the window closes after 2 minutes. This context is used in the assignment system (see figure 6.13) where it gathers together the `Delivery Bid` events that refer to a given `Bid Request`. It is associated with the `Assignment manager` and `Manual assignment preparation` agents.

Table 7.10a `Bid interval` **composite context**

Priority order	Member contexts
1	Request
2	Temporal bid interval

Table 7.10b shows the temporal member context, which lasts for 2 minutes from the `Bid Request`.

Table 7.10b `Temporal bid interval` **member context**

Identifier	Context type	Initiator event	Expiration time offset	Initiator policy
Temporal bid interval	event interval	Bid Request	+2 minutes	Ignore

Table 7.11a defines the `Response interval` composite context. This context opens a window when the assignment system sends a `Delivery Bid` event to a store that has chosen to perform manual driver assignment (separate windows are created for each delivery request); it ends 1 minute after the last `Delivery Bid` event. This context is associated with the `Assignment not done` agent (this agent generates an alert if the store doesn't complete its assignment process in time).

Table 7.11a `Response interval` **composite context**

Priority order	Member contexts
1	Request
2	Temporal response interval

Table 7.11b defines the temporal member context that runs from the first `Delivery Bid` event until 1 minute after the last `Delivery Bid` event.

Table 7.11b `Temporal response interval` **member context**

Identifier	Context type	Initiator event	Expiration time offset	Initiator policy
Temporal response interval	event interval	Delivery Bid	+1 minute	Extend

Table 7.12a defines the `Pickup interval` context; this context denotes the time interval in which a pickup is expected. It ends when the pickup is made or when the time-out occurs. This context is associated with the `Pickup alert` agent which detects pickups that weren't completed on time.

Table 7.12a `Pickup interval` **composite context**

Priority order	Member contexts
1	Request
2	Temporal pickup interval

Table 7.12b defines the temporal context member that runs until a maximum of 5 minutes after the required pickup time.

Table 7.12b `Temporal pickup interval` **member context**

Identifier	Context type	Initiator	Terminator	Expiration time offset	Initiator policy
Temporal pickup interval	event interval	Assignment	Pickup Confirmation	requiredPickUpTime +5 minutes	Ignore

Table 7.13a defines the `Driver evaluation` context; this context creates a new window for each driver every time the driver completes 20 deliveries, and it uses the `Driver` context (table 7.5) as its segmentation member. The `Ranking increase` and `Ranking decrease` agents (figure 6.15) operate in this context so they can reassess the driver's ranking after every 20 deliveries.

Table 7.13a `Driver evaluation` **composite context**

Priority order	Member contexts
1	Driver
2	Confirmations

Table 7.13b defines the `Confirmations` member context which partitions the `Delivery Confirmation` events into non-overlapping groups of 20 events.

Table 7.13b `Confirmations` **temporal member context**

Identifier	Context type	Event list	Interval size	Event period
Confirmations	sliding event interval	Delivery Confirmation	20	20

Table 7.14a defines the `Daily active driver` context; this context is used by the `Daily assignments calculator` agent, which counts the number of assignments per driver for each day when the driver is active. In addition to the `Driver` segmentation context (table 7.5) it contains two temporal contexts. The first of these is the `Daily` context (table 7.8) which would, by itself, open a new window every day. However, it is composed with the `When active` context, and this means that the composite context doesn't open a window until the driver bids to make a delivery that day. The `Daily` context member closes this window at the end of the day.

Table 7.14a `Daily active driver` **context**

Priority order	Member contexts
1	Driver
2	Daily
3	When active

Table 7.14b defines a temporal member of this composite context that is opened whenever a driver creates a `Delivery Bid` event. This is an indication that the driver is active on that day.

Table 7.14b `When active` **temporal member context**

Identifier	Context type	Initiator	Terminator	Initiator policy
When active	event interval	Delivery Bid	-	Ignore

Table 7.15 defines the composite Monthly driver context. This context partitions the relevant events according to the combination of month and driver, and is used by the reporting agents: Permanent weak driver, Idle driver, Improving driver, Consistent strong driver, and Consistent weak driver. It composes two contexts that we have already met, the Driver context (table 7.5) and the Monthly context (table 7.7).

Table 7.15 Monthly driver **composite context**

Priority order	Member contexts
1	Driver
2	Monthly

The following stateless event processing agents are not associated with a context. They therefore operate as if they are associated with the default context which classifies all events to a single partition: Location service, Request enrichment, Driver enrichment, Bid Request creator, Bid routing, and Bid enrichment.

These are the contexts used in the Fast Flower Delivery example. In the next couple of chapters we see how they're used in conjunction with various types of event processing agent, but we conclude this chapter with a quick look at how context is expressed in some event processing platforms.

7.9 Context definitions in practice

Many event processing languages have an explicit time window construct. In the Continuous Computation Language (CCL) language (Aleri/Coral8) a window is defined with a schema, like a stream, but has the ability to store records. This example shows the creation of a window called Book_w.

```
CREATE WINDOW Book_w SCHEMA Book_t KEEP ALL;
INSERT INTO Book_w
 SELECT * FROM Book_s;
```

The KEEP policy specifies the kind of window. Here are some examples:

```
KEEP LAST PER Id
KEEP 3 MINUTES
KEEP EVERY 3 MINUTES
KEEP UNTIL ("MON 17:00:00 ")
KEEP 10 ROWS
KEEP LAST ROW
KEEP 10 ROWS PER Symbol
```

The CCL window has many of the functions of context that we have mentioned in this chapter, including several types of temporal context, and the ability to compose with a segmentation context (see the PER Id and PER Symbol examples). For more information about the semantics of KEEP policies in CCL, refer to the *Event Processing in Action* website.

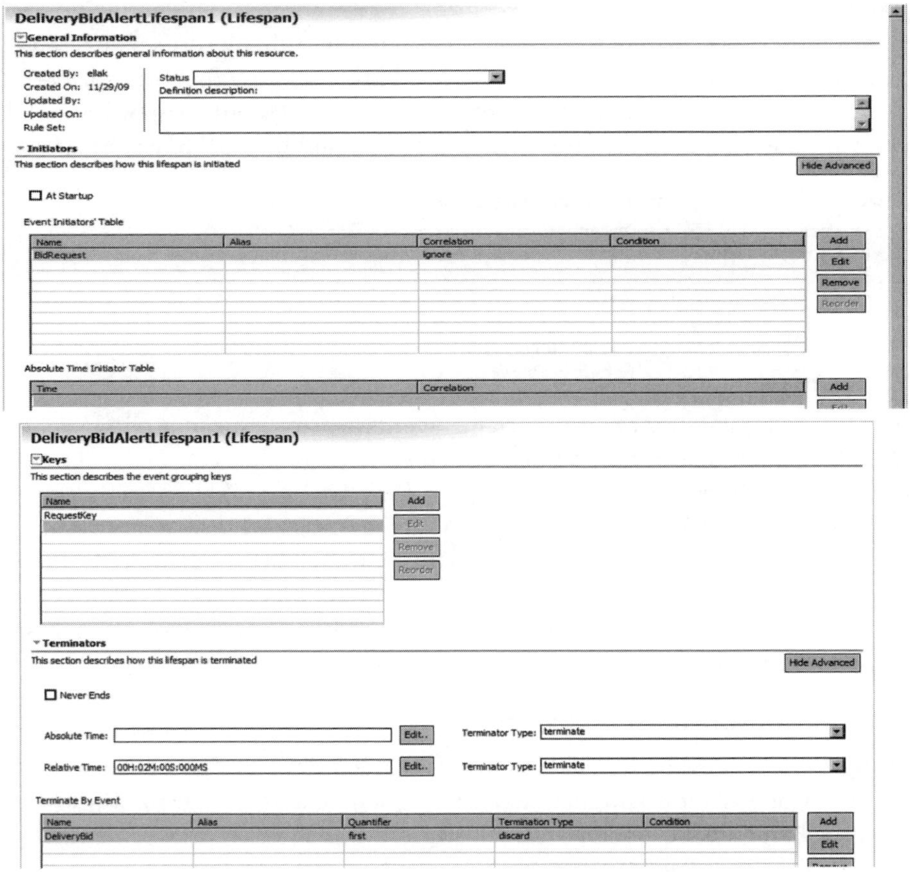

DeliveryBidAlertLifespan1 (Lifespan)

▽**General Information**

This section describes general information about this resource.

Created By: ellak   Status
Created On: 11/29/09   Definition description:
Updated By:
Updated On:
Rule Set:

▽ **Initiators**

This section describes how this lifespan is initiated   Hide Advanced

☐ At Startup

Event Initiators' Table

Name	Alias	Correlation	Condition	
BidRequest		ignore		Add
				Edit
				Remove
				Reorder

Absolute Time Initiator Table

Time	Correlation	
		Add

DeliveryBidAlertLifespan1 (Lifespan)

▽**Keys**

This section describes the event grouping keys

Name	
RequestKey	Add
	Edit
	Remove
	Reorder

▽ **Terminators**

This section describes how this lifespan is terminated   Hide Advanced

☐ Never Ends

Absolute Time: [   ] Edit..   Terminator Type: terminate

Relative Time: [00H:02M:00S:000MS] Edit.. Terminator Type: terminate

Terminate By Event

Name	Alias	Quantifier	Termination Type	Condition	
DeliveryBid		first	discard		Add
					Edit

Figure 7.8 An example definition of temporal segmentation using Amit. Note: Amit is not available through the *Event Processing in Action* website.

Figure 7.8 shows an example definition of a temporal segmentation using Amit,[1] a research project of the IBM Haifa Research Lab that started in 1998; the Amit language is not referred to on the book's website, but is shown here, because it is an interesting use of context.

This example shows the `Bid interval` context. The upper window defines the initiator event for this context. The second window gives a grouping key (a form of segmentation context) and specifies a terminator as an offset of 2 minutes.

Various other languages support some of the context options we have mentioned. We give some more examples in chapter 10, and you can find more on the *Event Processing in Action* website.

---

[1] *Amit* is an acronym for *Active Middleware Technology*; in some sources it is abbreviated as *AMiT*. For further information about the Amit language, refer to Asaf Adi and Opher Etzion: *Amit - the situation manager*. VLDB J, (VLDB) 13(2):177-203 (2004). http://www.springerlink.com/content/nb1qa1d02vvdre00/.

7.10 Summary

In this chapter we have discussed what we mean by context and how it is used in event processing applications. We have looked at the four dimensions of context: temporal, spatial, state-oriented, and segmentation-oriented, and have examined several different context types, both single-dimensional and multidimensional. These concepts were demonstrated using the contexts of the Fast Flower Delivery application.

In the chapters that follow we look in more detail at how context is used with various types of event processing agents. Chapter 8 looks at filtering and transformation event processing agents, and chapter 9 at pattern detection.

7.10.1 Additional reading

Adi, Asaf, and Opher Etzion. 2004. *Amit - the situation manager,* VLDB J. (VLDB) 13(2):177-203. http://www.springerlink.com/content/nb1qa1d02vvdre00/. This article, mentioned before, contains an early definition of context.

Chakravarthy, Sharma, and Qingchun Jiang. 2009. *Stream Data Processing: A Quality of Service Perspective: Modeling, Scheduling, Load Shedding, and* Complex Event Processing. Springer. http://www.amazon.com/Stream-Data-Processing-Perspective-Scheduling/dp/ 0387710027/ref=sr_1_1?ie=UTF8&s=books&qid=1259477906&sr=1-1. This book provides an introduction to stream processing, and discusses the notion of windows.

7.10.2 Exercises

7.1   Can you find other applications of the notion of context, besides event processing? Provide concrete examples.

7.2   Give an example of an event processing application that uses all the types of spatial context.

7.3   Give an example of a composite context that uses multiple segmentation contexts composed with other types of contexts.

7.4   Is it useful to have a context composition that composes two or more temporal contexts? Give an example, or explain why it doesn't make sense.

7.5   Can you think of additional spatial contexts? Give examples.

7.6   Take a specific stream processing language and show how its windowing expressions map to the context types discussed in this chapter.

7.7   Provide an example that employs spatio-temporal context that is the combination of spatial and temporal contexts.

7.8   Provide an example of an interesting use of state-oriented context, listing the cases in which different behavior is required in different states.

7.9   At the end of the section on composite contexts, we gave an example of composite context composed of three members: two segmentation contexts (driver and store) and one sliding temporal interval context (every 20 assignments). Show all the different interpretations of this context that occur using different priority orders, by taking a concrete example.

Filtering and transformation

There are painters who transform the sun to a yellow spot, but there are others who with the help of their art and their intelligence transform a yellow spot into the sun.

—Pablo Picasso

We now return to the examination of event processing networks that we started in chapter 6, to take a deeper look at the event processing agents (EPAs) that an event processing network can contain. The most important kinds of EPAs are Filter, Transformation, and Pattern detect. In this chapter we look at the first two of these. Pattern detection is a large topic, so we dedicate the entire next chapter to that. We also look at the general question of how context is applied to EPAs of all kinds.

In this chapter we will cover the following:

- The idea of a filter, the places where filtering can be performed in an event processing agent, and languages used to specify filter expressions
- The use of event context to perform filtering
- The different types of stateful and stateless transformation
- The effect of filtering and transformation on event header elements

As usual we illustrate the concepts with examples from the Fast Flower Delivery application and examples from other fictional applications. We start with the discussion of filtering and then move on to transformation later in the chapter.

8.1 Filtering in the event processing network

Many event processing applications perform event filtering. An application that involves event producers which produce large numbers of events, such as sensors or news feeds, might need to filter out irrelevant events. Similarly an application might have multiple consumers, all interested in different things, so the application needs to filter the events that it sends to each consumer. Also if the application is performing pattern detection (which we look at it in the next chapter), it may need to filter the events it receives to remove those that aren't relevant to the pattern that it is looking for.

All these cases use filters—a *filter* is an operation which takes an event instance as input and decides whether that instance is to be selected for further processing or not.

> **NOTE** We sometimes say that an instance that is selected has *passed* the filter, or has been *filtered in*, whereas an instance that has not been selected has *failed* or has been *filtered out*.

We can specify filter operations in three places in an event processing network definition:

- On the input terminals of any event processing agent or event consumer.
- As part of the definition of certain event processing agent types. In particular there is the Filter agent type which is specifically dedicated to the task of event filtering.
- As part of an event processing context definition.

At first sight it might seem unnecessary to have more than one place where you can specify a filter, however, our three places have slightly different uses, and having all three allows us to model applications in a more natural way.

A filter on an input terminal lets an event processing agent declare the set of events that it can accept in a way that is independent of its particular type or implementation; this is like declaring the interface of a request-response style service, for example, the portType of a WSDL web service. In some cases the application needs more advanced filters, such as rate-limiting filters or *if-then-else* filters where events that fail the filter are also processed; we provide an explicit Filter agent for use in these cases. Context definitions, as we saw in chapter 7, are about identifying sets of events that are related so that they can be processed together. This can result in a form of filtering, as events that don't get assigned to a context partition are effectively filtered-out, although that is not the main purpose of a context definition.

We now look at each of the three places where a filter may be used. We start with input terminal filters, and this also gives us an opportunity to discuss stateless filter expression languages.

8.1.1 Filtering on an input terminal

Figure 8.1 shows filtering on an input terminal. In this illustration we have represented the different events emitted by the producer as geometric objects, and have shown an English-language filter expression "allow only triangle and square events". We'll look at more formal filter expressions in a minute.

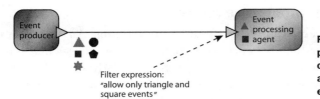

Filter expression:
"allow only triangle and
square events"

Figure 8.1   In this example the event
processing agent has a filter expression
on its input terminal that allows in only
a subset of the events emitted by the
event producer.

If a filter operation is attached to an input terminal, only event instances that pass the filter actually make their way through the terminal; other event instances are filtered-out. It is helpful to be able to specify a filter operation on an input terminal for several reasons:

- It keeps the specification of the filter separate from the definition of the rest of the event processing agent. This means that you can determine the set of events accepted by the agent, without having to know anything else about the agent. This makes it possible to separate the filtering process from the implementation of the agent. For example, filtering could be performed by the channel that transmits events from the producer to the consumer—or even by the producer itself.
- You will recall that we do not specify the internal behavior of an event consumer, so the input terminal is the only place on an event consumer where you can specify a filter.
- Some event processing agents have more than one input terminal, so you can specify different filter operations for each terminal.

The input terminal's filter operation is specified by means of one or more *filter expressions* (assertions). A filter expression is defined as follows.

FILTER EXPRESSION   A *filter expression* (assertion) takes the form of a predicate that is evaluated against an event. The event passes the filter if the predicate evaluates to TRUE, and fails the filter if the predicate evaluates to FALSE.

Several kinds of filter expressions can be attached to an input terminal, and it's possible to mix these different kinds of expressions on a single terminal:

- An *event type filter expression* lists one or more event types (we described event types in chapter 3). The expression evaluates to TRUE if the incoming event is an instance of any of these types.
- An *event header filter expression* is evaluated from the values of header attributes of the event instance.
- An *event content filter expression* is evaluated from the values of payload attributes of the event instance.

An event header or content filter is essentially a collection of attribute name/value assertions, for example, (attributeA == valueX) && (attributeB > valueC). Different event processing languages use different variations of syntax, with differing degrees of expressive power. Table 8.1 shows some of the features that you typically find in a filter expression language.

Table 8.1   Features typically found in filter expressions

Feature	Interpretation
Attribute inclusion	Checks whether the event instance contains an attribute with that name
Attribute has value	Checks that the value of the attribute is not null
Data type assertion	Checks that the attribute's value is valid with respect to its data type, for example, that it is valid as a number, string or timestamp
Binary relation	Tests the value of an attribute against a constant or against the value of another attribute, using a relation such as $<, >, =, \neq, \leq,$ or $\geq$
Conjunction	Expression is the conjunction ("AND") of two or more expressions
Disjunction	Expression is the disjunction ("OR") of two or more expressions
Negation	Expression is the negation of another expression

We use the World Wide Web Consortium (W3C) XML Path Language (XPath) standard as an example of a filter expression language. Not only does it demonstrate all these features, it is also used in event distribution standards such as WS-Notification and WS-Eventing and so is worth covering in some depth. You may be familiar with XPath as a language used to navigate around an Extensible Markup Language (XML) document, or with its use as part of the Extensible Stylesheet Language Transformation (XSLT) language that's used to transform XML documents, and you might now be wondering how it can be used to specify an event filter operation. Here's how it's done.

NOTE   There are two versions of XPath, the older XPath 1.0 version being the more widely used at the time of writing. Most of our discussion will assume XPath 1.0, though the newer XPath 2.0 has some advantages when it comes to handling dates and times.

We start by viewing the event instance's attributes (both header and payload) as XML documents. Note that we do this only to explain how the filter definition works—an implementation doesn't have to hold its event instances as real XML documents. The event instance's header attributes correspond to the top-level elements of the header XML document (the immediate children of the root element of that document), and the payload attributes correspond to the top-level elements of the payload document. The name of each XML element matches the name of the event attribute, and if the event attribute has a complex data type, the corresponding XML element contains child elements representing the structure of that complex data type.

If you have used the XPath language you will have encountered XPath path expressions. These are expressions of the form /chapter/paragraph that are used to point to parts of an XML document. These expressions return XML *node-sets* consisting of zero, one or more nodes from the XML document that match the path expression.

NODE-SET   A *node-set* is a collection of nodes from the document. XPath defines seven types of nodes (root, element, attribute, text, namespace, procedural instruction, and comment) but it's chiefly element nodes that we are interested in here.

We can use a path expression as a filter by interpreting the result as FALSE if the node-set is empty, and TRUE otherwise. As we have set up a correspondence between elements in our notional XML document and attributes in the event instance, a path expression can be used to test for the presence of one or more attributes in the event instance. This is best explained using examples:

```
/Driver
```

A simple path expression like this can be used as a content filter to test that the payload contains a `Driver` attribute. If there's an attribute of this name (whatever its value), the expression returns TRUE and the filter passes the event. A path expression can also contain multiple steps, like this:

```
/Location/Latitude
```

Expressions like this can be used if the event type is expected to contain structured attributes. This example checks that the event instance contains an attribute called `Location` and that it has a child attribute called `Latitude`. You can also test events which contain attribute arrays with filters like this:

```
/Itinerary/Point[7]
```

This expression checks that the document contains at least seven `Itinerary/Point` nodes and so, if you know that the event can't have more than one `Itinerary` attribute, you can use it to filter out any event that doesn't contain an `Itinerary` attribute with at least seven `Points` in it.

> **NOTE** XPath has no concept of an array, even though the syntax of our example expression might suggest that it does. All the expression does is test for the presence of seven `Itinerary/Point` nodes, so it would also be satisfied by an event that had seven `Itinerary` attributes each containing a single `Point`, or one that had two `Itinerary` attributes each containing four `Points`.

Path expressions can also be combined together with the union (`|`) operator:

```
/Driver | /Store
```

This operator combines the two node-sets and so it causes an event to be passed if either of the two path expressions is satisfied. In this example an event will be passed if it contains either a Driver attribute or a Store attribute (or both).

> **NOTE** Recall that if you were to supply separate `/Driver` and `/Store` filter expressions, then they would be ANDed together, so that an event instance would only be passed if it contained both attributes.

The path expressions we have looked at so far are all attribute inclusion tests. You might not need to use expressions like these if you already know the event type (for example, because you have included an event type filter) and if that event type completely dictates the shape of the message. However you can have event types that allow some attributes to be optional, or that permit lists containing a variable number of entries, and a path expression allows you to check that the attributes you need are there. They are also useful when filtering a stream that contains multiple event types; our first example will pass any event instance that contains a `Driver` attribute, regardless of its type.

The XPath language also allows you test the value of an XML node, so we can use that to filter events based on the values of one or more of their attributes.

```
/Ranking > 5
```

This is a simple numeric comparison; it selects events that contain a `Ranking` attribute that has a value greater than 5. An event instance would fail the filter if it had a `Ranking` value less than or equal to 5, and it would also fail if had an attribute called `Ranking` which had a non-numeric value (for example, a character string like "High") or if it had no attribute called `Ranking` at all.

```
/Store = "Exotic Flowers"
```

This selects events that have a character string attribute called `Store` with the value `Exotic Flowers`. If the event type contains a structured attribute, you can use a filter to select events based on a part of the attribute:

```
/Location/Latitude > 0
```

This selects events which have a `Location` that is in the Northern Hemisphere (positive latitude).

```
/Itinerary[1]/Point[7]/Latitude > 0
```

This selects events whose first (or only) `Itinerary` attribute has a seventh point that is in the Northern Hemisphere (the remaining points of course could be in either hemisphere).

The XPath expressions that we have looked at so far have just been path expressions and comparison expressions. We observed that a path expression returns an XML node-set, and we defined the interpretation of the corresponding filter to be such that it passes an event if (and only if) this node-set contains one or more nodes. Comparison expressions, when evaluated against an event instance, already return the value TRUE or FALSE, so the natural interpretation is to pass an event if the expression returns TRUE and to fail it otherwise. We can extend this line of reasoning to allow any XPath expression to be used as a filter. Table 8.2 shows how we do this.

Table 8.2 Interpreting XPath filter expressions

Expression returns	Success condition	Example
Node-set	Node-set contains at least one node	/occurrenceTime
Boolean	Value is TRUE	/ranking > 5
Number	Value is non-zero	25
String	String has non-zero length	"OK"

We aren't going to go into all the details of the XPath language or the things you can do with it. Plenty of tutorials and reference books are available that do that (we suggest one at the end of this chapter). However, we conclude this section with a few examples that show some of the power of the language. XPath has a number of built-in functions that return Boolean values, and we start with a couple of examples that show this:

```
true()
```

This filter passes every event regardless of its content. A more useful Boolean function is `not()` which inverts the logical value of its argument.

```
not(/Credit)
```

This passes every event unless it has one or more attributes called `Credit`. The logical operators `and` and `or` are also available and can be used to combine other Boolean expressions:

```
/Credit or /Ranking > 5
```

This example passes any event that contains a `Credit` attribute (recall that `/Credit` by itself would return TRUE in such a case) and also any event that has a `Ranking` attribute with a value greater than 5.

   The comparisons that we have looked at so far have all compared an attribute value against a literal constant contained in the filter expression, but it is also possible to compare the values of two attributes in the event with each other:

```
/Credit = /Debit
```

The XPath interpretation of this expression is a little tricky. If the event instance contains exactly one `Credit` attribute and exactly one `Debit` attribute, the event is passed, provided that the two attributes have the same value. If the event doesn't have `Credit` or `Debit` attributes, it is filtered-out. If the event contains more than one `Credit` or `Debit` attribute, the event is passed, provided there is a match between any one of the `Credit` and any one of the `Debit` attributes.

   Our remaining examples show the use of more XPath built-in functions:

```
count(/Credit) = count(/Debit)
```

The `count()` function returns the number of nodes present in the node-set, so this filter passes an event provided that it has exactly the same number of `Credit` and `Debit` attributes (possibly none).

```
count(/Credit) mod 2
```

This example passes an event if it has an odd number of `Credit` attributes (recall from table 8.2 that if an expression returns a numeric result, the event is passed if that result is non-zero).

```
/Itinerary/Point[last()]/Latitude > 0
```

The `last()` function can be useful when dealing with variable length arrays. This example passes any event containing an `Itinerary` which ends up in the Northern Hemisphere.

XPath has a number of string handing functions. The next example shows one:

```
contains(/Store, "Exotic")
```

This filter passes any event that has a `Store` attribute whose value contains the substring "Exotic". We conclude our examples by looking at a time comparison. The XPath 2.0 standard contains a number of useful time functions:

```
op:time-less-than(/occurrenceTime,xs:time(10:00:00))
```

This tests the `occurrenceTime` timestamp and passes an event if it occurred earlier than 10:00 A.M.

8.1.2 *Filtering in an event processing agent*

The filter expressions that we have looked at so far are placed on input terminals, and have two common characteristics:

- They are simple pass/fail filters. If an event instance fails the filter test, it is not processed by the event processing agent or event consumer.
- They are stateless, that is to say, the process of filtering one incoming event instance doesn't influence the way that any subsequent event instances are filtered by that terminal.

Some event processing agents involve a further filtering step that takes place logically after any input terminal filtering has been performed. This filtering forms part of the event processing logic itself and is not subject to the constraints that we just listed. These filters can be stateful, and events that fail them can continue to be processed, not just those that pass. We encounter one use of such filtering in the next chapter when we look at pattern detection, but here we take a closer look at the explicit Filter EPA which we introduced in section 6.2.3, and which is illustrated in figure 8.2.

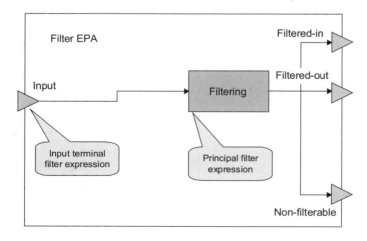

Figure 8.2 A schematic view of the Filter event processing agent

The Filter EPA has a single Input terminal which, like all input terminals, can have a filter expression associated with it. The output from this filter expression is then fed into the agent's main filtering step, as shown in figure 8.2. The output from this step is made available through three output terminals. Event instances that pass the filter are emitted through the *Filtered-in* terminal, but event instances that fail the filter are made available through the *Filtered-out* terminal. This means that the event processing application designer can use a Filter agent as a kind of if-then-else construct to route event instances to different parts of the event processing network, depending on whether they pass or fail a particular filter.

> **NOTE** Of course the event processing network designer is not required to connect either the Filtered-in, or Filtered-out output terminals to anything else (event instances that are passed to an unconnected output terminal are simply discarded).

Another way of thinking about it is that the Filter agent splits the incoming stream into two substreams, one containing the event instances that pass the filter, the other containing those that do not. You can subdivide the stream further by using a second Filter agent as shown in figure 8.3.

This example is taken from an imaginary loyalty card application. The application processes a stream of incoming events relating to card-holders, and applies different processing logic depending on a card-holder's membership status. In this fictional loyalty card scheme there are just three levels of membership, imaginatively called *Gold*, *Silver*, and *Bronze*.

The first filter separates out the Gold customer events from the others; these events are routed through its Filtered-in terminal. The stream coming out of its Filtered-out terminal could contain a mixture of Silver and Bronze customer

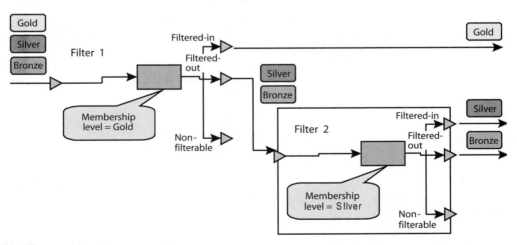

Figure 8.3 Using two successive Filter agents to divide an incoming event stream into three substreams

events, so the application passes them to a second agent which separates events relating to `Silver` customers from those relating to `Bronze`.

You'll have seen that the Filter EPA has an additional output terminal, which we refer to as the Non-filterable terminal. This output terminal is used for the case where the incoming event instance is incompatible with the filter expression, and the expression cannot be evaluated as either TRUE or FALSE, (some filter expression languages allow expressions that can fail when evaluated against certain input events, for example, if the input event results in a divide by zero). If this happens, the incoming event is routed to the Non-filterable terminal.

The Filter agent's principal filter expression can be one of the stateless expressions described in section 8.1.1 (topic filter, event header filter, or event content filter), but we also permit some simple stateful filters. Stateful filters need a context within which to operate, so in order to discuss them we need to return to the idea of an event processing context, which we introduced in chapter 7.

8.1.3   *Filtering and event processing contexts*

You will recall from chapter 7 that an event processing context groups event instances into one or more subsets called *context partitions*. The number of these partitions depends on the context definition:

- Some contexts give rise to just one context partition, for example, a spatial context definition that requires events to occur within a specific building.
- Some contexts can give rise to a fixed number of context partitions, for example, a context that separates events based on their location's zip code.
- Some contexts, in particular some temporal contexts, don't have a fixed number of instances; context partitions can be created and destroyed dynamically over time.

If an event processing agent is associated with a context, each context partition is handled by a separate instance of that agent. However, there might be event instances that are not classified into any of the context partitions (especially in the case where there's only one context partition). These event instances aren't handled by any instance of the agent, and so are automatically filtered out. This is true whether it's a Filter agent or any other kind of agent and it is separate from the filter, if any, on the input terminal.

Figure 8.4 shows the logical order of the three kinds of filtering that we have been talking about. Filtering specified on an input terminal applies to every instance of the event processing agent and takes place before the context is used to determine which instance of the agent (if any) is to process the event. Input terminal filtering is applied first because, as we saw in chapter 7, some contexts count the number of events received and we don't want events that are filtered out by the input terminal to count towards the size of the window. In some cases (like the Filter agent that is illustrated in figure 8.4) further filtering is performed by the particular agent instance that was selected by the context step.

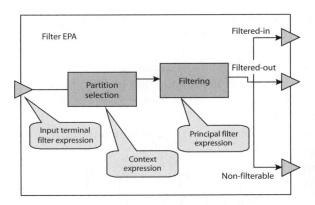

Figure 8.4   A Filter EPA showing the logical position of the partition filter, after the input terminal and before the internal filter step

Figure 8.4 shows the three filters that an incoming event has to negotiate in a Filter event processing agent. It's important to note that this is purely a logical view. An implementation is free to compile all the three filter steps together into a single operation provided that this achieves the same result. You should also note that this illustration relates to the entire event processing agent, and not to a specific instance of this agent. The input terminal filter expression applies to all of these agent instances and it's the instance selection step that hands off the event to the agent instance that is to process it.

Now that we have discussed context, we can return to the question of stateful Filter agents.

8.1.4   *Stateful filtering in an event processing agent*

Filtering is frequently stateless in nature; however, stateful filtering can be used to sample a stream of events, in order to reduce its data rate. Of course this is done only in applications where discarding events is acceptable. Stateful filtering can only be performed in a Filter agent (the filtering on input terminals is always stateless), and uses a combination of the agent's context and filter expression. We define three stateful filter expressions as follows:

- *First m*—This passes the first m event instances in the context partition window.
- *Last m*—This passes the last (most recent) m event instances in the window.
- *Random m*—This passes a random set of m instances.

These filters are always used with a temporal context. First m filters can pass events as soon as they are encountered; a last m filter has to buffer up the events and can't start passing them until the window has closed. If the window contains fewer than m events, all events in the window are passed. Here are some ways to use these expressions to sample a stream of events:

- First m out of n sample. The Filter agent has a first m filter expression, and it is associated with a sliding event interval with a window of size n. A new agent instance is created to handle every block of n successive event instances, so its event count is initialized to zero, and the agent instance passes the first m event instances out of the n in that block. As an example, a first 1 out of 2 filter would pass the first event that it receives, and every other event thereafter.

- Random m out of n sample. This filter is similar to the previous one, except it has a random m filter expression. Using this expression in combination with a sliding event window of size n, we obtain a filter that passes a random m out of every n event instances.
- Rate limiting k events per second sample. The first m filter expression can be used with a sliding fixed interval context to ensure that the rate at which events emerge from the Filtered-in output terminal doesn't exceed a specified value. If the rate at which events arrive at the agent (after passing through any input terminal filter) is less than the specified value of k events per second, they are all passed through to the Filtered-in output terminal, but if it is higher, excess event instances are diverted to the Filtered-out terminal.

These filters operate in an unsubtle fashion; we encounter more sophisticated stateful ways of filtering incoming events when we look at pattern detection in chapter 9. We now turn our attention to this chapter's other main focus area, transformation of event instances and event streams.

8.2 Transformation in depth

Transformation event processing agents take one or more input events and create different output events that are based on them. This transformation can be *stateless*, meaning that each incoming event instance is processed independently of any preceding event instances and each output event is derived from just one input event, or it can be *stateful*, in which case an output event may have been derived from multiple input events.

As we saw in chapter 6, we can classify Transformation agents, as in figure 8.5, depending on whether they are stateful or stateless and depending on their number of input and output terminals.

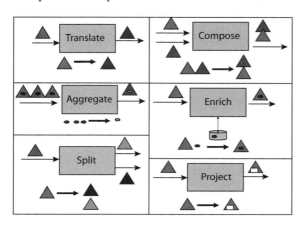

Figure 8.5 Classification of the different types of Transformation agents. The triangles represent event instances; the arrows show the number of input and output streams for each type.

We start by looking at the three stateless agents that have a single input and single output stream, and then move on to the Split, Aggregate, and Compose agents. Our discussion focuses initially on transformation of the event instance's payload attributes and we defer discussion of the header attributes until the end of this section.

8.2.1   *Project, translate, and enrich*

These three types have the same basic structure, which is shown in figure 8.6. They have a primary Input terminal which, just like all other input terminals, can have a filter expression assigned to it (an agent can have additional input terminals if the context uses initiator or terminator events that aren't processed by the agent). As with other agents, there is then an instance selection step; if the agent is associated with a context, this step filters and routes the incoming event to the appropriate agent instance in the way we discussed in section 8.1.3.

The heart of the Transformation agent is the derivation step, which generates the output event instance. If the derivation step is successful, the output event is emitted through the Output terminal. In some cases it's possible for the derivation step to fail. If this happens, the agent routes the original incoming event through the *Failure* terminal, allowing it to be processed by error handling logic downstream in the event processing network.

The agent specification includes the mapping or derivation rules that describe how the output event's attributes are to be derived from the input. We refer to this as the *derivation expression*.

> **DERIVATION EXPRESSION**   A *derivation expression* is an expression that assigns values to the attributes of a derived event. A derivation expression can refer to values of the input event attributes.

If the output event type just has simple attributes, things are relatively straightforward: each attribute in the output event is either copied across from the input event, set to a fixed value, or set to a value computed from the input event and/or other input data. In simple transformation cases the output event instance can have the same type as

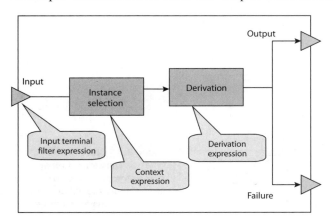

Figure 8.6   Internal logic of a transformation agent

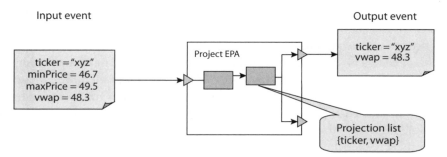

Figure 8.7   A Project agent can be used to simplify an event by removing one or more of its attributes.

the corresponding input event, although a Transformation agent is permitted to make more radical modifications, resulting in an output event instance that is of a different type from the input.

THE PROJECT EPA

The *Project* EPA is the simplest kind of transformation agent. In this agent the payload of the output event instance is made up of a subset of the attributes from the input event; the derivation expression of the Project EPA is the list of input attributes to be copied over. Figure 8.7 shows an example of an event being processed by a Project agent.

This example comes from a stock trading application, where the input event contains a `ticker` attribute that identifies the stock in question, with attributes that give the maximum-, minimum-, and volume-weighted average price (vwap). The derivation expression lists the attributes to be projected in to the output event—in this case we are interested only in the `ticker` and `vwap` attributes, so the `minPrice` and `maxPrice` are left out of the output event.

THE TRANSLATE EPA

The *Translate* EPA can copy attributes to the output event, like the Project agent, but it can also modify the values of copied attributes or even insert new attributes into the output event. The derivation expression for a Translate EPA specifies how each output attribute is to be computed.

Figure 8.8 shows a simple example.

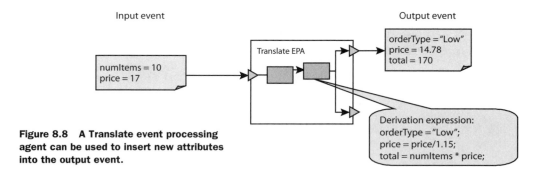

Figure 8.8   A Translate event processing agent can be used to insert new attributes into the output event.

In this example the EPA inserts the new attribute `orderType` with a fixed value ("Low"). It adjusts the value of the `price` attribute from the value supplied in the input event, and it adds a new attribute called `total`, computed from two attributes of the input event. The derivation expression in this example is made up of simple arithmetic assignments where the left-hand side of an assignment identifies an attribute in the output event, and the right-hand side refers to attributes in the input event. The syntax we have used is just for illustration. In practice, an event processing language may implement such translations as part of the language itself, as shown in examples later in this chapter. In some cases event processing platforms allow transformations to be written using conventional languages such as the following:

- Scripting languages like JavaScript, PHP, or PERL. These have powerful string handling functions, which are useful if you want to manipulate the values of the input attributes
- General purpose programming languages such as Java
- XSLT (Extensible Stylesheet Language Transformations)

These languages can be used just to express simple assignments, one for each attribute in the output event, but when handling event types that have more complex structures such as lists, arrays, and structured elements, it is sometimes helpful to be able to use loops and other program control structures in the language itself.

The XSLT language was designed for the purpose of converting one XML document into another, or for converting an XML document into a non-XML format. However, it can be used to derive the output event from the input event, regardless of whether the events in question are actually serialized as XML documents. We can use it in a manner similar to the way that XPath is used for filtering (see section 8.1.1). We start by viewing the attributes of the input event instance as an XML document, regardless of whether it is actually serialized as such. The event instance's attributes correspond to the top-level elements of the header XML document (the immediate children of the root element of that document). The name of each XML element matches the name of the event attribute, and if the event attribute has a complex data type, the corresponding XML element contains child elements representing the structure of that complex data type. We take a similar approach with the output event, and then map the effect of our XSLT stylesheet onto the underlying attributes in the input and output event instances.

We illustrate this with the example that was shown in figure 8.8. Our input event, represented as a document, looks like this:

```
<event>
    <numItems>10</numItems>
    <price>17</price>
</event>
```

Remember that this is a logical representation, and an implementation doesn't necessarily create this document at runtime. Similarly the output event can be represented like this:

```
<event>
    <orderType>Low</orderType>
    <price>14.78</price>
    <total>170</total>
</event>
```

Listing 8.1 shows an XSLT stylesheet that can be used to transform this input event to the output event.

Listing 8.1   XSLT stylesheet performing the transformation

```
<xsl:stylesheet xmlns:xsl="http://www.w3.org/1999/XSL/Transform"
    version="1.0" >

  <xsl:template match="/event">
     <event>
        <orderType> Low </orderType>
        <price>
           <xsl:value-of select="round (100*//price div 1.15) div 100" />
        </price>
        <total>
           <xsl:value-of select="//price * //numItems" />
        </total>
     </event>
  </xsl:template>
</xsl:stylesheet>
```

This stylesheet uses an XSLT template to construct the output event. The `<order-Type>`, `<price>` and `<total>` tags insert the corresponding XML tags into the output. The `<xsl:value-of>` elements fill in the computed values. Note the computation of price includes a rounding operation, as otherwise it would be set to the value 14.782608695652176.

THE ENRICH EPA

The *Enrich* EPA can copy, modify, or insert new attributes, just like the Translate agent, but its derivation step can take input from a global state element, as well as from the input event. It can thus add data to the output event that was not present in the input. As you can see from figure 8.9, the Enrich EPA has a reference to a global state element that contains the information used by the enrichment operation.

You will recall from chapter 6 that the global state element encapsulates data that can be accessed by one or more event processing agents. The Enrich EPA can use a global state element as a source of *reference data* (this is data that changes relatively slowly, and is often external to the event processing application itself). The agent uses this reference data when building the output event.

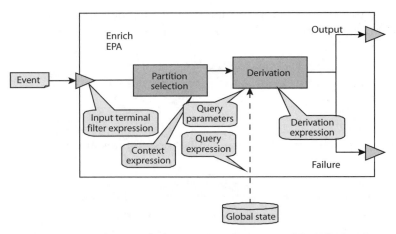

Figure 8.9   The Enrich agent augments the output event with attribute values derived by querying a global state element.

In figure 8.10 we show an example—the `Request enrichment` agent—from the Fast Flower Delivery application. This should help explain both the concept and the specification of an Enrich agent. You will see that it is quite straightforward—a single attribute from the input event is used as a key to return a couple of values from a database table which are then added to the output event.

The enrichment operation shown here happens right at the start of the Fast Flower Delivery event flow. A flower store (in this case, Exotic Flowers) submits a

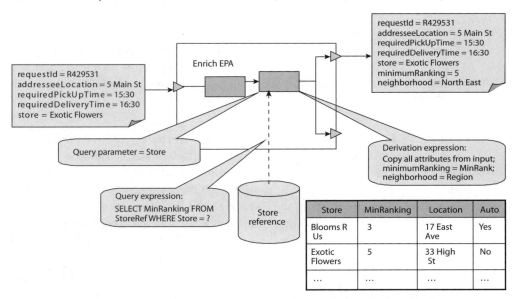

Figure 8.10   The `Request enrichment` agent from the Fast Flower Delivery application. This agent uses the `store` attribute of the input event to find the flower store's neighborhood and the minimum driver ranking that is acceptable to it, and adds these values as attributes to the output event.

Delivery Request event, shown at the top left of the figure. When the Exotic Flowers store signed up for the Fast Flower Delivery application a profile record was created for it, and this is held centrally, with profiles from other stores, in the Store refer-ence table shown at the bottom of the figure. Among these details is the minimum ranking that the store is prepared to accept (you will recall that the Fast Flower Deliv-ery application assigns rankings to its drivers).

When it comes time to assign a driver to this request, the Fast Flower Delivery application needs to know the minimum ranking acceptable to the store but, as you can see from figure 8.10, this information is not contained in the original Delivery Request. The application therefore uses the Enrich agent shown to look up this value from the Store reference table and add it as a new output to the Delivery Request event. The agent also looks in the Store reference table to find out what part of the city the flower store is in. You can see the result in the output event at the top right.

Now let's look at the three bits of specification needed to make this work (remem-ber that this agent has to work for all stores, not just for Exotic Flowers). Each time it receives an input event, the agent issues a query to the global state element, and the first bit of specification we encounter is the *query parameter* list. This identifies one or more attributes from the input event that are to be used in the query. In our example we just need one, the store attribute, because this is used as the key to look up the data we need. Note that the agent could identify the attributes simply by attribute name, or (if more complex input event types are being used) by XPath expressions.

Next we come to the query expression, which specifies the query itself. Different global state implementations support different kinds of queries, the simplest being a basic keyed lookup like that provided by a Java hash table. In our example we assume that the store reference data is held in a relational database table and that access to this data is through a SQL statement:

```
SELECT MinRank, Region FROM StoreRef WHERE Store = ?
```

This is a very simple query, which just looks up the reference data for a single store and returns the ranking and neighborhood values of that store. The ? is a placeholder for a parameter, and each time an input event is received, a parameter from the input event, as specified by the query parameter list, is substituted in place of the ?. In the example of figure 8.10 it's the value Exotic Flowers that is used. This query returns just one result containing the two values we are interested in.

Lastly we come to the derivation expression, which indicates how the output event is to be constructed. This is similar to the Translate EPA except that the computation can now use values returned by the query as well as the values of attributes in the input event. In our example we copy across the attributes from the input event and add the two new attributes that were returned by the query.

Before we leave the Enrich agent, you should note that our query returned exactly one row from the table. What should an agent do if the query returns more than one row, or none at all? The case where no rows are returned is likely to be an error, so in that case the agent routes the original unchanged event through to the Failure output terminal. (If your application actually expects that some events don't get enriched, that's fine. There's nothing to stop it from continuing to process events that are emitted through the Failure terminal.)

The Enrich agent can take several actions if the query returns multiple rows, and what's appropriate depends on the nature of the query and the meaning of the data in the table. The Enrich agent specification contains a policy that indicates which one to take.

> **MULTIPLE RESULTS POLICY** The *multiple results* policy defines the behavior of an Enrich event processing agent when its query returns more than one result. The possible policy values are first, last, every, and combine.

The four values for this policy are defined as follows:

- *First*—Use only the first row that is returned.
- *Last*—Use only the last row that is returned.
- *Every*—A separate output event is generated, one for each row that is returned.
- *Combine*—A single output event is returned, but the derivation rules have access to all the rows when preparing the output.

The combine option is useful if the output event type supports structured data types, as it can be used to build a list of data items in that event. For example, suppose the input event is an indication that there's been a power failure in a floor of a building. An Enrich agent could augment that event with the list of all the systems impacted by that failure, obtained by querying a facilities database. We now look at partial converse of this, the Split EPA, which can be used to pull a single event apart into constituent parts.

8.2.2 Split

The *Split* event processing agent takes a single input event and breaks it apart to produce multiple events as output. As you can see from figure 8.11, a Split agent can have multiple output terminals. In an application you might want the various output events (which could be of different types) to be processed differently, so it is convenient to have them presented on different output terminals.

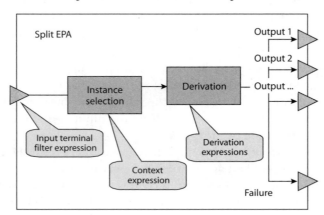

Figure 8.11   A Split event processing agent

A Split agent can have filtering on its Input terminal and multiple context partitions, just like every other EPA. The difference between Split and Translate is that a Split agent's derivation expressions are capable of producing multiple output events.

A Split agent can be used when an application receives a complicated event object and has multiple consumers, each interested in seeing only one particular aspect of the original event; an extreme example is a split that extracts each individual attribute from the original event and forwards it as a separate event instance in its own right. A split is also useful when the input event instance is a batching together of several individual events, for example, a composite event or the result of the enrich-with-combine operation that we looked at in the previous section. We might need to split such an event into its constituent parts so that each part can be processed individually.

There are three ways of specifying a Split EPA, depending on the nature of the split to be performed. We start by describing the *static* approach, which is useful when the input event has a fixed structure, or where there's a well understood set of events that we wish to pull out of it. We then describe the *iterative* approach, which is useful if the input event contains lists and repeating structures of arbitrary length (both these approaches can use the same transformation languages that we discussed in section 8.2.1). Finally there is the special case of splitting a composite event type.

STATIC SPLITTING

A static split specification looks just like a translate specification with these exceptions:

- It consists of multiple derivation expressions, instead of just one.
- Each derivation expression is associated with a particular output terminal.

When an input event is received it is processed independently by all of the derivation expressions, so if you have five derivation expressions, the process will result in five output events. These event instances are then routed to their associated output terminals. Note that you can have more than one derivation expression assigned to the same terminal; in particular you can have them all assigned to Output 1. This would mean that the five output events would be emitted, one after the other, through Output 1. In this example we have chosen to call the terminals Output 1, Output 2, and so on. However, these names are not significant, as the semantics of the terminal are defined by its derivation expression. An agent designer can therefore choose to give them more meaningful names.

The derivation expressions could be projection expressions, extracting different attributes from the input event. Each expression could extract a completely different set of attributes from all the others but this doesn't have to be the case. For example, in a stock trading application you might want all the output events to contain a Tick Symbol attribute.

ITERATIVE SPLITTING

A static splitting specification will always (except in failure cases) produce the same number of output events. In contrast, in an iterative split the number of output events is determined by the content of the input event. Iterative splits are useful if the input event type contains variable length lists or repeating structures of variable length.

An iterative split has a single derivation expression typically written in XSLT, a scripting language (like JavaScript, PERL, or PHP), or a general purpose programming language such as Java. These languages contain loops or other program control structures that make it possible to walk through the incoming event instance and unpack it into a variable number of output events.

You encounter a slight difficulty when using XSLT, as this language generates only a single output file, yet we want to use it to generate multiple output events. We can get around this problem by using a single XSLT stylesheet to output a kind of composite event. This takes the form of a single event, but its attributes are themselves all events—in fact they are the events that make up the output of the iterative split operation. The agent can obtain this output from XSLT and unpack it mechanically, routing the events that it extracts out through the appropriate output terminals. This unpacking process is a special case of our third kind of split, the composite event split.

SPLITTING COMPOSITE EVENTS

In chapter 3 we came across the idea of a composite event type. This is a special type of event which is actually made up of a collection of other event types. As a result, an instance of a composite event contains a collection of other event objects, bundled together either for convenience, or because there is a causal or other connection between them. There's enough information contained in the composite event type definition to let someone extract the member events from a composite, and so a Split EPA can be configured to decompose a composite event just by being given its type; no XSLT stylesheet or further derivation expression is required.

8.2.3   *Aggregate*

All the transformations we've looked at so far have been stateless. Each input event is processed independently of any others and gives rise to zero or more output events. In contrast our two remaining kinds of transformation, *Aggregate* and *Compose*, are stateful. An output event from one of these kinds of agent can contain information derived from more than one input event. As they are stateful, they operate within an event processing context, like the stateful filters that we discussed in section 8.1.4.

The Aggregate EPA is widely used in stream processing. It takes a single stream of input events from its Input terminal, groups the event instances from this stream into context partitions, and then derives output events from them. Figure 8.12 shows that the logical structure of an Aggregate EPA is similar to that of a Translate EPA, except that there is an additional step between the partition selection and output event derivation.

In this additional step the input events that belong to the current context partition (or in some implementations data derived from these events) are gathered together so that they are available when the derivation step runs. Note that the derivation step doesn't necessarily run every time an input event is received; by default it only runs when a temporal context partition closes.

There are two kinds of Aggregate EPA. One of these is the reverse of the composite event split that we mentioned in the previous section; it takes the events in the current

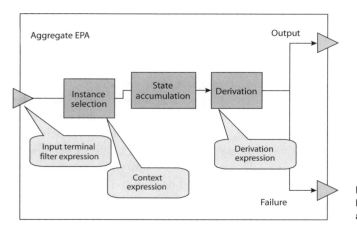

Figure 8.12 An Aggregate EPA, showing the state accumulation step

context partition and when that partition closes it combines them to form a single composite event, which it then routes through the Output terminal.

For the remainder of this section we concentrate on the other kind of Aggregate EPA. This kind doesn't simply bundle the events that are waiting in the context partition; instead it uses a derivation expression to construct an output event. This derivation expression is similar to a derivation expression for the Translate EPA except that instead of reading attributes from a single input event, the expression has a repertoire of *derivation functions* that it can use to compute information from the events in the context partition. To see what that means, let's look at the example in figure 8.13, which is the Daily assignments calculator agent from the Fast Flower Delivery application.

The Fast Flower Delivery application uses this agent to count the number of assignments that each driver receives during the course of each day. This information is then used to help assign a ranking to each driver. Note that phrase "each driver receives during the course of each day": this means that the application needs to maintain a separate total for each driver, and the counting process needs to start

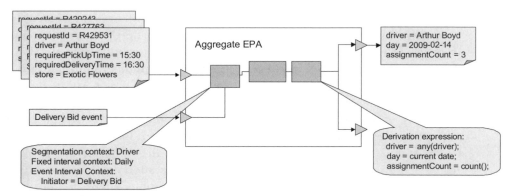

Figure 8.13 The Daily assignments calculator agent from the Fast Flower Delivery application. This shows how an Aggregate agent can be used to count the number of Assignment events associated with a given driver on any one day.

afresh every day. That suggests that we need to use a separate instance of the agent for each driver and that we need to track each day separately. By now you've probably realized that the way to do this is through a context definition, and you can see the one that we're using at the bottom left of figure 8.13. It is the `Daily active driver` context that we looked at in chapter 7. This is a composite context that includes a segmentation context and two temporal contexts. The segmentation part assigns each driver to a separate partition. The temporal part includes a fixed interval context that ensures that a new instance of the agent (for each driver) is created each day and that this instance outputs its result at the end of the day. In fact, that's not quite what happens in this example because we've decided we don't want to receive any output event if a given driver has chosen to take the day off. To do this we include an event-initiated temporal context so that a new agent instance, for any particular driver, is created only when that driver makes his or her first delivery bid of the day. The agent needs to receive `Delivery Bid` events, but these events are used only to trigger new partitions and aren't included in the aggregation. The agent therefore receives them on a separate input terminal (only events received through the main Input terminal participate in the aggregation).

As we approach the end of each day, we should have as many instances of this agent as there have been active drivers. Each instance has been collecting its input events, and at the end of the day they each run their derivation step and output their results. The cleverness of this agent specification lies mainly in the context definition. The derivation expression, shown at the bottom right of figure 8.13, is relatively simple. We want the output event to contain the name of the driver and the count for that day, and to produce these we use a couple of derivation functions. Note that some implementations save all the input event instances and aggregate them at the end, and others compute partial totals as they go along. Either way the result is as if the events have all been saved.

The driver's name can be taken from any of the event instances in the context partition. Because the segmentation context uses the `driver` attribute to segment the input events, all the events in a given context partition will have the same `driver` attribute value. The `any()` derivation function instructs the derivation step to pick an arbitrary instance and extract the value of the named attribute from it. The `count()` derivation function, as you might expect, returns the number of instances in the current context partition. In our example you can see that driver Arthur Boyd received three assignment events.

Several of our derivation functions take an attribute name or XPath expression as an input parameter. Such a function takes all the event instances in the current context partition that contain this attribute, extracts the values of the given attribute from each event, and then performs a specific operation on this set of attribute values. Note that Aggregate EPAs are often used in situations where all input events have the same type, in which case the attribute is likely to be present in all the events in the context partition.

We've already discussed a couple of derivation functions. Table 8.3 contains a longer list.

Table 8.3 Derivation functions that can be used in an Aggregate event processing agent

Name	Argument	Returns
first	Attribute Name	Attribute value taken from the first event that arrived in the context partition
last	Attribute Name	Attribute value taken from the last event that arrived in the context partition
any	Attribute Name	Attribute value taken from an arbitrary event in the context partition
min	Attribute Name	Smallest of all the values of the attribute
max	Attribute Name	Largest of all the values of the attribute
sum	Attribute Name	Sum of all the values of the attribute
avg	Attribute Name	Arithmetic mean of all the values of the attribute
stdev	Attribute Name	Standard deviation of all the values of the attribute
distinct	Attribute Name	Number of distinct values of the attribute
concat	Attribute Name	A list that contains all the attribute values
dConcat	Attribute Name	A list that contains all the distinct attribute values
count	-	Number of event instances in the current context partition
partitionCount	-	Number of active partitions for the current context
globalCount	-	Number of event instances in all active partitions of the current context

In the example in figure 8.13 each agent instance runs its derivation step only once, when the temporal context partition ends (in this case, at the end of a day). This is the default behavior for an Aggregate agent, but in some situations you might want to receive intermediate output results before the end of the context partition. To allow this, the Aggregate agent has one further configuration parameter—the *aggregation frequency*. A frequency value of one means that the derivation step runs every time a new input event is received into the context partition. A frequency value of two means it runs for every second event, and so on. Note that you would normally only use this parameter if your temporal context has non-overlapping windows.

8.2.4 *Compose*

Our final transformation EPA is the *Compose* agent. This is stateful, like Aggregate, but instead of operating on successive events in one stream it takes in two input streams, which we refer to as the *left stream* and the *right stream*. It matches event instances from

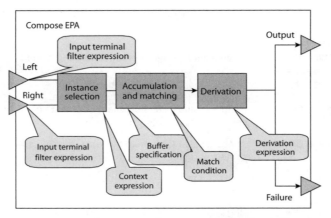

Figure 8.14   The Compose event processing agent

one stream against event instances from the other, in other words, it performs a *join* operation on the two streams. Figure 8.14 shows the logical construction of a Compose EPA. Note that the terminology *left, right,* and *join* is borrowed from relational algebra, as the effect of this EPA is similar to a SQL JOIN operation on a pair of database tables.

As with all EPAs, there is an optional filter step on the input terminals, followed by a context step that routes incoming events to the appropriate agent instance (or instances). Each instance accumulates events and runs a matching operation that compares event instances from one input stream against those from the other. The matching operation runs like this: each time a new event instance is received, through either one of the two input terminals, it is paired with events that have previously been received through the other terminal. This pair of events is then tested to see if they meet a specified *match condition*. If they do meet the condition, the derivation step runs and produces an output event, based on the two event instances that make up the pair.

We illustrate this using the simple example of figure 8.15. In this example suppose that a highway authority wishes to measure the speed of vehicles traveling over

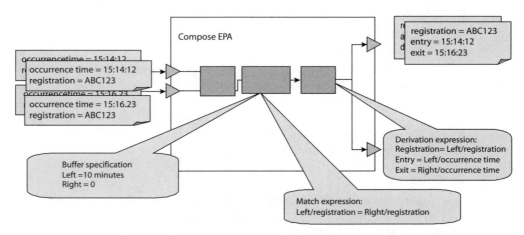

Figure 8.15   Use of a Compose event processing agent to match up vehicle arrival and departure times

a particular section of highway. It installs a camera at either end, one to produce an `arrival` event whenever a vehicle enters the section, and the other to produce a `departure` event when a vehicle leaves, and then has to match the `arrival` event for a particular vehicle with the `departure` event for the same vehicle so that it can see how long the vehicle has spent in the section of road.

You can see some `arrival` and `departure` events at the top left. They both have the same format, containing a vehicle registration mark and an occurrence timestamp (for simplicity we only show the time part of this timestamp). The `arrival` events come into the agent through the Left terminal and the departure events through the Right one. The match condition in this example is a simple equality test (we are interested in matching up `arrival` and `departure` events for the same vehicle). Note that the attributes we are matching on have the same name in both events in the pair, so we have to distinguish them by referring to them as `Left/registration` and `Right/registration`. Similarly the derivation expression has to distinguish between `Left/occurrenceTime` and `Right/occurrenceTime` when constructing an output event.

Regardless of whether a match has been found or not, the Compose agent instance can then retain the incoming event so that it can be matched against future events from the other stream. However, if it were to hold on to every event that it received it could, over time, build up a huge number of events. Not only would this be bad for performance (each time a new event is received it has to be matched against all the accumulated events from the other stream), it's often the case that we only want to see matches that happen reasonably close to each other in time. In our example, suppose that this section of highway were to lie on a driver's way to work and she drives along it every day. We wouldn't want arrivals from Monday to be matched with departures from Tuesday, or—even worse—for departures from Monday to be matched with arrivals from Tuesday. To cope with this, the agent has a buffer specification which controls how many (or how long) events from each input terminal are kept. In this example we have asked for `arrival` events to be kept for 10 minutes (it's only a short section of road that is being monitored and there's nowhere to stop along it), and we have asked for `departure` events not to be accumulated at all. This means that each `departure` event is tested against the last 10 minutes' worth of `arrival` events and is then discarded.

The matching and accumulation step is controlled by a number of parameters. We have met a few in the example that we have just looked at, but here is a fuller list:

- *Left buffer specification*—This controls how many event instances from the Left input terminal should be retained. It can be specified either as a count of instances or as a time interval.

- *Right buffer specification*—This controls how many event instances from the Right input terminal should be retained. It can be specified either as a count of instances or as a time interval.

- *Unmatched left policy*—This states what should happen when an event is evicted from the left buffer if that event hasn't been matched with anything prior to eviction.

- *Unmatched right policy*—This states what should happen when an event is evicted from the right buffer if that event hasn't been matched with anything prior to eviction.
- *Match condition*—This is the condition used to judge whether an event from the left stream matches one from the right stream. It can be a simple equality test, such as `Left/A = Left/B`, or a more complex expression involving both events, such as the XPath expression `count(Left/A) = count(Right/B) + 7`.

If the left or right buffer is specified to have a fixed size and that size is exceeded, the oldest event in the buffer is evicted in order to make room for the new event. Events are also evicted if they have been in the buffer too long (in cases where it is specified with a time interval) and when the context window closes.

The default behavior for an unmatched policy is simply to drop the unmatched event and not produce an output event. However the policy can be set to *forward*, in which case it is forwarded to the derivation step as part of a pair with a null event from the other stream, or to *fail* in which case it is processed by the failure derivation expression and emitted by the Failure terminal. In our example, if we had set an unmatched left policy of forward, an unmatched arrival event would result in an output event containing the vehicle registration and the arrival time, but no departure time. A Compose EPA with an unmatched policy of forward is sometimes called an *outer join*.

Some buffer size settings are particularly noteworthy. If one of the buffer sizes is set to zero (as in our example), the operation becomes a *one-way join*. Events from that stream are compared against earlier events from the other stream, but not the other way around. If both buffer sizes are non-zero, the operation is a *two-way join*. If one of the buffer sizes is set to one, only the last event is retained for that stream. This is useful in circumstances where each incoming event on that stream invalidates any earlier event, making a match against such events worthless.

8.2.5   *Header attributes and validation*

You will recall that in chapter 3 we described a number of header attributes that may (and in some cases must) be present in an event instance. These header attributes, if present, can be read and used as input by context expressions, derivation expressions, and the Compose agent's match condition, but we have been a bit vague as to how their values get set in an output event. That is the question that we tackle in this section, and which concludes our discussion of event transformation.

The first attribute to consider is the event identity. You will recall that this is a system-generated value used to distinguish a particular event instance from any other. It is clear that in a complex transformation, for example, an aggregation, the output event is different from any of the input events and so must have a different identity, whereas in the case of a Filter EPA you would expect an event to preserve its original identity. We take the view that events that emerge from the Output terminal of a Transform EPA are different from the events that go in, even in cases where the transform doesn't actually result in any change to the input event. This means that they should have distinct system-generated event identity values. However, in cases where a Transform EPA detects an error and routes an incoming event to its Failure terminal, the event should keep its original event identity, with all its other header attributes. For the rest of this discussion we concern ourselves only with events that emerge from the Output terminal.

You may recall from chapter 2 that output terminals can specify the types of event that they emit, so if the output terminal lists just one type, by default this is used as the output event type. In some special cases, it's possible that the derivation step might wish to override this at runtime and indicate that the event that it emits is a more specialized subtype of that type, and so it does have power to do this. However, even if it doesn't do this, it is important that the event emitted by the output terminal does conform to the event type that is advertised by that terminal. As we have seen, the derivation step has complete power to set the payload attributes of an event. So how do we make sure that the event instance conforms to the type? The two approaches are listed here. Note that we discuss validation of event processing networks in more detail in section 10.5.

- *Static analysis of the derivation expression*—In simple cases it's relatively easy to detect cases where the derivation expression won't produce the correct output. For example, if the derivation expression consists of a set of output attribute assignments, and there's a mandatory attribute in the event with no corresponding assignment, the output event instance is not going to be valid. Static analysis techniques can be built into a tool used to construct the derivation expression in the first place, or they can be applied by a separate verification tool.

- *Runtime validation*—In cases where the output of the derivation step is highly variable (for example, where the derivation expression is an XSLT program dealing with highly variable input) it's not always easy to perform static analysis, so the alternative is to have the agent implementation perform a validation step at runtime. This checks the output event instance against the output terminal's type definition and only allows the event to pass through the terminal if it is valid. Runtime validation can be costly in performance terms, so implementations don't always offer this; if they do they usually provide a mechanism for turning validation off. Note that you would not want to use runtime validation if you have performed satisfactory static analysis. Also it's common practice to have it turned on during testing, but turned off when putting the application into production.

Because the output event is a new event instance, the event processing agent has to provide values for its occurrence time and detection time timestamps. The detection time, if there is one, is set implicitly, and its value can't be overridden by the derivation expression. It is generally set to show the time at which the derivation step ran. There is, however, an important qualification to this when the event processing agent is associated with a fixed interval or sliding fixed interval context. You will recall from chapter 7 that these contexts have windows, which are half-open time intervals with well-defined start and end times (an interval starting at time Ts and ending at Te includes events with timestamp τ where $Ts \leq \tau < Te$). We want to ensure that derived events also qualify as members of the window in which they are derived, so that they can continue to be processed by other event processing agents that use the same context. For example, suppose we have a context in which every day is a separate window; any event derived from Tuesday's events is itself also a Tuesday event, but implementation considerations may mean that the derivation step doesn't actually run until Wednesday. In order to qualify as a member of the window $[Ts, Te)$, the latest possible detection time that a derived event can have is Te - g, where g is the event's temporal granularity. We therefore state that, if the derivation step executes at Te or later, the detection time is to be set to Te - g. This can be summarized in the following rule.

> **DETECTION TIME VALUE**   If an event processing agent is associated with a *fixed interval* or *sliding fixed interval* context then any new event derived by the agent instance for the window $[Ts, Te)$ is assigned a detection time of $min(Td, Te\text{-}g)$ where Td is the time of derivation and g is the temporal granularity of the derived event.

By default the occurrence time, if there is one, is set to the same value as the detection time. However in the simpler transformation cases, for example, Project or Enrich, where there's a clear relationship between input and output events it may make sense for the output event to keep the occurrence time value from the input event, and in an aggregation you might want to compute the occurrence time in some other way. You may therefore want to set the occurrence time explicitly as part of the derivation step. We discuss the derivation of occurrence time further in section 11.1.2.

One can go through a similar reasoning process with regard to the remaining attributes. This is summarized in table 8.4 which shows the values set by default (if the derivation expression says nothing) and indicates which of these values can be overridden in a derivation expression.

Table 8.4   The interaction of a Transform event processing agent with event header attributes

Attribute name	Default output value	Settable by derivation step?
eventIdentity	New system-generated identity	No
event Type	Specified by output terminal definition	Yes
detectionTime	See earlier discussion	No
occurrenceTime	As detectionTime	Yes[a]
eventAnnotation	Not present	Yes
eventCertainty	Not present	Yes
eventSource	Identity of the event processing agent	Yes

a. See section 11.1.2 for further discussion.

Having concluded our in-depth look at both stateless and stateful transformation, it's time to turn once more to the Fast Flower Delivery application and give more details of the Filter and Transformation agents that were mentioned in the chapter 6.

8.3 *Examples in the Fast Flower Delivery application*

Chapter 6 mentioned that the Fast Flower Delivery application involves several Filter andTransformation agents. We have looked at two of them already:

- The `Request enrichment` agent was illustrated in figure 8.10.
- The `Daily assignments calculator`, an Aggregate EPA, was illustrated in figure 8.13.

The remaining examples are the `Location service`, `Bid Request creator`, `Driver enrichment`, `Assignment manager`, `Bid enrichment`, `Bid routing`, `Daily statistics creator` and `Performance evaluation` agents.

LOCATION SERVICE EPA

This is a Translate EPA whose job is to compare the raw latitude/longitude readings that come from a driver's GPS device against a set of geofences to determine what part of the city the driver is currently in. We show a version of this in figure 8.16 where we have assumed, appropriately enough, that our flower delivery application is set in the city of Florence. The various regions of the city are stored as geospatial objects in the `Neighborhoods` global state element. For simplicity we have divided the city into four regions, meeting at the point with latitude 44.778° North, longitude 11.259° East.

This process of converting a latitude/longitude reading to a geographical point or region is technically known as *reverse geocoding,* and there are number of commercial products and online services that offer it. Listing 8.2 shows how you can do it, in our simple case, using JavaScript. A more realistic example might have irregular shaped regions (for example, regions bounded by the river) and would retrieve the region boundaries from a database table.

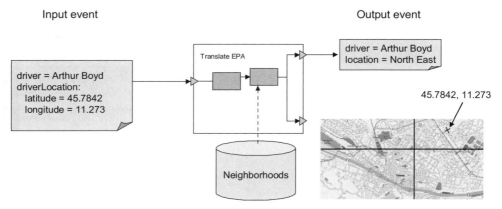

Figure 8.16   Locating a Fast Flower delivery driver in the city of Florence

Listing 8.2   JavaScript implementation of a simple reverse geocode translation

```
output.Region = reverse_geocode(input.Latitude, input.Longitude);

function reverse_geocode(latitude, longitude) {
    if (latitude > 43.7783)
            if (longitude > 11.259)
                    return "North East";
            else
                    return "North West";
    else if (longitude > 11.259)
            return "South East";
    else
            return "South West";
}
```

Conversion function ❷   **Derivation expression** ❶

This tests the latitude and longitude values from the input event against the borders of the four regions (conveniently these are lines of constant longitude and latitude so the tests are simple). For clarity we have split the conversion code out from the derivation expression ❶ into a separate function ❷.

BID REQUEST CREATOR EPA

This is an Enrich agent that queries the Driver status global state element, finds out which drivers are in the neighborhood of the store who meet the minimum ranking assignment and then creates a Bid Request event ready to be sent out to those drivers as shown in figure 8.17.

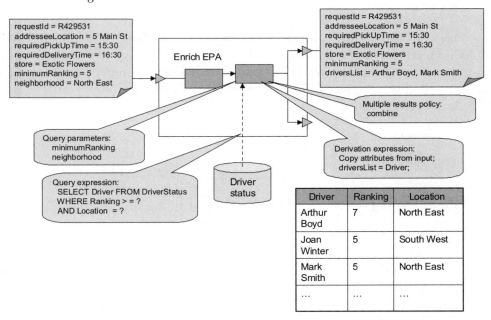

Figure 8.17   The Bid Request creator agent from the Fast Flower Delivery application. This agent queries the Driver status table to find suitable drivers and creates a Bid Request event containing the names of these drivers in its drivers list attribute.

There are three things about this Enrich agent that make it different from our earlier example (figure 8.10). First, it uses two attributes from the incoming event in its query. You can see that there are two parameters in the query parameter list. These get substituted in order for the two ? placeholders in the query expression. This means the example shown in figure 8.17 results in the following query:

```
SELECT Driver FROM DriverStatus WHERE Ranking >= 5 AND Location = "North
    East"
```

In addition, the query can find more than one driver, so you can see that the agent uses a multiple results policy. In this case the policy is *combine*, which means that it produces a single output event containing names of all the matching drivers. Finally the output and input events are of different types, so in this example the derivation expression copies across only attributes that are common to both events.

DRIVER ENRICHMENT EPA

This is another Enrich agent. Its specification is straightforward, with a single query parameter, the driver attribute from the Delivery Bid event. It queries the Driver status global state element with the following query expression:

```
SELECT Ranking FROM DriverStatus WHERE Driver = ?
```

Its job, as you can see from figure 6.13, is to take a Delivery Bid event and add the ranking of the driver who submitted the bid. The assignment system can then check that the driver has the appropriate ranking level to make the delivery.

ASSIGNMENT MANAGER EPA

The Assignment manager, shown in figure 8.18, is a Compose agent that receives Delivery Bid events from the drivers. It checks that the committed pickup times in these bids match the pickup time from the corresponding Bid Request.

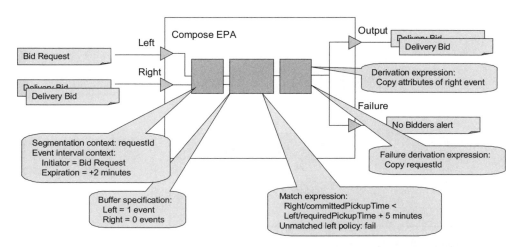

Figure 8.18 The Assignment manager agent monitors incoming delivery bids. It rejects them if the committed pickup time is too far out. If no bids are received it raises a No Bidders alert.

The context specification for this agent means that a new window is created each time a new `Bid Request` is detected. Each window is active for 2 minutes and contains only one `Bid Request`, which is received into the left buffer. Delivery bids, if any, are received into the right buffer. As soon as one is received it is tested against the `Bid Request`, and if the match expression is satisfied the pair of events is passed to the derivation step; this results in the `Delivery Bid` being emitted through the Output terminal. The buffer specifications mean that only one `Bid Request` event is retained, but as there is only one `Bid Request` in each window, it stays in the left buffer for the lifetime of the agent instance. When the window closes, the unmatched left policy value means that the agent will check to see if any valid matches were found. If not (in other words, if there were no valid `Delivery Bid` events) it runs the failure derivation expression against the `Bid Request`. This causes it to generate a `No Bidders` alert, which it then emits through the Failure terminal.

BID ENRICHMENT AND BID ROUTING EPAS

When a driver submits a `Delivery Bid` event in the Fast Flower Delivery application, the system has to decide whether to forward the event to the requesting flower store, or whether to send it to the automatic assignment process. This is performed by the two EPAs shown in figure 8.19.

After leaving the `Assignment manager` agent, `Delivery Bid` events are sent to the `Bid enrichment` agent. This uses the same `Store reference` global state element that

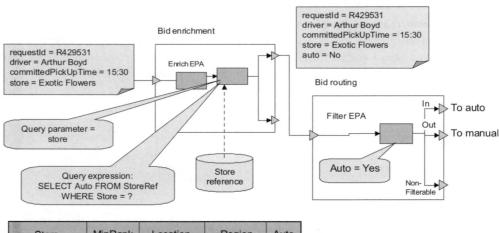

Store	MinRank	Location	Region	Auto
Blooms R Us	3	17 East Ave	South East	Yes
Exotic Flowers	5	33 High St	North East	No
...	...	...	...	...

Figure 8.19   The `Delivery Bid` event is first enriched with the store's automatic/manual assignment preference and then routed using a Filter agent.

we met in section 8.2.1. It adds an additional attribute to the event, to show whether the store wishes to do its own assignment or not. The output from this EPA is then passed to the `Bid routing` agent. This is a Filter agent which routes the event based on this attribute.

DAILY STATISTICS CREATOR AND PERFORMANCE EVALUATION EPAS

Our final Fast Flower Delivery examples come from the ranking and reporting system, shown in figure 6.15. The `Daily statistics creator`, shown in figure 8.20, is an Aggregate agent. It takes `Daily assignments` events (from the `Daily assignments calculator` agent shown in figure 8.13) and, once a day, it calculates statistics relating to all the drivers. The output from this agent is used by the ranking agents.

This agent uses the `Daily` fixed interval context and the default aggregation frequency. This means that it accumulates the `Daily Assignments` events (one for each active driver) and then computes the aggregation at the end of each day. The derivation step uses derivation functions from table 8.3 to compute the mean number of assignments that day and their standard deviation. Note that this agent receives events from the `Daily assignments calculator` which also runs only once a day. The rule we gave in section 8.2.5 means that that agent assigns them a detection time of 23:59:00 and so they qualify to be processed in the corresponding day's instance of this agent.

The `Daily Statistics` events from this agent are also used as input to our final EPA, the `Performance evaluation` agent. This is a Compose agent that compares the performance of each driver against the cohort of drivers active that day. Like the `Daily statistics creator`, it uses the `Daily` fixed interval context, and so each day is handled by a separate instance of the agent. Each instance receives one `Daily Statistics` event through its Right input terminal, and multiple `Daily Assignments` events (one for each active driver) through its left terminal. The match expression is `true()` as we want to compare every `Daily Assignments` event against the single `Daily Statistics` event. The derivation expression computes how far the driver's assignment count is away from the mean for that day, as follows:

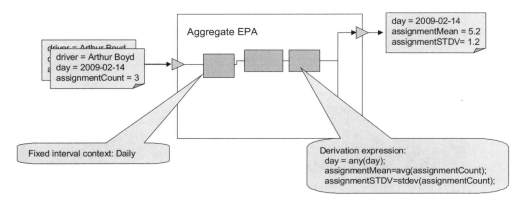

Figure 8.20 The `Daily statistics creator` agent. This runs once a day to calculate statistics for the whole cohort of drivers, so that the performance of an individual driver can be assessed.

```
driver = Left/driver;
day = Right/day;
deviation =(Left/assignmentCount-Right/assignmentMean) /
                   Right/assignmentSTDV;
```

As we saw earlier, all the events processed by an agent instance have a detection time of 23:59:00, and they can logically arrive at the agent in any order. This is not a problem, as the agent buffers all the events. Both left and right buffer sizes are specified as unbounded, though in practice the right buffer will contain at most one event, and the left buffer will contain only as many events as there are drivers active that day. All events will get matched, so the unmatched policies are irrelevant.

This concludes our review of the Filter and Transformation agents used in the Fast Flower Delivery application. We end this chapter with a few words on filtering and transformation in some of today's event processing languages.

8.4   *Filtering and transformation in practice*

In this chapter we discussed the use of XPath and XSLT, but have mentioned the fact that some products use different languages. In this section we provide examples of filtering and transformation from current event processing languages. As a reminder, you can find more detail on some of these languages and see examples of them being used by visiting the *Event Processing in Action* website.

We start with figure 8.21, which shows an example of filtering from StreamBase. This example shows the filter from the Fast Flowery Deliver application that is used to

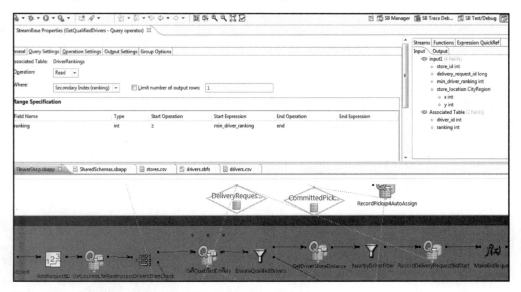

Figure 8.21   Example of a filter from the StreamBase product

select those drivers who satisfy the requesting store's ranking constraint. The filter expression can be seen at the top left. Our second filter example, in listing 8.3, is a rule-based programming example taken from ruleCore.

Listing 8.3   Example of filtering using ruleCore

```
<Rule name="CreateAutomaticAssignments" limit="?" evalMode="once" level="2">
<Description>This is rule CreateAutomaticAssignments</Description>
<Initialize>
  <Assert>
    <Event>
      <base:XPath>sim:EventDef[@eventType="BidRequest"]</base:XPath>
    </Event>
    <Expression>
      <Property name="Store">
        <InList name="AutomaticAssignmentStore"/>
      </Property>
    </Expression>
  </Assert>
</Initialize>
<Views>
  <ViewRef name="CreateAutomaticAssignments">
    <base:XPath>sim:ViewDef[@name="CreateAutomaticAssignments"]
        </base:XPath>
  </ViewRef>
</Views>
<Situations>
  <SituationRef name="CreateAutomaticAssignments">
    <base:XPath>sim:SituationDef[@name="CreateAutomaticAssignments"]
        </base:XPath>
  </SituationRef>
</Situations>
<Actions>
  <SituationDetected situationName="CreateAutomaticAssignments">
   <ActionRef name="CreateAutomaticAssignments" eventVisibility="external">
     <base:XPath>sim:ActionDef[@name="CreateAutomaticAssignments"]
         </base:XPath>
   </ActionRef>
  </SituationDetected>
</Actions>
</Rule>
```

The rule shown in listing 8.3 implements the Bid routing agent that we mentioned in the previous section.

Finally we show a transformation example. Figure 8.22 shows part of the Apama MonitorScript implementation of the Fast Flower Delivery application. This example shows some code that enriches a Delivery Request event by adding a location attribute to it.

```
70    /**
71     * Update the driver's current location, in region.
72     */
73    action updateCurrentLocation(string loc) {
74        edrListener.quit();
75        currentDriverRegion:=loc;
76        // because the current location is changed so what enriched delivery
77        // requests to care for is also changed -- therefore re-establish edr
78        // listener based on the changed current location
79        EnrichedDeliveryRequest edr;
80        edrListener:=on all EnrichedDeliveryRequest(region=loc, ranking<=currentDriverRanking):edr {
81            route BidRequest(edr.dr.requestId, edr.dr.store, driver,
82                    edr.dr.requiredPickupTime, edr.dr.requiredDeliveryTime);
83        }
84
85        updateGUI(driver, loc);
86    }
```

Figure 8.22   A transformation example in MonitorScript

As you can see, a variety of language styles are used to express similar functionality. We examine these various programming styles further in chapter 10.

8.5   *Summary*

Filtering and transformation are two of the three main intermediary functional capabilities provided in an event processing network. You should now have a good understanding of the different ways filters can be used and the places where filtering can be specified (on an input terminal, in a context expression, or in a dedicated Filter event processing agent) and how XPath can be used to give a standardized way of describing common filter operations.

We have also looked at the various kinds of stateful and stateless transformation, and examined the logical internal structure of these different kinds of agents. We have observed how XSLT can be used in many of these transformation agents to derive the output event. We have also discussed the treatment of event header attributes and touched on the issue of event validation.

Our final stateful EPA was the Compose EPA, used to join a pair of input event streams by looking for matches or correlations between events in these streams. We develop this idea of matching events further in the next chapter when we complete a detailed review of our modeling language by turning to the final group of event processing agents, the *Pattern detect* EPAs.

8.5.1   *Additional reading*

Hohpe, Gregor, and Bobby Woolf. 2004. *Enterprise Integration Patterns: Designing, Building, and Deploying Messaging Solutions*. Addison Wesley. This book is primarily about the use of message-oriented middleware to deliver enterprise application integration solutions, but in many cases there is a direct read-across between the messaging patterns it describes and the way that events are handled in an event processing network. In particular the stateless filter and transformation patterns described in this chapter have counterparts described in this book.

DuCharme, Bob. 2001. *XSLT Quickly.* Manning Publications. http://www.manning.com/ ducharme/. This book is a tutorial for XSLT and XPath. In this chapter we showed how these languages can be used for filtering and transformation.

8.5.2   Exercises

8.1   Would the *Non-filterable* output terminal ever be used in an EPA that has an XPath filter expression? Explain the reasons for your answer.

8.2   The filtering example shown in figure 8.3 uses two Filter agents connected in series, that is to say, one after the other, to separate Gold, Silver, and Bronze customer events. Show how the same effect can be achieved using agents connected in parallel to one other. What are the advantages and disadvantages of these two approaches?

8.3   Can you think of an example of a Filter EPA where it would be useful to have a filter expression on the Input terminal in addition to the EPA's principal filter?

8.4   Some event processing applications can encounter situations in which there are multiple event instances corresponding to a single event occurrence, or where there are multiple event instances that aren't sufficiently different from each other to merit separate consideration. Explain how the concepts described in this chapter can be used to remove such duplicate event instances from a single stream of incoming events. How would you have to change this to handle multiple incoming streams (for example, streams from different event producers)?

8.5   The Compose example we showed in figure 8.15 could have used a segmentation context to partition incoming events by vehicle registration. What would the match condition look like in this case? Are there any implementation considerations that would favor one approach over the other?

8.6   A Compose EPA implementation can be made more efficient if the match condition contains only simple equality tests. Explain why this is the case.

8.7   Can you suggest more derivation functions to be added to the list in table 8.3?

8.8   What are the advantages and disadvantages of having a derived event which is the result of filtering, translation, enrichment, and projection keep the identity of the original event identity as opposed to having it gain a new event identity?

Detecting event patterns   9

Art is the imposing of a pattern on experience, and our aesthetic enjoyment is recognition of the pattern.

—Alfred North Whitehead

It's no exaggeration to say that event pattern detection is the jewel in the crown of event processing. Pattern detection lets us go beyond individual events to look for specific collections of events and the relationship between them; a pattern that is detected can have a meaning that goes beyond the individual events that it comprises. Consider a personalized healthcare system where a patient is hooked up to multiple monitors. The individual events reported by the monitors might not in themselves be significant, but by considering the events from all the monitors you might spot a problem that you would miss by looking at each monitor separately. In this example you would be looking for particular combinations of events occurring in particular orders, particular trends emerging from the events, or situations where an expected event did not occur. These are all examples of what we call an event *pattern*.

In this chapter we shall discuss patterns and the pattern detection process, in particular:

- The definition of an event pattern, and the Pattern detect event processing agent
- Categories of event patterns

214

- Specific patterns of various types
- The use of pattern policies
- Pattern detection examples from the Fast Flower Delivery application

Our discussions of patterns in this chapter is language independent, using our building block approach, but at the end of the chapter we show a few examples in various languages. You can also refer to the *Event Processing in Action* website to see how patterns are implemented in the language of your choice. Before you get to that point, however, we should explain what we mean by an event pattern in more detail.

9.1 Introduction to event patterns

Imagine that you have just taken a flight, and you are in the baggage reclaim hall, watching the various pieces of luggage travel past you on the carousel. In your mind's eye you have a picture of your suitcase, with the ribbon you attached to distinguish it from the others, and you are trying to match this mental picture with each piece of luggage as it flows past you. You are, without thinking about it, performing a pattern matching process. Pattern detection in event processing is similar. Instead of luggage on a carousel you have a stream of incoming event instances, and instead of a passenger you have a piece of event processing logic, which we model as a Pattern detect EPA. This agent is equipped with a pattern (the equivalent of the passenger's mental picture), and it examines the incoming event stream looking for an event, or sometimes a combination of events, that matches this pattern.

9.1.1 The Pattern detect event processing agent

In chapter 6 we showed that an event processing agent can be considered as having three steps:

- The filtering step, in which relevant events are selected
- The matching step that selects subsets of these events
- The derivation step that takes the output from the matching step and uses it to derive new events

Many EPA types leave out the matching step and just do filtering or derivation. The Pattern detect agent, which we illustrate in figure 9.1, uses the matching step to perform its pattern detection. Its filtering step includes input terminal filtering and content-based instance selection, just like every other event processing agent. However, the agent is equipped with a further list of event types (the *relevant event types list*), and any input events that pass the input filters are then checked against this list. If the event's type is on the list, it's classified as a *participant event.*

The matching step takes these participant events, examines them to see if they match the specific conditions of the pattern that it's looking for, and if they do, it outputs one or more subsets of the events. These subsets are called *pattern matching sets* and are passed to the derivation step. A pattern matching set is often a proper subset of the participant events, although it can be the entire participant event set.

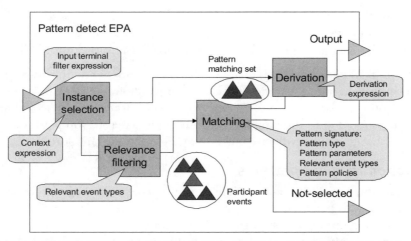

Figure 9.1   The logical structure of a Pattern detect agent, showing its three logical parts, with the "pattern signature" that controls the pattern detection process. The triangular objects represent event instances.

The derivation step emits one or more events through the agent's Output terminal, and is similar to the derivation steps we looked at in the previous chapter. It can combine the events into a single derived event, or it can emit them as individual events. It can also base derived events on other events received by the agent—this is important as some patterns, such as *absence*, can have matching sets that are empty even when the pattern has been matched successfully. We don't discuss the derivation step further, as this chapter concentrates on the matching step.

Figure 9.1 shows the logical structure of a Pattern detect EPA. The event processing *pattern signature*, shown at the bottom right, specifies the particular pattern detection process that is to be performed by the matching step. In this example the relevance filtering step creates a set of five participant events. The pattern detection process takes this set and creates a matching set containing two events of two different types, which then serves as an input to the derivation step.

You will see from figure 9.1 that a Pattern detect agent also has a *Not-selected* terminal. If the agent is associated with a temporal context (or a composite context that has a temporal member), all events that are in the participant set, and which have not been included in any matching set, are emitted through this terminal when the temporal window closes.

9.1.2   *Pattern definitions*

We're going to spend most of this chapter describing common types of event patterns, but before we can get to that we need to define some of the terms that we use. We start with a definition of an event pattern itself.

EVENT PATTERN   An *event pattern* is a template specifying one or more combinations of events. Given any collection of events, you may be able to find one or more subsets of those events that match a particular pattern. We say that such a subset *satisfies* the pattern.

The matching step of a Pattern detect agent examines the participant events set to see if it can find a subset of those events that satisfies its pattern. If it finds one, we say that it has *detected* the pattern.

Our definition is rather general, and as you look at the patterns described later in the chapter you'll see that they fall into groups:

- Some patterns, such as the *threshold* patterns we meet in section 9.2.2, require the pattern to be satisfied by the entire participant event set.
- Other patterns, such as the *any* pattern that we discuss in 9.2.1, allow the pattern to be satisfied by a proper subset of the participant events. In some cases there could be several subsets that satisfy the pattern; we discuss what happens when we look at *pattern policies* in section 9.4.

The pattern that is being looked for is defined by a pattern signature which consists of the *pattern type*, the *relevant event types*, and, in some cases, *pattern parameters* and *pattern policies*. We now give formal definitions for each of these components of the signature.

PATTERN TYPE The *pattern type* is a label that determines the meaning and intention of the pattern and specifies the particular kind of matching function to be used.

Some examples of pattern type are *sequence, absence* and *moving north*. We discuss pattern types further in section 9.1.3, and give detailed definitions of important pattern types in sections 9.2 and 9.3.

RELEVANT EVENT TYPES LIST The *relevant event types list* is a list of event types, and it forms part of the pattern matching function. The order of these event types has importance for some pattern functions.

The relevant event types list is used to filter incoming events, and has a further role in some of the pattern types. You'll see how it's used when we describe the way the different pattern types work in sections 9.2 and 9.3.

Some pattern types require additional values to be provided in the form of *pattern parameters.*

PATTERN PARAMETERS *Pattern parameters* provide additional values used in the definition of the pattern function. The parameters that may be specified, and their meanings, vary depending on the pattern type.

We describe these parameters when we go through each of the different pattern types. They are summarized in table 9.1, which appears towards the end of this chapter. The pattern signature can also contain a number of pattern policies.

PATTERN POLICY A *pattern policy* is a named parameter that disambiguates the semantics of the pattern and the pattern matching process.

Pattern policies fine-tune the way the pattern detection process works. We discuss them in section 9.4.

We have already been using a couple of general terms that apply to all pattern types: they are *participant events* and *pattern matching set.*

> **PARTICIPANT EVENTS** The *participant events* are those event instances that occur within the Pattern detect agent's context partition, and which are instances of the event types mentioned in the relevant event types list.

You can see from figure 9.1 that the relevant event types list filters the incoming events to create the participant events set. We're now ready for our last definition, the *pattern matching set.*

> **PATTERN MATCHING SET** A *pattern matching set* is the output of the pattern matching process; it's a subset of the participant events.

A pattern matching process takes the participant events as an input and creates a pattern matching set, consisting of the event instances that satisfy the pattern. Let's look at some examples:

- The Fast Flower Delivery application uses a Pattern detect agent to assign a delivery task to the first driver to make an acceptable bid. In this case the participant events set contains all the `Delivery Bid` events that have an appropriate pickup time, while the pattern matching set consists of the single `Delivery Bid` event that has been selected.
- An event processing application designed to detect speculative traders. This application looks for traders that have bought and later sold more than $1M of the same security in the same day. In this case, the participant events are `security buy` and `security sell` events with a value of at least $1M. The pattern matching set consists of a pair of events {`security buy`, `security sell`} which satisfy an additional condition (same customer, same day, and same security). Note that this pattern may yield multiple pattern matching sets in any given day.

In both these examples the pattern type allows matching by a proper subset of the participant events; however, we noted earlier that there are some pattern types which only detect a match if the entire participant set satisfies the pattern. For such patterns the matching set (if there is one) is the entire participant event set.

We conclude this section with an example of a pattern signature, taken from the Fast Flower Delivery application. You'll recall that in this application a store can ask for the system to send it the five highest ranking bids so that it can choose the driver itself. In such cases the system takes the `Delivery Bid` events from drivers that relate to a particular `Bid Request` and applies the following pattern:

- Pattern name: Manual assignment preparation
- Pattern type: relative n highest values

- Pattern parameters: Count = 5, Attribute = Ranking
- Relevant event types: {Delivery Bid}
- Pattern policies: cardinality = single, evaluation = deferred, repeated type = every.

This pattern is satisfied by the five Delivery Bid events that have the highest ranking value. In the Fast Flower Delivery application, this pattern is associated with a temporal context; the pattern policies mean that the pattern is tested at the end of the time interval, and creates a single matching set. All these concepts are explained later in this chapter.

9.1.3 Event pattern types

The semantics of the pattern matching operation are determined by the pattern type, and in sections 9.2 and 9.3 we describe a number of different pattern types. The patterns defined in this book are ones that we have found in use while surveying a relatively large sample of applications; however, we don't claim that it's a complete list, and we expect new pattern types to emerge over time. We divide these pattern types into two categories:

- *Basic patterns*—These are simple patterns that relate to basic operations on event types or on collections of event types and are described in section 9.2. They are divided into logical operator patterns, threshold patterns, subset selection patterns, and modal patterns. An example of a basic pattern is the *all* pattern that designates a conjunction of event types.
- *Dimensional patterns*—These are patterns that relate to time, space, or a combination of time and space. This category is described in section 9.3 and is divided into temporal patterns, spatial patterns, and spatiotemporal patterns. Examples are as follows: *sequence* (temporal), *min distance* (spatial), and *constantly moving north* (spatiotemporal).

Support for these patterns varies by event processing platform. Some event processing languages provide built-in support for patterns as primitive constructs in the language, whereas in other languages patterns are detected using a mixture of language constructs. Either way, the pattern abstraction plays a major part in the design of event based applications. Now let's meet the patterns themselves.

9.2 Basic patterns

These pattern types are frequently found in event processing applications. Although they can be used with temporal contexts, these patterns don't depend on the timing or ordering of the participant events. For convenience we describe them in the following groups: logical operator patterns, threshold patterns, subset selection patterns, and modal patterns. We start with the logical operator patterns.

9.2.1   *Logical operator patterns*

These are the most basic patterns, based on the three common logical operators: conjunction, disjunction, and negation. The patterns discussed here are *all* (conjunction), *any* (disjunction), and *absence* (negation). The all and any patterns can be matched by proper subsets of the participant event set, whereas absence is always matched by an empty participant event set.

THE ALL PATTERN

This pattern looks for subsets of the participant event set containing occurrences of all the types that appear in the relevant event types list. If this pattern is used, the relevant event types list should contain more than one entry.

> **ALL PATTERN**   The *all* pattern is satisfied when the participant event set contains at least one instance of each event type that is mentioned in the relevant event types list. The pattern matching set is made up of the event instances (one for each relevant event type) that cause the pattern to be satisfied.

As an example, suppose we have an all pattern with relevant event types {flight reserved, car reserved, hotel reserved}. This pattern is matched if at least one instance of each of these event types occurs within the context partition; the order of event occurrences is immaterial. If the pattern is matched the pattern matching set contains the three events, though it's up to the agent's derivation step to determine what it does with them.

We illustrate this example in figure 9.2. Let's assume that we asked a travel agent to make these three reservations and send us an email when finished. There could be different people in the travel agency dealing in parallel with these three types of reservations, and each of them creates an event when their particular reservation has been made. These events are processed by a Pattern detect agent, which uses its derivation step to trigger the email if the pattern is satisfied. In the example in figure 9.2 the pattern is satisfied at 11:02.

In this example there is only one instance of each of the three event types, but what should the Pattern detect do if there are multiple hotel reservations? The answer to this question is determined by pattern policies. We return to this question in section 9.4.

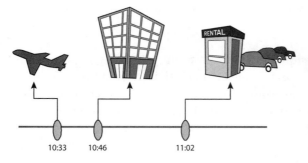

Figure 9.2   Illustration of the all pattern—an instance of every event type listed as a relevant event type must be present for the pattern to be matched. In this case there are three relevant event types (flight reservation, car reservation, and hotel reservation), and you can see that the participant event set includes an instance of each type.

10:33   10:46   11:02

The relevant event types list is allowed to contain more than one copy of a particular type. If we changed the list in our example to be {flight reserved, car reserved, car reserved}, we would need two car reservations (and wouldn't need any hotel reservations) for the pattern to be satisfied.

The all pattern can be augmented with a *pattern assertion* parameter. This is an additional condition that the matching set is required to meet for the pattern to be satisfied. We represent the assertion using a syntax that refers to members of the matching set by their event type. This is best explained with a simple example. Suppose the relevant event types are {E1, E2, E3} and the pattern assertion is

```
E1.A > E2. B and E2.B > E3.C
```

As this is an all pattern the matching set must contain an event of each of the three types, but in addition the A attribute of the E1 event must be greater than the B attribute of the E2 event, which must in turn be greater than the C attribute of the E3 event. If the relevant event types list requires the matching set to contain more than one event of a particular type, the assertion must be met by all instances of that type.

We take this opportunity to explain the Not-selected terminal. Figure 9.3 shows an example of the all pattern from a used book trading application. The application has created a market for a popular textbook, and accepts two types of event: book offer events, which contain a lower limit on the price, and book order events, which have an upper limit on the price. During the course of the day the application uses an all pattern to match book offers to book orders. At the end of the day, when trading has closed, there may be some unmatched events, either because there were more of one kind of event than the other, or because some orders or offers contained unrealistic price limits. In figure 9.3 book offer 1 was matched against order 2, and book offer 2 was matched against order 3. This leaves three unpaired events: book offer 3, book order 1, and book order 4. These three events flow out through the Not-selected terminal at the end of the auction interval.

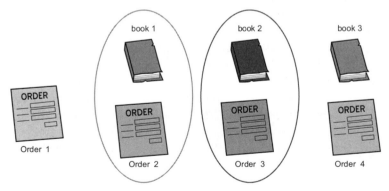

Figure 9.3 A used book selling application that shows use of the Not-selected terminal. Book offer events are shown at the top, and book orders at the bottom. Two orders and one offer are left unpaired, and these will be routed through the agent's Not-selected output terminal.

The Not-selected terminal can be used to catch exceptions of various kinds, or to trigger the creation of an alert. For example, you can use it to alert a customer that his orders are never matched as he always makes unrealistic bids.

Next we discuss the any pattern.

THE ANY PATTERN

This pattern looks for occurrences of any of the relevant event types. A matching set for the *any* pattern contains just one member.

> **ANY PATTERN**   The *any* pattern is satisfied if the participant event set contains an instance of any of the event types in the relevant event types list. The pattern matching set consists of the event instance that causes the pattern to be satisfied.

As an example, suppose you are purchasing a new house but have not yet sold your old one. You need funds to complete the payment on the new house which you will get when you sell your old house, but you could arrange a bridging loan or you might luckily win the lottery. In this example the relevant event types are {lottery win, loan advanced, old house sold}. Any of these events would match the pattern and the matching set is a singleton, consisting of the event in question.

THE ABSENCE PATTERN

This pattern is sometimes referred to as the "non-event pattern"; it detects the absence of any events with certain specified characteristics.

> **ABSENCE PATTERN**   The *absence* pattern is satisfied when there are no participant events. The matching set is empty.

For example, the absence pattern is satisfied if we have relevant event types {E1, E2, E3} but there are no instances of these types in the context partition. Note that because the participant set in this case is an empty set, the Not-selected terminal is meaningless for this pattern.

If this pattern is associated with a temporal context, it can be used to detect timeouts, and in such cases it's sometimes called the "timeout" pattern. We use it as a way of generating the various timeout alerts in the Fast Flower Delivery application. For example, there is a Pickup alert agent, which detects when a driver misses the pickup deadline. This is modeled using the absence pattern; the relevant events set consists of a single event, Pickup Confirmation, and the temporal context starts with the Assignment event and terminates after a time offset, specified as 5 minutes after the required pickup time. If no Pickup Confirmation event occurs within the time window, the absence pattern is detected.

For another example, look at figure 9.2 and suppose we use the absence pattern with one relevant event type {car reserved} in an event interval context that has flight reserved as its initiator event and hotel reserved as its terminator event. The pattern is satisfied in this example, because the context interval lasts from 10:33 to 10:46, and there is no car reservation in that time period.

Next we discuss threshold patterns.

9.2.2 *Threshold patterns*

A threshold pattern involves an aggregation operation which is performed against the set of participant events. The result of the aggregation operation is then compared against a threshold value.

> **THRESHOLD ASSERTION** A *threshold assertion* comprises two pattern parameters, the *threshold relation* and *threshold value*. An aggregation function is performed and the relation is used to compare the result of the aggregation against the threshold value. The pattern is matched if this comparison returns TRUE. If the pattern is matched, the matching set is the entire set of participant events.

Unlike the any or all patterns, the threshold patterns are satisfied only by the entire participant event set. If the pattern is satisfied, no events are emitted through the Not-selected terminal, whereas if the pattern is not satisfied, the entire participant event set is emitted through that terminal. We define several specific threshold patterns, which we describe next.

THE COUNT PATTERN

The *count* pattern counts the number of participant event instances and tests this value using a threshold assertion. This assertion uses one of the relations, $>$, $<$, $=$, $\geq$, $\leq$, $\neq$, to test the value against a constant threshold value.

> **COUNT PATTERN** The *count* pattern is satisfied when the number of instances in the participant event set satisfies the pattern's threshold assertion.

The matching set in this case includes all the events that were counted; thus it may include multiple events of the same type. Note that in some cases this pattern can be detected while the collection is incomplete. For example, if the threshold assertion is >5 and we get a sixth participant event, the threshold assertion is satisfied, regardless of what happens later.

An example of the use of such a pattern is a customer satisfaction application that detects when a customer sends at least ($\geq$) three complaints to a call center within a single day, as this indicates that the customer is likely to be unhappy with the service being offered. Figure 9.4 illustrates this example.

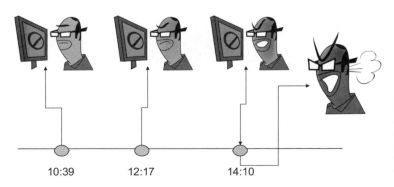

10:39   12:17   14:10

Figure 9.4 A count pattern where three instances of the same event type—customer complaint—match the pattern and suggest the likelihood of a frustrated customer

In this case the context is a single working day. If the pattern match is evaluated each time a new event is received, it's possible to detect the pattern at 14:10. If the Pattern detect agent does not run the match operation until the context window has closed, detection doesn't occur until this has happened—in this case that is at the end of the working day.

THE VALUE MAX PATTERN

In the *value max* pattern the matching operation examines a given attribute of each event instance in the participant event set and tests its maximum value against the threshold assertion.

> **VALUE MAX PATTERN**   The *value max pattern* is satisfied when the maximal value of a specific attribute over all the participant events satisfies the value max threshold assertion.

Figure 9.5 shows an example that we use to demonstrate value max and the next two threshold patterns.

The threshold assertion can use the binary relations >, <, =, ≥, ≤, ≠. The relevant events should all contain a numeric attribute with a name identical to the attribute mentioned in the assertion. Any events which do not contain this attribute are ignored when the maximum value is computed. As with the count pattern, it's sometimes possible to determine whether the pattern is going to be matched before the full set of participant events has been assembled.

To see the value max pattern in use, suppose we're interested in identifying high-spending daily investors. We decide to look, each day, for an investor who makes either a security buy or a security sell transaction with a value of $10M or more. The relevant event types are {security buy, security sell}, the attribute to be used is amount and the threshold assertion is ≥ 10M. In figure 9.5 we see an example of a customer who

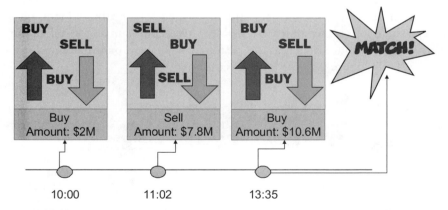

Figure 9.5   A trading example where the participant event set contains three events (two buy events and one sell event). The value max pattern will detect a match as the third event exceeds the $10M threshold.

made two buy transactions and one sell transaction in the same day. The last transaction was for a sum of $10.6M and so this customer matches the pattern.

This pattern has a twin, the value min pattern.

THE VALUE MIN PATTERN

The *value min* pattern is similar to the value max pattern except that this time it's the minimal value of a specific numeric attribute that is tested against the threshold assertion. The assertion can use the relations $>, <, =, \geq, \leq, \neq$.

> **VALUE MIN PATTERN** The *value min* pattern is satisfied when the minimal value of a specific attribute over all the participant events satisfies the value min threshold assertion.

As with *value max*, all the relevant events should contain the numeric attribute used by the pattern. Again this pattern can be matched before the full set of participant events has been assembled.

We can look at the same example in figure 9.5 and see what would happen using value min with the threshold assertion > 5M. We would now be looking for customers whose minimal transaction amount for the day is more than $5M. The customer described in figure 9.5 does not match the pattern because this customer has a transaction with an amount of $2M, which is less than the $5M threshold.

THE VALUE AVERAGE PATTERN

The *value average* pattern belongs to the same threshold family, but differs from the two we have just looked at, as its final outcome can never be determined until all the participant events have been assembled. In this pattern the average (arithmetic mean) value of a specific numeric attribute over the event instances is tested against the threshold assertion. Again the threshold assertion can use the relations $>, <, =, \geq, \leq, \neq$.

> **VALUE AVERAGE PATTERN** The *value average* pattern is satisfied when the value of a specific attribute, averaged over all the participant events, satisfies the value average threshold assertion.

As with *value max* and *value min*, all relevant events should contain the numeric attribute used by the pattern; any events that do not have the attribute are excluded from the computation.

For an example, refer again to figure 9.5. Suppose that we have a value average pattern for the amount attribute, with a threshold assertion > $5M. In this case the average amount is $6.8M, so the pattern is satisfied.

THE FUNCTOR PATTERN

The threshold patterns we have just looked at are special cases of the more general *functor* pattern. In the functor pattern the threshold assertion can use any of the derivation functions shown in table 8.3, for example, the standard deviation function.

The threshold patterns we have looked at all have the property that they aren't *always* satisfied, but when they *are,* the matching set contains all the participant events.

In contrast, our next set of patterns are always satisfied, regardless of the contents of the participant set, but the matching set doesn't have to contain all the events from the participant event set.

9.2.3   *Subset selection pattern*

The threshold patterns previously described compare a statistical function of an event collection with a threshold value; a subset selection pattern, on the other hand, is concerned with selecting a subset from the set of events using various criteria. We have two such patterns to discuss: relative n highest values and relative n lowest values.

THE RELATIVE *n* HIGHEST VALUES PATTERN

The *relative n highest values* pattern looks for the event instances that contain the n highest values of a given attribute. The pattern has a parameter called *Count* that provides the value of n. This pattern is sometimes referred to as *Top-n* or *Top-k*.

> **RELATIVE *n* HIGHEST VALUE PATTERN**   The *relative n highest values* pattern is satisfied by the events which have the n highest values of a specific attribute over all the participant events, where n is supplied as a pattern parameter. The matching set contains these n events. If there are fewer than n events, the matching set contains all the participant events.

If there's a tie for n^{th} place the matching set includes all the events that are in n^{th} place. This means that the matching set could contain more than n values. This pattern could be used to find the bid events that offer the highest prices in an auction. The definition of the relative n lowest values pattern is similar.

THE RELATIVE *n* LOWEST VALUES PATTERN

The *relative n lowest values* pattern looks for the event instances containing the n lowest values of a given attribute. The pattern has a parameter called *Count* that provides the value of n.

> **RELATIVE *n* LOWEST VALUES PATTERN**   The *relative n lowest values* pattern is satisfied by the events which have the n lowest values of a specific attribute over all the participant events, where n is supplied as a pattern parameter. The matching set contains these n events. If there are fewer than n events, the matching set contains all the participant events.

As with the previous pattern, all n^{th} placed events are included if there's a tie for n^{th} place. Going back to the example in figure 9.5, the participant event set contains three events. The relative n lowest values pattern for the attribute Amount with Count = 1 would select the Buy event that occurred at 10:00 as, at only $2M, this event contains the smallest value of amount. The relative n highest values pattern for the same attribute with Count = 1 would select the Buy event that occurred at 13:35 with the amount of $10.6M.

We now move on to our last set of basic patterns, the modal patterns.

9.2.4 Modal patterns

Modal patterns are patterns that take an assertion and check to see if it's satisfied by the entire participant event set or just by some members of the set. The modal patterns described here are similar to the operators used in modal logic: necessity corresponds to the always pattern, and possibility to sometimes.

To explain modal patterns we return to the world of call centers and problem handling and use the example shown in figure 9.6. In this example problems can be reported through web, email, phone, and fax and are converted to instances of a single `Problem assignment` event type. In the course of the morning in question a service representative has been assigned four different problems. Each problem has a problem type, a severity (1 – critical, 2 – urgent, 3 – regular) and a customer type (gold or silver).

THE ALWAYS PATTERN

Always is a modal pattern which is matched if all event instances in the participant event set satisfy an assertion.

> **ALWAYS PATTERN**   The *always* pattern is satisfied when the participant event set is non-empty, and all the participant events satisfy the always pattern assertion. If the pattern is satisfied, the matching set is the entire participant event set.

Consider the scenario illustrated in figure 9.6, with the following pattern specification (operating in the context of the morning shift for a particular service representative).

```
Pattern: always
Relevant event types: {Problem assignment}
Pattern assertion: "reportedBy = Web"
```

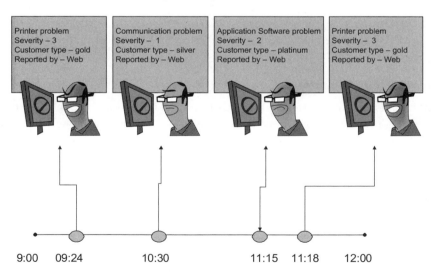

Figure 9.6   This example illustrates modal patterns. The problems are assigned to a particular service representative, during the morning shift from 9:00 – 12:00.

In this case the pattern would detect a match as all problems were indeed reported by the web. The outcome of this pattern can be detected only when all participant events are available.

THE SOMETIMES PATTERN

The *sometimes* pattern is another modal pattern.

> **SOMETIMES PATTERN**   The *sometimes* pattern is satisfied when at least one participant event satisfies the pattern assertion. The matching set, if the pattern is satisfied, is the entire participant event set.

As you can see from the definition, the sometimes pattern generates a match if any event instance in the participant event set satisfies the assertion. Returning to figure 9.6, suppose we have the following pattern specification (operating in the context of the morning shift for this particular service representative).

```
Pattern: sometimes
Relevant event types: {Problem assignment}
Pattern assertion: "Severity = 1"
```

This pattern is satisfied, as a severity 1 problem was assigned at 10:30. The example shows that this pattern can be detected incrementally and not necessarily at the end of the shift. This concludes the discussion of basic event patterns; now we move on to the dimensional patterns.

9.3   *Dimensional patterns*

Dimensional patterns are patterns that relate to the time dimension, to the space dimension, or to a combination of both. Whereas temporal patterns are common, spatial and spatio-temporal dimensions have not been explored in traditional event processing applications, but we observe that the use of these dimensions is growing and so we have included examples of these patterns. We expect that the list of patterns will grow with time.

9.3.1   *The temporal order patterns*

Temporal patterns are patterns in which time plays a major role. In this chapter we assume that every event happens at a single point in time, although we revisit this assumption briefly in chapter 11. We start the discussion of temporal patterns by looking at the most common pattern, the *sequence* pattern.

THE SEQUENCE PATTERN

The *sequence* pattern is similar to the all pattern except that it requires the event instances to occur in the order implied by the relevant event types list.

> **SEQUENCE PATTERN**   The *sequence* pattern is satisfied if the participant event set contains at least one instance of each event type mentioned in the relevant event types list, and if the order of these event instances matches the order of their types in the list. The pattern matching set is made up of the event instances (one for each relevant event type) that cause the pattern to be satisfied.

For most patterns the order in which event types appear in the relevant event types list is insignificant. However, with the sequence pattern, the relevant event types list is treated as an ordered list, and the participant event set has to be a totally ordered set. Like the all pattern, the sequence pattern can be satisfied by a proper subset of the participant events. This means that consecutive types in the relevant event types list can be matched by nonconsecutive participant event instances. The sequence pattern is satisfied if instances of the relevant event types appear in the right order within the participant event set, and if all the types in the list are matched.

Figure 9.7 shows an example. The pattern in this example is satisfied if a patient is released from hospital and then readmitted to the hospital within 48 hours for the same reason as the original admission. The relevant event types are <patient discharge, patient admission>, in that order.

As with the all pattern, the relevant event types list can contain more than one occurrence of a particular event type. As an example, suppose the relevant event types list is <patient discharge, patient admission, patient discharge>. If this pattern is to be satisfied the participant event set must contain two discharge events, separated by an admission event (and possibly by other events). A sequence can be further constrained by a pattern assertion parameter, just like that used with the all pattern.

As we saw with the temporal context discussion in chapter 7, there are several ways to define the ordering of the participant event set (for example, by occurrence time, by detection time, or by the event's position in the stream). We define an *order policy* parameter that specifies which approach is to be used. This is discussed further in section 9.4.

THE FIRST *n* PATTERN

This pattern is always detected, regardless of the contents of the participant event set. It returns at most *n* events according to the following definition.

> **FIRST *n* PATTERN**   The *first n* pattern is satisfied by the first *n* events within the participant event set. The matching set contains these *n* events. If there are fewer than *n* events, the matching set contains all the participant events. The pattern has a parameter called *Count* that provides the value of *n*.

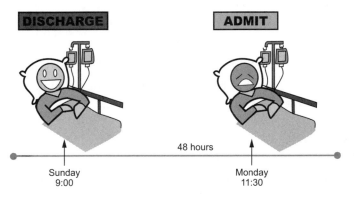

Figure 9.7   A sequence pattern example—a patient who is readmitted to the hospital within 48 hours of having been discharged

We use this pattern in the Fast Flower Delivery's `Automatic assignment` event processing agent. This agent uses Count = 1 to assign the delivery task to the first bidder.

THE LAST *n* PATTERN

A similar pattern is the *last n* pattern.

> **LAST *n* PATTERN** The *last n* pattern is satisfied by the last *n* events within the participant event set. The matching set contains these *n* events. If there are fewer than *n* events, the matching set contains all the participant events. The pattern has a parameter called *Count* that provides the value of *n*.

This pattern also selects up to *n* events and can be used in cases where the later events are more significant than earlier ones.

9.3.2 *Trend patterns*

Trend patterns are patterns that trace the value of a specific attribute over time. These patterns relate only to a single event type, so the relevant event types list must have only one entry. In addition the instances of this event type must make up a time series, meaning that they must be temporally totally ordered. This order may be based either on occurrence time or detection time or position in the input stream (the ordering approach to be used is determined by the order policy that we discuss in section 9.4). We use the notation e1 << e2 to denote that input event instance e1 is before event instance e2 in this temporal order. If a trend pattern is satisfied, the matching set contains all the participant events.

The trend patterns are increasing, decreasing, stable, non-increasing, non-decreasing, and mixed. We start by discussing the increasing pattern.

THE INCREASING PATTERN

The *increasing* pattern is satisfied if the value of a given attribute increases strictly monotonically as we move forwards through the sequence of participant events.

> **INCREASING PATTERN** The *increasing* pattern is satisfied by an attribute A if for all the participant events, e1 << e2 $\Rightarrow$ e1.A < e2.A. The symbol $\Rightarrow$ denotes implication.

The remaining definitions are quite similar.

THE DECREASING PATTERN

The *decreasing* pattern is satisfied if the value of a given attribute decreases strictly monotonically as we move forwards through the sequence of participant events.

> **DECREASING PATTERN** The *decreasing* pattern is satisfied by an attribute A if for all the participant events, e1 << e2 $\Rightarrow$ e1.A > e2.A.

THE STABLE PATTERN

The *stable* pattern is satisfied if the given attribute has the same value in all the participant events. Note that in this case the order of the event instances is irrelevant.

> **STABLE PATTERN** The *stable* pattern is satisfied by an attribute A if for all the participant events, e1 << e2 $\Rightarrow$ e1.A = e2.A.

THE NON-INCREASING PATTERN

The *non-increasing* pattern is satisfied if the value of a given attribute does not increase within the given context.

> **NON-INCREASING PATTERN** The *non-increasing* pattern is satisfied by an attribute A if for all participant events e1 << e2 $\Rightarrow$ e1.A $\geq$ e2.A.

THE NON-DECREASING PATTERN

The *non-decreasing* pattern is satisfied if the value of a given attribute does not decrease within the given context.

> **NON-DECREASING PATTERN** The *non-decreasing* pattern is satisfied by an attribute A if for all participant events e1 << e2 $\Rightarrow$ e1.A $\leq$ e2.A.

The complement to all these patterns is the mixed pattern. This is matched if none of the trends defined so far is satisfied.

THE MIXED PATTERN

The *mixed* pattern is satisfied if the value of a given attribute both increases and decreases in different portions of the time series.

> **MIXED PATTERN** The *mixed* pattern is satisfied by an attribute A, if the participant event set contains event instances e1, e2, e3, e4 such that
>
> e1 << e2 and e1.A < e2.A and e3 << e4 and e3.A > e4.A.
>
> Note that e1, e2, e3, and e4 don't have to be four distinct instances, for example, e2 could be the same event as e3.

We use the example shown in figure 9.8 to illustrate these trend patterns. In this example a patient's vital signs, including a subjective pain scale, are taken every 3 hours. Note the following patterns in figure 9.8:

- The value of the `fever` attribute satisfies the decreasing pattern.
- The value of the systolic `blood pressure` attribute (the first of the pair) satisfies the increasing pattern.

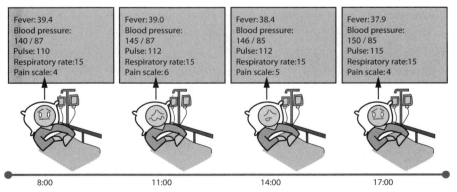

Figure 9.8   A health monitor example used to illustrate various temporal trend patterns

- The value of the diastolic `blood` `pressure` (the second of the pair) satisfies the non-increasing pattern.
- The value of the `pulse` attribute satisfies the non-decreasing pattern.
- The value of the `respiratory` `rate` attribute satisfies the stable pattern.
- The value of the `pain` `scale` attribute satisfies the mixed pattern.

The only trend that may be detected without having all the event instances is the mixed pattern. All other patterns require the entire relevant portion of the time series, but it may make sense for the agent implementing a trend pattern to emit intermediate results.

Trend patterns are commonly used in stream processing systems that process continuous time series, typically in batches.

9.3.3   *Spatial patterns*

Spatial patterns are patterns that are satisfied based on the distance between the locations of the events. They include the distance patterns: *min distance, max distance,* and *average distance.* These distance patterns can be either absolute or relative. Absolute distance patterns are concerned with the distance of an event's location from a fixed point, typically the location of a particular object. Relative distance patterns are concerned with the distances between events in the participant event set. These patterns assume that every event contains an attribute that gives its location as a point (not a line or area). Any events that do not contain this attribute are ignored when determining whether the pattern is matched or not. The name of the attribute is supplied as a pattern parameter.

Distance patterns can be implemented using the standard threshold patterns that we discussed in section 9.2.2, but for reasons of convenience we present them here as patterns in their own right. We define the absolute distance patterns first.

THE MIN DISTANCE PATTERN

The *min distance* pattern deals with the distance between events and a given object.

> **MIN DISTANCE PATTERN**   The *min distance* pattern is satisfied when the minimal distance of all the participant events from a given point satisfies the min distance threshold assertion.

To determine whether this pattern is matched or not, you take all the participant events and find out which one occurred closest to the given point. The pattern is satisfied if its distance satisfies a threshold assertion (like the patterns in 9.2.2, this is expressed as a threshold relation and threshold value). In the Fast Flower Delivery example, we could discover whether there were any delivery vans less than 20 km from a given florist in a particular time period. This can be done by using the min distance pattern with a threshold assertion of `<` `20` `km`.

In a similar fashion we define the max distance and average distance patterns.

THE MAX DISTANCE PATTERN

The *max distance* pattern is similar, except that it's concerned with the maximal distance of all events from the given object.

> **MAX DISTANCE PATTERN**   The *max distance* pattern is satisfied when the maximal distance of all the participant events from a given point satisfies the max distance threshold assertion .

The average distance pattern definition is next.

THE AVERAGE DISTANCE PATTERN

The *average distance* pattern again relates to the distance between events and entities.

> **AVERAGE DISTANCE PATTERN**   The *average distance* pattern is satisfied when the average distance of all the participant events from a given point satisfies the average distance threshold assertion.

Figure 9.9 uses the Fast Flower Delivery application to demonstrate these three patterns. To keep the figure 9.9 illustration simple, we assume that the relevant context partition contains just two GPS readings, one for each van. The distances are calculated as part of this pattern evaluation relative to the fixed locations of stores A, B, C. The following patterns are satisfied:

- Min distance relative to Store A > 10 km
- Max distance relative to Store B < 5 km
- Average distance relative to Store C ≤ 7 km

Next we move to discuss relative distance patterns. These relate to distances between pairs of events in the participant event set. The first of these is relative min distance.

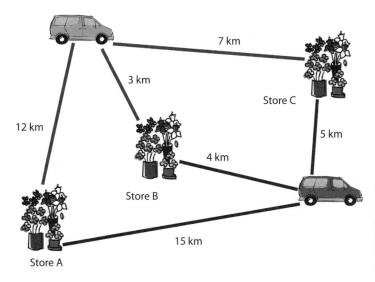

Figure 9.9   An example showing the location of two delivery vans and three flower stores in the Fast Flower Delivery application. This demonstrates absolute distance patterns.

THE RELATIVE MIN DISTANCE PATTERN

The *relative min distance* pattern, as its name suggests, evaluates the minimal distance between all pairs of events in the participant event set.

> **RELATIVE MIN DISTANCE PATTERN**   The *relative min distance* pattern is satisfied when the minimal distance between any two participant events satisfies the min distance threshold assertion.

To show this in use, we consider a law enforcement application that analyzes burglary reports looking for patterns of similar-looking burglary events. One hypothesis is that there could be a burglar who never commits two crimes in the same neighborhood, to camouflage his tracks. To look for this the application uses a relative min distance pattern to detect when there is a set of similar burglaries always separated by a distance of at least 20 km.

THE RELATIVE MAX DISTANCE PATTERN

The definition of the next pattern, *relative max distance*, is similar.

> **RELATIVE MAX DISTANCE PATTERN**   The *relative max distance* pattern is satisfied when the maximal distance between any two participant events satisfies the max distance threshold assertion.

Using the burglary story again, the relative max distance pattern can be used to look for lazy burglars who always operate within a single neighborhood. We could, for example, look for a maximal distance of 5 km between similar burglaries.

THE RELATIVE AVERAGE DISTANCE PATTERN

Our third relative distance pattern looks at the average distance between events:

> **RELATIVE AVERAGE DISTANCE PATTERN**   The *relative average distance* pattern is satisfied when the average distance between any two participant events satisfies the relative average threshold assertion.

This pattern could be useful looking for a burglar who generally stays in a particular neighborhood, but now and then takes a journey further afield.

Figure 9.10 illustrates these three relative patterns. In this figure, crime reports are being processed by Pattern detect agents that use a segmentation-oriented context. This context has three partitions. One of them relates to burglaries where a door is broken, one relates to burglaries where the burglar gains entry by breaking a window, and the third includes the theft of heavy appliances. Looking at the figure you can see that these partitions satisfy the following patterns:

- The *relative max distance* pattern with threshold assertion < 5 km is satisfied in the door breaking partition.
- The *relative min distance* pattern with threshold assertion > 20 km is satisfied in the window breaking partition.

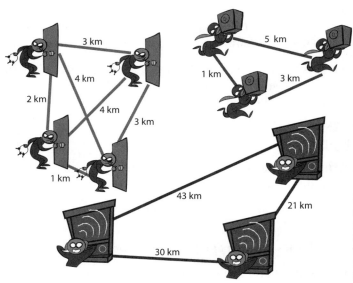

Figure 9.10 Examples that demonstrate three relative distance patterns. Going clockwise from the top right they are relative max distance, relative min distance, and relative average distance.

- The *relative average distance* pattern with threshold assertion ≤ 3 km is satisfied in the heavy lifter partition.

9.3.4 *Spatiotemporal patterns*

Spatiotemporal patterns look at time series of events and determine spatial trends over time. These patterns are of the following types: *moving in a constant direction*, *moving in a mixed direction*, *stationary*, and *moving toward*.

As with temporal trend patterns we assume that there is just one relevant event type, so all the participant events are instances of this one type. Moreover, the patterns require that the participant events themselves constitute a time series, meaning that they are temporally totally ordered (as with temporal trend patterns; the definition of this order depends on the ordering policy, which we discuss in section 9.4). We use the notation: e1 << e2 to mean that event instance e1 comes before e2 in this ordering.

THE MOVING IN A CONSTANT DIRECTION PATTERN

This pattern is actually a family of patterns, such as *moving north*, or *moving south*. For example, the moving south pattern would be satisfied by a vehicle that is transmitting GPS readings of its position while it's traveling from Bologna to Florence.

> **MOVING IN A CONSTANT DIRECTION PATTERN** The *moving in a constant direction* pattern is satisfied if there exists a direction from the set {north, south, east, west, northeast, northwest, southeast, southwest} such that for any pair of participant events e1, e2 we have e1 << e2 ⇒ e2 lies in that direction relative to e1.

The complementary pattern is the pattern moving in a mixed direction, discussed next.

THE MOVING IN A MIXED DIRECTION PATTERN

This pattern is the complementary pattern indicating that no consistent direction can be found among the participant events in the time context being considered.

> **MOVING IN A MIXED DIRECTION PATTERN**   The *moving in a mixed direction* pattern is satisfied if there are at least three events with different locations and if none of the eight moving in a constant direction patterns is satisfied.

THE STATIONARY PATTERN

This pattern is self-explanatory.

> **STATIONARY PATTERN**   The *stationary* pattern is satisfied if the location of all participant events is identical.

We have one final spatiotemporal pattern, and this one refers to an external object.

THE MOVING TOWARD PATTERN

This is a pattern that indicates movement towards some object.

> **MOVING TOWARD PATTERN**   The *moving toward* pattern is satisfied when for any pair of participant events e1, e2 we have e1 << e2 ⇒ the location of e2 is closer to a certain object than the location of e1.

Note that this pattern may be true for several objects at the same time.

We illustrate these patterns in figure 9.11, which shows movements of aircraft (the events in question are periodic position reports from these aircraft). In this figure, the helicopter flies across Central America from the Pacific Ocean to the Atlantic Ocean. This satisfies the moving east pattern. It also satisfies moving toward France (and also, for that matter, moving toward Germany). The biplane is going around in circles over the Pacific Ocean, and so it satisfies the mixed direction pattern, while the small helicopter is hovering stationary over Greenland.

One can imagine many more patterns, for example, patterns that refer to medians, quartiles, and other statistical measurements. The list we have given in this chapter contains the most commonly used patterns, and will probably grow over time. We now turn to pattern policies. These are an integral part of pattern interpretations and they are discussed next.

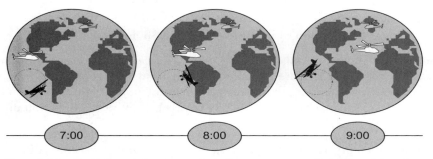

Figure 9.11   Spatiotemporal patterns where the events are reports of aircraft location

9.4   *Pattern policies*

Some patterns in the previous sections, such as any, all, and sequence, look for particular subsets of the participant events. What should a Pattern detect agent do if there's more than one subset that satisfies the pattern? Should it generate all the possible matching sets, or should it generate only one—in which case which one? The right thing to do here varies by application, as it depends on what the pattern is being used for. So we allow the application to specify this, and other behavior, through *pattern policies*.

The role of a pattern policy is to disambiguate the semantics of a pattern matching operation, and in this chapter we discuss five kinds of policies:

- *Evaluation policy*—This determines when the matching sets are produced.
- *Cardinality policy*—This determines how many matching sets are produced within a single context partition.
- *Repeated type policy*—This determines what happens if the matching step encounters multiple events of the same type.
- *Consumption policy*—This specifies what happens to a participant event after it has been included in a matching set.
- *Order policy*—This specifies how temporal order is defined.

We now discuss these policies in depth.

9.4.1   *Evaluation policies*

The *evaluation* policy lets you choose whether a Pattern detect agent generates output incrementally, or only at the end of the temporal context.[1]

EVALUATION POLICY   An *evaluation* policy is a semantic abstraction that determines when the matching process is to be evaluated.

The two evaluation policies are

- *Immediate*—The pattern is tested for each time a new event is added to the participant event set.
- *Deferred*—The pattern is tested for only when the agent's temporal context partition (window) closes.

In immediate mode we could have a matching set generated each time a new event is received. Moreover, if the pattern is one that can be matched by multiple subsets, we could have several matching sets generated each time a new event is received. The cardinality policy, which we look at next, can be used to limit the number of matching sets that are generated, and thus the number of derived events that are produced.

---

[1]   For a thorough discussion of coupling modes see David Botzer and Opher Etzion, *Self-Tuning of the Relationships among Rules' Components in Active Databases System,*. IEEE Trans. Knowl. Data Eng. 16(3): 375-379 (2004). http://www.computer.org/portal/web/csdl/doi/10.1109/TKDE.2003.1262191.

9.4.2 *Cardinality policies*

A Pattern detect agent can find itself able to generate more than one matching set, either because the pattern is one (like all or any) that can be satisfied by a proper subset of the participant events, or because there is an immediate evaluation policy, or both. A *cardinality* policy can be used to control how many matching sets are actually created.

> **CARDINALITY POLICY**   A *cardinality* policy is a semantic abstraction that controls how many matching sets are created. The possible policies are *single, unrestricted,* and *bounded.*

The various policies are as follows:

- *Single*—Only one matching set is generated. When this has been done, no further action is performed within this context partition, so no more matching sets are generated.
- *Unrestricted*—Under this policy there are no restrictions on the quantity of matching sets that can be generated.
- *Bounded*—This policy specifies an upper bound on the number of matching sets that can be generated within a context partition. The Pattern detect agent continues generating matching sets until it reaches this bound.

You'll see that with the single and bounded policies we can still be left with the problem of deciding which matching set or sets are to be generated. To answer this question we introduce two further kinds of policies, repeated type policies and consumption policies.

9.4.3 *Repeated type policies*

You will recall that every Pattern detect agent has a relevant event types list, specifying the types of events that qualify as participant events. This list also specifies how many instances of a particular type are needed in order to satisfy an all pattern or a sequence pattern.

> **EXCESS TYPE CONDITION**   An *excess type* condition occurs when a Pattern detect agent encounters more instances of a given event type than are specified by the relevant event types list.

Excess type conditions are normal for some patterns, including patterns that operate on time series like the spatiotemporal patterns, but they are the reason why there can be multiple subsets that satisfy an all or sequence pattern. Consider the travel agent example that we used to illustrate the all pattern. We show a variation of this in figure 9.12; this time there are two `flight reserved` events, two `car reserved` events, and three `hotel reserved` events.

With an all pattern, each matching set has to include a single instance of each of these event types, and by counting up the possibilities in figure 9.12 you can see that

Figure 9.12 An example of the all pattern where there are multiple events of the same type

twelve matching sets could be created. This might be what you want, but if it isn't you can use the *repeated type* policy to limit the number.

> **REPEATED TYPE POLICY** A *repeated type* policy is a semantic abstraction that defines the behavior of a Pattern detect agent when an excess type condition occurs. The possible policies are override, every, first, last, with maximal value, and with minimal value.

The interpretation of these various policies is as follows:

- *Override*—The participant event set keeps no more instances of any event type than the number implied by the relevant event types list. If a new event instance is encountered and the participant set already contains the required number of instances of that type, the new instance replaces the oldest previous instance of that type.
- *Every*—Every instance is kept in the participant event set, so that all possible matching sets can be produced.
- *First*—Every instance is kept in the participant event set, but only the earliest instances of each type are used for matching.
- *Last*—Every instance is kept, but only the latest instances of each type are used for matching.
- *With maximal value <attribute name>*—Every instance is kept, but only the event or events with the maximal value of the specified attribute are used for matching.
- *With minimal value <attribute name>*—Every instance is kept, but only the event or events with the minimal value of the specified attribute are used for matching.

With the exception of every, all these policies ensure that the matching step returns at most one matching set. This means that they can be used with the single policy without ambiguity. If every is used in combination with the single or bounded cardinality policy, our modeling language does not specify which sets are to be generated.

We now describe the effects of these policies in the example shown in figure 9.12:

- With the override policy there is always at most one participant event for each relevant event type. This means that at the end of the time interval there are just three events {Continental flight reservation, Sheraton hotel reservation, Avis car reservation}, so only one matching set is produced.

- The every policy, if used in combination with the unrestricted cardinality policy, would generate twelve matching sets containing all twelve combinations.
- The first policy generates the matching set {Hertz car reservation, Hilton hotel reservation, United flight reservation}.
- The last policy generates the matching set {Continental flight reservation, Sheraton hotel reservation, Avis car reservation}.
- A with minimal value policy could be used to select the cheapest option for each of the three reservations.

You could be wondering why we have *first* and *last*. In this example, *override* with *immediate* seems to do the same as *first*, and *override* with *deferred* the same as *last*. The reason for having them should become clear when we introduce consumption policies.

9.4.4   *Consumption policies*

Up to now our focus has been on policies you can use with an all or sequence pattern to get the number of matching sets down to one. However, consider an application that uses a pattern to match together related events, like the book selling example we saw in figure 9.3. In this case the application wants to find as many matching sets as possible, but with the constraint that no event can be in more than one matching set. You can specify this using a *consumption* policy,

> **CONSUMPTION POLICY** A *consumption policy* is a semantic abstraction that defines whether an event instance is consumed as soon as it's included in a matching set, or whether it can be included in subsequent matching sets. Possible consumption policies are *consume, reuse,* and *bounded reuse.*

The consumption policies are quite straightforward:

- *Consume*—Under this policy each event instance is removed from the participant event set after it has been included in a matching set. This means that it can't take part in any further matching for this particular pattern within the same context.
- *Reuse*—Under this policy, an event instance can participate in an unrestricted number of matching sets.
- *Bounded reuse*—Under this policy, you can specify the number of times that an event can be used in matching sets for this particular pattern within the same context.

The choice of consumption policy is irrelevant if the cardinality policy is single because that means that the matching step runs only once. However, if the cardinality policy does permit another matching set to be generated, the removal of events by the consumption policy immediately triggers a reevaluation of the pattern. This means that you can use first with consume or last with consume to generate a sequence of non-overlapping matching sets.

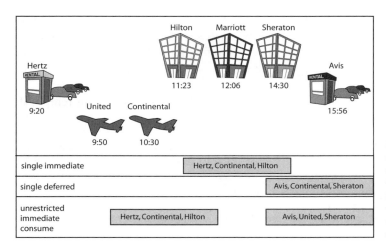

Figure 9.13 The effect of different evaluation and cardinality policies, when the repeated type policy is last. The events shown at the top of the figure give rise to the matching sets shown at the bottom.

Figure 9.13 takes our travel reservation example, which you will recall involves an *all* pattern, and uses it to show a repeated type policy of *last* with different combinations of evaluation, cardinality, and consumption policies.

- Under the *immediate* and *single* policies, a single matching set is created as soon as all the three event types have been detected. This happens at 11:23, when the Hilton hotel reservation is made. Note that there have been two airline reservation events at this point, so under the *last* policy it's the Continental reservation that is selected. The consumption policy is irrelevant in this case, as the *single* policy has been used.

- Under the *deferred* and *single* policies, the matching set is not created until after the last event has been received. As the repeated type policy is *last*, this means that the matching set consists of the Avis, Continental, and Sheraton reservations, being the last instances of their respective event types. You can see that this has produced a different result as more events have occurred.

- Under the *immediate* and *unrestricted* policies, the first matching set is the same as the one generated in the immediate and single case, namely {Hertz, Continental, Hilton}. Processing then continues, but what happens next depends on the consumption policy. If the policy is *reuse* (indicating that the same event instance can appear in more than one matching set), three more matching sets will be generated, the last of them being the same as the one generated under the deferred and single policies. However, if the policy is *consume*, as shown in figure 9.13, the Hertz reservation is used up, so no more matching sets get generated until the Avis reservation is encountered. You will see that the second matching set is {Avis, United, Sheraton} even though the United reservation came earlier than the Continental one. This is because the Continental reservation was consumed in the first matching set, leaving the United flight reservation as the last (and only) flight reservation.

Some of our pattern functions rely on the participant events having an order. As we saw in chapter 7, an order can be established in several ways, and our final policy lets you specify which one is to be used when testing to see if the pattern is matched or not.

9.4.5 *Order policies*

The last type of policy is the order policy, which follows the various temporal ordering possibilities presented in chapter 7.

> **ORDER POLICY**   An *order policy* is a semantic abstraction that defines the meaning of the << temporal order of the event instances in the participant event set. The possible policies are by occurrence time, by detection time, by user-defined attribute, or by stream position.

The order policy is applicable to all temporal or spatiotemporal patterns. The possible policies are

- *By occurrence time*—The order of events in the participant event set is determined by comparing their occurrence time attributes, so that the order reflects the order in which the events happened in reality (as accurately as the temporal granularity allows).
- *By detection time*—The order of events in the participant event set is determined by comparing their detection time attributes, that is the order in which events are detected by the event processing system. Note that this order may not be identical to the order in which events happened in reality.
- *By user-defined attribute*—Some event payloads contain a timestamp, sequence number, or another attribute that increases over time, and this can be used to determine the order. For example, the `Delivery Request` events in the Fast Flower Delivery application could be ordered using their `required delivery time` attribute.
- *By stream position*—In this case the order to be used is the order in which the events are delivered to the EPA from the channel that feeds it. Some channel implementations are designed so that this order is the same as the order in which events were delivered to the channel.

Note that the first three of these policies don't guarantee that the order is unique as there could be two or more participant events that have the same timestamp or user-defined attribute value.

9.5   *Patterns reference table*

To summarize the previous sections we bring information about all the patterns that we have mentioned into a single table.

Table 9.1   Event pattern reference table

Category	Pattern	Pattern parameters	Matching set
Basic	all	Pattern assertion (optional)	One event for each type in the participant set
	any		One matching event
	absence		Empty
Threshold	count	Relation, Threshold value	Entire participant event set
	value max	Attribute, Relation, Threshold value	Entire participant event set
	value min	Attribute, Relation, Threshold value	Entire participant event set
	value average	Attribute, Relation, Threshold value	Entire participant event set
	functor	Function, Relation, Threshold value	Entire participant event set
Subset Selection	relative n lowest values	Attribute, Count (value of n)	n (or fewer) events with the lowest values for the given attribute
	relative n highest values	Attribute, Count (value of n)	n (or fewer) events with the highest values for the given attribute
Modal	always	Always assertion	Entire participant event set
	sometimes	Sometimes assertion	Entire participant event set
Temporal	sequence	Pattern assertion (optional)	One event for each type in the participant set
	first n	Count (value of n)	The first n (or fewer) events
	last n	Count (value of n)	The last n (or fewer) events
	increasing	Attribute	Entire participant event set
	decreasing	Attribute	Entire participant event set
	stable	Attribute	Entire participant event set
	non-increasing	Attribute	Entire participant event set
	non-decreasing	Attribute	Entire participant event set
	mixed	Attribute	Entire participant event set
Spatial	min distance	Location attribute, Spatial entity, Relation, Threshold value	Entire participant event set
	max distance	Location attribute, Spatial entity, Relation, Threshold value	Entire participant event set

Table 9.1   Event pattern reference table *(continued)*

Category	Pattern	Pattern parameters	Matching set
Spatio-temporal	average distance	Location attribute, Spatial entity, Relation, Threshold value	Entire participant event set
	relative min distance	Location attribute, Relation, Threshold value	Entire participant event set
	relative max distance	Location attribute, Relation, Threshold value	Entire participant event set
	relative average distance	Location attribute, Relation, Threshold value	Entire participant event set
	moving in a constant direction	Location attribute, Direction	Entire participant event set
	moving in a mixed direction	Location attribute	Entire participant event set
	stationary	Location attribute	Entire participant event set
	moving toward	Location attribute, Spatial entity	Entire participant event set

These comments may help you interpret table 9.1:

- The parameters column shows which additional parameters must (or in a couple of cases may) be provided in order to specify the pattern. Many of the patterns require a relation parameter (one of the relations $>, <, =, \geq, \leq, \neq$).
- The relative *n* highest values, relative *n* lowest values, first *n* and last *n* patterns generally produce a matching set containing *n* events. However, if the participant event set contains fewer than *n* events, the matching set contains all the participant events.

As indicated before, this set of patterns is extendable, and will be updated periodically on the *Event Processing in Action* website. We now look at some of these patterns being used in the Fast Flower Delivery application.

9.6   *The Fast Flower Delivery patterns*

In this section we list all the Pattern detect agents used in the Fast Flower Delivery application. Each of these agents will be presented in a separate table, followed by comments where required. In this table we only show the policies that are significant.

Table 9.2 Automatic assignment

Pattern type	Context	Relevant types	Parameters	Policies
first n	Request	Delivery Bid	Count = 1	cardinality = single evaluation = immediate

This agent is responsible for picking the driver who is going to be assigned to a particular delivery. The `Delivery Bid` events from the drivers have already been checked by other agents, so all this agent has to do is pick one. It uses the simple strategy of picking the first event that it encounters. It uses the immediate evaluation policy, as it makes sense to match as soon as it receives its first event, and a single cardinality policy as we don't want to continue the process after this first event has been selected.

Table 9.3 `Manual assignment preparation`

Pattern type	Context	Relevant types	Parameters	Policies
relative n highest values	Bid interval	Delivery Bid	Attribute = ranking Count = 5	cardinality = single evaluation = deferred repeated type = every

This pattern selects the highest (at most) five bids with respect to their driver's `rank-ing` value. These bids are then forwarded to the flower store, so that it can choose the driver who is to be assigned to the delivery. The selection of bids is done once, at the end of the `Bid interval` window.

Table 9.4 `Assignment not done`

Pattern type	Context	Relevant types	Parameters	Policies
absence	Response interval	Manual Assignment		

This is a timeout detection, indicating that the manual assignment decision was not performed on time. There are no parameters for the absence pattern, and none of the pattern policies have any effect on it.

Table 9.5 `Pickup alert`

Pattern type	Context	Relevant types	Parameters	Policies
absence	Pickup interval	Pickup Confirmation		

This is a timeout detection indicating that a pickup was not done on time.

Table 9.6 `Delivery alert`

Pattern type	Context	Relevant types	Parameters	Policies
absence	Delivery interval	Delivery Confirmation		

This is another timeout detection; this one detects that a delivery was not made on time.

Table 9.7 `Ranking increase`

Pattern type	Context	Relevant types	Parameters	Policies
absence	Driver evaluation	Delivery Alert		

This agent detects drivers who did not have any delivery alerts within the `Driver evaluation` context. It's used to decide whether to give the driver a ranking increase.

Table 9.8 `Ranking decrease`

Pattern type	Context	Relevant types	Parameters	Policies
count	Driver evaluation	Delivery Alert	Relation: > Threshold 5	repeated type = every evaluation = deferred

This agent detects drivers who had more than five delivery alerts within the driver evaluation context.

Table 9.9 `Improving note`

Pattern type	Context	Relevant types	Parameters	Policies
sequence	Driver	Ranking Decrease, Ranking Increase		repeated type = override evaluation = immediate cardinality= unrestricted consumption = consume

This agent detects when a driver had a ranking increase after a ranking decrease. The override policy guarantees that there will be at most one of each of these events in the participant event set, and the consume policy means that the set is cleared each time the pattern is detected. This agent doesn't have a temporal context, so it has to use an immediate evaluation policy.

Table 9.10 `Permanent weak driver`

Pattern type	Context	Relevant types	Parameters	Policies
always	Monthly driver	Daily Assignments	Assertion: assignmentCount < 5	evaluation = deferred

This agent detects when a driver has had fewer than five assignments in each of his working days during the month.

Table 9.11 `Idle driver`

Pattern type	Context	Relevant types	Parameters	Policies
sometimes	Monthly driver	Daily Assignments	Assertion: assignmentCount = 0	evaluation = deferred

This agent detects drivers who had at least one working day during the month without any assignment.

Table 9.12 `Consistent weak driver`

Pattern type	Context	Relevant types	Parameters	Policies
always	Monthly driver	Relative Performance	Assertion: deviation< -2	evaluation = deferred

This agent detects when a driver has a consistently low number of assignments. It takes a month's worth of `Relative Performance` events (for a given driver) and sees if that driver is always more than two standard deviations under the mean number of assignments on that day.

Table 9.13 `Consistent strong driver`

Pattern type	Context	Relevant types	Parameters	Policies
always	Monthly driver	Relative Performance	Assertion: deviation > 2	evaluation = deferred

This pattern detects that a driver has a consistently high number of assignments. It takes a month's worth of `Relative Performance` events (for a given driver) and sees if that driver is always more than two standard deviations above the mean number of assignments on that day.

Table 9.14 `Improving driver`

Pattern type	Context	Relevant types	Parameters	Policies
non-decreasing	Monthly driver	Daily Assignments	Attribute = assignmentCount	evaluation = deferred

This agent detects drivers whose daily assignment rate stays level or increases over the month, so as to designate them as improving. This assessment is performed on a monthly basis.

These examples from the Fast Flower Delivery application don't cover all types of patterns that we have mentioned in this chapter. We hope that solving the exercises at the end of the chapter will provide the interested reader an opportunity to experiment with additional patterns.

9.7 *Pattern detection in practice*

In this section we show some examples of pattern detection in current event processing languages. Note that further details about the languages can be found on the *Event Processing in Action* website.

```
// keep count of deliveries the driver made
on all DeliveryConfirmation(driver=driver) {
    deliveriesMade:=deliveriesMade+1;

    // every time when driver completes 20 delivers
    if deliveriesMade=20 then {
        // if the driver didn't have a delivery alert
        if alertsReceived=0 then {
            // then generate a RankingIncrease event
            route RankingIncrease(driver);
            // if the previous evaluation generated a ranking decrease
            if prevDecrease then {
                // then generate an Improvement Note
                route ImprovementNote(driver);
            }
        }
    }
}
```

Figure 9.14   An Apama example that shows the code for the `Ranking increase` and `Improving note` Pattern detect agents from the Fast Flower Delivery application

In figure 9.14 we can see an implementation, using Apama MonitorScript, of the `Ranking increase` and `Improving note` agents. This figure shows the use of the imperative language style. Here are some observations about this example:

- The `Driver evaluation` sliding event interval context is implemented by incrementing a variable called `deliveriesMade`, and then testing to see when 20 events have been received.
- The `Ranking increase` agent (an absence pattern) is implemented by the second `if` statement. The route statement causes the derived event to be emitted.
- The `Improving note` agent (a sequence pattern) is implemented by the third `if` statement.

We now look at a different language style. In figure 9.15 we show a StreamBase implementation of the `Automatic assignment` agent.

Like all the StreamBase examples, the bottom part of the window shows the event flow, which is a similar concept to our event processing network. The `Automatic assignment` agent, a first *n* Pattern detect EPA, is called `SelectFirstBidder` in this example and is shown in the "Additional Expression" form in the middle of the window.

The following snippet shows the `Pickup alert` absence pattern in Esper. This is a SQL- oriented programming example.

```
/**
* Not picked up after 5 mins (300 secs) of the driver proposed pickup time
*/
insert into AlertW(requestId, message, driver, timestamp)
select a.requestId, "not picked up", a.driver, current_timestamp()
from pattern[
every a=Assignment -> (timer:interval(300 + (a.pickupTime-current_timestamp)/
    1000) and
not PickUpConfirmation(requestId = a.requestId))
];
```

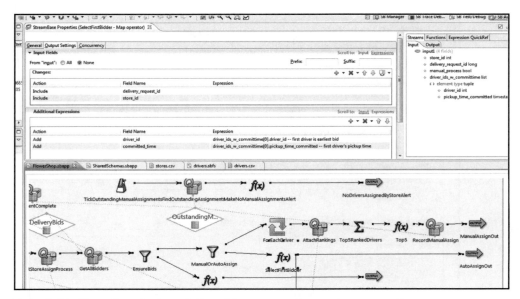

Figure 9.15 StreamBase implementation of the `Automatic assignment` pattern

You can see that this includes an explicit pattern clause that contains a timer and a "not" clause, designating the absence.

The following snippet is the `Automatic assignment` agent implemented in Prova, an agent-oriented logic programming based language.

```
process_automatic(RequestId,StoreId) :-
    @group(bids)
    rcvMsg(RequestId,Protocol,VanId,response,delivery_bid(VanId,RequestId)),
    sendMsg(RequestId,esb,VanId,request,assignment(RequestId,StoreId)).
process_automatic(RequestId,StoreId) :-
    % Exit channel to define the operator, timeout 2 seconds for fast
      testing, limit to one result
    @and(bids) @timeout(2000) @count(1)
    rcvMsg(RequestId,Protocol,From,and,[Events]).
```

This example receives `Delivery Bid` events, using the rcvMsg clause, and creates a single derived event (denoted by the sendMsg clause).

Figure 9.16 shows an example of IBM WebSphere Business Events, which has an active (ECA) rule language. In this language all activities that are triggered by the same input event are grouped into one logical unit called an *interaction set*. This consists of the event to which it responds, in this case a `Perform Evaluation` event, and a collection of action blocks. In this example the first block emits a derived event if no ranking change is needed, and the second block implements the `Improving note` agent (this has a sequence pattern). The last two blocks implement the `Ranking decrease` pattern (a count threshold pattern) and the `Ranking increase` pattern (an absence pattern).

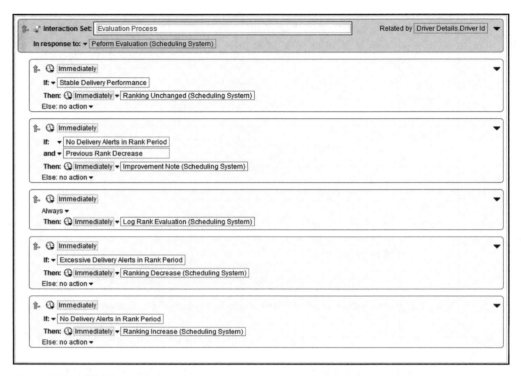

Figure 9.16   IBM WebSphere Business Events example showing some patterns from the Fast Flower Delivery example

As you can see, these different programming styles can all express the same functionality, and in chapter 10 we survey the various programming styles.

9.8   Summary

In this chapter we discussed the notion of event processing patterns, the central concept in contemporary event processing. We explained the idea of patterns and gave formal definitions of the terms used. We looked at a number of different pattern types, and you should have noticed that there are two things that Pattern detect agents can be used for. They can be used to examine a collection of events and simply decide whether the events match the pattern or not, and they can be used to extract one or more subsets of the events that are related to one another by matching a pattern. A Pattern detect agent may need some guidance when finding subsets, and this is provided via a number of pattern polices which tune up the semantics of patterns.

This chapter concludes this part of the book, the "deep dive" into all the concepts and building blocks used when constructing event-based applications. The final part of this book deals with advanced topics related to implementing applications and looks at some future directions of event processing.

9.8.1 *Additional reading*

Luckham, David. 2002. *The Power of Events: An Introduction to Complex Event Processing in Distributed Enterprise Systems.* Addison-Wesley Professional. http://www.amazon.com/Power-Events-Introduction-Processing-Distributed/dp/0201727897/ref=sr_1_2?ie=UTF8&s=books&qid=1258816511&sr=8-2. This book introduces the notion of event patterns, and the Rapide language for event patterns.

Etzion, Opher. 2008. "Event processing architecture and patterns," Tutorial in DEBS. http://www.slideshare.net/opher.etzion/tutorial-in-debs-2008-presentation. This is a tutorial about event processing patterns in the form of a slide presentation.

9.8.2 *Exercises*

9.1 Add three more EPAs to the Fast Flower Delivery example that use patterns that were not used in section 9.7.

9.2 Which pattern would you use if the only thing that needs to be done is an assertion over different attributes of different events, such as: E1.A > E2.B > E3.C ?

9.3 What are the relationships among these event collections: the collection of input events to the EPA, the matching set, and the collection of output events?

9.4 What are the relationships among these event type collections: the collection of input event types, the relevant event types, and the collection of output event types?

9.5 The set of patterns we have given is not minimal. If you had to reduce the set of patterns by expressing some of the patterns in terms of other patterns, which patterns could you have removed in this way?

9.6 Can you think of a new EPA related to the Fast Flower Delivery application that would show the use of the Not-selected terminal? Write the exact pattern signature, and explain what it could be used for.

9.7 Is it useful to allow entities that are external to the EPA to query the internal state of the pattern matching process (for instance to see the collection of participant events that have arrived so far and that have not yet been matched)? If yes, to what purpose? Show an example.

9.8 A higher level pattern, or template, is a construct that packages one or more patterns with their parameters. State how you could define timeout as a higher level pattern. Can you find another such higher level pattern, by looking at the patterns of the Fast Flower Delivery example? Can you think of additional cases outside this example in which using this idea would be useful?

9.9 List the cases in which the value max and value min patterns would give the same results when run with either single and immediate, or single and deferred policies.

9.10 For some patterns all the participant events need to be present in order for it to be possible to evaluate the pattern. The meaning of *all* in that sentence is clear when a pattern is being used with a temporal context, but what does it mean in the case of a spatial only context? Is there a way to know that the participant event set is complete in that case?

9.11 Show examples of the sequence pattern where it makes sense to order the events according to each order policy.

9.12 Can you think of additional spatiotemporal patterns? If so, define such patterns.

9.13 Show an example where the mixed trend pattern could be used.

9.14 Explain the benefit of externalizing policies to be separate entities.

9.15 What is the difference between the override and last repeated type policies? Give an example where they produce the same result and an example where they produce different results.

9.16 What is the difference between the immediate and deferred evaluation policies? Give an example where they produce the same result, and an example where they produce different results.

9.17 Give an example where a deferred evaluation policy can be done before the end of the temporal context, with a guarantee that the result can't change. Can you describe the necessary conditions for this?

Part 3

Pragmatics

Finally, the wedding event has been planned and is about to take place. There are pragmatic decisions to be made concerning the duration of the event, weather problems anticipated for the day (which might necessitate a move indoors), table seating arrangements, and more.

In this part of the book we discuss some of the pragmatics behind the implementation of an event processing system. Chapter 10 deals with the engineering aspects. It looks at the various programming languages that are available, and some of the engineering questions involved in implementing the non-functional properties of event processing. Chapter 11 deals with pragmatic challenges involved in implementing event processing applications using the current state of the practice, in areas like getting events in the right order and dealing with inexact events.

Chapter 12 completes the book by discussing current usage trends and looks at emerging directions in event processing.

Engineering and implementation considerations

In theory, there is no difference between theory and practice; in practice, there is.

—Chuck Reid

In the second part of this book, we concentrated on the principles of event processing, giving examples to show how these principles are used in practice. In this chapter we change our emphasis and focus explicitly on the implementation of event processing applications. The implementation-related topics we discuss are language styles, non-functional properties, performance optimizations, and validation. These are the major engineering topics behind implementation of event processing applications. In summary, this chapter discusses the following topics:

- Event processing programming in practice surveying various programming styles found in current products
- Non-functional requirements of event processing applications
- Performance metrics for event processing applications
- Optimization techniques in event processing

NOTE We discuss some specific performance optimizations in section 10.3, but before we get there we point out a couple of reasons why an event processing approach can eliminate bottleneck issues that you might encounter if you were to use a centralized server approach, such as loading all the events into a database management system (DBMS) server. The first of these is asynchronous execution, which we mentioned in chapter 1. The processing of events can be split into a chain of operations (event processing agents in our model), which can execute asynchronously to one another on separate processors. The second reason is that you can often implement a single event processing operation using multiple runtime artifacts executing on different processors.

10.1 *Event processing programming in practice*

At the time of writing this book, there are no standards for event processing programming languages, although there are various programming styles and approaches. The building block approach that we use in this book is a kind of modeling language and, as you can see from the different code samples, there are various ways to implement each of these building blocks. In this section we survey some of the most common event processing programming styles, both the language itself and the type of development environment used with it.

In this section we look at two styles, which we term the stream-oriented style and the rule-oriented style. We also survey different types of development environments. There is a third style, the imperative style, where the logic is coded in a C- or Java-style language. There are several languages like this, but they vary quite a bit from one another, so we suggest you look at examples of specific languages. The Apama MonitorScript language is a good representative of the imperative style and we showed an example of it in chapter 8.

This section is based on the tutorial made by the Event Processing Technical Society (EPTS) Language Analysis group[1] in July 2009.

10.1.1 *Stream-oriented programming style*

The stream-oriented programming style is rooted in data flow programming. In essence a data flow graph is a directed graph that consists of nodes and edges. The nodes represent processing elements, and the edges represent data flowing between these nodes. The paradigm is one of continuous queries, sometimes called *operators*, that are constantly running in the nodes, while their results flow through the edges in the data flow graph. Note that the EPN discussed in this book can be represented as a data flow graph.

The languages used to describe the queries are inspired by SQL and relational algebra, though not all of them are based on SQL. As noted when we discussed stream computing in chapter 2, streams are not necessarily streams of events, and indeed some of the roots of stream programming come from signal processing. When we are using a data flow graph for event processing, the data flowing in the streams are event instances and have the appropriate event semantics.

These event instances are represented as records, and are often referred to as *tuples* following the relational model's terminology. A stream is a continuous flow of events,

---

[1] The full tutorial made by the EPTS language analysis group in ACM DEBS 2009 is available in http://www.slideshare.net/opher.etzion/debs2009-event-processing-languages-tutorial.

```
stream PointOfSaleTransactions(...) := Source()[...]{...}
stream Sales(...) := operator1(PointOfSaleTransactions)[...]{...}
stream TaxableSales(...) := operator2(Sales)[...]{...}
stream TaxPaymentsDue(...) := operator3(TaxableSales)[...]{...}
Null := Sink(TaxPaymentsDue)[...]{...}
stream Deliveries(...) := Source()[...]{...}
stream InventoryCounts(...) := operator4(Sales;Deliveries)[...]{...}
stream RestockOrders(...) := operator5(InventoryCounts)[...]{...}
Null := Sink(RestockOrders)[...]{...}
```

Figure 10.1   An example of a data flow graph with streams on the edges and operators on the nodes

in most cases all of the same event type, and are considered to be tuples of the same relation. The stream may be unbounded and be active forever. This means that, unlike the conventional relational model where a query is executed against an entire table of data, in the continuous query model a query can execute only against a bounded subset of the stream. The stream is therefore broken up into a sequence of *windows* and the query is performed successively against each window. Windows in stream processing correspond to the temporal context concept that we defined in chapter 7 (and for this reason we sometimes refer to temporal context partitions as windows).

Figure 10.1 shows a data flow graph, in which the edges represent streams, and operations on streams are represented by the nodes. This data flow graph is taken from the SPADE language.[2]

There is another way of representing the graph, shown in figure 10.2, which is taken from the Aleri language. In this representation the nodes represent derived streams (and so incorporate a derivation operation) and the edges show the flow of events by indicating which streams provide input to the derivation operation. In figure 10.2 you can see an example in which the ValueByBook stream is derived by an aggregation operation performed on the IndividualPosition stream.

You can see from these examples that there are several ways to model stream processing. We now show some examples of stream processing code. Note that these are just samples; to learn the details of a particular language refer to the fuller examples and references on the book's website.

---

[2] Bugra Gedik, Henrique Andrade, Kun-Lung Wu, Philip S. Yu, Myungcheol Doo: SPADE: the system's declarative stream processing engine. SIGMOD Conference 2008: 1123-1134. http://portal.acm.org/citation.cfm?doid=1376616.1376729.

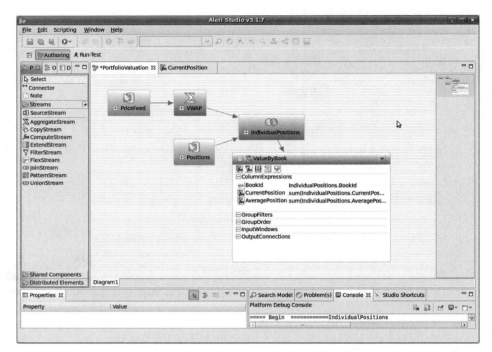

Figure 10.2   An example of data flow with a node as a record and associated operation taken from the Aleri language

Here is an example of a query in the CQL language (developed in the Stanford Stream project).

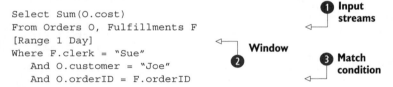

```
Select Sum(O.cost)
From Orders O, Fulfillments F
[Range 1 Day]
Where F.clerk = "Sue"
    And O.customer = "Joe"
    And O.orderID = F.orderID
```

1 Input streams

2 Window

3 Match condition

This query composes the two input streams shown at **1**, applying a temporal context **2** to the second input stream and using the match condition **3**. This query adds up the total cost of orders placed each day by customer "Joe" that were fulfilled by clerk "Sue".

Our next example is a more complex CQL query; this one includes a segmentation context and sampling. Sampling is a form of filtering used in stream computing as the number of events in each window may be high.

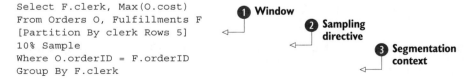

```
Select F.clerk, Max(O.cost)
From Orders O, Fulfillments F
[Partition By clerk Rows 5]
10% Sample
Where O.orderID = F.orderID
Group By F.clerk
```

1 Window

2 Sampling directive

3 Segmentation context

This query takes a 10 percent sample of the Fulfillments stream, and extracts the five most recent fulfillments for each clerk (this is specified by the window specification ❶ and the sampling directive ❷). As in regular SQL, the Group By ❸ means that the query then computes the maximum order cost for each of these groups of five fulfillments. The combination of Partition By and Group By is equivalent to a segmentation context in our model.

Here's an example of a different language, also SQL-based. This one uses Continuous Computation Language (CCL), the language used by Coral8 (now part of Aleri).

```
CREATE STREAM Vwap_s                              ❶ Output stream
   SCHEMA (Symbol STRING, Vwap FLOAT);                and its schema
INSERT INTO Vwap_s                                       ❷ Derivation
   SELECT Symbol, sum(Qty * Price)/sum(Qty)                 rules
FROM Trades_s
KEEP 30                      ❸ Window
GROUP BY Symbol;                definition   ❹ Segmentation
                                                context
```

This query takes as an input a stream of Trade events, and produces an output stream of derived events ❶ containing volume weighted average prices. The calculation is specified by the derivation rules ❷, which follow standard SQL syntax (as was the case with the CQL examples). There is a 30-minute time window ❸, and the GROUP BY clause ❹ establishes a segmentation context meaning that volume-weighted average price (VWAP) calculations are performed independently for every different stock symbol encountered in the input stream.

We end with listing 10.1, which shows an example of an operator written in a stream processing language that does not look like SQL.

Listing 10.1   An example of an operator written in a stream processing language

```
stream VWAPAggregator@day                    ◁        Output
(ticker:String, svwap:Float, svolume:Float)        ❶ stream

                                                           ❷ Window
:= Aggregate                                                  definition
(TradeFilter@day <count(15), count(1), pergroup>)    ◁

[ticker                    ◁  ❸ Segmentation
                                 context

{ Any(ticker),                              ❹ Derivation
Sum(myvwap),                                   rules
Sum(volume) }

 partitionFor(TradeQuote@day),          ❺ Partitioning
 ComputingPool[mod(@day-1,NCNT)]           directive
```

This is a SPADE aggregate operator, which takes a set of VWAP values as input and then adds them up ❹. As with the CCL example, it starts with a definition of the output stream (in this example it's called VWAPAggregator@day) and its schema ❶. The window definition ❷ means that the operator takes input from the TradeFilter@day stream, and calculates its aggregate every time a trade occurs, using the last 15 trades (this is similar to our sliding event temporal context). The operator also includes a segmentation context ❸ that means that the calculation is performed separately (and in parallel) for every distinct value of the `ticker` attribute. The last lines ❺ tell the system where to locate this processing for optimal performance in a multiprocessor system.

To summarize, stream-oriented languages are one of the common event processing language styles. Although several of these languages extend SQL, different languages extend it in different ways.[3] We now look at another style: rule-oriented languages.

10.1.2 *Rule-oriented languages*

The other dominant style of event processing languages is the style we call *rule-oriented*. The *rules* word is overloaded, as there are several distinct types of rules: production rules, active (event-condition-action) rules, and rules based on logic programming. We briefly survey each of these styles.

PRODUCTION RULES

Production rules are rules of the type *if condition then action*. They operate in a forward chaining way: when the condition is satisfied, the action is performed. Production rules are rooted in expert systems; the operational processing of production rules may be either declarative or procedural:

- Declarative production rule execution is typically based on a variation of the Rete[4] algorithm which matches facts against the patterns contained in the rules to determine which rule conditions are satisfied. Information about the antecedents (conditions) of each rule is stored in an internal state, and in every execution cycle changes to these states are evaluated.
- Procedural production rule execution is based on sequential execution of compiled rules.

Production rules are based on state changes and not on events; however, some event processing languages extend Rete-based production rules to support event processing. This is done by making events an explicit part of the model, so that event occurrences can be used as part of the conditions for invoking an inference rule. Thus the event processing is done through an inference process.

Figure 10.3 shows the Object Management Group (OMG) Production Rule Representation classes. This figure comes from part of an OMG standard for modeling production rules in UML. As noted, events are modeled as part of the rule conditions.

---

[3] This article, presented by owners of different languages, discusses the semantic differences among stream SQL extensions: Namit Jain, Shailendra Mishra, Anand Srinivasan, Johannes Gehrke, Jennifer Widom, Hari Balakrishnan, Ugur Çetintemel, Mitch Cherniack, Richard Tibbetts, Stanley B. Zdonik: *Towards a streaming SQL Standard*. PVLDB 1(2): 1379-1390 (2008). http://www.vldb.org/pvldb/1/1454179.pdf.

[4] The Rete algorithm was introduced in Charles Forgy: *Rete: A Fast Algorithm for the Many Patterns/Many Objects Match Problem*. Artif. Intell. 19(1): 17-37 (1982).

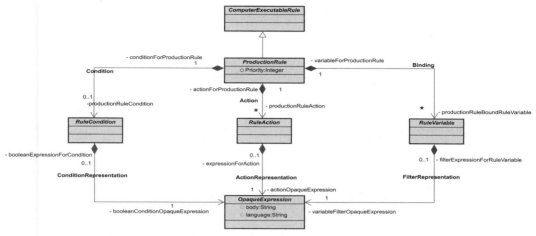

Figure 10.3   OMG Production Rule Representation

ACTIVE RULES

Active rules, also known as event-condition-action (ECA) rules, are descended from work on active databases.[5] Active rules operate according to the following execution pattern: when an event occurs, evaluate conditions and, if they are satisfied, trigger an action.

The event may be primitive or composite. The action can be one that derives an additional event, in which case an active rule maps directly onto an EPA in our model. In cases where the action performs some external activity, such as invoking an external service, the rule maps to the combination of an EPA and an event consumer. In listing 10.2 we show the general structure for active rules.

Listing 10.2   General structure for active rules

```
<Rule style="active" eval="strong">
     <on>
                     <!-- event -->
     </on>

     <if>
                     <!-- condition -->
     </if>

     <do>
                     <!--  action -->
     </do>

     <ifPost>
                     <!-- postcondition -->
     </ifPost>
```

---

[5] Norman W. Paton, *Active Rules in Database Systems*, Springer, 1998, http://www.amazon.com/Database-Systems-Monographs-Computer-Science/dp/0387985298/ref=sr_1_11?ie=UTF8&s=books&qid=1259266096&sr=8-11.

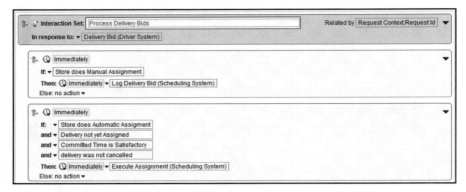

Figure 10.4   An example of an active rule in IBM WebSphere Business Events

```
<doAlternative>
                <!-- alternative/else action -->
</doAlternative>
</Rule>
```

This is a general structure for active rules; particular rule languages are variations of this structure. An example of a particular active rule language is IBM WebSphere Business Events, as illustrated in figure 10.4.

This is an active rule taken from the Fast Flower Delivery application that filters the bids according to the store's preference to perform manual or automatic assignments and routes to the appropriate action.

The third kind of the event processing rule language is the logic programming rule style.

LOGIC PROGRAMMING RULES

Logic programming is a programming style based on logical assertions. The most well-known example of a logic programming language is Prolog. The application of the logic programming style to event processing is rooted in the work done in the deductive database area.[6]

Listing 10.3 shows an example of event processing based on logic programming, taken from the ETALIS implementation of the Fast Flowers Delivery application. Refer to the *Event Processing in Action* website for more information on the syntax and semantics of the language.

Listing 10.3   Example based on ETALIS logic programming

```
no_bid_alert(DeliveryRequestId)<-                          ← ┐  Automatic
        start_automaticAssignment(                          ❶  assignment
                DeliveryRequestId,
                StoreId,
```

---

[6] A good source of knowledge about deductive databases is Stefano Ceri, Georg Gottlob, Letizia Tanca, *Logic Programming and Databases*, Springer-Verlag, 1990. http://www.amazon.com/Programming-Databases-Surveys-Computer-Science/dp/0387517286/ref=sr_1_7?ie=UTF8&s=books&qid=1259274738&sr=8-7.

```
                ToCoordinates,
                DeliveryTime) fnot
            delivery_bid(
                DeliveryRequestId,
                _DriverId,
                _CurrentCoordinates,
                _PossiblePickupTime).
no_bid_alert(DeliveryRequestId)<-
        start_manualAssignment(
                DeliveryRequestId,
                StoreId,
                ToCoordinates,
                DeliveryTime) fnot
            delivery_bid(
                DeliveryRequestId,
                _DriverId,
                _CurrentCoordinates,
                _PossiblePickupTime).
```

Manual ❷ assignment

This assertion is intended to derive the No Bidders Alert event (called no_bid_alert in this example). It identifies two cases: the automatic assignment case ❶, and the manual assignment case ❷.

10.1.3 *Development environments*

There are two types of development environments: text-based and graphically based. These two are not mutually exclusive, as development environments can consist of a mixture of graphical and text-oriented tools. The various environments reflect different assumptions about developers' preferences. In some cases developers prefer a

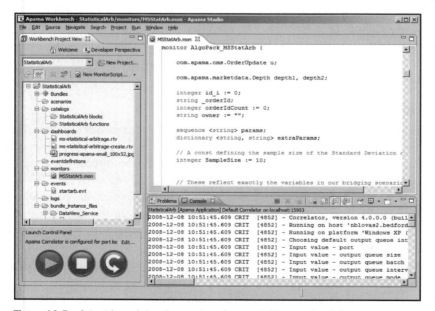

Figure 10.5 A text-based development environment (Apama Studio)

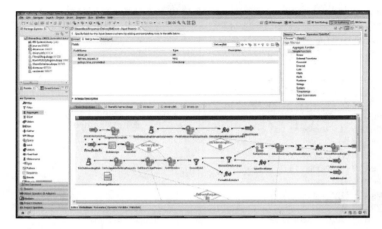

Figure 10.6   Combined graphical- and form-based development environment

more familiar text-based interface, whereas others prefer a more visual style of development. Text-oriented tools can provide a "fill a form" type of interface, as shown in figure 10.4, or they can offer full text entry, like the example in figure 10.5. This is taken from Apama's Eclipse-based IDE, which is called Apama Studio.

StreamBase also has an Eclipse-based IDE, but as you can see from figure 10.6, this has a graphically based development environment, with some functions being provided in a textual manner. In this tool (StreamBase Studio) the EPN is constructed graphically, while event types and individual functions are then built using form-oriented text.

The environments we have looked at here are geared mainly towards technical developers. In chapter 12 we discuss the trend towards having semi-technical event processing developers.

The language and development environment is just one facet of the event processing implementation; next we discuss the non-functional properties of event processing systems.

10.2   *Non-functional properties*

An important aspect of the engineering and implementation considerations in any system is the non-functional aspect. Non-functional requirements are concerned not with *what* a system does but *how well*. It is often the non-functional properties that make or break a specific application. In this section we briefly survey the main non-functional aspects of event processing systems and explain the particular requirements imposed by event processing systems that the system designer should be aware of. Not all of these requirements apply equally to all applications, so when designing an event processing application one needs to consider which of them are important for the case in hand. In the next section we deal with various optimizations and relate them back to these requirements.

The non-functional requirements that we discuss in this section are scalability, availability, and security. There are further non-functional properties, such as reliability and usability. We touch on reliability in chapter 11 when discussing inexact event processing, and usability requirements are closely related to the programming styles and development environments discussed earlier in this chapter.

10.2.1 *Scalability*

We start with our definition of *scalability*.

> **SCALABILITY** *Scalability* is the capability of a system to adapt readily to a greater or lesser intensity of use, volume, or demand while still meeting its business objectives.

Scalability has several dimensions. The dimensions relevant to us here are the volume of events, the number of agents, producers, consumers and contexts, the complexity of computation, and the processor environment.

SCALABILITY IN THE VOLUME OF PROCESSED EVENTS

High event throughput is often considered one of the characteristics and main motivations for the use of event processing software. This is certainly true in some application segments. However, our experience has been that event processing software is employed mainly to increase agility and reduce the total cost of ownership. So the range of applications that are likely to employ generic event processing software is much wider than those that need high event throughput. In these applications scalability means the ability to handle variable event loads efficiently; the quantity of events may go up and down over time.

That being said, some applications require high event throughput, for example, some financial market applications, weather-related event processing, and telephony call tracking. These can encounter extremely high volumes of input events which may require special treatment and optimization. Some systems have been specifically designed with high event throughput in mind, and we discuss performance further in section 10.3.

SCALABILITY IN THE QUANTITY OF AGENTS

In some applications there is a significant amount of processing applied to the events, so the major scalability issue is the ability of the EPN to grow substantially and have a large number of EPAs. An example is a banking system that lets each customer create his or her own sophisticated alerts. Each customer could end up with a unique EPA and this could result in the dynamic creation of a large and complex EPN. When designing an event processing system, estimates about the number of EPAs and their growth curve may impact the way the system is implemented and deployed. Related optimizations are discussed in section 10.4.

SCALABILITY IN THE QUANTITY OF CONSUMERS

In some cases the number of event consumers may become high, for example, the personal banking application that we just mentioned. The event processing system has the challenge of tracking which consumers are active and has to route events to the active consumers and possibly hold them for subsequent delivery to inactive ones. In some cases a single event emitted from the event processing system may have to be routed to many consumers. This could benefit from optimizations at the routing level, such as the use of multicasting[7] Related optimizations are discussed in section 10.4.

SCALABILITY IN THE QUANTITY OF PRODUCERS

In some cases the number of event producers can grow substantially. Consider a web bookstore that tracks events related to all the customers who browse and buy books to determine patterns of use. If we view every customer as a separate event producer the number of event producers can grow large. Even though the number of events from each customer may be small, the total number of customers can be high and the system has to be able to cope with this. This can also lead to a high number of context partitions, which we discuss next.

SCALABILITY IN THE QUANTITY OF CONTEXT PARTITIONS

In some event processing applications, the number of context partitions that are concurrently active may become large. Consider an internet retail store, with an application which has a context partition that tracks each order from the time it is placed until the items are delivered. Such orders may be numerous, and if we assume that each context partition has an internal state, this requires the event processing system to store a large amount of state information. If each context partition is implemented by a distinct runtime artifact, this also leads to a scale-up in number of these artifacts that the runtime has to manage.

SCALABILITY IN CONTEXT STATE SIZE

Another context-related scalability issue is the ability of a single EPA instance to acquire the space needed to store its internal state, especially if it is associated with a long-running context partition. For example, a sequence pattern running over a 24-hour period might need to accumulate and retain a large number of events each day.

SCALABILITY IN THE COMPLEXITY OF COMPUTATION

The complexity of the EPAs themselves may have substantial impact on the overall performance of the system. Cases where the EPAs implement highly complex logic may require different types of optimization than the other scalability aspects that we have mentioned. We return to this point in section 10.4.

SCALABILITY IN THE PROCESSOR ENVIRONMENT

Event processing systems may run in heterogeneous environments. At one extreme they may run on multiprocessor supercomputers; at the other extreme they may run on small devices that have footprint limitations. Both ends, as well as those in the middle, require specific optimizations, and an implementation that works well at a certain point in this spectrum may need significant redesign to work well on a different size processor.

A system designer should be aware of all these scalability issues when designing an application, as well as the corresponding optimizations discussed in the next section.

---

[7] Multicasting is the ability to transmit a single stream to multiple subscribers at the same time. For more information refer to http://www.tcpipguide.com/free/t_IPMulticasting.htm.

10.2.2 *Availability*

Availability is one of the notable quality of service requirements in current systems, and we start by defining this term.

AVAILABILITY The *availability* of a system is the percentage of the time its users perceive it to be functioning.

Event processing systems can use existing standard high availability practices like logging, failover, and disaster recovery practices. The designer of an event processing system must, however, make decisions related to high availability. These considerations relate to whether it is cost effective to employ high availability practices, as they have a cost associated with them and they may not be fully required in some applications. An example of such a consideration is the issue of recoverability, as discussed in the sections that follow.

Some event processing agents (such as those that perform aggregation, composition, and pattern detection) are stateful. The internal state of such an agent has to be kept as long as the particular EPA instance is active, meaning as long as its context partition is valid. For example, a sequence Pattern detect EPA running with the reuse policy over a 24-hour window might need to retain all the participant events that occurred during that period. This brings us to the issue of *recoverability*.

RECOVERABILITY *Recoverability* is the ability to restore the state of a system to its exact value before a failure occurred.

If you are interested in learning more about well-known techniques for achieving recoverability, refer to the reading list at the end of the chapter. Recoverability incurs some additional processing overhead as changes in state need to be logged and the entire state needs to be written to a persistent store, at least periodically. This overhead may take a toll on the processing latency and total throughput of processed events. Note that typically states are persisted in checkpoints, and logs are kept between checkpoints.

In some applications recoverability is a must. If the event processing is part of a mission-critical application, and decisions are made using the results of this processing, losing some of the system's state may have critical implications, such as the following: ignoring an order, missing a pattern in a specific customer's behavior, losing the location of a consignment of goods, or making an incorrect decision due to ignorance of a new trend.

For other applications, it might not be cost effective to apply recoverability. Consider a network management system that receives events about observable faults in the system and attempts to find the root cause. Because the events are symptoms of an underlying problem, they will recur anyway until the problem is resolved. In this case recoverability could help identify a problem faster, but it is not vital and might not be cost effective. Likewise, systems which look for statistical trends may be based on sampling or on analysis of a large number of events; in these cases recoverability may not be required.

In conclusion, event processing systems should support recoverability as an optional property with various tuning alternatives (for example, full persistence of state and checkpointing) and the designers of each application should consider the cost effectiveness of recoverability for their applications and decide whether recoverability is required.

From availability we move on to discuss security in event processing systems.

10.2.3 *Security*

Security requirements relate both to ensuring that operations are only performed by authorized parties, and that privacy considerations are met. Specifically this means the following functions:

- Ensuring only authorized parties are allowed to be event producers or event consumers.
- Ensuring that incoming events are filtered so that authorized producers can't introduce invalid events, or events that they are not entitled to publish.
- Ensuring that consumers only receive information to which they are entitled. In some cases a consumer might be entitled to see some of the attributes of an event but not others.
- Ensuring that unauthorized parties can't add new event processing agents to the system, or make modifications to the EPN itself (in systems where dynamic EPN modification is supported).
- Keeping auditable logs of events received and processed, or other activities performed by the system.
- Ensuring that all databases and data communications links used by the system are secure.

Some people[8] view security and privacy issues as barriers for the trust and utilization of event processing systems. Authentication and authorization issues are a concern because attacks that send false events could be devastating to safety-critical systems, such as those that support air traffic control, or a smart electricity grid. Privacy issues are also a serious concern for people; some people won't install electronic vehicle toll payment devices, such as the E-ZPass[9] system that exists in some of the U.S. states, because they are sensitive to privacy issues and don't want anyone recording information about their whereabouts. Privacy is also a concern in healthcare applications, and in many jurisdictions legislation requires organizations to safeguard the privacy of personal data in all application domains. Trust is particularly significant in applications where sensitive data is passed between different organizations.

---

[8] The view on security and privacy as barriers is taken from Chandy and Schulte's book (K. M. Chandy and W. R. Schulte, *Event Processing: Designing IT Systems for Agile Companies*, McGraw-Hill Osborne Media, 1 edition (September 24, 2009).

[9] http://www.ezpass.com/.

Event processing systems can have various levels of sensitivity to security and privacy issues. If the collection of event producers is a closed set in which security practices are trusted, the problem is reduced. On the other hand, if anybody can be a producer (for example, when events come from Twitter feeds), the security issues may be pervasive.

Studies on related security issues[10] have been conducted, but people mainly deal with security and privacy issues that are specific to event processing in an ad hoc way. The additional reading section at the end of this chapter refers you to material on database security, which shares many common issues with event processing security.

In conclusion, when designing an event processing application, you should be aware that non-functional requirements may have a major impact on the way the system should be implemented and you must make the choices appropriate to your particular application. We now discuss optimization techniques to address some of these non-functional requirements.

10.3 Performance objectives

Some non-functional requirements can be translated to performance objectives which can then be the subject of various optimization approaches. In this section we discuss some of the major performance objectives for event processing relating to throughput, latency, and time-constraint objectives. Table 10.1 summarizes these objectives, and we discuss each objective in this section.

Table 10.1 Performance objectives and their associated metrics

Number	Objective name	Objective metrics
1	Max input throughput	Maximize the quantity of input events processed by a certain system or subsystem within a given time period
2	Max output throughput	Maximize the quantity of derived events produced by a certain system or subsystem within a given time period
3	Min average latency	Minimize the average time it takes to process an event and all its consequences in a certain system or subsystem
4	Min maximal latency	Minimize the maximal time it takes to process an event and all its consequences in a certain system or subsystem
5	Latency leveling	Minimize the variance of processing times for a single event or a collection of events in a certain system or subsystem
6	Real-time constraints	Minimize the deviation in latency, from a given value, for the processing of an event and all its consequences in a certain system or subsystem.

---

[10] An early article about security issues in pub/sub system is the following: Mudhakar Srivatsa, Ling Liu, *Securing Publish-Subscribe Overlay Services with EventGuard*. ACM Conference on Computer and Communications Security 2005: 289-298 http://portal.acm.org/citation.cfm?doid=1102120.1102158.

All these objectives are intended to address scaling issues, but each addresses them using different assumptions and may be served by different optimizations. As you can see from table 10.1, each objective may apply to an entire system, or to any part of a system. In some systems there is a single performance objective for all the processing in the system, for example, latency leveling for each event type in that system. In other systems there may be mix of performance objectives; some of the events may have real-time constraints associated with them, whereas others may have another metric. Performance objectives may also be composed of several separate metrics. We now briefly discuss each of the six performance objectives defined in table 10.1 and then move on to metric composition.

MAX INPUT THROUGHPUT

This is the performance metric most often mentioned as a motivation for high performance stream processing systems.[11] This metric is strongly related to the requirement for scalability in the quantity of events. This metric measures the number of input events that the system can accept within a given timeframe while continuing to function correctly. It is sometimes referred to as *events per second*. Note that although this metric asserts that the system can absorb events, it does not say anything about the latency of processing. To specify a required latency, this metric has to be composed with a latency-oriented metric.

MAX OUTPUT THROUGHPUT

This is a performance metric that refers to the output throughput rather than the input throughput. It is also measured in events per second, but in this case the measure relates to the number of events that the system generates and not to the input events.

MIN AVERAGE LATENCY

This is the first of the latency metrics. It is a statistical metric that refers to the average latency of all events, and it is measured as a time unit (for example, 10 milliseconds). Because different event types may have different levels of processing complexity, it's sometimes useful to measure the latency of a single event type, rather than the overall metric, which is the average of all the average event type latencies.

MIN MAXIMAL LATENCY

This metric relates to the maximal latency for a certain event type or collection of event types. Note that this is a different objective than the previous one, and there are optimizations that improve one of these metrics, and make the other one worse.

LATENCY LEVELING

This metric is also known as a *deterministic performance* metric, and is sometimes identified with real-time processing. This metric is used by applications that need predictable and low variance performance processing for each event type or collection of event types.

---

[11] An example of an article showing an optimization related to this performance metric is the following: Joel L. Wolf, Nikhil Bansal, Kirsten Hildrum, Sujay Parekh, Deepak Rajan, Rohit Wagle, Kun-Lung Wu, and Lisa Fleischer: *SODA: An Optimizing Scheduler for Large-Scale Stream-Based Distributed Computer Systems*. Middleware 2008: 306-325. http://www.springerlink.com/content/9h772844u5875757/.

REAL-TIME CONSTRAINTS

Although latency leveling is identified with real-time systems, these systems may also need to impose particular performance upper limits for either processing of a certain event type, or a certain EPA. This can be achieved through a real-time constraints metric that specifies just such an objective. Note that real-time constraints may be hard real-time, in which case compliance with these constraints is a must, because lack of compliance may have disastrous consequences, or soft real-time constraints that are considered quality of service goals.

COMPOSING METRICS

In some cases there is a need to develop a performance objective that includes more than one metric. This composition may be related to a specific part of the system; for example, there might be an event type which has both throughput- and latency-related metrics. Alternatively, there could be different performance metrics for different parts of the system. An optimization plan might have to take into account different objectives, with some weight factors applied to them, when creating an objective function.

This takes us to the various types of optimization available to help meet such objective functions.

10.4 *Optimization types*

In this section we discuss various types of optimization that have either been used or have been proposed for use with event processing systems. These can serve as building blocks for an optimization plan that is particular to a specific performance function. We discuss optimizations in the following areas:

- Optimizations related to EPA assignment: partitioning, parallelism, distribution, and load balancing
- Optimizations related to the coding of specific EPAs: code optimization and state management
- Optimization related to the execution process: scheduling and routing optimizations

It should be noted that the optimization considerations are quite complex, and this area is still in need of more established methods and practices. The purpose of this section is to make applications designers aware of optimization opportunities, rather than to provide a recipe to optimize a specific application.

10.4.1 *EPA assignment optimizations*

In chapter 6 we stated that an event processing agent represents a logical function, and that there are various ways to map these logical functions to physical runtime artifacts. This is the basis for EPA assignment optimizations, as the choice of assignment can influence the performance metrics that we listed earlier.

These optimizations are also known as *black box* optimizations, because the EPA's implementation is assumed to be fixed. They deal with factors external to the EPA such as its location and relative scheduling. The following sections survey the most common assignment optimizations.

PARTITIONING OF EPA INSTANCES TO RUNTIME ARTIFACTS

The way that EPA instances are mapped to runtime artifacts can have a major effect on the various performance metrics. We refer to this as *partitioning* the EPAs, and the idea is to group EPA instances so that they execute together for better performance. The two extremes are one where there's a single centralized runtime artifact that embeds all the EPA instances, and one where there's a separate runtime artifact for each EPA instance. The centralized solution has benefits for cases where the volume of events is not an important measure, because it saves the overhead of communication between the different EPAs. Partitioning is the key both to parallel execution and to distributed execution.

Partitioning decisions can be driven by the EPN topology as this determines the dependencies between the EPAs, although some languages, such as SPADE, let the programmer make partitioning decisions. One approach to partitioning is based on assigning EPAs to strata, where the EPAs in each stratum are independent of one another and can run in parallel. If EPA1 produces events that are consumed by EPA2, then EPA2 is placed in a higher stratum. We show an example of stratification in figure 10.7, where the EPN is partitioned into three strata, each of which contains independent EPAs.

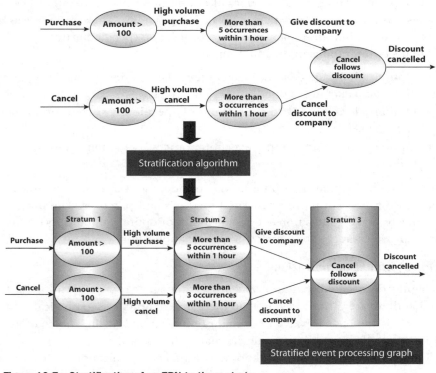

Figure 10.7   Stratification of an EPN to three strata

Note that this is a simple example, and for EPNs in which there are many interdependencies between EPAs the stratification process is more complex. We reference an article describing stratification-based optimization at the end of this chapter.

This stratification process tells us which EPAs can run in parallel, but to decide which of them should be grouped together in the same runtime artifact we have to consider other factors, such as the number of available cores/processors, the level of distribution, the communication overhead, and of course the performance objective function. We discuss some of these aspects in the sections that follow.

PARALLEL PROCESSING

One of the major ways to achieve various performance metrics is parallel processing. There are three levels of parallelism: first, parallelism inside a single core using multithreading; second, parallelism by partitioning the work within a multicore machine where the threads running in different cores have access to shared memory; and third, partitioning the work to multiple machines within a cluster. Decisions on which activities should be run in parallel are difficult, and are usually made automatically by a system optimizer, rather than being performed manually. You may find it interesting to look into research performed on such parallel processing.[12]

DISTRIBUTED PROCESSING

An additional optimization method involves moving the processing close to the producers and consumers where applicable. Consider an example where there are multiple sensors within the same location, and the event processing involves aggregation of events that are emitted by these sensors. Placing the aggregation EPA close to the sensors can eliminate a substantial amount of network traffic. Likewise, if the EPN contains an EPA that creates many events that are all consumed by a certain consumer, or a set of consumers that are located in a certain location, it might be useful to locate this EPA close to the consumer or consumers. This optimization approach can also complement the parallel processing approach. If the parallel event processing is executed over a grid of machines within various geographic locations (instead of being on a physical cluster or co-located set of multicore machines) it might be sensible to co-locate a group of agents if there's a substantial amount of communication between them.

LOAD BALANCING

Static optimization techniques, such as stratification, involve analysis of the EPN dependencies, making some assumptions about the traffic load and available resources. However, these assumptions, as well as the topology of the EPN, may change over time. The introduction of more resources, the temporary unavailability of computing resources, as well as unexpected changes in the distribution and load of events, are all reasons for reevaluating the partitioning scheme. Answering the general question of how and

---

[12] An example of such optimization for stream processing is in the following article: Rohit Khandekar, Kirsten Hildrum, Sujay Parekh, Deepak Rajan, Joel L. Wolf, Kun-Lung Wu, Henrique Andrade, and Bugra Gedik, *COLA: Optimizing Stream Processing Applications via Graph Partitioning,*Middleware 2009: 308-327. http://www.springerlink.com/content/aw817m13m4536001/.

when to rebalance the load in this way requires more work, although there are some ad hoc solutions in use today.

Another approach, used in high throughput event applications, is to discard events if there aren't sufficient resources available to process them all. This form of load balancing, which results in approximate event processing, is called load shedding.[13] The book by Chakravarthy and Jiang that is referenced at the end of this chapter surveys load shedding techniques used in stream processing.

Some performance objectives require us to go further than the *black box* approaches we have discussed so far, and optimize the actual EPA code itself. We discuss a couple of such *white box* optimizations next.

10.4.2 *EPA code optimizations*

White box optimizations are optimizations that modify the internal execution of EPAs. This area is less developed than the black box optimizations. We briefly discuss some of the possibilities in this area starting with code generation and then moving on to the more developed area of state management.

OPTIMIZED CODE GENERATION

Query optimization is a vital part of relational database execution; substantial research and development have been invested over the years in this area. The core idea behind query optimization is that although queries may look similar, different queries have different optimized execution plans, and thus an optimizer might generate totally different code.

The equivalent of this idea is also valid for event processing, and you might hope that if you have a language that is an extension of SQL, you could adjust the SQL query optimization to include continuous queries. However, it turns out that these adjustments are not trivial.

To see why this might be not trivial, consider the sequence Pattern detect EPA shown in figure 10.8.

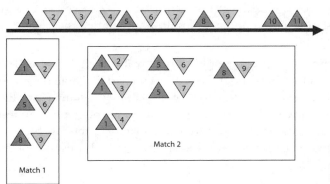

Match 1

Match 2

Figure 10.8   A sequence Pattern detect example showing the results of two different policies

---

[13] For example, refer to the following article: Nesime Tatbul, Ugur Çetintemel, and Stanley B. Zdonik, *Staying FIT: Efficient Load Shedding Techniques for Distributed Stream Processing*, VLDB 2007:159-170. http://www.vldb.org/conf/2007/papers/research/p159-tatbul.pdf.

In this example, there are two types of events. The first type (E1) is shown as a triangle pointing upwards, and has five instances: 1, 5, 8, 10, 11. The second type (E2) has six instances: 2, 3, 4, 6, 7, 9. These instances arrive in the order shown at the top of the diagram, and the pattern is looking for the sequence <E1, E2>. As we saw in chapter 9, the output of a Pattern detect EPA depends on the matching policies being used. Suppose that the EPA uses the immediate, override, and consume policies. This means that it matches each E1 event with the next occurring E2 event to produce three matching sets: <1, 2>; <5, 6>; <8, 9>. However, if it were to use the reuse policy rather than consume it would match each E1 event with multiple subsequent E2 instances to create the six matching sets shown as "Match 2" in figure 10.8. These two results are quite different, and it is conceivable that the optimal data structure and implementation code will also be different. Code optimization should take account of this.

Another optimization that is being used by some event processing implementations is the use of Real-time Java,[14] which allows for thread priorities and smoothes the memory management.

STATE MANAGEMENT

State management optimization relates to the way that an internal state is held by EPAs, and in some cases also to global state elements. The basic trade-off is between performance and recoverability. Memory-based state provides better performance, but recoverability requires some overhead and implementation complexity. Persistence-based state (for example, one where state is held in a database) provides better recoverability, but may conflict with performance goals. The implementation of state management is a function of the requirements, both for performance and recoverability. Use of in-memory state can also be problematic when there is a need for scalability in the number of context partitions or in the quantity of events accumulated within a context partition.

The choices in this area include the following:

- Using disk-based persistence. This resolves space scalability issues and recoverability; however, it may harm performance goals.
- Using in-memory databases that provide caching capabilities while guaranteeing recoverability. This is a way to balance between the two sides of the trade-off. There are various tuning possibilities that can be made, based on assumptions about mean time between failures (MTBF) and mean time to recovery (MTTR).
- Using grid memory instead of persistence. The idea here is to replicate the state in memory held on multiple machines, to get recoverability without having to use disk-based persistence. This solution has an overhead of network traffic, and the complexity of synchronizing among the different replicas.
- Using a mixture of these approaches, for example, persistent storage for states that have space scalability issues, and in-memory for others. You can also allow different levels of recoverability for different EPAs.

---

[14] http://www.rtsj.org/

We complete our survey of optimization techniques with a discussion of execution optimization.

10.4.3 Execution optimizations

Some additional optimizations can be performed at execution time.

SCHEDULING

Scheduling optimization deals with planning the order of EPA execution, in cases where there is no natural order of precedence, but the EPAs concerned compete with each other for computing resources. Scheduling optimizations can be done when there are different performance requirements for different EPAs, for example, when one EPA has real-time constraints while the other does not. In such cases you might use a preemptive schedule that delays the execution of a runtime artifact that has already started in order to execute another runtime artifact that needs to run to comply with its real-time constraints. Scheduling can also be done by analysis of the EPN topology, giving priority to EPAs that are in a critical path to achieve performance criteria.[15]

ROUTING

Various optimizations that relate to the transport layer deal with the manner and physical implementation of routing between the various components of the systems (producers, EPAs, and consumers). This relates to the way that event channels are implemented and the routing method used (anycast, broadcast, multicast, and unicast). Routing optimizations are typically assumed to be the role of the transport infrastructure.

There is no comprehensive methodology for event processing optimization, so performance tuning of event processing applications is still an art rather than a precise science. This section provided a quick look at some techniques that a system designer can use in order to optimize an application. Some of these optimizations are provided, to some extent, by today's event processing platforms. However, this is still an active area of research and development, and we expect that more optimization tools and methodologies will be provided in the future. Next, we move from optimization to our last engineering topic: event processing validation.

10.5   Event processing validation and auditing

We have noted that event processing programming differs in some ways from regular programming and thus needs its own validation tools. Validation consists of static analysis and dynamic analysis of event processing networks. In essence, these analyses provide observations about EPNs that point out possible problems in the design of event processing applications. We briefly describe some of the main observations that can be obtained from such analyses and conclude this section with a discussion of auditing of event processing applications.

---

[15] The following article shows an optimization related to scheduling: Joel L. Wolf, Nikhil Bansal, Kirsten Hildrum, Sujay Parekh, Deepak Rajan, Rohit Wagle, Kun-Lung Wu, and Lisa Fleischer, *SODA: An Optimizing Scheduler for Large-Scale Stream-Based Distributed Computer Systems*, Middleware 2008: 306-325. http://www.springerlink.com/content/9h772844u5875757/.

10.5.1 *Static analysis of event processing networks*

Static analysis observation is analysis that is performed on the EPN model, as described by our building block language. It can serve to validate the design of an event processing application. In some cases observations at the static analysis level can point out possible problems that might not actually happen in reality; thus, to complete the validation picture you need to complement it with dynamic analysis (this is analysis that examines what happens at runtime). It should be noted that static analysis can be used in the design phase, and also as part of change management, where it can be used to check whether a proposed change might introduce a problem.

TERMINATION PROBLEM OBSERVATION

A termination problem is a case in which the system (in this case, the flow of events in the event processing network) does not terminate due to an infinite loop. Recall that the edges in the EPN denote events that are emitted by one node in the network and serve as input to another node. The event processing network may be cyclic. For example, an event that is derived by EPA1 serves as input to EPA2, which derives an event that serves as input to EPA1. This is a simple cycle that consists of two EPAs, but a cycle can be a longer cycle that consists of multiple EPAs. A cycle in the EPN may or may not indicate a design problem. It may indicate a design problem if indeed it creates an EPN that never terminates where this was not the intention of the designer. It may not be a problem, if the system is really cyclic in nature, like a state machine that always returns to the initial state after getting to its final state. It may also not be a problem if this infinite loop is only theoretical, and the combination of conditions in which it occurs can't occur in reality or doesn't occur even if it could.

A validation tool can find cycles in the EPN. In some cases it can also check whether the conditions in the cycle have internal contradictions, so that this cycle can't occur in reality, and make this observation visible to the designer. Note that the general issue of discovering whether a set of conditions can be satisfied together is an NP-complete problem, but in some cases this can be detected more easily.

Figure 10.9 illustrates an EPN containing five EPAs, called R1,...,R5. There are two cycles, a smaller cycle consisting of R2 and R3, and a bigger cycle consisting of R2, R3, R4, and R5. Figures 10.9, 10.10, and 10.11 are taken from an event processing validation research project done in the IBM Haifa Research Lab by Ella Rabinovich and Sarit Arcushin.

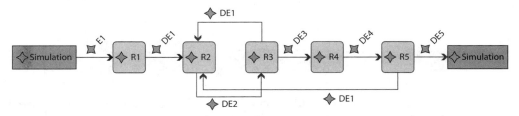

Figure 10.9 An example of two loops detected within a path in EPN

EVENT NOT USED

This observation discovers events that are produced and not used. A producer may produce an event that is not consumed by any consumer or EPA. An EPA may derive an event that again is not consumed by any EPA or consumer. This may indicate a design problem, or it could be caused by a change that results in a certain event no longer being required. Events that are not used can be observed by a static analysis tool and be flagged up to the user of the tool.

EPA IS NOT REACHABLE

This type of observation traces the fact that an EPA never executes because one or more of its input events never flows. This may be a design flaw or the result of a change that eliminates some event from being produced, derived, or routed to the EPA. This observation can be obtained by static analysis of the EPN, and the EPN designer can be alerted.

EPA IS A DEAD END

This type of observation identifies the fact that an EPA does not produce any derived events. This may be a design flaw or the result of a change. Again this observation can be obtained by static analysis of the EPN, so as to warn the designer. Figure 10.10 shows an example of a dead end; this is an EPN with several consumers, producers, and EPAs. The marked EPA, whose label is "Handle Low Inventory with No PO", does not have outgoing edges, which means it does not produce any derived events.

POSSIBLE NONDETERMINISTIC PROCESSING

This type of observation identifies the fact that two or more EPAs can execute in any order, and may yield different results depending on their order of execution. This can

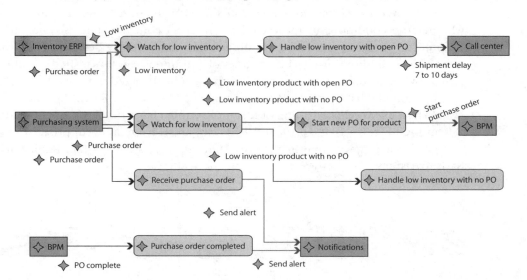

Figure 10.10   A dead end example. The EPA Handle Low Inventory with No PO **does not have any outgoing events.**

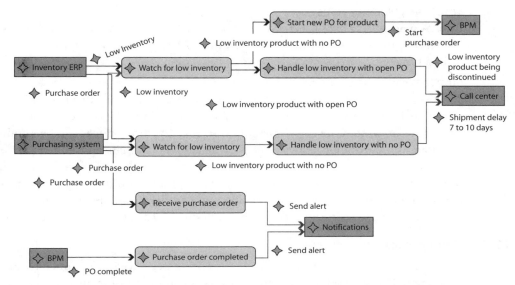

Figure 10.11 An example of provenance—finding the path in the EPN that contains all the antecedents of the derived event "`Shipment Delay 7 to 10 Days`"

serve as an indication to the designer to specify priority ordering of those EPAs, if this is supported by the event processing system, or to redesign the EPN flow, should this nondeterministic order actually matter to the application.

Validation tools may also provide information about event provenance. They can operate forwards, showing all consequences of a certain event or node in the EPN, or backwards, showing all antecedents of a certain derived event or node in the EPN. Figure 10.11 shows an example of tracing back to see the path in the EPN that leads to the fact that a derived event "`Shipment Delays 7 to 10 Days`" has been obtained.

Static analysis tools may provide textual or graphical output. They are complemented by dynamic analysis techniques, which are discussed next.

10.5.2 Dynamic analysis of event processing networks

Dynamic analysis is an analysis that is based on observation of runtime execution and not on the static model. There are two types of dynamic analysis for EPNs: simulation and tracing. Simulation creates simulated events and scenarios and runs the application using this simulation, which may provide observations. Tracing takes traces of runtime executions and analyzes them. Dynamic analysis may provide observations that can't be obtained in static analysis. We briefly explain some of these observations.

ACTUAL TERMINATION ISSUES

Whereas static analysis indicates the possibility of termination issues, dynamic analysis may detect that a termination problem actually exists. In the simulation mode we can observe that a loop is actually realized; in tracing mode we can observe that loops indeed happened.

ACTUAL REACHABILITY ISSUES

An EPA may be reachable, as far as the static analysis is concerned, and there is a visible path in the EPN to the EPA; however, this EPA is never activated in the simulation or in a trace.

OUTPUT TERMINAL IS UNUSABLE

The events that flow out of an output terminal of a certain producer or EPA could be unusable, in the sense that none of them is consumed by an EPA or consumer. This may be an indication that the events produced by this EPA or producer can be eliminated.

In addition, dynamic analysis can provide actual provenance for a specific instance of an event or any EPN node, backwards or forwards, and observation about quantities of raw and derived events that may be used in optimization decisions. Validation and debugging tools are important to making new paradigms usable in practice.

Our final engineering topic concerns the auditing of an event processing application.

10.5.3 *Event processing auditing*

Auditing is the ability to investigate whether processes have been applied in an appropriate way. This may refer to whether a process complies with external regulations, or internal policies, or whether a decision has been made in an appropriate way. Whereas validation is intended to validate the implementation, auditing is intended to validate the usage of the system and the work processes behind a certain information system. In chapter 5 we stated that one of the event consumer kinds is an event log which retains raw or derived events for further processing. The events persisted in the event log may be used as the audit trail that is required for performing auditing functions.

The audit itself is done by querying this event log. Queries may be similar to the dynamic analysis we have just discussed. The kind of query that can be used depends on the amount of information that is stored in the event log, alongside the events themselves. If the entire path in an EPN is retained, queries like the following can be made:

- Trace all antecedents of a certain event or EPA instance activation
- Trace all consequences of a certain event.

Other types of audit queries may require temporal queries of the type demonstrated by the following query:

- Since the beginning of 2010, have all the manual assignments made by the Exotic Flowers store used only the same five drivers?

This type of query may be more easily answered if the event store is a temporal database. You can find more material about temporal databases in the additional reading section at the end of this chapter.

This ends our engineering-oriented discussion and is a good time to summarize this chapter.

10.6 Summary

In this chapter we've discussed some of the engineering aspects of event processing. We looked at software engineering and reviewed various programming styles and development environments. We then talked about non-functional aspects of event processing, followed by a discussion of performance objectives and optimization techniques, and event processing validation. Current engineering practices provide solid foundations for many existing applications, but as the area of event processing is evolving, its software engineering aspects and the various optimization techniques will also evolve. The next chapter discusses challenges within the current state of the practice.

10.6.1 Additional reading

Schmidt, Klaus. 2006. *High Availability and Disaster Recovery: Concepts, Design, Implementation.* Springer. http://www.amazon.com/High-Availability-Disaster-Recovery-Implementation/dp/3540244603/ref=sr_1_2?ie=UTF8&s=books&qid=1259392209&sr=8-2. This book is recommended if you want to fully understand high availability techniques.

Bernstein, Philip A., Vassos Hadzilacos, and Nathan Goodman. 1987. *Concurrency Control and Recovery in Database Systems.* Addison Wesley. The book can be freely downloaded from Phil Bernstein's homepage: http://research.microsoft.com/en-us/people/philbe/ccontrol.aspx. This is a classic book and an excellent source for anyone who wants to understand the principles of recoverability and the techniques needed to implement it.

Ben-Natan, Ron. 2005. *Implementing Database Security and Auditing: Includes Examples for Oracle, SQL Server, DB2 UDB, Sybase.* Digital Press. http://www.amazon.com/Implementing-Database-Security-Auditing-Examples/dp/1555583342/ref=sr_1_2?ie=UTF8&s=books&qid=1259399581&sr=1-2. This book deals with the state of the practice in database security, and provides insights on approaches to security issues.

Chandy, K. M., and W. R. Schulte. 2009. *Event Processing: Designing IT Systems for Agile Companies.* McGraw-Hill Osborne Media, 1 edition. http://www.amazon.com/Event-Processing-Designing-Systems-Companies/dp/0071633502/ref=sr_1_1?ie=UTF8&s=books&qid=1258816511&sr=8-1. This book, which we have mentioned before, is included here as it describes security and privacy issues as barriers to the adoption of event processing (chapter 12: The Future of Event Processing).

Liu, Jane W. S. 2000. *Real-Time Systems.* Prentice Hall. http://www.amazon.com/Real-Time-Systems-Jane-W-Liu/dp/0130996513/ref=sr_1_5?ie=UTF8&s=books&qid=1259439073&sr=1-5. This book explains the basic concepts of real-time systems.

Lakshmanan, Geetika T., Yuri G. Rabinovich, and Opher Etzion. "A stratified approach for supporting high throughput event processing applications." DEBS 2009. http://portal.acm.org/citation.cfm?doid=1619258.1619265. This article describes partitioning of EPAs using the stratification approach.

Chakravarthy, Sharma, and Qingchun Jiang. 2009. *Stream Data Processing: A Quality of Service Perspective: Modeling, Scheduling, Load Shedding, and Complex Event Processing.* Springer. http://www.amazon.com/Stream-Data-Processing-Perspective-Scheduling/dp/0387710027/ref=sr_1_1?ie=UTF8&s=books&qid=1259477906&sr=1-1. This book provides an introduction to stream processing, and discusses several load shedding and scheduling optimizations.

Etzion, Opher. "Reasoning About the Behavior of Active Database Applications." Rules in Database Systems 1995: 86-100. http://www.springerlink.com/content/f81uw237j1151663/. This paper provides discussion on validation in active database applications and explains some of the concepts being discussed in the event processing validation section.

Etzion, Opher, Sushil Jajodia, and Suryanarayana Sripada (editors). 1998. *Temporal Databases: Research and Practice.* Springer. http://www.amazon.com/Temporal-Databases-Research-Practice-Computer/dp/3540645195/ref=sr_1_1?ie=UTF8&s=books&qid=1262847152&sr=8-1. This book provides a collection of articles about various aspects of temporal databases, including a glossary.

10.6.2 *Exercises*

10.1 How do continuous queries and rules relate to the concept of an EPA?

10.2 In the EPN model we present in this book, we associate processing functions with the EPN nodes. Some stream processing representations associate functions with edges. Can you describe an alternative EPN representation in which the functions are associated with edges? Can the functionality be spread between nodes and edges?

10.3 What are the pros and cons of graphical- versus text-oriented development environments?

10.4 State the non-functional requirements, performance metrics, and optimizations for the Fast Flowers Delivery application used in this book.

10.5 Devise guidelines for using the various performance metrics that we list.

10.6 Which of the optimizations mentioned can be controlled by an application designer, and which depend on capabilities provided by event processing middleware?

10.7 Are the various event-processing programming styles and non-functional requirements related or totally orthogonal to each other? Provide examples to justify your answer.

Today's event processing challenges 11

Challenges are gifts that force us to search for a new center of gravity. Don't fight them. Just find a different way to stand.

—Oprah Winfrey

Up to this point we have focused on what might be called state-of-the-art event processing practices. Event processing applications are being developed successfully using the patterns and approaches that we have discussed, but application developers should be aware that there are some challenging topics that are not fully resolved within the current state of the practice. These topics might not have any bearing on your particular application, but you should consider their implications to see if they raise any issues that you need to avoid. The purpose of this chapter is to inform you of these challenges. The chapter covers the following topics:

- The temporal semantics of event processing
- Inexact event processing
- Event retraction and event causality

We start the chapter with the topic of *temporal semantics*. Time plays an important part in nearly all event processing applications, but there are subtleties and complications in the way it needs to be handled. Some of these can only be resolved using *inexact event processing*, which is our second topic. As its name suggests, this concerns the handling of uncertainty in event processing. In some applications you can use a probabilistic approach to deal with uncertainty, but in other cases you may need to allow for an event to be retracted by your application. *Retraction*, and the related subject of *event causality*, is our final topic.

We take you through each topic, explaining the problem and outlining possible solutions and their implications.

11.1   *The temporal semantics of event processing*

In part 2 of the book, we saw that time plays a major role in event processing. In chapter 3, while discussing event types and structures, we noted that an event instance can have two temporal attributes: the detection time, which is the time that the event processing system becomes aware of the event; and the occurrence time, which is the time, often provided by the event producer, at which it is thought that the event occurred in reality. In chapter 7, while discussing context dimensions, we saw that the temporal dimension is often the dominant context dimension, and also plays a role in most composite contexts. In chapter 8 we saw that the temporal dimension had an important influence on stateful filtering and transformations. In our examination of event processing patterns in chapter 9 we noticed that many patterns rely on the temporal order of events, and that furthermore these patterns are often used within a temporal context.

We can summarize this by saying that, in many cases, the outcome of a piece of event processing is affected by the timestamps associated with the input messages, and the order in which these messages are processed relative to one another. In this section we go deeper into the temporal dimension, and discuss three major issues:

- Occurrence time: time points versus intervals
- Temporal issues with derived events
- Issues related to event ordering

We start with occurrence time.

11.1.1 *Occurrence time: time point versus interval*

When we defined the occurrence time attribute we defined it as a single point in time, the only ambiguity being the precision with which it is recorded, and we set a bound on this imprecision through the temporal granularity (chronon) attribute. This definition is in keeping with a view of events as being transitions between states of an external system; in models that handle transitions between states, a transition is typically considered as instantaneous, that is, something that occurs at a specific point in time, and so has zero time duration. Now is the time to review this assumption, and raise the question of whether events do indeed follow this definition and are instantaneous, or whether instead they really occur over a time interval. Here are three examples that demonstrate the ambiguity of occurrence time, and suggest that events can actually have non-zero time durations.

- The event `Flight BA0238 landed`. Landing is a process that starts with the descent of the aircraft, and ends when the aircraft parks at the gate. (Some might say it doesn't end until the aircraft door is open.) This is clearly an interval. One could argue that landing is a state and not a transition, and so there are two point-in-time events: one when the aircraft starts landing, and one (the `landed` event) when it arrives at the gate. However, how people understand the `landed` event is still ambiguous. Some might understand it to mean the time when the first wheel makes contact; others might view it as occurring when all the wheels make contact, or when the aircraft leaves the runway.

- A medical application uses a derived event called `call physician` produced if the patient's blood pressure is constantly raised during a 2-hour period with a temperature > 104° F (40° C). When does this event occur? You could say that its occurrence time should be taken to be the time when the derived event is detected, which is typically some time after the 2-hour interval has ended). Alternatively you could reasonably argue the event occurs during the entire 2-hour interval.

- The financial crisis that started in 2008 is an event made up of many atomic events, and spans an interval that had not really ended when this book was written.

In reality many events take place over a period of time, contrary to the view of an event as an instantaneous state transition. Such events have an occurrence *time interval* with a start time and an end time. Why does this matter? The answer is that for computational purposes it is often easier to deal with events that occur at a single point in time, and so many systems today assign a single timestamp to the event, rather than giving it separate start and end times. Many event processing operations depend on knowing the order in which events occur, and it is much more obvious how to define an order if each event has a single occurrence time. This gap between reality and computational convenience is sometimes bridged by selecting a relatively coarse temporal granularity so that an event time interval can be approximated by a single time point.

This approach of approximating time intervals to time points is good enough for some applications, particularly when the event time intervals are short relative to other timescales in the application, but in other cases it would be better to have an explicit representation of event time intervals. To do this, we introduce support for time interval as an explicit data type; a time interval is designated by the two time points that serve as its start point and end point. A time point t is part of a time interval $[Ts, T)$ if $Ts \leq t < Te$.[1]

> **TIME INTERVAL**   A time interval is a data type that designates a continuous segment in time. It is a half-open interval, starting at a time point Ts and ending at a time point Te.

A temporal context, as defined in chapter 7, establishes a set of (possibly overlapping) context partitions (windows), each of which is a time interval. If an event instance is associated with a single time point, it is clear whether it is to be included with a given

---

[1]   We define it as a "half-open interval" where the ending boundary is not included in the interval.

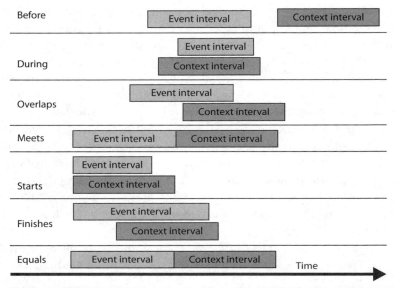

Figure 11.1   Relationships between the context partition's time interval and an event occurrence interval

context partition or not. When the event itself occurs within an interval and not at a single point in time the relationship becomes an interval-to-interval relationship and not a point-to-interval relationship.

Because intervals are partially ordered, the patterns that are based on order (for example, the sequence pattern, or the trend-oriented patterns) can't be used as currently defined with events that have a time interval, and so their definitions have to be adjusted. Interval-oriented patterns are outside the scope of this book.

Figure 11.1 shows some of the possible ways in which a temporal context interval can relate to the event occurrence interval (for each of the first six there is also the converse relation, for example, context interval before event interval). When using a temporal context to process events with time intervals you need to state what relationship is to be used. For example, a travel expenses application might define a context to be the year 2010, but with a relationship of finishes, meaning that all business travel events that end in 2010, even if they started earlier, are to be included in this context.[2]

11.1.2 *Temporal issues concerned with derived events*

The occurrence time and detection time event attributes are important when determining whether an event instance falls within a certain context instance. In some systems these temporal event attributes are also used to determine the order of an event relative to other events, which is important when using a pattern whose semantics

---

[2] The interval-to-interval relationships were introduced in Allen's seminal paper: James F. Allen, *Maintaining Knowledge about Temporal Intervals*, Communications of the ACM 26(11): 832-843 (1983).

depend on that order. In this section we discuss the semantics of issues related to the ordering of derived events.

In an event processing network we do not make a fundamental distinction between derived events (events generated by event processing agents in the network) and raw events (events introduced by an event producer). An event processing agent may take either or both kinds of events as input. The way it processes an event depends on the event's type and content, not on whether it is raw or derived. This means that we need to have an approach to occurrence time and detection time that is consistent between raw and derived events.

Recall that the order used when processing events may be determined either by using the time at which the events occurred in reality (occurrence time), or the order in which the events arrived at the system (detection time). The issue before us is how we should assign these timestamps to a derived event, and how we should order the processing of a derived event relative to other events, both raw and derived.

Let's look at some examples. In the Fast Flower Delivery example, things start when a store sends a `Delivery Request` event (a raw event) to the application. The application then creates the derived event `Bid Request`, which is sent to the drivers. Let's assume that the first `Delivery Request` has occurred, but that a second `Delivery Request` occurs before the application has been able to issue the first `Bid Request`. The implementation now has choices: it could queue up the second `Delivery Request`, so that `Bid Request 1` is issued before `Bid Request 2`; it could suspend processing of `Delivery Request 1` until after it has dealt with `Delivery Request 2` (so the `Bid Requests` are issued in the opposite order from the `Delivery Requests`); or it could use separate processing threads to handle both `Delivery Requests` in parallel. In this last case the two `Bid Requests` could be issued in either order, depending on processor loads or other conditions out of the direct control of the application. In the Fast Flower Delivery application, the relative order of the two `Bid Requests` is not that important, because they are independent of each other and can be dealt with in parallel. The worst that can happen is that a driver can get a pair of `Bid Requests` that are not in the same order as the original `Delivery Requests`. You might try this yourself and experiment using the various implementations on the *Event Processing in Action* website in order to see whether the order of requests is preserved or not. To remind you, the book's website is http://www.ep-ts.com/EventProcessingInAction.

Although the order may not matter in the Fast Flower Delivery application, in other examples it may influence the result that is produced by an event processing agent further downstream in the event processing network.

To see how this can happen, let's consider an event processing system that processes auctions. Bidders can place bids within an auction interval, and at the end of this interval the highest bid wins. If multiple bidders issue the highest bid, the first bidder to have issued this bid wins the auction. Let's assume that each bid starts as a raw event, but there is a validation process that involves checking the bidder's history and credit,

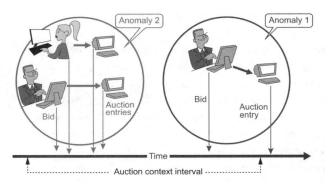

Figure 11.2   **Two anomalies that may stem from setting occurrence time for derived events in a naïve way**

and an enrichment process which provides more information on the bidder. These two processes result in a derived event that enters the bid into the auction process.

Now let's suppose that we take the most intuitive approach and say that the occurrence time of a derived event is always the point in time at which the derived event was emitted by the enrichment process. This sounds reasonable, as it is the time that the derived event is created, but doing this can lead to a couple of anomalies, which are shown in figure 11.2.

- In the first anomaly (shown at the right of figure 11.2) we suppose that a bid event was issued, within the auction interval, but that the interval ended before the validation and enrichment had completed. An auction system using this as the occurrence time would reject the bid, even though it was validly submitted and might actually have been the highest bid.
- In the second anomaly we suppose that two equal highest bids were submitted one shortly after the other, both well within the deadline. They were both processed before the auction interval ended but, as we saw earlier, the processing of the second bid might complete first, resulting in its being assigned an earlier occurrence time. This means that it would win the auction, although according to the rules it should not.

We can conclude from this that the occurrence time of a derived event should itself be a derived value. In our example, if we were to assign the occurrence time of the auction entry event to have the same value as the occurrence time of the corresponding bid event, these two anomalies disappear. Of course, this is not always the desired solution. In some cases we may explicitly want to impose the order based on the time in which the system derived the events.

So how do you decide when a derived event actually occurs? Let's look at a couple of pattern detection examples. Our first example is the sequence pattern example shown in figure 9.7. In this example we are looking for patients who are discharged from hospital and then readmitted for the same reason within 48 hours. We show such a case in table 11.1.

Table 11.1 An example use of the sequence pattern that illustrates possible alternatives for the semantics of occurrence time for derived events

Event identity	Event type	Patient	Cause of hospitalization	Detection time	Occurrence time
E232243	patient discharge	Pierre Warner	High fever	September 14, 2009 15:04	September 14, 2009 14:50
E291126	patient admission	Pierre Warner	High fever	September 16, 2009 08:20	September 16, 2009 08:18
E291244	patient readmission (derived)	Pierre Warner	High fever	September 16, 2009 08:21	?

In this example the detection time of the derived event E291244 is the timestamp applied by the system when it was emitted by the event processing agent that detected the pattern. The question is what value its occurrence time should have. We can think of three possible values:

1 occurrence time = detection time = September 16, 2009, 08:21.
   Rationale: Because this event is a virtual one, and does not occur in reality, its occurrence time should be identical to the time it is detected.

2 occurrence time = occurrence time of the last event that completed the pattern, in this case, the `Patient-Admission` event, which we see had an occurrence time of September 16, 2009, 08:18.
   Rationale: The `Patient-Admission` event was the one which completed the pattern; thus it was the direct reason for the derivation of event E291244.

3 `occurrence time` is the interval of all events participated in its derivation = [September 14, 2009 14:50, September 16, 2009 08:18).
   Rationale: Because all three events were responsible for the derivation of the event derivation, the derived event must have occurred within the interval bounded by the occurrence times of these three events.

We can't say that one of the interpretations is more valid than the other two, so the choice as to which value to set for occurrence time should be left to the system designer as a policy decision, similar to the pattern policies that we have seen before in chapter 9.

We validate these three policy options by looking at another example. Let's take an absence pattern from the Fast Flower Delivery application, shown in table 11.2.

Table 11.2   The absence pattern example used to illustrate possible alternatives for the semantics of occurrence time for derived events

Event identity	Event type	Request id	Detection time	Occurrence time
E234143	Assignment	R302291	October 8, 2009 11:30	October 8, 2009 11:30
E812134	Pickup Alert (derived)	R302291	October 8, 2009 12:04	?

This pattern detection process is looking for cases where a driver fails to make a pickup on time. The Pattern detect EPA (in this case the `Pickup alert` agent) generates a `Pickup Alert` derived event when the `Pickup interval` window terminates and no `Pickup Confirmation` event has been detected. The `Pickup interval` terminates 5 minutes after the required pickup time; let's suppose that that is at 12:05. You will recall from chapter 8 that the detection time of the derived event is set to the latest possible time within the context interval, which in this case is 12:04. The question again is, what value should be set as the occurrence time of the `Pickup alert` derived event? Let's examine the three policies discussed in the previous example to determine whether they make sense:

- occurrence time = detection time = October 8, 2009, 12:04.
  The rationale here is similar to the rationale for setting detection time that we gave in chapter 8; it means that the `Pickup alert` is included within the context partition that was used to derive it.
- occurrence time = end of the interval time = October 8, 2009, 12:05.
  The rationale here is that the time at which we know that there aren't going to be any bidders is the time in which the context interval expired. This is similar to the case of the last event completing the pattern in the previous example.
- occurrence time = time when the EPA detected the pattern; in our case this could be October 8, 2009, 12:06. The rationale here is similar to the previous example. `Pickup Alert` is a virtual event, and as such it occurs when its derivation takes place.
- `occurrence time` is the interval of all events that participated in the derivation = [October 8, 2009 11:30, October 8, 2009 12:05). The rationale here is that the `Pickup Alert` event relates to the entire interval as the `Pickup Confirmation` event did not occur at any one of the time points during this interval.

NOTE TO USERS OF SYSTEMS THAT DON'T SUPPORT OCCURRENCE TIME   There is an important practical problem that you may encounter. Some event processing platforms do not support ordering of events by *occurrence time*, and instead they process events in an order determined by a system-generated *detection time*. In such cases it may not be enough just to set an occurrence time value (indeed your language might not even have an explicit occurrence time concept), and you may need to take other steps to detect and work around anomalies like the ones we have discussed.

To conclude, putting derived events in order may not be trivial, and the system designer should be aware of possible semantic anomalies here and make the appropriate policies carefully.

In our discussion of figure 11.2 we noted that one of the cases shown there also results in events that need to be processed out of order. Our next section deals with this and other issues of event ordering.

11.1.3 *Event order and out-of-order semantics*

This section deals with the issue of guaranteeing that events are processed in the correct order. There are many cases where the ordering of events is significant, and it is important that they are processed in the correct order. Here are three examples:

- An event is part of a time-series event stream, and we are looking for a trend pattern that is based on the order of events as occurred in reality (for example, we might be checking to see if the value of a particular attribute is increasing). A disturbance to the order of the event stream will affect whether this pattern is detected or not.
- A public library has a limited number of workstations available to library users. When all the workstations are occupied, the library institutes a timeout protocol terminating a user's session so that he or she hands over the workstation to the person waiting next in line. This is implemented by an event processing application that processes events of the following types: workstation becoming free, workstation becoming occupied, person entering the queue, and person leaving the queue. The application depends on the relative order of these events being correct in order to operate the protocol.
- In the auction example shown in figure 11.2, the winner depends on the order in which the events are received by the application.

In this section we discuss the difficulties associated with determining the correct order in which to process events, keeping the events in that correct order in a distributed network, and processing events if they are not in the correct order. The difficulties in ordering stem from several causes: the occurrence time synchronization problem, synchronization of the processing order with occurrence time ordering, and keeping processing order consistent in a distributed environment. In addition, as we saw in the previous section, when you are dealing with derived events, the time taken to generate a derived event may mean that it is not available for processing until some time after its logical occurrence time.

OCCURRENCE TIME SYNCHRONIZATION

The problem of occurrence time synchronization relates to the fact that there may be many event producers in an application, each using its own internal clock to generate event occurrence times. These internal clocks might not be synchronized with each other or with the servers that are running the event processing logic or other analytics. In some cases a producer's clock might be wildly incorrect, but even if it is not there could be enough inaccuracy to yield incorrect results for any order-sensitive processing that uses these occurrence times as the basis for determining the order of the events. Two approaches that can be used to mitigate this problem are clock synchronization and the use of a time server.

- Clock synchronization is a well researched topic in distributed computing, starting with Lamport's 1978 seminal paper,[3] and progressing over the years. The idea is that the various event producers exchange messages among each other to establish a logical order to the events that they collectively produce. The major problem with this approach is that it requires a degree of central control and also cooperation between event producers. This might be feasible in a bounded environment, where all the relevant event producers can be controlled, but becomes difficult if there is a large number of producers, or if they are owned and managed independently.

- An alternative solution is that all event producers set the occurrence time timestamp from the same time server,[4] and not from their own internal clocks. One obvious example is a GPS device which gets a timestamp from the GPS satellites at the same time that it is getting a fix on its position. There are similar time servers available through the internet, and some organizations provide time servers in their intranets. This solution may have some latency, and may not be applicable when the temporal granularity is small; the time server solution is typically considered good enough, and is used by several event processing implementations. This approach requires that producers of order-sensitive events work under an agreement that they all use the same time server, which, again, requires some level of control over the event producer implementations.

In cases where it is not feasible to apply either of these approaches, an ordering based on occurrence time order may be inexact. Section 11.2 discusses this and other sorts of inexact event processing.

ORDERING IN A DISTRIBUTED ENVIRONMENT

Event processing platforms frequently base the order of processing not on the event *occurrence time*, but on the *detection time* (the time when they first become aware of an event). In a distributed environment, where there is a central event processing platform and a collection of event producers that are remote from that platform, you must choose where the detection time is to be assigned.

- In some systems it is assigned by the central platform when the events arrive there. In such cases the order in which events occurred may not be identical to

---

[3] Leslie Lamport, *Time, Clocks, and the Ordering of Events in a Distributed System*, Communications of the ACM 21(7): 558-565 (1978).

[4] NIST time server is an example of such: see http://tf.nist.gov/service/its.htm.

the order in which they arrive in the system. This could be because the time taken to propagate event messages through the system varies from message to message, or because the system uses multiple threads to process events.

- In some systems the detection time is assigned by the producers or by the channels[5] that bring the events from the event producers. In these cases we can't rely on event detection times to give us a completely accurate ordering, because we have the same synchronization issue that we encountered with occurrence time.

This means we can encounter the following anomalies:

- The occurrence time of an event is accurate, but the event arrives out of order and processing that should have included the event might already been executed.
- Neither the occurrence time nor detection time can be trusted, so the order of events can't be accurately determined.

Attempts have been made in various systems to cope with the out-of-order issue. The most common solution uses a timeout buffering technique; it is based on the following assumptions:

- Events are reported by the producers as soon as they occur.
- The delay in reporting events to the system is relatively small, and can be bounded by a timeout offset.
- Events arriving after this timeout can be ignored.

Based on these assumptions, timeout reordering is performed by putting the incoming events into a buffer prior to assigning them a detection time and sending them to be processed. Let τ be the timeout offset. According to the assumptions it is safe to assume that at any time point t, all events whose occurrence time is earlier than $t - \tau$ have already arrived. Each event whose occurrence time is To is kept in the buffer until $To+\tau$, at which time the buffer can be sorted by occurrence time, and events can be processed in this sorted order. The main benefit of this technique is that it guarantees that the processing order will be the same as the occurrence time order. In some cases systems assign detection time attributes to the events after the sorting has been performed, so that detection time can also be used as an accurate metric for temporal order.

This method has two main deficiencies that may or may not be important for a particular application:

- Each event has to be delayed by time τ, thus increasing the end-to-end latency of the processing system.
- Events may be ignored due to late arrival, which may impact the quality of the processing results.

The assumptions behind this method may also be invalid for some realistic cases. There are cases in which the producers do not themselves sense or instrument the

---

[5] For example, a timestamp assigned by a message oriented middleware system.

events, but instead simply forward events from their original sources, so the delay in reporting might not be negligible; also it might not be acceptable to ignore events that arrive after the timeout.

Another similar method, used by some messaging systems is to assign sequence numbers to events when they are produced, so that gaps in an incoming event stream can be detected and events buffered until the gaps have been filled. This approach has the benefit of not having to unnecessarily delay everything by τ, however, the delay may not be bounded (unless a timeout is imposed again). It can also be difficult to assign sequence numbers if there are multiple producers, unless there is a natural sequence number in the event data itself.

RETROSPECTIVE COMPENSATION

The issues involved with ordering in a distributed system may mean that the event processing application has to deal with the case where events miss the processing that they should have participated in because they arrived late. This can be the case even in nondistributed systems because of the general problem of sequencing derived events that we looked at earlier in the chapter.

One way to solve the problem is to compensate for it retrospectively, providing the effect of undo and redo. Rather than delaying the processing of all events just in case some happen to be late, the application goes ahead and processes events that arrive on time, and then uses a compensation approach to deal with any latecomers there might be.

The idea of compensation is used in transaction processing, when dealing with long-running business transactions (for example, processing of an insurance claim which might take several days). It's not practical to have a database transaction running for the entire period as you cannot afford to leave data items locked for that long. Instead, applications take an optimistic approach and release data locks when some subtransaction concludes, and if it turns out that the entire transaction needs to abort, it compensates by generating transactions that undo the original transaction and redo dependent transactions. A similar principle, known as *eventual consistency*, applies in distributed systems, in which consistency inside the system (for example, among replicas of the same data item) may be sacrificed temporarily, but the system is eventually brought back to consistency.

We can borrow from these ideas by arranging for the following actions to occur each time an out-of-order event is detected:

- Find out all the event processing agents that have already sent derived events which would have been affected by the out-of-order event if it had arrived at the right time.
- Retract all the derived events that should not have been emitted in their current form. See further discussion on event retraction in section 11.3.
- Replay the original events with the late one inserted in its correct place in the sequence so that the correct derived events are generated.

This logic is similar to the logic of truth maintenance in artificial intelligence systems. In practice there are several difficulties when applying it to the "out-of-order" issue:

- Event processing operations may result in actions done by event consumers. Those actions are not part of the event processing system, and so the event consumers need to be able to accept event retractions and perform the appropriate compensation actions. This might not be feasible either because some actions are not undoable, or because the consumer's software does not support compensation.
- The execution of retrospective processing requires the system to maintain past states. If an event processing agent is to be able to redo a function, it needs to have access to all relevant information, both the historical events that it was processing, and the past state of any global state elements (e.g., reference data, global variables) that it was using. This requires both keeping the history and finding the right events and data items (temporal databases can help with these issues, but they are not in general commercial use today).
- A compensation process may have a cascading effect in the sense that a single compensation for an out-of-order event can trigger a large number of compensation actions, putting a high burden on the system's performance.

For these reasons this solution, while theoretically appealing, is difficult to implement. It might, however, still be worth considering as an option in some cases, especially when the undo and redo of all consequences are feasible, the information is still available, and the compensation process is bounded.

To conclude, those who develop order-sensitive applications should be aware of the possible anomalies that can occur, their solutions, and the possible problems associated with these solutions. When it is not possible to determine the order of events accurately you can use *inexact event processing* techniques. We discuss these, in the context of a more general discussion of inexact event processing, in the next section.

11.2 Inexact event processing

Developers and users of event processing systems should be aware of points where event processing may become inexact. The cases that we discuss are the following:

- Uncertainty whether an event actually occurred
- Inexact content in the event payload
- Inexact matching between derived events and the situations they purport to describe

We first explain each of these three issues, and then discuss possible solutions. This whole area is handled in an ad hoc way, or not handled at all, in current systems.

11.2.1 Uncertain events and inexact event content

Although you may be certain that a particular event either occurred or did not occur in the real world, there can still be uncertainty in the event objects that report on it in a computer system. Events that occur in the real world may not get reported, whereas events that have been reported might not have occurred. Several reasons may induce this kind of uncertainty:

- *An unreliable or imprecise source*—An event producer (such as a sensor) may malfunction and indicate that an event has occurred even if it has not. Similarly, an event producer may fail to signal the occurrence of an event which has in fact occurred. In the case of derived events, problems in the design or the implementation of the agent deriving this event can cause it to create false derived events or not create logically valid ones.
- *A malicious source*—An event could be the direct or indirect result of an act that is intended to sabotage the system.
- *Projection of temporal anomalies*—In the previous section we discussed a number of anomalies which can cause order-sensitive event processing agents to process events in an order that is not consistent with the true order of event occurrence. This can cause an agent to create derived events that should not have been created, or to skip events that should have been created.

Inexact event content occurs when the content of an event object's header or payload is not consistent with one or more of the characteristics of the event that happened in reality. The reasons for inexact event content are similar to the reasons for uncertain events:

- The source may be imprecise, for example, a badly calibrated thermometer being used to measure someone's temperature could yield an incorrect result.
- Temporal anomalies can also lead to incorrect event content in derived events.
- Raw events may contain estimated or sampled data, which are inherently inaccurate.

When an event processing agent derives further events from inexact input events, this can cause it to propagate uncertainty or inexact content to subsequent phases of the event processing network.

Figure 11.3 illustrates the reasons for inexactness and uncertainty in events.

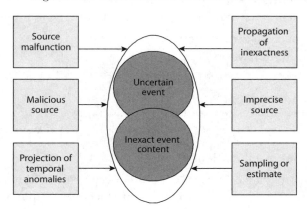

Figure 11.3 Reasons for uncertainty and inexactness in events.

Before talking about possible solutions, we need to talk about the other aspect of inexact event processing, which is inexact matching between events and situations.

11.2.2 *Inexact matching between events and situations*

In chapter 1 we defined a *situation* to be an event that might require a reaction. This definition sits squarely in the domain of users, not computers. In the user domain consideration of what should trigger a reaction depends on the user's perspective; this is rather different from the computer domain in which everything is determined according to computational processes.

In most cases you might assume that an event in the computer domain (either a raw event detected by an event processing system, or a derived event produced by an event processing system) is exactly what you should use to trigger the reaction; however, in reality this might not be so. Consider the case in which an event processing system generates a derived event signaling that a network denial of service (DoS) attack has occurred. In this case the `network DoS attack` event is the situation we are looking for, because it obviously requires a reaction. However, the computational process that created this derived event is not an exact science, and can have two phenomena associated with it: false positive and false negative situation detection.

> **FALSE POSITIVE** *False positive situation detection* refers to cases in which an event representing a situation was emitted by an event processing system, but the situation did not occur in reality.

False positives may lead to reactions that should not be performed, and may be damaging. Shutting down activities because of false DoS attacks may be costly. Other cases may be even more damaging: false detection of a missile attack might trigger a counterattack. The converse to false positive situation detection is false negative situation detection.

> **FALSE NEGATIVE** *False negative situation detection* refers to cases in which a situation occurred in reality, but the event representing this situation was not emitted by an event processing system.

False negatives may also be damaging. In the DoS attack example, failure to detect this situation may inflict even more damage than the false positive in this area, and the same is true for the other example of failing to detect a missile attack.

False positives and false negatives may result from uncertain and inexact events. In cases where situations are detected through derived events, they may also occur because the pattern detection (or other computational process) used in the derivation does not guarantee that the situation occurred, but just indicates that it is likely that it occurred. In the DoS attack example, the derived event that detects this situation may be the result of matching one or more patterns known to indicate likely attacks; however, these patterns may just approximate the situation and not indicate it with complete certainty.

Now that we have completed our discussion of the issues, we briefly touch on ways that they can be mitigated.

11.2.3 *Handling inexact event processing*

The way that systems deal with inexact event processing often depends on assumptions about how common these inexact cases are and how important it is to deal with them when they occur. There is a spectrum of views, with two extreme positions:

- The first extreme position, which is quite common in current systems, assumes that these are rare cases, which can be considered as exceptions and can be handled manually. Based on this assumption, the event processing system does not include any feature to handle inexact event processing.
- The other extreme is based on the assumption that inexact event processing is frequent and important enough that every part of the system should behave as if it is inexact. So inexactness is an integral part of the event processing infrastructure.

Clearly there can also be systems that are in the middle of this spectrum. For example, they could assume that inexact event processing is always required for some event types or event patterns, whereas for others it can be ignored. In some cases this decision can depend on the context in which the processing occurs.

Techniques to handle inexact event processing may be based on known uncertainty handling frameworks, such as probability-based methods (for example, Bayesian networks), evidential reasoning (Dampster-Shafer), and fuzzy logic. Probability-based methods are the most common. They work by associating a probability both to the occurrence of an event and to the accuracy of its content.

Table 11.3 shows examples of the sorts of probability that can be attached to an event instance.

Table 11.3   Probability indicators associated with an event instance

Inexact indicator	Probability
Event did not occur	0.4
Event occurred before T1	0.1
Event occurred in [T1, T2]	0.45
Event occurred after T2	0.05

You can see that we can track not only the likelihood of the event occurrence, but also estimate the accuracy of some of its temporal characteristics. We can also assign probabilities to patterns and to derived events, for example, assessing the occurrence probability of events produced by a given pattern detection operation, as a function of the certainty or exactness of its input events.

It should be noted that existing tools like Bayesian nets can cope with probabilistic networks and the propagation of such probabilities through an event processing network. However, in practice, assigning the probabilities is not an easy task to do manually. Some research projects have used machine learning to derive these probabilities, but at present there is no readily available solution that can be applied to the general case.

To summarize, developers and users of event processing systems should be aware of the different cases of inexact event processing and the fact that many current systems view them as rare exceptions that can be dealt with using ad hoc solutions.

In this section we mentioned the use of quantitative approaches to deal with uncertainty such as the use of probability. There are, however, cases where you may need to allow for events to be *retracted*, that is to say, cancelled or withdrawn, as discussed in the next section.

11.3 Retraction and causality

In this section we discuss two challenging issues related to the relationships between events. The first of these is the issue of *retraction*, and the second is the *causality*, which is something that can provide traceability in event processing systems.

11.3.1 Event retraction

The Fast Flower Delivery example application includes a facility to allow a customer to cancel an order; we use this example to demonstrate the challenges involved in retracting events. First let's consider what we want to happen when an order is cancelled. The customer who sent the flower delivery order is not interested in pursuing the order anymore, so you might think that we should treat this like a database transaction and roll back all the operations that have been performed thus far. In practice, however, some actions are undoable and some are not. Furthermore there may be different ways to perform an undo, depending on the state we happen to be in when the cancellation event is received. Figure 11.4 illustrates the retraction possibilities along the lifecycle of the delivery.

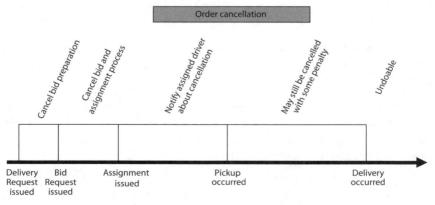

Figure 11.4 Order cancellation implications over the delivery lifecycle

The implications of cancellation are contingent on the phase in the delivery lifecycle:

- After the `Delivery Request` has been issued, but before the `Bid Request` has been issued, the cancellation is realized by aborting the `Bid Request` preparation process.
- Between the time that the `Bid Request` was issued and the time that the driver was assigned, the cancellation is realized by cancelling the bid and assignment process. In this case, as with the previous one, no action is required to change any plans in the real world.
- Between the time that the `Assignment` was issued and the pickup occurred, the cancellation may be realized by notifying the assigned driver about the cancellation.
- Between the pickup time and delivery time, the driver can be called to return and not finish the delivery; however, this depends on the store's policy. Some stores might allow it, and some might allow it but charge a penalty to the customer.
- After the delivery has been made it can't be cancelled.

Although this analysis is quite reasonable, and in principle might be inferred by the system, no current systems provide built-in support for retraction as an automated process. Furthermore, you can see that the actions required at some points in the delivery lifecycle go beyond the event processing system, and it is not easy to track the logical implications of retracting an event at these points.

To conclude this discussion: developers and users of event processing systems should be aware that retraction needs to be hardcoded, and carefully determine the exact cases of retraction required by their applications. Retraction is a challenge whose inexact nature can't be handled by quantitative approaches. Another challenge which can't be handled in this way is event causality, and that is the last area that we discuss in this chapter.

11.3.2 *Event causality*

Event causality is described as a key term in David Luckham's book *The Power of Events*. Its definition is quite simple.

> **EVENT CAUSALITY** *Event causality* is a relation between two event instances e1 and e2, designating the fact that the occurrence of the event e1 caused the occurrence of event e2.

The practical importance of this concept is that through causality relations it's possible to trace back the events and computing elements that led to the execution of an action, or the detection of a situation. Looking deeper at the notion of causality we can observe three types of event causality:

- *Predetermined causality*—This type of causality refers to raw events, e1 and e2 where we know that event e2 always occurs as a result the occurrence of e1. We may thus assume that if e1 has been reported, e2 occurred whether reported or not. This occurrence may also be conditioned, for example, a time offset or interval may be attached to this causality.

- *Induced causality*—The event e1 is an input to an event processing agent a1, and the derived event e2 is the output of a1.
- *Potential causality*—The event e1 is an event that is sent from an event processing network to a consumer c1. The actions of c1 are beyond the borders of the event processing system, but c1 also acts as an event producer and can produce events of type e2. The event processing system can't know, without further information, whether there is indeed causality between events e1 and e2, but can't rule out this possibility.

Note that only induced causality can be automatically inferred from knowledge of the event processing network. We need additional information to detect the other two types. This can be done by adding event-to-event relationship information to the event type definition. Such information can be entered as domain knowledge, or in some cases determined using machine learning techniques, which can learn statistical correlations between events that may approximate causality.

Developers and users of event processing systems should determine whether causality tracing is important to their systems, and if so they need to establish the right causality relations to be able to find the lineage of events in the system.

11.4 Summary

This chapter provided system developers and users insights into the challenges they may encounter when using current state-of-the-art event processing tools and techniques. The challenges discussed in this chapter included various types of temporal issues, issues related to inaccuracy of events and event processing, and issues of traceability and retraction of events. System designers should check whether any of these issues apply, and determine how to resolve or mitigate the specific issues they have. The next chapter, which concludes this book, deals with event processing of the future and a summarizes what this book is and isn't.

11.4.1 Exercises

11.1 Give an example of an event whose occurrence time is best represented by a time interval.

11.2 Take each of the relationships between context interval and occurrence time intervals described in figure 11.1, and provide an example in which this relationship occurs.

11.3 Determine the appropriate detection time and occurrence time for each of the derived events in the Fast Flower Delivery application.

11.4 Which of the various pattern detection event processing agents in the Fast Flower Delivery application are order sensitive? Suggest a way to handle out-of-order anomalies in each of them.

11.5 Devise a scenario in which it is practical to use retrospective processing to handle out-of-order events.

11.6 Devise a scenario in which all types of inexact processing exist, and show how a probabilistic method can be applied.

11.7 Provide examples of false positives and false negatives in the Fast Flower Delivery application, and explain how you would mitigate these anomalies.

11.8 Devise a retraction scenario (not related to the Fast Flower Delivery application), and explain the different retraction steps and how you would handle them.

11.9 Can you find examples of each of the three types of event causality in the Fast Flower Delivery application? If so, show what they are. If any of them can't be found in the application, devise a scenario in which this causality type does occur.

Emerging directions of event processing 12

You cannot escape the responsibility of tomorrow by evading it today.

—Abraham Lincoln

We started this book by stating that event processing is an emerging technology, and you can experience the current state-of-the-practice using the *Event Processing in Action* website. Emerging technologies keep moving, and this chapter reflects the personal opinions of the authors about the emerging directions of event processing.

This chapter covers the following topics:

- The authors' reflections on current trends in event processing
- The authors' prediction on the future directions of event processing
- A short epilogue to this book

12.1 Event processing trends

In this section we discuss several trends that we anticipate will have the strongest impact on the direction that event processing will take. The trends we discuss show the technology moving in the following directions: from narrow to wide, from monolithic to diversified, from proprietary to standards-based, from programmer-centric development to semi-technical development, from stand-alone to embedded, and from reactive to proactive.

12.1.1 Going from narrow to wide

Every new area starts with its early adopters, often centered on one or two specific industries or application types. Event processing is no different; the early adopters of this type of technology were capital market trading applications. Event processing is now spreading to other industries and is being employed by many different types of applications, fitting all the classes of application that we showed in figure 1.2. The use cases working group of the Event Processing Technical Society (EPTS)[1] has collected some examples:

- Border security radiation detection
- Mobile asset tracking
- Logistics and scheduling
- Detecting unauthorized use of heavy machinery
- Hospital patient and asset tracking
- Activity monitoring for tax and fraud detection
- Intelligent customer relationship management in banking
- Event-driven architecture and asynchronous business process management (BPM) in retail
- Situation awareness in energy utilities
- Situation awareness in airlines
- Reducing cost of injection therapy
- Next generation navigation
- Real-time management of hazardous materials
- Finding anomalies in retail point of sales
- Monitoring the behavior of the elderly

This variety has wide implications to the technology. These implications start with the languages; additional use cases result in the extension of event processing languages to include more primitives. In addition there are architectural implications, driving the shift from centralized architectures to distributed architectures and from monolithic to diversified architectures. Generalization can also be a driver for standards. The trend of going from narrow to wide also triggers other trends that we discuss in this chapter.

12.1.2 Going from monolithic to diversified

"One Size Fits All: An Idea Whose Time Has Come and Gone" is the title of a famous paper by Michael Stonebraker and Uğur Çetintemel,[2] that discusses relational databases and explains why the authors think that the single solution approach is no longer valid. In the event processing area we are still in the one-size-fits-all era. As a consequence of

---

[1] http://www.ep-ts.com/
[2] Michael Stonebraker and Uğur Çetintemel, "One Size Fits All: An Idea Whose Time Has Come and Gone," ICDE 2005: 2-11. http://www.computer.org/portal/web/csdl/doi/10.1109/ICDE.2005.1ok.

going from narrow to wide, the range of new applications to be supported will require diversity in implementation technology. This diversity includes the following:

- *Variety of function*—Particular application segments will require particular functions, such as specific types of transformation and aggregation or trend patterns that are based on advanced statistical functions.
- *Variety of quality of service (QoS) requirements*—Different event processing agents may have different QoS requirements, which require different implementations, such as the following examples: one EPA might require its internal state to be fully recoverable, whereas another might not; part of the event processing network may have hard real-time constraints, while the rest of it does not.
- *Variety of platforms*—Different EPAs may reside on different platforms so the EPN is spread across these platforms. For example, in a radio frequency identification (RFID) application, one of the agents might be embedded inside an RFID reader, while others run on a server.

This diversity will lead to the development of heterogeneous event processing agent implementations, and lead to a component-based approach in which an EPN can be built from a collection of EPAs selected from a library of components. Some of these components are generic and some specific to a particular industry or application and provided by niche suppliers. Obviously, standards are vital for achieving diversity, as we discuss in the section that follows.

12.1.3 *Going from proprietary to standards-based*

Some level of standardization will be required if we are to get to the position where event processing applications can be assembled out of diverse sets of components instead of being developed for specific monolithic event processing engines. Standardization in the event processing area is a challenge because of the different starting points and approaches that have been taken so far, as will be evident to you if you have already experimented with the various implementations on this book's website. However, standards often emerge when an area of technology starts to mature, and although currently there doesn't seem to be strong pressure towards standardization, we anticipate that there will be a shift towards it in the event processing of tomorrow.

There are several avenues for standardization related to event processing:

- *Event structure and metadata representation*—As seen from the examples in chapter 3, there are various ways to represent event metadata, and differences between products when it comes to header attributes and the kind of data that can be included in an event payload. Standards covering exchange of event type metadata and runtime event instances would enable interoperability among various components.
- *Domain-specific event metadata*—By this we mean standardization of specific event types for specific applications or subject areas, for example, system management symptoms, insurance claims, workflow state transitions, and medical

device events. Many of these areas have standards today; however, in the absence of the generic standards, each standard has developed its own way to represent event type metadata and its own decisions about event structures.

- *EPA component model*—These standards would define the terminal interfaces used by an EPA to emit and receive events, as well as other runtime interfaces used by an agent during its lifecycle. They would let someone produce an event processing component that could be hosted in any software environment that supported the model.

- *EPA assembly model*—This would standardize the language used to express how event producers, EPAs, and event consumers are linked to form event processing networks. We have presented a basic assembly model in this book.

- *Event distribution standards*—These are standards for transporting events between event processing platforms, and for exchanging metadata about events and event processing. They include publish/subscribe protocol specifications. There are already some evolving standards in this area like WS-Notification[3] and WS-Eventing.[4]

- *Event processing specification meta-models*—These are standards to allow modeling of event processing functionality. These standards could build on existing standards such as Unified Modeling Language or Business Process Modeling Notation.

- *Event processing language*—Standardization of the language used to express what an event processing agent does. This is the toughest area for getting agreement on. Standardization here might be achieved in a phased approach, with the first phase being standardization at the modeling level, such as the building blocks that have been presented in this book. We think it likely that a standard language will be adopted at some stage, but it might have to wait until the event processing of the day after tomorrow.

Next we discuss a trend affecting the types of users of event processing.

12.1.4 *Going from programming-centered to semi-technical development tools*

The first generation of event processing application development tools is largely programming centered in the sense that you must possess programming skills in order to use them to develop event processing applications. We see an increasing trend towards allowing business users and business analysts, who might not have deep programming skills, to compose all or part of an event processing application. Figure 12.1 shows a part of a customer survey conducted by ebizQ that indicates that the majority of customers surveyed would like to have *event rules* defined by business analysts and business specialists.

---

[3] http://www.oasis-open.org/committees/tc_home.php?wg_abbrev=wsn
[4] http://www.w3.org/Submission/WS-Eventing/

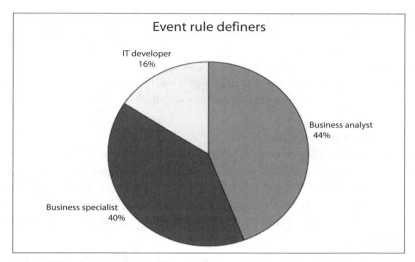

Figure 12.1   A chart of an ebizQ customer survey taken from ebizQ Event Processing Market Pulse 2007; chart can be found at http://complexevents.com/2007/10/30/event-processing-market-pulse-2007/

This trend implies the need for user interfaces and abstraction levels that fit this population. Figure 12.2, showing the interface of IBM WebSphere Business Events, is an early example of this trend.

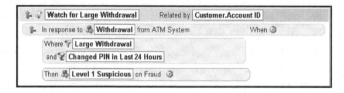

Figure 12.2   An example of a user interface aimed at business users

We believe that the level of abstraction will increase, and future business-oriented languages will be based on assertions, intentions, and goals. We expect that more work will be dedicated to this topic in the next few years, as it will continue to grow in importance. Next we discuss how event processing fits into a bigger picture.

12.1.5 *Going from stand-alone to embedded*

Today event processing technology is delivered in two ways. The first of these is as a specialist event processing platform, whose primary goal is to support event processing applications. With the second, event processing functionality is embedded inside another piece of software, either middleware or a packaged application, that needs event processing capabilities. Some analysts predict that in the future up to 80 percent of the event processing market will be embedded. We discussed some related technologies in chapter 1, and here we provide examples of this trend.

BUSINESS PROCESS MANAGEMENT (BPM)

The combination of event processing and business process management is sometimes called ED-BPM[5] (event-driven business process management). The idea is to use event processing logic to analyze events and detect situations, and the BPM part of the system can then react by triggering a new BPM workflow instance, or by stopping or modifying an existing workflow instance. BPM systems can also act as producers of events, as we saw in chapter 4.

BUSINESS ACTIVITY MONITORING (BAM)

Business activity monitoring has emerged in recent years as a category of software in its own right. Although early BAM products were batch oriented, the newer generation monitors and analyzes information in real time, so as to be able to give up-to-date information about the state of the business that is being monitored. Many modern BAM products, therefore, are event driven and embed event processing capabilities.

BUSINESS INTELLIGENCE (BI)

In the business intelligence area we have also seen some movement from batch-oriented to online-oriented analytics, so that businesses can detect and react to fast-changing situations in a timely fashion. We expect that BI products will follow the example of BAM products and start to include event processing functionality, and there are signs that this is already starting to happen.

MOM AND ESBS

Message-oriented middleware (MOM) may be embedded in event processing platforms to provide an event transport layer, but the converse could also be the case, with event processing being embedded inside a messaging system to detect patterns in message traffic, and to provide efficient routing decisions based on such patterns (for example, a messaging system that saw three messages from a customer to a service center within two hours could route the third message to a supervisor).

Enterprise service buses (ESBs) typically perform filtering and transformation functions, among other enterprise integration patterns, and as we saw in chapter 8 there is a partial overlap between them and event processing platforms, although the primary role of an enterprise service bus is to provide communication between services. Event processing can assist in some ESB functions, such as selection of services, routing decisions, and validation decisions, as these can be based on event processing patterns.

PACKAGED APPLICATIONS

Event processing functions may also be embedded inside packaged applications. Notable examples include the use of event processing in network and system management applications and its use in trading platforms found in capital markets. More examples are emerging.

---

[5] http://complexevents.com/2009/12/16/integrating-complex-events-for-collaborating-and-dynamically-changing-business-processes/

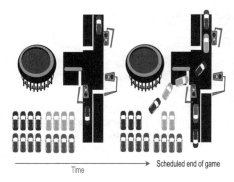

Time   Scheduled end of game

Figure 12.3 An example of proactive computing; traffic light policies are modified according to the expected end of a basketball game

12.1.6 Going from reactive to proactive

Event processing today is used mainly in a reactive manner, where a system needs to take an action as a result of an event or a series of events that have already happened. Event processing is used in such applications to analyze events and detect situations that need to be handled.

In *proactive computing*, on the other hand, the emphasis is on detecting undesirable states so that they can be eliminated, or at least mitigated, before they give rise to unwanted (usually negative) consequences. A good example of proactive computing is its use in predicting traffic congestion before traffic actually comes to a standstill so that steps can be taken to manage the traffic flow to prevent a jam. This can be done at a city level, but in figure 12.3 we show a smaller scale example where proactive computing is used to set traffic light policies (the timings for red, yellow, and green traffic lights) within an area of a city.

Traffic management like this can be performed simply by reacting to observed traffic conditions. For example, if the system sees that there is a heavy buildup of traffic in one direction, while other directions have relatively sparse traffic, it can adjust to give more time to the busy traffic stream. Traffic light policies can also be based on other information. In the example shown in figure 12.3, a specific traffic light policy is set when a basketball game is due to end, to limit congestion caused by spectators leaving the game. If the game goes into extra time, the system might switch back to the original policy until the extension is over.

Proactive computing involves other technologies besides event processing, such as predictive analytics to identify possible future outcomes and to select between appropriate courses of action.

Now that we've looked at these trends, we survey some of the developments in technology that we anticipate will affect event processing platforms and products.

12.2 Future directions in event processing technology

In this section we discuss some of the emerging technology directions. We start with the idea of a virtual event processing platform, discuss optimization and software engineering, and conclude with an introduction to intelligent event processing.

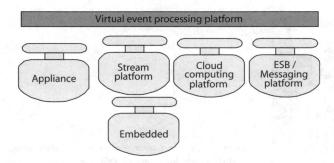

Figure 12.4   A virtual event processing platform can replace today's multiple event processing platforms.

12.2.1 *Event processing virtual platforms*

Figure 12.4 shows some of the many different kinds of platforms that are used to run today's event processing applications.

These event processing platforms include the following:

- *Hardware appliance platforms*—These are specialist hardware platforms, often with many processor cores, dedicated to running event processing. The event processing software that runs on them is usually specially tuned to the hardware capabilities. In multicore machine cases, the system can perform automatic parallelization of the event processing logic.

- *Stream platforms*—A stream platform is a platform for processing streams of information, such as video, audio, or news information. The applications that run on these platforms, for example, surveillance or traffic offence detection applications, frequently use event processing.

- *Cloud computing*—Cloud computing platforms are growing in use. It is expected that many event processing applications will run on cloud platforms.

- *ESB/messaging platforms*—As event processing becomes part of service-oriented architecture (SOA) applications, the connection between events and services is performed by enterprise service bus (ESB) platforms.

- *Embedded platforms*—There are many specialized platforms in which event processing may be embedded. For example, robotic platforms, RFID readers, home appliance gateways, and more. As we saw in the previous section, there is a trend towards having more embedded event processing.

It is clear that it is not cost effective to build different event processing software for each of these platforms, so the alternative is to construct a virtual event processing platform that can be mapped to each of the hosting platforms in an efficient way. This is already beginning to happen.

12.2.2 *Event processing optimization*

Relational databases became pervasive after the introduction of query optimization. The trend of going from narrow to wide will necessitate more work on optimization issues in event processing. An optimization decision is relative to an objective function (the metric that we are trying to optimize); we discussed such optimization metrics in chapter 10.

Note that each of these objective functions entails a different type of optimization. For example, with a Java implementation you might minimize maximal latency by smoothing the Java garbage collection process, making it continuous rather than discrete. However, this raises the average latency, so if the objective function is to minimize average latency, other methods should be used.

The most common optimization approach being used at present is black box optimization. In this approach you take the implementation of the event processing agents as given, and optimize the assignment of EPAs to threads, cores, and machines, and their relative scheduling. We anticipate a trend towards white box optimization, where the optimization process has the ability to vary the code used to implement the agents themselves in order to obtain an implementation that best meets the requirements of the objective function given the particular circumstances of the application.

12.2.3 *Event processing software engineering*

Event processing requires a slightly different type of thinking than traditional computing. We have covered some of this thinking in this book, starting from the decoupling principle that we discussed in chapter 2, and moving through the other concepts that we introduced. There is a need to devise software engineering methodologies and tools to support this kind of thinking. This will be realized through methodologies and supported tools, design patterns, and collections of best practices, and also be assisted by modeling and meta-modeling standards.

12.2.4 *Intelligent event processing*

Intelligent event processing is a subject that brings together a number of extensions to the event processing technologies we have covered in this book. These include pattern acquisition, handling inexact and uncertain events, and handling predicted events.

- The pattern detection EPAs that we discussed in chapter 9 all have to be programmed with details of the specific pattern that they are to detect. We have been assuming that the application designer is aware of what these patterns are when developing the application, and that the patterns form part of the application specification. In many cases, for example, patterns used to monitor compliance with regulations, this is a fair assumption. However, there are other cases, for example, fraud detection or the traffic congestion prediction example we mentioned earlier, where you may not know exactly what you are looking for when first designing the application. Acquisition of event processing patterns in these cases is not always straightforward. Several techniques that might be used have originated from artificial intelligence. These are knowledge acquisition techniques that have been used in expert systems, and machine learning techniques can be used to examine historical events and learn the patterns from them. Machine learning can be assisted by data mining tools, neural networks, and other similar techniques.

- In chapter 11 we discussed inexact and uncertain event processing issues. These issues can be dealt with using techniques devised to handle uncertain reasoning, such as Bayesian networks.

- The from-reactive-to-proactive trend requires the prediction of events, and the handling of such predicted events. Another branch of intelligent event processing is the handling of causality networks. These are networks consisting of semantic relations between events and entities. These causality relations have to be acquired (in similar methods to pattern acquisition) and processed. Causality relations also have a temporal dimension that represents the delay between cause and effect. Extensions in this area will take event processing further towards the support of proactive computing.

These trends and technology advancements are some of what we anticipate in the event processing of the future. Of course, as time passes the future will become the present, and new trends and features will be seen on the horizon. With this glance to the future, it is now time to summarize this book.

12.3 *Epilogue*

This is the end of our journey through this book, but the event processing journey is only starting. Event processing is still a young subject, and will most certainly evolve in the future. We hope that this book has provided a solid foundation for the understanding of the concepts and facilities of event processing. The building block approach and modeling language we have used is intended to help you understand the concepts and to serve as a gateway to future programming of event processing systems, which we believe will be done using this level of abstraction. If you wish to get hands-on experience with some of the various approaches to event processing, you are welcome to use the different languages through our website. This website will also help to keep this book a living entity with updates, a live forum, and contact with other readers.

appendix A
Definitions

This appendix is a glossary of the special terms we use in this book.

A The **absence pattern** is satisfied when there are no participant events. The matching set is empty (see section 9.2.1).

An **Aggregate EPA** is a Transformation EPA that takes as input a collection of events and creates a single derived event by applying a function over the input events (6.2.4).

The **all pattern** is satisfied when the participant event set contains at least one instance of each event type that is mentioned in the relevant event types list. The pattern matching set is made up of the event instances (one for each relevant event type) that cause the pattern to be satisfied (9.2.1).

The **always pattern** is satisfied when the participant event set is non-empty and all the participant events satisfy the always pattern assertion. If the pattern is satisfied, the matching set is the entire participant event set (9.2.4).

The **any pattern** is satisfied if the participant event set contains an instance of any of the event types in the relevant event types list. The pattern matching set consists of the event instance that causes the pattern to be satisfied (9.2.1).

The **availability** of a system is the percentage of the time its users perceive it to be functioning (10.2.2).

The **average distance pattern** is satisfied when the average distance of all the participant events from a given point satisfies the average distance threshold assertion (9.3.3).

C   A **cardinality policy** is a semantic abstraction that controls how many matching sets are created. The possible policies are single, unrestricted, and bounded (9.4.2).

A **common attribute** is an event attribute whose semantics are defined by the attribute name. All common attributes with the same name in a given application domain are considered to be semantically equivalent (3.3.2).

A **Compose EPA** is a Transformation EPA that takes groups of events from two input terminals, looks for matches using a matching criterion, and creates derived events based on these matched events (6.2.4).

A **composite context** is a context that is composed from two or more contexts, known as its **members**. The set of context partitions for the composite context is the Cartesian product of the partition sets of the member contexts (7.7.1).

A **consumption policy** is a semantic abstraction that defines whether an event instance is consumed as soon as it's included in a matching set, or whether it can be included in subsequent matching sets. Possible consumption policies are consume, reuse, and bounded reuse (9.4.4).

A **context** is a named specification of conditions that groups event instances so that they can be processed in a related way. It assigns each event instance to one or more **context partitions**. A context may have one or more **context dimensions** and can give rise to one or more context partitions (7.1).

A **context initiator policy** is a semantic abstraction that defines the behavior required when a window has been opened and a subsequent initiator event is detected. The possible policies are open another window, ignore the new initiator event, refresh the window, or extend the window (7.6).

The **count pattern** is satisfied when the number of instances in the participant event set satisfies the pattern's threshold assertion (9.2.2).

D   The **decreasing pattern** is satisfied by an attribute A if for all the participant events, e1 $\ll$ e2 $\Rightarrow$ e1.A > e2.A (9.3.2).

A **derivation expression** is an expression that assigns values to the attributes of a derived event. A derivation expression can refer to values of the input event attributes (8.2.1).

A **derived event** is an event that is generated as a result of event processing that takes place inside the event processing system (2.2.1).

The **detection time** attribute is a timestamp (in the event type's temporal granularity) that records the time at which the event became known to the event processing system (3.2.2).

E An **Enrich** EPA is a Translate EPA that takes a single input event, uses it to query data from a global state element, and creates a derived event which includes the attributes from the original event, possibly with modified values, and can include additional attributes. The new and changed values are calculated using the results from the global state query (6.2.4).

An **entity distance location context** assigns events to context partitions based on their distance from a given entity. This entity is either specified by an event attribute or is given as part of the context specification (7.3.2).

An **evaluation policy** is a semantic abstraction that determines when the matching process is to be evaluated (9.4.1).

An **event** is an occurrence within a particular system or domain; it is something that has happened, or is contemplated as having happened in that domain. The word *event* is also used to mean a programming entity that represents such an occurrence in a computing system (1.1.1).

The **event annotation** attribute provides a free-text explanation of what happened in this particular event (3.2.2).

An **event attribute** is a component of the structure of an event. Each attribute has a name and a data type (3.1.1).

Event-based programming, also called event-driven architecture (EDA), is an architectural style in which one or more components in a software system execute in response to receiving one or more event notifications (2.1.6).

Event causality is a relation between two event instances e1 and e2, designating the fact that the occurrence of the event e1 caused the occurrence of event e2 (11.3.2).

The **event certainty** attribute denotes an estimate of the certainty of this particular event (3.2.2).

An **event channel** is a processing element that receives events from one or more source processing elements, makes routing decisions, and sends the input events unchanged to one or more target processing elements in accordance with these routing decisions (6.3.1).

The **event composition** attribute is a Boolean attribute that denotes whether the specific event type is the composition of other events or not (3.2.1).

An **event consumer** is an entity at the edge of an event processing system that receives events from the system (2.2.1).

An **event distance location context** assigns events to context partitions if they occurred within a specific distance from the location of the event that triggered the creation of the partition (7.3.3).

An **event entity reference** is an event attribute whose value is a reference to a particular entity external to the event (3.3.2).

The **event generalization** and **event specialization** relationships indicate that an event type is a generalization or specialization of another event type, possibly conditioned by a predicate (3.4).

The **event identity** attribute is a system-generated unique ID for each individual event instance (3.2.2).

In an **event interval context** each window is an interval that starts when the associated event processing agent receives an event that satisfies a specified predicate. It ends when the EPA receives an event that satisfies a second predicate, or when a given period has elapsed (7.2.2).

Event processing is computing that performs operations on events. Common event processing operations include reading, creating, transforming, and deleting events (1.2.1).

An **event processing agent** is a software module that processes events (2.2.1).

An **event processing network** is a collection of event processing agents, producers, consumers, and global state elements, connected by a collection of channels (2.2.2).

An **event producer** is an entity at the edge of an event processing system, that introduces events into the system (2.2.1).

The **event source** attribute is the name of the entity that originated this event. This can be either an event producer or an event processing agent (3.2.2).

An **event stream** is a set of associated events. It is often a temporally totally ordered set (that is to say, there is a well-defined timestamp-based order to the events in the stream). A stream in which all the events must be of the same type is called a homogeneous event stream; a stream in which the events may be of different types is referred to as a heterogeneous event stream (2.2.3).

An **event type** is a specification for a set of event objects that have the same semantic intent and same structure; every event object is considered to be an instance of an event type (3.1).

The **event type identifier** attribute uniquely identifies the event type described by an event type definition element (3.2.1).

A **excess type** condition occurs when a Pattern detect agent encounters more instances of a given event type than are specified by the relevant event types list (9.4.3).

F **False negative situation detection** refers to cases in which a situation occurred in reality, but the event representing this situation was not emitted by an event processing system (11.2.2).

False positive situation detection refers to cases in which an event representing a situation was emitted by an event processing system, but the situation did not occur in reality (11.2.2).

A **Filter agent** is an EPA that performs filtering only and has no matching or derivation steps, so it does not transform the input event (6.2.3).

A **filter expression** (assertion) takes the form of a predicate that is evaluated against an event; the event passes the filter if the predicate is evaluate to TRUE, and fails the filter if the predicate evaluate to FALSE (8.1.1).

The **first n pattern** is satisfied by the first n events within the participant event set. The matching set contains these n events. If there are fewer than n events, the matching set contains all the participant events. The pattern has a parameter called *Count* that provides the value of n (9.3.1).

In a **fixed interval context** each window is an interval that has a fixed time length; there may be just one window or a periodically repeating sequence of non-overlapping windows (7.2.1).

A **fixed location context** has predefined context partitions based on specific spatial entities. An event is included in a partition if its location attribute indicates that it is correlated with the partition's spatial entity (7.3.1).

I The **increasing pattern** is satisfied by an attribute A if for all the participant events, e1 $\ll$ e2 $\Rightarrow$ e1.A $<$ e2.A (9.3.2).

L The **last n pattern** is satisfied by the last n events within the participant event set. The matching set contains these n events. If there are fewer than n events, the matching set contains all the participant events. The pattern has a parameter called *Count* that provides the value of n (9.3.1).

A **location** data type is used to designate a real-world location associated with the event; it can refer to the location using domain-specific geospatial terms, for example, lines and areas that are defined in a particular geospatial domain (3.3.1).

M The **max distance pattern** is satisfied when the maximal distance of all the participant events from a given point satisfies the max distance threshold assertion (9.3.3).

An event type is said to be a **member** of a composite event type if its instances can be included in instances of the composite event type. The **membership** relationship applies only to composite event types. It indicates that the related event type is a member of the composite event type (3.4).

The **min distance pattern** is satisfied when the minimal distance of all the participant events from a given point satisfies the min distance threshold assertion (9.3.3).

The **mixed pattern** is satisfied for a value of an attribute A, if the participant event set contains event instances e1, e2, e3, e4 such that e1 << e2; e1.A < e2.A; e3 << e4; and e3.A > e4.A (9.3.2).

The **moving in a constant direction pattern** is satisfied if there exists a direction from the set {north, south, east, west, northeast, northwest, southeast, southwest} such that for any pair of participants events e1, e2 we have e1 << e2 $\Rightarrow$ e2 lies in that direction relative to e1 (9.3.4).

The **moving in a mixed direction pattern** is satisfied if there are at least three events with different locations and if none of the eight moving in a constant direction patterns is satisfied (9.3.4).

The **moving toward pattern** is satisfied when for any pair of participant events e1, e2 we have e1 << e2 $\Rightarrow$ the location of e2 is closer to a certain object than the location of e1 (9.3.4).

The **multiple results policy** defines the behavior of an Enrich event processing agent when its query returns more than one result. The possible policy values are first, last, every, and combine (8.2.1).

N The **non-decreasing pattern** is satisfied by an attribute A if for all participant events e1 << e2 $\Rightarrow$ e1.A $\leq$ e2.A (9.3.2).

The **non-increasing pattern** is satisfied by an attribute A if for all participant events, e1 << e2 $\Rightarrow$ e1.A $\geq$ e2.A (9.3.2).

O The **occurrence time** attribute is a timestamp with a precision given by the event type's temporal granularity (chronon). It records the time at which the event occurred in the external system (3.2.2).

An **order policy** is a semantic abstraction that defines the meaning of the << temporal order of the event instances in the participant event set. The possible policies are by occurrence time, by detection time, by user-defined attribute, or by stream position (9.4.5).

P The **participant events** are those event instances that occur within the Pattern detect agent's context partition, and which are instances of the event types mentioned in the relevant event types list (9.1.2).

An event **pattern** is a template specifying one or more combinations of events. Given any collection of events you may be able to find one or more subsets of those events that match a particular pattern. We say that such a subset **satisfies** the pattern (9.1.2).

A **Pattern detect EPA** is an EPA that performs a pattern matching function on one or more input streams. It emits one or more derived events if it detects an occurrence of the specified pattern in the input events (6.2.5).

A **pattern matching set** is the output of the pattern matching process; it's a subset of the participant events (9.1.2).

Pattern parameters provide additional values used in the definition of the pattern function. The parameters that may be specified, and their meanings, vary depending on the pattern type (9.1.2).

A **pattern policy** is a named parameter that disambiguates the semantics of the pattern and the pattern matching process (9.1.2).

A **pattern type** is a label that determines the meaning and intention of the pattern and specifies the particular kind of matching function to be used (9.1.2).

A **Project EPA** is a Translate EPA that takes an input event and creates a single derived event containing a subset of the attributes of the input event (6.2.4).

R A **raw event** is an event that is introduced into an event processing system by an event producer (2.2.1).

Recoverability is the ability to restore the state of a system to its exact value before a failure occurred (10.2.2).

The **relative average distance pattern** is satisfied when the average distance between of any two participant events satisfies the relative average threshold assertion (9.3.3).

The **relative max distance pattern** is satisfied when the maximal distance between any two participant events satisfies the max distance threshold assertion (9.3.3).

The **relative min distance pattern** is satisfied when the minimal distance between any two participant events satisfies the min distance threshold assertion (9.3.3).

The **relative n highest values pattern** is satisfied by the events which have the n highest values of a specific attribute over all the participant events, where n is supplied as a pattern parameter. The matching set contains these n events. If there are fewer than n events, the matching set contains all the participant events (9.2.3).

The **relative n lowest values pattern** is satisfied by the events which have the n lowest values of a specific attribute over all the participant events, where n is supplied as a pattern parameter. The matching set contains these n events. If there are fewer than n events, the matching set contains all the participant events (9.2.3).

The **relevant event types** list is a list of event types, and it forms part of the pattern matching function. The order of these event types has importance for some pattern functions (9.1.2).

A **repeated type policy** is a semantic abstraction that defines the behavior of a Pattern detect agent when an excess type condition occurs. The possible policies are override, every, first, last, with maximal value, and with minimal value (9.4.3).

A **retraction** event relationship is a property of an event type referencing a second event type. It indicates that the second type is a logical reversal of the referencing event type (3.4).

A **routing scheme** denotes the type of information used by a channel to make a routing decision. The possible routing schemes are fixed, type-based, and content-based (6.3.2).

S **Scalability** is the capability of a system to adapt readily to a greater or lesser intensity of use, volume, or demand while still meeting its business objectives (10.2.1).

A **segmentation-oriented context** assigns events to context partitions based on the values of one or more event attributes, either using the value of these attribute(s) to pick a partition directly, or using predicate expressions to define context partition membership (7.5).

The **sequence pattern** is satisfied if the participant event set contains at least one instance of each event type mentioned in the relevant event types list, and if the order of these event instances matches the order of their types in the list. The pattern matching set is made up of the event instances (one for each relevant event type) that cause the pattern to be satisfied (9.3.1).

In a **sliding event interval context** the opening of each new window and its duration are determined by counting the number of events received by the event processing agent (7.2.4).

In a **sliding fixed interval context** each window is an interval with fixed temporal size or a fixed number of events. New windows are opened at regular intervals relative to one another (7.2.3).

A **situation** is an event occurrence that might require a reaction (1.1.2).

The **sometimes pattern** is satisfied when at least one participant event that satisfies the pattern assertion. The matching set, if the pattern is satisfied, is the entire participant event set (9.2.4).

A **Split EPA** is a Transformation EPA that takes as an input a single event and creates a collection of events. Each of them can be a clone of the original event, or a projection of that event containing a subset of its attributes (6.2.4).

The **stable pattern** is satisfied by an attribute A if for all the participant events e1 << e2 ⇒ e1.A = e2.A (9.3.2).

An EPA is a **stateful event processing agent** if the way it processes events is influenced by more than one input event (2.2.3).

An EPA is a **stateless event processing agent** if the way it processes one event does not influence the way it processes any subsequent events (2.2.3).

A **state-oriented context** has a single partition. It is controlled by an external entity, and the decision of whether to include an event in the partition is based on the state of the external entity at the time when the event occurs or is detected (7.4).

The **stationary pattern** is satisfied if the location of all participant events is identical (9.3.4).

A **synchronous interaction** is a service interaction style in which the service requestor's thread of execution blocks waiting for a response from the service provider without doing anything else in the interim. The service provider is expected to send a response back fairly promptly. This usually means a few tenths of a second at the longest, though response times of several seconds are sometimes encountered in web applications (2.1.1).

T A **temporal context** consists of one or more time intervals, possibly overlapping. Each time interval corresponds to a context partition, which contains events that happen during that interval (7.2).

The **temporal granularity** (or chronon) attribute denotes the *atom of time* from a particular application's point of view, for example, second, minute, hour, or day (3.2.1).

A **threshold assertion** comprises two pattern parameters, the **threshold relation** and **threshold value**. An aggregation function is performed and the relation is used to compare the result of the aggregation against the threshold value. The pattern is matched if this comparison returns TRUE. If the pattern is matched, the matching set is the entire set of participant events (9.2.2).

A **time interval** is a data type that designates a continuous segment in time. It is a half-open interval, starting at a time point *Ts* and ending at a time point *Te* (11.1.1).

A **timestamp** is a data type that denotes a certain point in time; its precision is given by the temporal granularity that applies to the event type (3.2.1).

A **Transformation EPA** is an EPA that includes a derivation step, and optionally also a filtering step (6.2.4).

A **Translate EPA** is a stateless Transformation EPA that takes a single event as its input, and generates a single derived event which is a function of the input event, using a derivation formula (6.2.4).

The **value average pattern** is satisfied when the value of a specific attribute, averaged over all the participant events, satisfies the value average threshold assertion (9.2.2).

The **value max pattern** is satisfied when the maximal value of a specific attribute over all the participant events satisfies the value max threshold assertion (9.2.2).

The **value min pattern** is satisfied when the minimal value of a specific attribute over all the participant events satisfies the value min threshold assertion (9.2.2).

appendix B
The Fast Flower
Delivery application

This appendix gives a description of the Fast Flower Delivery application using the definition elements provided in this book. It contains material taken from various chapters of the book, describing event types, contexts, event consumers, event processing agents, event producers, and channels.

B.1 Specification of the Fast Flower Delivery application

This specification is taken from chapter 1, section 1.5.

Figure B.1 gives a high-level summary of the application. The arrows represent event flows, and the icons represent the producers, consumers, and the various processing systems (made up of event processing agents) that comprise the application.

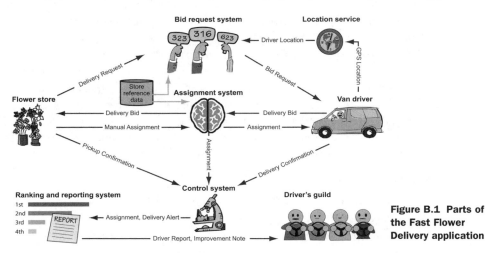

Figure B.1 Parts of the Fast Flower Delivery application

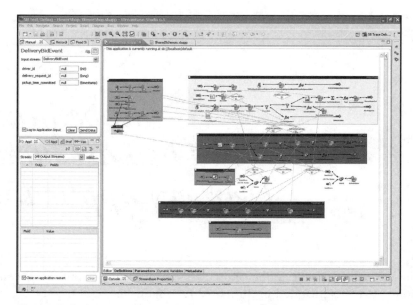

**Figure B.2
StreamBase
representation of
the Fast Flower
Delivery application**

Figure B.2 shows an event processing network representation of the application—this example uses the StreamBase Studio development tool.

We now describe the application itself.

B.1.1   General description

A consortium of flower stores in a large city has established an agreement with local independent van drivers to deliver flowers from the stores to their destinations. When a store gets a flower delivery order, it creates a request which is broadcast to relevant drivers within a certain distance from the store, with the time for pickup (typically *now*) and the required delivery time. A driver is then assigned, and the customer is notified that a delivery has been scheduled. The driver makes the pickup and delivery, and the person receiving the flowers confirms the delivery time by signing for them on the driver's mobile device. The system maintains a ranking of each individual driver based on his or her ability to deliver flowers on time. Each store has a profile that can include a constraint on the ranking of its drivers; for example, a store can require its drivers to have a ranking greater than 10. The profile also indicates whether the store wants the system to assign drivers automatically, or whether it wants to receive several applications and then make its own choice.

B.1.2   Skeleton specification

The sections that follow describe the five phases of the application.

PHASE 1: BID PHASE

The communication between the store and the person who makes the order is outside the scope of the system, so as far as we're concerned a delivery's lifecycle starts when a store places a `Delivery Request` event into the system. The system *enriches* the `Delivery Request` event by adding to it the minimum ranking that the store is prepared to accept (each store has a different level of tolerance for service quality). Each van is equipped with a GPS modem which periodically transmits a GPS Location event. The system *translates* these events, which contain raw latitude and longitude values, into events that indicate which region of the city the driver is currently in. When it receives a Delivery Request event, the system matches it to its list of drivers. It selects only those authorized drivers who satisfy the ranking requirements and who are currently in nearby regions. A Bid Request event is then broadcast to all these drivers.

PHASE 2: ASSIGNMENT PHASE

A driver responds to the Bid Request by sending a Delivery Bid event designating his or her current location and committing to a pickup time. Note that here the term *request* means a message that asks drivers to bid; it should not be confused with a service request issued in a request-response protocol. Two minutes after the Bid Request broadcast, the system starts the assignment process. This is either an automatic or a manual process, depending on the store's preference. If the process is manual the system collects the Delivery Bid events that match the original Bid Request and sends the five highest-ranked to the store. The store chooses one of these five drivers and creates the Assignment event itself. If the process is automatic, the first bidder among the selected drivers wins the bid, and the Assignment event is created by the event processing application. The pickup time and delivery time are set and the Assignment is sent to the driver.

There are also alerts associated with this process: if there are no bidders, an alert is sent both to the store and to the system manager; if the store has not performed its manual assignment within 1 minute of receiving its Delivery Bid events, both the store and system manager receive an alert.

PHASE 3: DELIVERY PROCESS

When the driver arrives to pick up the flowers from the store, the store sends a Pickup Confirmation event; when the driver delivers the flowers, the person receiving them confirms by signing the driver's mobile device, and this generates a Delivery Confirmation event. Both Pickup Confirmation and Delivery Confirmation events have associated timestamps, and this allows the system to generate alert events:

- A Pickup Alert is generated if a Pickup Confirmation wasn't reported within 5 minutes of the committed pickup time.
- A Delivery Alert is generated if a Delivery Confirmation wasn't reported within 10 minutes of the required delivery time.

PHASE 4: RANKING EVALUATION

The system evaluates each driver's ranking every time that driver completes 20 deliveries. If the driver didn't have any Delivery Alerts during that period, the system generates a Ranking Increase event indicating that the driver's ranking has increased by one point. Conversely, if the driver has had more than five delivery alerts during that time, the system generates a Ranking Decrease to reduce the ranking by one point. If the system generates a Ranking Increase for a driver whose previous evaluation had been a Ranking Decrease, it generates an Improvement Note event.

PHASE 5: ACTIVITY MONITORING

The system aggregates assignment and other events and counts the number of assignments per day for each driver for each day in which the driver has been active. Once a month the system creates reports on drivers' performance, assessing the drivers according to the following criteria:

- A permanently weak driver is a driver with fewer than five assignments on all the days on which the driver has been active.
- An idle driver is a driver with at least one day of activity that had no assignments.
- A consistently weak driver is a driver whose assignments, when active, are at least two standard deviations lower than the average assignments per driver on that day.
- A consistently strong driver is a driver whose daily assignments are at least two standard deviations higher than the average number of assignments per driver on each day in question.
- An improving driver is a driver whose assignments increase or stay the same day by day.

B.2 *The event processing network for Fast Flower Delivery*

This section copies section 6.2.7 showing the event processing network for the Fast Flower Delivery application. For simplicity, each of the different parts of the network is shown in a different illustration. Please note that where these illustrations include explicit channels, they only show the connections from these channels to other entities in the figure concerned. For example, in figure B.3 you can see that the Bid Request channel receives events from the Bid Request creator agent, but to see what happens to them you'll need to look at figure B.5 where you'll see that this same channel delivers events to agents in the assignment system.

B.2.1 *Bid request system*

We start with the bid request system, illustrated in table B.1.

Table B.1 Event processing agents in the bid request system

Identifier	EPA type	Input event types	Output event types	References
Request enrichment	Enrich	Delivery Request	Delivery Request	Store reference
Bid Request creator	Enrich	Delivery Request	Bid Request	Driver status

These two EPAs are connected to each other, as shown in figure B.3

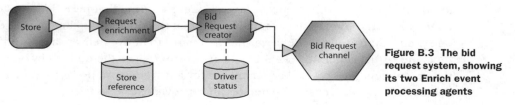

Figure B.3 The bid request system, showing its two Enrich event processing agents

The `Request enrichment` agent takes a `Delivery Request` event, submitted by a flower store's `Store` producer, and queries the store's preferences (held in the `Store reference` global state element) to find the minimum ranking that the store is prepared to accept. This is added to the event instance, which is then forwarded to the `Bid Request creator` agent. This is another Enrich agent. It queries the `Drivers` global state element, finds out which drivers are in the neighborhood and meet the minimum ranking requirement (this is the attribute supplied by the `Request enrichment` agent), and creates a `Bid Request` event. This contains details from the original `Delivery Request` along with the IDs of the chosen drivers. It sends this event, through the `Bid Request` channel, to the `Driver` consumer, which distributes it to the drivers registered with those IDs.

B.2.2 The location service

In order to know which drivers are in the right neighborhood, the application needs to know where the drivers are at any point in time. The drivers are tracked by the location service, which includes a single event processing agent, shown in table B.2.

Table B.2   Event processing agents in the location service

EPA identifier	EPA type	Input event types	Output event types	References
Location service	Translate	GPS Location	Driver Location	Neighborhoods

This is a Translate EPA whose job is to compare the raw latitude/longitude readings that come from a vehicle's GPS device against a map of the city to determine what part of the city the driver is currently in. It is shown in figure B.4.

This agent inserts the name of the neighborhood into the output event, which is then used to update the `Driver status` global state element.

B.2.3 The assignment system

The core of the application is the assignment system, which takes each `Bid Request` from the bid request system and matches it against the `Delivery Bid` events that come back from the drivers. The system either selects a driver itself, or gets the flower store to select one. Table B.3 lists the assignment system's event processing agents, and figure B.5 shows how they are connected.

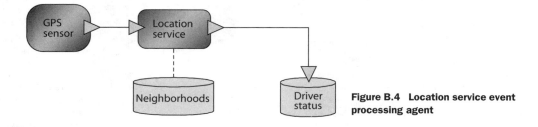

Figure B.4   Location service event processing agent

Table B.3   Event processing agents in the assignment system

EPA identifier	EPA type	Input event types	Output event types	References
Driver enrichment	Enrich	Delivery Bid	Delivery Bid	Driver status
Assignment manager	Compose	Delivery Bid, Bid Request	Delivery Bid, No Bidders Alert	
Bid enrichment	Enrich	Delivery Bid	Delivery Bid	Store reference
Bid routing	Filter	Delivery Bid	Delivery Bid	
Manual assignment preparation	Pattern detect	Delivery Bid, Bid Request	Delivery Bid	
Automatic assignment	Pattern detect	Delivery Bid	Assignment	

The Assignment manager is a Compose agent. It takes Bid Request events from the bid request system, and also receives Delivery Bid events from the drivers (after these have been enriched with driver rankings by the Driver enrichment agent). It checks that the committed pickup times in these bids match the pickup times from the corresponding Bid Requests. If it doesn't find any acceptable bids in the 2-minute period, it generates a No Bidders Alert. If it does find bids, it forwards the Delivery Bid events to the Bid enrichment agent. This takes each event and looks up the flower store's preference, adding an attribute to the event to indicate whether the store wishes to assign the driver itself or not, before passing it to the Bid routing agent. This is a Filter agent that routes the event either to the Manual assignment preparation agent or to the Automatic assignment agent, depending on the value of this attribute. The Manual assignment preparation agent accumulates the Delivery Bid events from

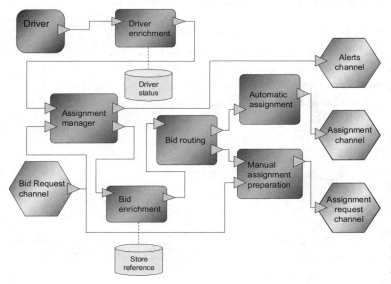

Figure B.5   Event processing agents that make up the assignment system

the top five ranked drivers and forwards them to the `Store` consumer, through the `Assignment Request` channel. The `Automatic assignment` agent picks the first `Bid Request` that it encounters and converts it into an `Assignment` event. It is then forwarded, through the `Assignment` channel, to the driver and other interested parties.

B.2.4 *The control system*

The control system is responsible for checking that drivers and stores are using the application correctly. It has three Pattern detect agents, listed in table B.4.

Table B.4 Event processing agents in the control system

EPA identifier	EPA type	Input event types	Output event types
Assignment not done	Pattern detect	Delivery Bid, Manual Assignment	Manual Assignment Timeout Alert
Pickup alert	Pattern detect	Pickup Confirmation, Assignment	Pickup Alert
Delivery alert	Pattern detect	Delivery Confirmation, Assignment	Delivery Alert

These agents take `Assignment` events from the `Assignment` channel, `Pickup Confirmation` events from the stores, and `Delivery Confirmation` events from the drivers, as shown in figure B.6.

The `Assignment not done` agent monitors stores to make sure that they are performing manual assignments on time when they are sent `Delivery Bids`. The `Pickup alert` and `Delivery alert` agents monitor the delivery after it has been assigned. They raise alert events if the driver doesn't pick up the flowers or deliver them by the times stated in the `Assignment` event.

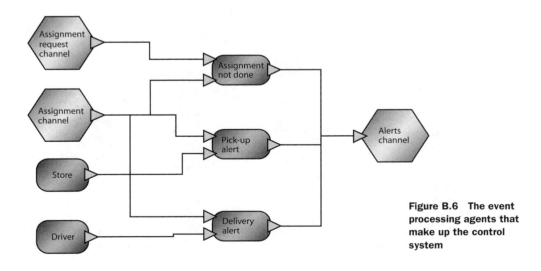

Figure B.6 The event processing agents that make up the control system

B.2.5 *The ranking and reporting system*

The ranking and reporting system contains a number of event processing agents, shown in table B.5 and figure B.7, that assess driver performance.

Table B.5   Event processing agents in the ranking and reporting system

EPA identifier	EPA type	Input event types	Output event types
Ranking increase	Pattern detect	Delivery Alert	Ranking Increase
Ranking decrease	Pattern detect	Delivery Alert	Ranking Decrease
Improving note	Pattern detect	Ranking Increase, Ranking Decrease	Improvement Note
Daily assignments calculator	Aggregate	Assignment, Delivery Bid	Daily Assignments
Daily statistics creator	Aggregate	Daily Assignments	Daily Statistics
Performance evaluation	Compose	Daily Assignments, Daily Statistics	Relative Performance
Permanent weak driver	Pattern detect	Daily Assignments	Driver Report
Idle driver	Pattern detect	Daily Assignments	Driver Report
Consistent strong driver	Pattern detect	Relative Performance	Driver Report
Consistent weak driver	Pattern detect	Relative Performance	Driver Report
Improving driver	Pattern detect	Daily Assignments	Driver Report

The agents at the top of figure B.7 perform the phase 4 ranking evaluations, which are conducted every 20 deliveries; the others do the phase 5 activity monitoring, which generates reports once per month.

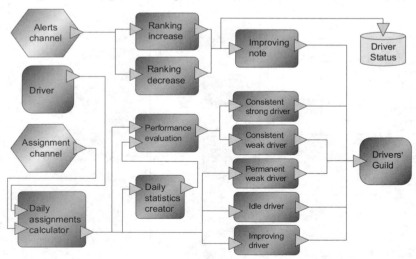

Figure B.7   The event processing agents in the ranking and reporting system

After showing the general picture, we list the details, starting with the event types.

B.3   *Event type definitions*

Table B.6 lists all event types in the application in alphabetical order.

Table B.6   Event types

Event type	Raw	Derived
Assignment		✓
Bid Request		✓
Daily Assignments		✓
Daily Statistics		✓
Delivery Alert		✓
Delivery Bid	✓	✓
Delivery Bid Alert		✓
Delivery Confirmation	✓	
Delivery Request	✓	✓
Delivery Request Cancellation	✓	
Driver Location		✓
Driver Report		✓
GPS Location	✓	
Improvement Note		✓
Manual Assignment	✓	
Manual Assignment Timeout Alert		✓
No Bidders Alert		✓
Pickup Alert		✓
Pickup Confirmation	✓	
Ranking Decrease		✓
Ranking Increase		✓
Relative Performance		✓

You'll see that most of these types are either used only for raw or only for derived events. Two of the event types (`Delivery Request` and `Delivery Bid`) have instances that are raw and instances that are enriched by an EPA, and so they are derived.

Table B.7 shows the application defaults for event types.

Table B.7   Application defaults for the Fast Flower Delivery application

Attribute type	Default setting
temporalGranularity	minute
eventAnnotation	optional
eventCertainty	not applicable
eventIdentity	required
occurrenceTime	required
detectionTime	required
eventSource	required

Tables B.8 through B.29 show the payloads of the event types.

Table B.8   Assignment

Attribute name	Data type	Occurrence	Semantic role
requestId	Integer	required	Common attribute
store	String	required	Reference to store entity
driver	String	required	Reference to driver entity
addresseeLocation	Location	required	Common attribute
requiredPickupTime	DateTime	required	Common attribute
requiredDeliveryTime	DateTime	required	Common attribute

Table B.9   Bid Request

Attribute name	Data type	Occurrence	Semantic role
requestId	Integer	required	Common attribute
store	String	required	Reference to store entity
addresseeLocation	Location	required	Common attribute
requiredPickupTime	DateTime	required	Common attribute
requiredDeliveryTime	DateTime	required	Common attribute
minimumRanking	Integer	required	
driversList	Collection of strings	required	References to driver entity

Table B.10 `Daily Assignments`

Attribute name	Data type	Occurrence	Semantic role
driver	String	required	Reference to driver entity
day	Date	required	
assignmentCount	Integer	required	

Table B.11 `Daily Statistics`

Attribute name	Data type	Occurrence	Semantic role
day	Date	required	
assignmentMean	Decimal	required	
assignmentSTDV	Decimal	required	

Table B.12 `Delivery Alert`

Attribute name	Data type	Occurrence	Semantic role
requestId	Integer	required	Common attribute
driver	String	required	Reference to driver entity

Table B.13 `Delivery Bid`

Attribute name	Data type	Occurrence	Semantic role
requestId	Integer	required	Common attribute
driver	String	required	Reference to driver entity
store	String	required	Reference to store entity
committedPickupTime	DateTime	required	
ranking	Integer	optional	

Table B.14 `Delivery Bid Alert`

Attribute name	Data type	Occurrence	Semantic role
requestId	Integer	required	Common attribute

Table B.15 `Delivery Confirmation`

Attribute name	Data type	Occurrence	Semantic role
requestId	Integer	required	Common attribute
driver	String	required	Reference to driver entity

Table B.16 `Delivery Request`

Attribute name	Data type	Occurrence	Semantic role
requestId	Integer	required	Common attribute
store	String	required	Reference to store entity
addresseeLocation	Location	required	Common attribute
requiredPickupTime	DateTime	required	Common attribute
requiredDeliveryTime	DateTime	required	Common attribute
minimumRanking	Integer	optional	
neighborhood	Location	optional	Reference to neighborhood entity

Table B.17 `Delivery Request Cancellation`

Attribute name	Data type	Occurrence	Semantic role
requestId	Integer	required	Common attribute

Table B.18 `Driver Location`

Attribute name	Data type	Occurrence	Semantic role
driver	String	required	Reference to driver entity
driverLocation	Location	required	

Table B.19 `Driver Report`

Attribute name	Data type	Occurrence	Semantic role
driver	String	required	Reference to driver entity
consistentStrongDriver	Boolean	optional	
improvingDriver	Boolean	optional	
permanentWeakDriver	Boolean	optional	
consistentWeakDriver	Boolean	optional	
idleDriver	Boolean	optional	

Table B.20 `GPS Location`

Attribute name	Data type	Occurrence	Semantic role
driver	String	required	Reference to driver entity
driverLocation	Location	required	

Table B.21 `Improvement Note`

Attribute name	Data type	Occurrence	Semantic role
driver	String	required	Reference to driver entity

Table B.22 `Manual Assignment`

Attribute name	Data type	Occurrence	Semantic role
requestId	Integer	required	Common attribute
store	String	required	Reference to store entity
driver	String	required	Reference to driver entity
addresseeLocation	Location	required	Common attribute
requiredPickupTime	DateTime	required	Common attribute
requiredDeliveryTime	DateTime	required	Common attribute

Table B.23 `Manual Assignment Timeout Alert`

Attribute name	Data type	Occurrence	Semantic role
requestId	Integer	required	Common attribute
store	String	required	Reference to store entity

Table B.24 `No Bidders Alert`

Attribute name	Data type	Occurrence	Semantic role
requestId	Integer	required	Common attribute

Table B.25 `Pickup Alert`

Attribute name	Data type	Occurrence	Semantic role
requestId	Integer	required	Common attribute
driver	String	required	Reference to driver entity

Table B.26 `Pickup Confirmation`

Attribute name	Data type	Occurrence	Semantic role
requestId	Integer	required	Common attribute
store	String	required	Reference to store entity
driver	String	required	Reference to driver entity

Table B.27   `Ranking Decrease`

Attribute name	Data type	Occurrence	Semantic role
driver	String	required	Reference to driver entity

Table B.28   `Ranking Increase`

Attribute name	Data type	Occurrence	Semantic role
driver	String	required	Reference to driver entity

Table B.29   `Relative Performance`

Attribute name	Data type	Occurrence	Semantic role
driver	String	required	Reference to driver entity
day	Date	required	
deviation	Integer	required	

Next we show the context definitions.

B.4   *Context definitions*

The Fast Flower Delivery application uses several segmentation-oriented, temporal, and composite contexts. The first of these is the straightforward segmentation-oriented context shown in table B.30.

Table B.30   `Driver` **context**

Context identifier	Context dimension	Context type	Attribute list
Driver	segmentation-oriented	segmentation	driver

This groups events that relate to a given driver. The only event processing agent that is directly associated with this context is the `Improving note` agent that traces the driver's ranking modifications to check whether the driver has improved; in addition, this context participates in several composite contexts.

The application also uses a segmentation context, shown in table B.31, which groups events that are related to a particular delivery request.

Table B.31   `Request` **context**

Context identifier	Context dimension	Context type	Attribute list
Request	segmentation-oriented	segmentation	requestId

This context makes use of the fact that many of the events in the application contain the `request id` common attribute. The one agent directly associated with this context is the `Automatic assignment` agent from the assignment system (see figure B.5). This context is also used as part of composite contexts.

We now look at the temporal contexts used by the application. The first of these is shown in table B.32. This context assigns events into contiguous month-long windows. This context doesn't have any event processing agents directly associated with it, but is used as part of composite contexts.

Table B.32 `Monthly` **context**

Context identifier	Context dimension	Context type	Interval start	Interval end	Recurrence
Monthly	Temporal	fixed interval	2000-01-01	2000-02-01	Monthly

The `Daily` context, shown in table B.33, assigns events into contiguous day-long windows. The `Daily statistics creator` and `Performance evaluation` agents are directly associated with this context; these agents calculate aggregates for all drivers on a daily basis.

Table B.33 `Daily` **context**

Context identifier	Context dimension	Context type	Interval start	Interval end	Recurrence
Daily	temporal	fixed interval	2000-01-01	2000-01-02	Daily

The remaining contexts are all composite contexts that combine temporal contexts with one of the segmentation contexts that we have already defined. The first of these is the `Delivery interval` context, shown in tables B.34a and B.34b. The context denotes the time interval within which delivery is expected. It expires when the delivery is confirmed, or when the timeout occurs. The `Delivery alert` agent is directly associated with this context; this agent creates an alert if no confirmation is received in the interval.

Table B.34a shows the composite context; the `Request` context member (which we met earlier in table B.31) ensures that a new window is opened for each separate bid request, whereas the temporal member (table B.34b) opens a window each time that an `Assignment` event is encountered.

Table B.34a `Delivery interval` **context**

Priority order	Member contexts
1	Request
2	Temporal delivery interval

Table B.34b shows the temporal member context, which lasts for up to 10 minutes from the `required delivery time`.

Table B.34b `Temporal delivery interval` **member context**

Identifier	Context type	Initiator	Terminator	Expiration time offset	Initiator policy
Temporal delivery interval	event interval	Assignment	Delivery Confirmation	requiredDeliveryTime +10 minutes	Ignore

The next composite context, shown in table B.35a, is the `Bid interval` composite context; the `Request` context member (which we met earlier in table B.31) ensures that a new window is opened for each separate bid request, whereas the temporal member (table B.35b) opens a window each time that a bid request is encountered; the window closes after 2 minutes. This context is used in the assignment system (see figure B.5) where it gathers together the `Delivery Bid` events that refer to a given `Bid Request`. It is associated with the `Assignment manager` and `Manual assignment preparation` agents.

Table B.35a `Bid interval` **composite context**

Priority order	Member contexts
1	Request
2	Temporal bid interval

Table B.35b shows the temporal member context, which lasts for 2 minutes from the `Bid Request`.

Table B.35b `Temporal bid interval` **member context**

Identifier	Context type	Initiator event	Expiration time offset	Initiator policy
Temporal bid interval	event interval	Bid Request	+2 minutes	Ignore

Table B.36a defines the `Response interval` composite context. This context opens a window when the assignment system sends a `Delivery Bid` event to a store that has chosen to perform manual driver assignment (separate windows are created for each delivery request); it ends 1 minute after the last `Delivery Bid` event. This context is associated with the `Assignment not done` agent (this agent generates an alert if the store doesn't complete its assignment process in time).

Table B.36a `Response interval` **composite context**

Priority order	Member contexts
1	Request
2	Temporal response interval

Table B.36b defines the temporal member context that runs from the first `Delivery Bid` event until 1 minute after the last `Delivery Bid` event.

Table B.36b `Temporal response interval` **member context**

Identifier	Context type	Initiator event	Expiration time offset	Initiator policy
Temporal response interval	event interval	Delivery Bid	+1 minute	Extend

Table B.37a defines the `Pickup interval` context; this context denotes the time interval in which a pickup is expected. It ends when the pickup is made or when the timeout occurs. This context is associated with the `Pickup alert` agent which detects pickups that weren't completed on time.

Table B.37a `Pickup interval` **composite context**

Priority order	Member contexts
1	Request
2	Temporal pickup interval

Table B.37b defines the temporal context member that runs until a maximum of 5 minutes after the committed pickup time.

Table B.37b `Temporal pickup interval` **member context**

Identifier	Context type	Initiator	Terminator	Expiration time offset	Initiator policy
Temporal pickup interval	event interval	Assignment	Pickup Confirmation	requiredPickupTime +5 minutes	Ignore

Table B.38a defines the `Driver evaluation` context; this context creates a new window for each driver every time the driver completes 20 deliveries, and it uses the `Driver` context (table B.30) as its segmentation member. The `Ranking increase` and

`Ranking decrease` agents (figure B.7) operate in this context so they can reassess the driver's ranking after every 20 deliveries.

Table B.38a `Driver evaluation` **context**

Priority order	Member contexts
1	Driver
2	Confirmations

Table B.38b defines the `Confirmations` member context which partitions the `Delivery Confirmation` events into non-overlapping groups of 20 events.

Table B.38b `Confirmations` **temporal member context**

Identifier	Context type	Event list	Interval size	Event period
Confirmations	sliding event interval	Delivery Confirmation	20	20

Table B.39a defines the `Daily active driver` context; this context is used by the `Daily assignments calculator` agent, which counts the number of assignments per driver for each day when the driver is active. In addition to the `Driver` segmentation context (table B.30) it contains two temporal contexts. The first of these is the `Daily` context (table B.33) which would, by itself, open a new window every day. However, it is composed with the `When active` context, and this means that the composite context doesn't open a window until the driver bids to make a delivery that day. The `Daily` context member closes this window at the end of the day.

Table B.39a `Daily active driver` **context**

Priority order	Member contexts
1	Driver
2	Daily
3	When active

Table B.39b defines a temporal member of this composite context that is opened whenever a driver creates a `Delivery Bid` event. This is an indication that the driver is active on that day.

Table B.39b `When active` **temporal member context**

Identifier	Context type	Initiator	Terminator	Initiator policy
When active	event interval	Delivery Bid	-	Ignore

Table B.40 defines the composite `Monthly driver` context. This context partitions the relevant events according to the combination of month and driver, and is used in the reporting agents: `Permanent weak driver`, `Idle driver`, `Improving driver`, `Consistent strong driver`, and `Consistent weak driver`. It composes two contexts that we have already met, the `Driver` context (table B.30) and the `Monthly` context (table B.32).

Table B.40 `Monthly driver` **composite context**

Priority order	Member contexts
1	Driver
2	Monthly

The following stateless event processing agents aren't associated with a context. They therefore operate as if they are associated with the default context which classifies all events to a single partition: `Location service`, `Request enrichment`, `Driver enrichment`, `Bid Request creator`, `Bid routing`, and `Bid enrichment`.

B.5 *Producers in the Fast Flower Delivery application*

This section lists the event producer definition elements for the Fast Flower Delivery application. There are four event producers: `Store`, `Driver`, `GPS sensor`, and `Vehicle`. We look briefly at each of these in turn.

THE STORE EVENT PRODUCER

We start with the definition element for the `Store` event producer. Its definition element type is *producer class* because the application treats all the participating flower stores in a similar manner, so we can have a single event producer definition that represents them all.

Its event producer category is *human interaction*, as personnel in the flower store enter its events, and it has four output terminals, as shown in table B.41.

Table B.41 Output terminals for the `Store` **event producer**

Identifier	Event types	Targets
Request	Delivery Request	Request enrichment EPA
Assignment	Manual Assignment	Assignment channel
Confirm Pickup	Pickup Confirmation	Pickup alert EPA
Cancellation	Delivery Request Cancellation	Delivery cancellation channel

The `Assignment` and `Cancellation` terminals have explicit channels as their targets. The other two terminals are connected through implicit channels and so they are shown as directly targeting event processing agents.

We have chosen to model the event store with four output terminals, one for each event type. This is because there is no direct logical connection between them (for example, it doesn't make sense to think of a stream made up of `Request` and `Assignment` events). It's also convenient to use separate terminals in this application, because we want the different types of events to go to different targets. This would still have been possible with a single output terminal, but we would have had to include filter specifications to make sure that the right events go to the right targets.

THE DRIVER EVENT PRODUCER

The `Driver` event producer definition element represents all the drivers using the application, so it too has *producer class* as its definition element type. Although the driver uses a handheld device to submit events, we still give the definition element an event producer category of *human interaction*, because it is the driver that we are modeling, not the device (we are assuming here that there's a one-to-one association of drivers to devices). Table B.42 shows the event producer's output terminals.

Table B.42   The output terminals for the `Driver` event producer

Identifier	Event types	Targets
Bid	Delivery Bid	Driver enrichment EPA, Daily assignments calculator EPA
Confirm	Delivery Confirmation	Delivery alert EPA

Again, we have chosen to use separate output terminals for the two types of events emitted by this event producer.

THE GPS SENSOR EVENT PRODUCER

We have included the `GPS sensor` event producer to illustrate producer specialization. This event producer is abstract so, naturally, its definition element type is *abstract type,* and, as you might expect, its event producer category is *sensor.* The type has just one output terminal, as shown in table B.43.

Table B.43   Output terminal for the `GPS sensor` abstract event producer

Identifier	Event type	Targets
Report	GPS location	-

As this is an abstract type, its terminals aren't connected to any targets.

THE VEHICLE EVENT PRODUCER

Our final event producer is the `Vehicle`. Its definition element type is *producer class* as it represents all the vehicles that are being used for flower delivery. It is a specialization of the `GPS sensor` type, reflecting the fact that there is a physical GPS sensor in each vehicle, and the events are actually produced by that sensor. Its event producer category is therefore *sensor*, just like the GPS sensor type and, as you can see from table B.44, it has the same output terminal.

Table B.44 Output terminal for the `Vehicle` **event producer**

Output terminal	Event type	Targets
Report location	GPS Location	Location service EPA

As this definition element isn't an abstract type, this time we can supply a target for its output terminal.

B.6 *Consumers in the Fast Flower Delivery application*

This section contains a short discussion of the different event consumer definition elements that can be found in our model of the Fast Flower Delivery application. The Fast Flower Delivery application contains three event consumer definition elements: Driver, Store, and Drivers' Guild. We show the consumer details and input terminals for each of these in turn.

THE DRIVER EVENT CONSUMER

The Driver definition element represents the class of all drivers and so it has a definition element type of *consumer class.*

Its event consumer category is *human interaction*, and it has two input terminals as shown in table B.45.

Table B.45 The input terminals for the `Driver` **event consumer class**

Input terminal	Event types	Source
Bids	Bid Request	Bid Request channel
Assignments	Assignment	Assignment channel

Drivers have to handle two different types of events: Bid Request events, issued during the bid phase, and Assignment events, if they are selected during the assignment phase. We have chosen to model this event consumer with two separate input terminals, though we could also have combined both event types on a single input terminal.

Bid Request and Assignment events don't go out to all the drivers represented by the class. Both these event types contain driver attributes which indicate which drivers are to receive the event in question. When a new driver joins the Drivers' Guild, part of the joining process involves registering a new concrete event consumer instance with the system. This instance is registered only to receive event instances that contain the driver's name.

THE STORE EVENT CONSUMER

The Store definition element represents all the florist stores that participate in the program, and so it too has *consumer class* as its definition element type.

Its event consumer category is *human interaction*, and it has two input terminals, as shown in table B.46.

Table B.46   The input terminals for the Store event consumer class

Input terminal	Event types	Source
Bids	Delivery Bid	Assignment request channel
Alerts	No Bidders Alert Manual Assignment Timeout Alert Pickup Alert Delivery Alert	Alerts channel

A store that has elected to do manual assignment will receive Delivery Bid requests from drivers bidding for work on its Bids input terminal. Stores also receive alert events if something goes wrong in the process, and we have chosen to have all alerts handled by a single input terminal.

THE DRIVERS' GUILD EVENT CONSUMER

The Drivers' Guild event consumer feeds evaluation reports to the guild. Its definition element type is *consumer instance*, as there is only one guild.

Its event consumer category is *human interaction*, and it has a single input terminal, as shown in table B.47.

Table B.47   The input terminals for the Drivers' Guild event consumer

Input terminal	Event types	Source
Evaluation	Improvement Note Driver Report	Improving note EPA Consistent strong driver EPA, Consistent weak driver EPA, Permanent weak driver EPA, Idle driver EPA, Improving driver EPA

This consumer receives all its input events through this single input terminal.

B.7 Global state elements

Table B.48 shows the three global state elements used in the Fast Flower Delivery application.

Table B.48 Global state elements in the Fast Flower Delivery application

Element identifier	Element type	Metadata	Input event type
Neighborhoods	Reference data	Geospatial database schema	
Driver status	Event processing state	Driver ID, Driver ranking, Current neighborhood	Ranking Increase Ranking Decrease Driver Location
Store reference	Reference data	Store name, Minimum ranking, Store location, Store region, Automatic assignment flag	

B.8 Channels

Table B.49 shows the simple channels used in the Fast Flower Delivery application. These appear as edges in the event processing network diagram.

Table B.49 Implicit channels in the Fast Flower Delivery application

Input terminal sources	Output terminal targets	Event types
Store	Request enrichment EPA	Delivery Request
Request enrichment EPA	Bid Request creator EPA	Delivery Request
Vehicle	Location service EPA	GPS Location
Location service EPA	Driver status global state element	Driver Location
Driver	Driver enrichment EPA	Delivery Bid
Driver enrichment EPA	Assignment manager EPA	Delivery Bid
Assignment manager EPA	Bid enrichment EPA	Delivery Bid
Bid enrichment EPA	Bid routing EPA	Delivery Bid
Bid routing EPA	Automatic assignment EPA	Delivery Bid
Bid routing EPA	Manual assignment preparation EPA	Delivery Bid
Store	Pickup alert EPA	Pickup Confirmation
Driver	Delivery alert EPA	Delivery Confirmation
Driver	Daily assignments calculator EPA	Delivery Bid
Ranking increase EPA	Improving note EPA, Driver status global state element	Ranking Increase

Table B.49   Implicit channels in the Fast Flower Delivery application *(continued)*

Input terminal sources	Output terminal targets	Event types
Ranking decrease EPA	Improving note EPA, Driver status global state element	Ranking Decrease
Improving note EPA	Drivers' Guild	Improvement Note
Consistent strong driver EPA, Consistent weak driver EPA, Permanent weak driver EPA, Idle driver EPA, Improving driver EPA	Drivers' Guild	Driver Report
Daily assignments calculator EPA	Daily statistics creator EPA, Permanent weak driver EPA, Idle driver EPA, Improving driver EPA	Daily Assignment
Daily statistics creator EPA	Performance evaluation EPA	Daily Statistics
Performance evaluation EPA	Consistent strong driver EPA, Consistent weak driver EPA	Relative Performance

This table shows the type of events that flow across each channel, and the names of the processing elements attached to the channel.

Table B.50 shows the explicit channels that are used in the application. We have chosen to use explicit channels to link the various systems illustrated in figures B.3 through B.7.

Table B.50   Explicit channels in the Fast Flower Delivery application

Channel identifier	Routing scheme	Event type	Input terminal sources	Output terminal targets
Bid Request channel	Fixed	Bid Request	Bid Request creator EPA	Driver, Assignment manager EPA, Manual assignment preparation EPA
Alerts channel	Fixed	All Alert types	Assignment manager EPA, Assignment not done EPA, Pickup alert EPA, Delivery alert EPA	Ranking increase EPA, Ranking decrease EPA
Assignment channel	Fixed	Assignment	Store, Automatic assignment EPA	Driver, Assignment not done EPA, Pickup alert EPA, Delivery alert EPA, Daily assignments calculator EPA
Assignment request channel	Fixed	Delivery Bid	Manual assignment preparation EPA	Store, Assignment not done EPA

Table B.50   Explicit channels in the Fast Flower Delivery application *(continued)*

Channel identifier	Routing scheme	Event type	Input terminal sources	Output terminal targets
Delivery cancellation channel	Fixed	Delivery Request Cancellation	Store	Cancellation EPA *(not described in this book)*

B.9   *Event Pattern detect agents*

Tables B.51 through B.63 show the Pattern detect agents used in the application. Each of these agents will be presented in a separate table, followed by comments where required. In each table we show only the policies that are significant.

Table B.51   Automatic assignment

Pattern type	Context	Relevant types	Parameters	Policies
first n	Request	Delivery Bid	Count = 1	cardinality = single evaluation = immediate

This agent is responsible for picking the driver who is going to be assigned to a particular delivery. The Delivery Bid events from the drivers have already been checked by other agents, so all this agent has to do is pick one. It uses the simple strategy of picking the first event that it encounters. It uses the immediate evaluation policy as it makes sense to match as soon as it receives its first event, and a single cardinality policy as we don't want to continue the process after this first event has been selected.

Table B.52   Manual assignment preparation

Pattern type	Context	Relevant types	Parameters	Policies
relative n highest values	Bid interval	Delivery Bid	Attribute = ranking Count = 5	cardinality = single evaluation = deferred repeated type = every

This pattern selects the highest (at most) five bids with respect to their driver's ranking value. These bids are then forwarded to the flower store, so that it can choose the driver who is to be assigned to the delivery. The selection of bids is done once, at the end of the Bid interval window.

The next agent, shown in table B.53, uses the absence pattern to detect timeouts.

Table B.53   Assignment not done

Pattern type	Context	Relevant types	Parameters	Policies
absence	Response interval	Manual Assignment		

This is a timeout detection, indicating that the manual assignment decision wasn't performed on time. There are no parameters for the absence pattern, and none of the pattern policies have any effect on it. The Pickup alert agent shown in table B.54 is similar.

Table B.54 `Pickup alert`

Pattern type	Context	Relevant types	Parameters	Policies
absence	Pickup interval	Pickup Confirmation		

This is a timeout detection indicating that a pickup wasn't done on time. Our final timeout pattern is the `Delivery alert` agent, shown in table B.55.

Table B.55 `Delivery alert`

Pattern type	Context	Relevant types	Parameters	Policies
absence	Delivery interval	Delivery Confirmation		

This is another timeout detection; this one detects that a delivery wasn't made on time. Table B.56 shows that the absence pattern can be used for things other than timeout detection.

Table B.56 `Ranking increase`

Pattern type	Context	Relevant types	Parameters	Policies
absence	Driver evaluation	Delivery Alert		

This agent detects drivers who didn't have any delivery alerts within the `Driver evaluation` context. It's used to decide whether to give the driver a ranking increase. Its counterpart, the agent that decides when to decrease a driver's ranking, uses a different pattern, as you can see in table B.57.

Table B.57 `Ranking decrease`

Pattern type	Context	Relevant types	Parameters	Policies
count	Driver evaluation	Delivery Alert	Relation:> Threshold 5	repeated type = every evaluation = deferred

This agent detects drivers who had more than five delivery alerts within the driver evaluation context. The `Ranking Decrease` and `Ranking Increase` events that are derived by these two Pattern detect agents are themselves used as input to the Improving note agent, which is shown table B.58.

Table B.58 Improving note

Pattern type	Context	Relevant types	Parameters	Policies
sequence	Driver	Ranking Decrease, Ranking Increase		repeated type = override evaluation = immediate cardinality= unrestricted consumption = consume

This agent detects when a driver had a ranking increase after a ranking decrease. The override policy guarantees that there will be at most one of each of these events in the participant event set, and the consume policy means that the set is cleared each time the pattern is detected. This agent doesn't have a temporal context, so it has to use an immediate evaluation policy.

Table B.59 Permanent weak driver

Pattern type	Context	Relevant types	Parameters	Policies
always	Monthly driver	Daily Assignments	Assertion: assignmentCount < 5	evaluation = deferred

This agent detects when a driver has had fewer than five assignments in each of his working days during the month.

Table B.60 Idle driver

Pattern type	Context	Relevant types	Parameters	Policies
sometimes	Monthly driver	Daily Assignments	Assertion: assignmentCount = 0	evaluation = deferred

This agent detects drivers who had at least one working day during the month without any assignment.

Table B.61 Consistent weak driver

Pattern type	Context	Relevant types	Parameters	Policies
always	Monthly driver	Relative Performance	Assertion: deviation< -2	evaluation = deferred

This agent detects when a driver has a consistently low number of assignments. It takes a month's worth of Relative Performance events (for a given driver) and sees if that driver is always more than two standard deviations under the mean number of assignments on that day.

Table B.62 `Consistent strong driver`

Pattern type	Context	Relevant types	Parameters	Policies
always	Monthly driver	Relative Performance	Assertion: deviation > 2	evaluation = deferred

This pattern detects that a driver has a consistently high number of assignments. It takes a month's worth of `Relative Performance` events (for a given driver) and sees if that driver is always more than two standard deviations above the mean number of assignments on that day.

Table B.63 `Improving driver`

Pattern type	Context	Relevant types	Parameters	Policies
non-decreasing	Monthly Driver	Daily Assignments	Attribute = assignmentCount	evaluation = deferred

This agent detects drivers whose daily assignment rate stays level or increases over the month, so as to designate them as improving. This assessment is performed on a monthly basis.

index